*luttredge*

# Ancient Judaism and Christian Origins

"Based on his lifelong study of the complex world of early Christianity and its Jewish context, Nickelsburg demonstrates the remarkable similarities between the emergent faith and other Jewish movements, and also their decisive differences. The book is almost as significant for the questions it raises, unsettling many long-standing stereotypes, as for the answers it offers. A valuable resource for students of the New Testament and for all concerned to found Christian–Jewish dialogue today on a proper understanding of the original 'parting of the ways.'"

> —Franklin Sherman
> Associate for Interfaith Relations
> Evangelical Lutheran Church in America

D1110482

# Ancient Judaism and Christian Origins

## Diversity, Continuity, and Transformation

### George W. E. Nickelsburg

Fortress Press

Minneapolis

ANCIENT JUDAISM AND CHRISTIAN ORIGINS
Diversity, Continuity, and Transformation

Cover art: Menorah medallion in relief. Photo © Erich Lessing / Art Resource, N.Y. Chi-Rho, early Christian relief, from the Museo Pio Cristiano, Vatican Museums, Vatican State; and menorah medallion from the ruins of the synagogue of Aphek, Golan Heights, Israel, from the Golan Museum, photo © Art Resource, N.Y. Used by permission.
Author photo: Jon Van Allen, University of Iowa Foundation
Cover and interior design: Beth Wright

ISBN 0-8006-3612-0

Manufactured in the U.S.A.
07    06    05    04        2    3    4    5    6    7    8    9    10

# Contents

Preface      *xv*

Abbreviations      *xvii*

## Introduction / 1

The Renewed Study of Early Judaism      1

Implications for the Study of Christian Origins      3
     Historical / 4
     Theological / 4
     Methodological / 5

The Task and Scope of This Book      6

## 1. Scripture and Tradition / 9

The Situation in Early Judaism      9
     The Extent of the Authoritative Corpus / 9
         Manuscripts from the Caves of the Judean Desert / 9
         The Components of the Canon / 10
     The Developing Text of the Hebrew Bible / 11
     Scripture in Its Interpretive Context / 12
         The "Rewritten Bible": The Rise of Haggadah / 12
         Interpretation of the Prophetic Texts / 15
         The Servant of the Lord: A Multivalent Symbol / 17
     Summary / 20

Scripture in the Early Church      21
     The Biblical Canon of the Early Church / 22
     The Text of Scripture / 23

Biblical Interpretation in the Early Church      24
     The Church Read Scripture within Its Traditional Interpretations / 24
     The Use of Rabbinic Traditions in New Testament Exegesis / 25

**Jewish Precedents for the Rise and Development
  of the Jesus Tradition**                                                    **26**
   The Creation of Narrative Haggadah about Jesus / 26
   The Development of the Synoptic Tradition / 27
   Disagreements over the Bible and Its Interpretation:
     A Cause for "Unbelief" / 28

## 2. Torah and the Righteous Life / 29

**A Theological Problem for the Church**                                     **29**
**Torah in the Hebrew Scriptures**                                           **31**
   The Covenantal Context of Torah / 32
   Torah as Instruction Rather Than Simply Law / 33
   The Prevalence of Torah and Covenant in the Hebrew Scriptures / 34
   The Wisdom Literature: A Special Case / 34
   Divine Justice and Grace / 35
**Torah and the Righteous Life in Early Judaism**                           **36**
   The Role of Torah during the Antiochan Persecution / 36
   Faith and Obedient Action in the Jewish Texts / 38
   Torah and the Wisdom Tradition / 39
   Wisdom apart from the Mosaic Torah / 41
   Who Are "the Righteous" and "the Sinners"? / 42
   Summary: What the Texts Indicate and Do Not Indicate / 44
**The Development of Halakah and the Rise of Sectarianism**                  **44**
   A Note on Rabbinic Halakic Texts / 44
   The Heritage of Deuteronomic Theology: The Dynamics of Lawmaking
     and Legal Interpretation in the Book of Jubilees / 45
   Enochic Law / 46
   The Sectarian Torah of Qumran / 47
   Sect and Revealed Torah / 48
   Halakah as the Updating of Torah / 49
   Summary: The Responsibility to Act Righteously / 49
**Torah and Grace in Judaism**                                              **50**
**Torah and the Righteous Life in Early Christianity**                      **51**
   Divine Judgment on the Basis of Human Deeds / 51
   Justification and the Righteous Life in Paul / 53
   A Spectrum of Early Christian Attitudes about the Torah / 54
       Paul's Christian Predecessors and Contemporaries / 54
       Torah and Halakah in the Synoptic Jesus Tradition / 55

Wisdom Instruction and the Righteous Life / 57
Hellenistic Models for New Testament Ethical Instruction / 57
The Synoptics and Paul: Christological Models
    and Ethical Teaching / 58
**Summary**                                                    **58**


3. God's Activity in Behalf of Humanity / 61

**Models in Jewish Texts**                                     **61**
Deliverance Is a Pervasive Motif / 61
**Two Major Developments**                                     **62**
The Cosmic Character of Evil / 62
Locating Decisive Deliverance in the Eschaton / 64
**Salvation from Sin and Its Consequences**                    **64**
The Sacrificial System / 65
Exilic Alternatives to the Sacrificial System / 65
Continuations of These Developments / 66
    Suffering as Scourging, Discipline, or Chastisement / 66
    Martyrdom as Expiation and Propitiation / 66
    Righteous Deeds as a Means of Atonement / 67
    Prayers of Confession / 68
    Eschatological Cleansing and a Heavenly High Priest / 69
**Salvation from One's Enemies**                               **69**
Eschatological Judgment and Deliverance / 70
Salvation within History / 70
A Tension between Ideologies and Ambiguity about the Eschaton / 71
Healing and Rescue from Death / 72
Salvation as Revelation / 73
**The Scope of Divine Blessing and Salvation**                 **75**
A Spectrum of Biblical Attitudes / 75
Salvation for the Nations / 76
Israel versus the Nations / 77
Interpretations of Idols and Idolatry / 78
Sectarian Judaism / 78
**God's Interaction with Humanity according to Early Christianity**  **79**
Salvation from Sin / 79
    Jesus' Death for Others / 79
    Attitudes about the Temple / 80
    Salvation through Repentance / 80

The Humanity of the Son of God and the Transcendence of His Spirit:
A Solution for the Anthropological Problem of Sin  |  81
Rescue from One's Enemies  |  82
Salvation as Healing  |  83
Salvation as Revelation  |  83
The Scope of Salvation  |  85
Sectarianism in the Context of Universalism  |  87
**Summary**                                                                  **87**

## 4. Agents of God's Activity / 89

**God's Agents in Early Judaism**                                            **90**
When God Acts Alone  |  90
Human Agents  |  91
    The King  |  91
    The High Priest and Cult  |  93
    Prophets and Revealer Figures  |  96
Transcendent Agents  |  97
The Holy Watchers: Attendants and Agents of the Heavenly King  |  98
    The Four or Seven Holy Watchers  |  99
    Witnesses, Scribes, Intercessors  |  99
    Executors of God's Judgment  |  100
    General of the Army  |  100
    God's High Priest  |  100
    Melchizedek  |  101
    Raphael: God's Healer  |  101
    Messengers and Interpreters  |  101
    Facilitators of Righteousness  |  102
    Guardians and Governors of the Cosmos  |  102
    God's Vice-Regent: "One Like a Son of Man"  |  103
Two Major Transcendent Figures  |  103
    Wisdom  |  103
    The Enochic Son of Man/Chosen One/Righteous One  |  104
The Lord's Persecuted and Exalted Spokesman:
A Synthesis and Transition  |  106
Summary  |  108
**Early Christian Speculation about Jesus**                                  **108**
Jesus as God's Unique Agent  |  108

New Testament Models of the Messiah / 109
    Davidic King / 109
    Anointed Priest / 109
    Son of Man / 110
    The Righteous One and Servant of the Lord / 111
God's Spokesman, the Mouthpiece of Wisdom / 112
The Incarnation of Preexistent Wisdom and Logos / 113
Philippians 2:6-11: A Problematic Text / 113
The Gospel according to Mark: Son of Man and Son of God / 114
Jesus as Healer / 115
The Exaltation of Jesus: The Foundation of Christology / 115
Jewish "Unbelief" / 115
Jesus' "Messianic Consciousness" / 116

**Summary**                                                                   **116**


## 5. Eschatology / 119

**The Bible's Developing Eschatological Tendency**                            **120**
Jeremiah and Ezekiel / 120
Second and Third Isaiah / 121
The Legacy of Prophecy / 122
**Jewish Writings of the Greco-Roman Period**                                 **123**
The Apocalypses in *1 Enoch* and Daniel / 123
Teleology and the Fulfillment of Prophecy / 124
Pseudepigraphic Apocalypses and the Fulfillment of Prophecy / 125
Qumran: An Eclectic, Eschatologically Oriented Community / 126
The Eschatology of Some Heavily Hellenized Jewish Texts / 128
Eschatology: A Common Horizon Seen from Many Points of View / 129
Variations on a Common Theme / 130
    Messianism / 130
    The Kingdom of God / 130
    Resurrection, Immorality, and Eternal Life / 131
    The Locus of the New Age / 131
The Distinction between Eschatology and Apocalypticism / 132
Eschatological Timetables / 133
Realized Eschatology / 133
The Lack of Explicit Eschatology / 134
Summary / 134

**The Eschatological Orientation of Early Christianity**            135
  John the Baptist—Herald of the End Time / 135
  When the End Is Not Yet the End / 136
      The Tension between Present and Future
        in the Early Jesus Tradition / 136
      Fulfillment and Expectation in the Epistles of Paul / 137
      The Presence of Eschatological Realities
        in the Post-Pauline Tradition / 139
      Fulfillment and Postponement in Luke / 139
      The Presence of Judgment and Eternal Life
        in the Fourth Gospel / 140
**Resurrection, Immortality, and Eternal Life**            141
  The Resurrection and Exaltation of Jesus / 141
  Modes of Resurrection and Eternal Life / 142
**The Locus of Final Salvation**            144
**Jewish Responses to the Gospel: A Noneschatological Horizon**            144
**Summary**            145

## 6. Contexts and Settings / 147

**Ancient Texts as Historical Artifacts**            147
**Responses to Troubled Times**            149
**Geographic Location**            150
**Judaism and Hellenism**            150
**Temple, Cult, and Priesthood**            153
**The Synagogue**            154
**Religious Groups**            160
  Sources / 160
  Methodology / 161
  The Pharisees / 162
  The Sadducees / 166
  The Essenes and the Qumran Community / 167
  The Hasidim / 176
  Other Groups, Communities, and Sects / 178
**Summary**            181
  Variety among Jewish Groups and Sects / 181
  Early Christianity and Its Relationship to Sectarian Judaism / 182

## 7. Conclusions and Implications / 185

**Diversity within Early Judaism and Early Christianity:**
  **A Comparison**                                                185
  Scripture and Tradition  /  185
  Torah and the Righteous Life  /  186
  God's Activity in Behalf of Humanity  /  187
  Agents of God's Activity  /  189
  Eschatology  /  190
  Contexts and Settings  /  191
**Judaism and Early Christianity: Where They Differed**
  **and Why They Parted**                                         193
**The Consequences of These Events**                              195
  The Curious Irony of Gentile Christian Exclusivism  /  195
  The Triumph of Christianity without the Torah  /  195
  A Denigrating Comparison of Judaism and Christianity  /  196
  The Backwash of Christian Apocalyptic Eschatology  /  196
**Looking to the Future: Some Possibilities**                     197
  Three Axioms for Exegetical and Historical Study  /  198
  Exegetical and Historical Possibilities  /  198
  Theological and Practical Consequences  /  199

*Notes*                                                           201

*Index of Passages Cited*                                         245

*Index of Authors*                                                259

# Preface

Two questions have provided the framework for this volume. How have the discovery of the Dead Sea Scrolls and revolutions in the methodology of biblical scholarship in the past two generations changed our perceptions of Judaism in the Greco-Roman period, and how do—or should—these developments lead us to rethink the origins of Christianity? In attempting to answer these questions, I sought to highlight major aspects of the past fifty years of scholarship, and to synthesize my own work over four decades.

I intend the book for a broad audience consisting of biblical scholars who do not specialize in the study of Judaism; college, university, and seminary students; clergy; and laypeople who have some familiarity with the methods of modern biblical interpretation. I especially hope that it will engage persons participating in Jewish–Christian dialog.

The genesis of the book was a set of five seminar papers (chapters 1–5) prepared in 1993 for discussion in a number of venues in South Africa. After my return to the United States, the manuscript sat in the queue for eight years as I served as director of the University of Iowa School of Religion and then completed work on volume 1 of my commentary on *1 Enoch*. A month's fellowship at the Bellagio Study and Conference Center on Lake Como provided the occasion, the quiet environment, and the impetus to bring the task to fruition.

I cheerfully express my thanks to the Bellagio Committee of the Rockefeller Foundation for their support, and to the Universities of South Africa (UNISA), Potchefstroom, Bloemfontein, Stellenbosch, and Capetown, the New Testament Society of South Africa , and the Human Sciences Research Council of South Africa for the invitations and resources that made the trip possible. I remember with gratitude the gracious hospitality that Marilyn and I received from Pieter and Helen Botha, Pieter and Leona Craffert, Jaspar Burden, Fika van Rensburg, Hermie van Zyl, Jan Botha, Bernard

Lategan, Bernard Combrink, Daan Cloete, and Charles Wanamaker, as well as their concern and care for us during some very difficult days in South African history.

I wish also to thank colleagues and friends for their contributions to the completion of the book. Harold Rast, former director of Fortress Press, invited me to write the book and then waited a very long time to edit it. Erich Gruen, Hermann Lichtenberger, Eric Meyers, Jacob Neusner, Birger Pearson, and Norman Petersen read parts or all of the manuscript at various stages and offered helpful suggestions and corrections. Beth Wright designed the book and its cover with imagination and saw it through production. Gary Lee was a careful copy editor. To Marilyn, who always seems to stand and wait, once again I say "thank you; things will slow down!"

I dedicate the book, first, to Birger Pearson and Norman Petersen with appreciation and respect for our forty years of friendship and intellectual comradery. Many of the ideas expressed here percolated during our unofficial seminars at the Annual Meetings of the Society of Biblical Literature.

And finally there is this. More than twenty-five years after I began to publish on early Judaism and early Christianity, and a few years after I drafted the first five chapters of this book, I discovered my Jewish great grandfather. From archives in Germany, I learned that his father had sat on the praesidium of his synagogue and that, as far back as I could trace, the family had always married within the faith. Four gravestones bear the title *hakohen* ("the priest"). The timing of these discoveries was fortuitous, because it had allowed me to pursue my study of these two religious faiths and their interconnections with no hidden, existential agenda. What I had written, I had written because it interested me and it seemed intrinsically important. Nonetheless, the family silence about my Jewish roots has provided an additional compelling reason to publish the book. This is a probe into that misty time two millennia ago when a family that should have stayed together broke up. To the extent that we begin to understand the causes of the schism, we can find some of the means by which to heal it and in other ways to deal with it.

So, within the microcosm of my family, I dedicate the book to the memory of those of my direct ancestors whose names I have been able to recover and with whom I would have enjoyed some interesting theological discussions.

# Abbreviations

| | |
|---|---|
| AB | Anchor Bible |
| *ABD* | *Anchor Bible Dictionary.* Edited by D. N. Freedman. 6 vols. New York, 1992 |
| *Abot Rab. N.* | *Abot de Rabbi Nathan* |
| *Abr.* | Philo, *De Abrahamo* |
| *AbrN* | *Abr-Nahrain* |
| ad loc. | ad locum, at the place discussed |
| *Ag. Ap.* | Josephus, *Against Apion* |
| AGJU | Arbeiten zur Geschichte des antiken Judentums und des Urchristentums |
| AnBib | Analecta biblica |
| *ANRW* | *Aufstieg und Niedergang der römischen Welt: Geschichte und Kultur Roms im Spiegel der neueren Forschung.* Edited by H. Temporini and W. Haase. Berlin, 1972– |
| *Ant.* | Josephus, *Jewish Antiquities* |
| *AOT* | *The Apocryphal Old Testament.* Edited by H. F. D. Sparks. Oxford, 1984. |
| *Apoc. Abr.* | *Apocalypse of Abraham* |
| *1 Apol.* | Justin Martyr, *Apology 1* |
| *APOT* | *The Apocrypha and Pseudepigrapha of the Old Testament.* Edited by R. H. Charles. 2 vols. Oxford, 1913 |
| *Asc. Isa.* | *Ascension of Isaiah* |
| *b.* | Babylonian Talmud |
| *BA* | *Biblical Archaeologist* |
| Bar | Apocryphal Book of Baruch |
| *2 Bar.* | *Syriac Apocalypse of Baruch* |
| B.C.E. | Before the Common Era (= B.C.) |
| BETL | Bibliotheca ephemeridum theologicarum lovaniensium |

| | |
|---|---|
| BibOr | Biblica et orientalia |
| *BJRL* | *Bulletin of the John Rylands University Library of Manchester* |
| BZAW | Beihefte zur Zeitschrift für die alttestamentliche Wissenschaft |
| BZNW | Beihefte zur Zeitschrift für die neutestamentliche Wissenschaft |
| *Catech. Lectures* | Cyril of Jerusalem, *Catechetical Lectures* |
| *CBQ* | *Catholic Biblical Quarterly* |
| CBQMS | Catholic Biblical Quarterly Monograph Series |
| CD | Cairo Genizah copy of the Damascus Document |
| C.E. | Common Era (= A.D.) |
| chap(s). | chapter(s) |
| 1, 2 Chr | 1, 2 Chronicles |
| 1, 2 Cor | 1, 2 Corinthians |
| CRINT | Compendia Rerum Iudaicarum ad Novum Testamentum |
| CSCO | Corpus scriptorum christianorum orientalium. Edited by I. B. Chabot et al. Paris, 1903– |
| *CTM* | *Concordia Theological Monthly* |
| Dan | Daniel |
| *DBSup* | *Dictionnaire de la Bible: Supplément.* Edited by L. Pirot and A. Robert. Paris, 1928– |
| *De sacro chrism.* | Cyril of Jerusalem, *De sacro chrismate* |
| Deut | Deuteronomy |
| DJD | Discoveries in the Judaean Desert |
| *DSD* | *Dead Sea Discoveries* |
| EBib | Études bibliques |
| ed(s). | editor(s), edited by, edition |
| *1 En.* | *1 Enoch* |
| *EncJud* | *Encyclopaedia Judaica.* 16 vols. Jerusalem, 1972 |
| Exod | Exodus |
| *ExpTim* | *Expository Times* |
| Ezek | Ezekiel |
| Gal | Galatians |
| Gen | Genesis |
| Gk. | Greek |
| Hab | Habakkuk |

| | |
|---|---|
| *Haer.* | Hippolytus, *Refutatio omnium haeresium* (*Philosophoumena*) |
| HDR | Harvard Dissertations in Religion |
| Heb | Hebrews |
| Heb. | Hebrew |
| *HeyJ* | *Heythrop Journal* |
| HNT | Handbuch zum Neuen Testament |
| HO | Handbuch der Orientalistik |
| Hos | Hosea |
| HSM | Harvard Semitic Monographs |
| *HTR* | *Harvard Theological Review* |
| HTS | Harvard Theological Studies |
| *HUCA* | *Hebrew Union College Annual* |
| *Hypoth.* | Philo, *Hypothetica* |
| ICC | International Critical Commentary |
| *IDB* | *The Interpreter's Dictionary of the Bible.* Edited by G. A. Buttrick. 4 vols. Nashville, 1962 |
| *IDBSup* | *Interpreter's Dictionary of the Bible: Supplementary Volume.* Edited by K. Crim. Nashville, 1976 |
| *IEJ* | *Israel Exploration Journal* |
| Isa | Isaiah |
| Jas | James |
| JAL | Jewish Apocryphal Literature |
| *JBL* | *Journal of Biblical Literature* |
| Jer | Jeremiah |
| *JJS* | *Journal of Jewish Studies* |
| Josh | Joshua |
| *JQR* | *Jewish Quarterly Review* |
| *JSHRZ* | *Jüdische Schriften aus hellenistisch-römischer Zeit* |
| *JSJ* | *Journal for the Study of Judaism* |
| JSJSup | Journal for the Study of Judaism Supplements |
| *JSOT* | *Journal for the Study of the Old Testament* |
| JSOTSup | Journal for the Study of the Old Testament: Supplement Series |
| *JSP* | *Journal for the Study of the Pseudepigrapha* |
| JSPSup | Journal for the Study of the Pseudepigrapha: Supplement Series |

| | |
|---|---|
| *Jub.* | *Jubilees* |
| Judg | Judges |
| *J.W.* | Josephus, *Jewish War* |
| 1, 2 Kgs | 1, 2 Kings |
| *LAB* | *Liber Antiquitatum Biblicarum* (Pseudo-Philo) |
| LEC | Library of Early Christianity |
| Lev | Leviticus |
| *m.* | Mishnah |
| 1, 2, 3, 4 Macc | 1, 2, 3, 4 Maccabees |
| Mal | Malachi |
| Matt | Matthew |
| Mic | Micah |
| *Migr.* | Philo, *De migratione Abrahami* |
| MS(S) | manuscript(s) |
| MT | Masoretic text |
| *Nat.* | Pliny, *Naturalis historia* |
| *Neot* | *Neotestamentica* |
| *NIB* | *New Interpreter's Bible* |
| NovTSup | Novum Testamentum Supplements |
| NT | New Testament |
| NTL | New Testament Library |
| *NTS* | *New Testament Studies* |
| NTTS | New Testament Tools and Studies |
| Num | Numbers |
| OTL | Old Testament Library |
| *OTP* | *Old Testament Pseudepigrapha.* Edited by J. H. Charlesworth. 2 vols. New York, 1983 |
| *Par. Jer.* | *Paraleipomena Jeremiou* |
| 1 Pet | 1 Peter |
| Phil | Philippians |
| *Prob.* | Philo, *Quod omnis probus liber sit* |
| Prol. | Prologue |
| Ps | Psalm |
| *Ps(s). Sol.* | *Psalm(s) of Solomon* |
| PVTG | Pseudepigrapha Veteris Testamenti Graece |
| Q | Qumran MS, preceded by the number of the cave of discovery and followed by short title or MS number |

| | |
|---|---|
| 1QapGen ar | Genesis Apocryphon in Aramaic from Cave 1 |
| 1QH | *Hodayot* or Thanksgiving Hymns |
| 1QM | *Milḥamah* or War Scroll |
| 1QpHab | *Pesher* (commentary) on Habakkuk |
| 1QS | *Serek Hayaḥad* or Rule of the Community |
| 1QSa | Rule of the Congregation |
| 4QMMT | "Halakic Letter" from Cave 4 |
| 4QpIsa<sup>c</sup> | *Pesher* on Isaiah |
| 4QpNah | *Pesher* on Nahum |
| 4QPrNab | Prayer of Nabonidus |
| 4QTest | Testimonia (collection of proof texts) |
| 11QMelch | Melchizedek text from Cave 11 |
| 11QPs<sup>a</sup> | Psalms Scroll |
| *RAC* | *Reallexikon für Antike und Christentum.* Edited by T. Kluser et al. Stuttgart, 1950– |
| *RB* | *Revue biblique* |
| rec. | recension |
| *Rec.* | Pseudo-Clement, *Recognitions* |
| *RelSRev* | *Religious Studies Review* |
| Rev | Book of Revelation (New Testament) |
| rev. (ed.) | revised (edition) |
| *RevQ* | *Revue de Qumran* |
| Rom | Romans |
| 1, 2 Sam | 1, 2 Samuel |
| *Sanh.* | *Sanhedrin* |
| SANT | Studien zum Alten und Neuen Testaments |
| SBLDS | Society of Biblical Literature Dissertation Series |
| SBLEJL | Society of Bible Literature Early Jewish Literature |
| SBLMS | Society of Biblical Literature Monograph Series |
| SBLSCS | Society of Biblical Literature Septuagint and Cognate Studies |
| *SBLSP* | *Society of Biblical Literature Seminar Papers* |
| SBLTT | Society of Biblical Literature Texts and Translations |
| SBT | Studies in Biblical Theology |
| SC | Sources chrétiennes. Paris: Cerf, 1943– |
| *SCI* | *Scripta Classica Israelitica* |
| Sir | Sirach/Ecclesiasticus |

| | |
|---|---|
| SJLA | Studies in Judaism in Late Antiquity |
| SNTSMS | Society of New Testament Studies Monograph Series |
| *Soṭ.* | *Soṭah* |
| SP | Sacra pagina |
| SPB | Studia Post-biblica |
| STDJ | Studies on the Texts of the Desert of Judah |
| SUNT | Studien zur Umwelt des Neuen Testaments |
| Sup | Supplement |
| SVTP | Studia in Veteris Testamenti pseudepigraphica |
| *T. Job* | *Testament of Job* |
| *T. Jud.* | *Testament of Judah* |
| *T. Levi* | *Testament of Levi* |
| *T. Mos.* | *Testament of Moses* |
| TDNT | *Theological Dictionary of the New Testament.* Edited by G. Kittel and G. Friedrich. Translated by G. W. Bromiley. 10 vols. Grand Rapids, 1964–76 |
| 1, 2 Thess | 1, 2 Thessalonians |
| 2 Tim | 2 Timothy |
| Tob | Tobit |
| TSAJ | Texte und Studien zum antiken Judentum |
| v(v) | verse(s) |
| vol(s). | volume(s) |
| VTSup | Supplements to Vetus Testamentum |
| Wis | Wisdom of Solomon |
| WUNT | Wissenschaftliche Untersuchungen zum Neuen Testament |
| ZAW | *Zeitschrift für die alttestamentliche Wissenschaft* |
| Zech | Zechariah |
| ZNW | *Zeitschrift für die neutestamentliche Wissenschaft und die Kunde der älteren Kirche* |

# Introduction

In his oft-cited monograph *The Structure of Scientific Revolutions*, the historian of science Thomas S. Kuhn describes a phenomenon that is well known to scholars of the humanities.[1] When new evidence accumulates to the point that one can no longer sustain a current explanatory model, the scholar seeks to marshal old and new evidence into a new model that better accounts for *all* the data. Precisely such a restructuring of the evidence has occurred during the past half century among scholars of Second Temple Judaism.

## The Renewed Study of Early Judaism

Descriptions of early Judaism written by Christian scholars in the nineteenth and the first half of the twentieth century tended to contrast Judaism and Christianity. Judaism embodied, for the most part, the negative and inferior religious features that early Christianity would filter out. Dominating this picture was the rabbinic religion that these scholars extrapolated from the second- to fifth-century texts of the Mishnah, the Babylonian and Palestinian Talmudim, and the Midrashim. This allegedly "normative Judaism," projected back chronologically into the Hellenistic and early Roman periods, was legalistic; the Jews, these scholars claimed, were fixated on keeping the letter of the Law in the hope of receiving divine reward. Alongside this description scholars also found a set of dichotomies within Judaism, especially as ancient Jewish apocalyptic texts were discovered and published. One might contrast legalism with apocalypticism, praising the prophetic spirit of the latter and seeing in it some seeds for early Christian messianism, or one might criticize apocalyptic Judaism for its fanciful speculation and contrast it with the high ethical quality of the biblical prophets. Apocalyptic literature, with its eschatological focus, was a foil to the ethical emphasis in wisdom literature. In general, however, Christian scholarship—taught in seminaries and preached from the pulpit—portrayed Judaism as a whole as the dark religious backdrop before which were played out the liberating events of the life of Jesus and the rise of the early church. Jewish scholars, for their part, ignored the writings of the so-called Apocrypha and Pseudepigrapha, and focused their attention on the study of Scripture, especially the Torah, and its authoritative exposition in the ancient rabbinical corpus. Here one found God's will if one searched for it. Thus Jewish and Christian scholars were poles apart.

But since the 1950s a major shift has taken place among those concerned with the study of Judaism. At least four factors have contributed to the revolution. (1) Manuscripts discovered in the caves around the Dead Sea and the findings of Syro-Palestinian archaeology have supplied a wealth of new primary evidence about the history, religion, and culture of Judaism in this period. (2) Methods imported from literary studies and the social sciences have provided new tools for analyzing the sources, and scholars have become more self-conscious about their methods and methodology. (3) Related to this, the development of departments of religious studies in public and private universities in North America has created a context in which ancient religious texts and phenomena can be studied from a historical rather than a Christian theological perspective. (4) In part, these approaches have been encouraged by Christian reflection on the Holocaust, which has called into serious question the old polemical and denigrating descriptions of early Judaism that were generated, in large part, from Christian theological agendas.

These new data, new methods, and new settings have changed the face of scholarship. First, the publication of the initial Qumran Scrolls catalyzed renewed study of the old sources that had long been known, and the new methods and settings shed new light on them. Second, the discovery of these Hebrew and Aramaic scrolls in the Holy Land, just at the time of the founding of the State of Israel, piqued the interest of Jewish scholars, for whom these languages were their daily fare, and they began now to look also at the nonrabbinic texts to which they had previously paid little attention. Thus the combined work of scholars bringing to the sources a variety of interests, a multiplicity of religious and cultural perspectives, and significant differences in their training further enhanced the quest to shed new light on ancient times.

As a result of these developments, old stereotypes perpetuated in Christian literature about Judaism have collapsed, and the broader horizon has enriched the Jewish study of ancient Judaism. What is beginning to emerge is a picture of a variegated Judaism, a spectrum with many hues and blends, a religious and cultural phenomenon influenced by the specifics of the Jews' historical circumstances and inseparable from their non-Jewish environment.

It is important to emphasize that the picture is only *beginning* to emerge. The texts of most of the major Qumran Scrolls, to take one example, have been available for up to a half century now. However, the complex nature of the evidence, as well as the accidents of preservation, give pause to the careful historian. Indeed, the fragmentary condition of much of the Scroll material is a kind of parable for the shape and character of our evidence. We can see only bits and pieces of the reality, and we see it darkly through a glass. Nonetheless, a revolution in our understanding of antiquity has begun, and the old schemes and explanatory models no longer work. It is a time for cautious and conscientious construction of new models.

## Implications for the Study of Christian Origins

One of the corollaries of the emerging new picture of early Judaism is the need to reassess our hypotheses about the rise of Christianity. If the church developed in the matrix of Judaism and the mother was very different from what we have imagined and described, then we must reconsider the nature of the child, the circumstances of its birth, and the reasons for its youthful separation from its mother and its home. Yet it is fair to say that scholars of the New Testament and Christian origins devote relatively little time to major developments in the reinterpretation of early Judaism and even less time to the study of the ancient primary sources. Although many in the academy see themselves as historians of the religions of antiquity, in large part they focus their

efforts on the foundational, authoritative documents of Christianity—
the Hebrew Bible and the New Testament.

The reasons are understandable enough. The study of Judaism has
become a highly specialized endeavor. Add to the factors mentioned in
the previous paragraphs the fact that many of the primary texts have
been preserved in second- and third-hand translations written in relatively inaccessible ancient languages like Syriac, Ethiopic, Coptic, Church
Slavonic, Armenian, and Georgian, and the barrier can seem insur-
mountable. In addition, over the past decades the study of the Hebrew
Bible and the New Testament has grown like the stone of Daniel 2 into a
mountain of literature that defies the scholar to master it while challeng-
ing her or him to add to its mass. Given the law of inertia and the limits of
the workday, it is little wonder that important aspects of the renewed
study of early Judaism remain terra incognita for scholars whose professional responsibilities as teachers are centered on the study of early Christianity.[2] But the fact remains that a revolution in Judaic studies has
occurred, and it is imperative for students of early Christianity to take this
into account.

The renewed study of early Judaism has three kinds of implications for
the study of Christian origins.

## Historical

As the new evidence helps us to construct new models of early Judaism, it
requires, in turn, that we reshape our understanding of the rise of early
Christianity and the circumstances of its separation from Judaism. On the
one hand, Christianity arose from a particular strand of a variegated first-
century Judaism. On the other hand, earliest Christianity, attested in the
New Testament, brought with it much of the diversity of first-century
Judaism. New Testament studies in the past decades have, indeed,
emphasized the diversity of early Christianity.[3] Attention to the diversity
of early Judaism helps us better to perceive, understand, and appreciate
this early Christian diversity.

## Theological

As we make substantial adjustments in our writing of the history of this
period, some equally significant theological questions arise for those con-

cerned about such matters. The writings of the New Testament are thoroughly confessional, substantially apologetic, and significantly polemical. To no small extent these apologetic and polemical edges are directed toward and against contemporary Judaism. Much of the New Testament's picture of Judaism is governed by a desire to prove that the church, not the synagogue, is the true embodiment and continuation of the religion of Israel. While this is an interesting historical phenomenon in its own right, it has had massive and deleterious effects on human history. The past nineteen centuries of Jewish–Christian interactions are complex from every point of view, but much of the dark side of this history is a function of the portrayal of Judaism in the authoritative documents of the New Testament. And much Christian theology and preaching have not caught up with historiography.

## Methodological

Several methodological implications follow from these observations and pertain both to the writing of history and to the construction of theology. The purely accidental discovery of the Qumran Scrolls has taught us historians something that we neglect at our own professional peril. Our evidence is spotty, and the preservation and recovery of much of it are the result of accident and serendipity. Where the configuration of the evidence is systematic, this is due largely to ancient purposeful decisions to preserve one text or to destroy another and has little to do with the modern scientist's concern to collect a "representative sample." We are at the mercy of weather, worms, invading armies, and the zeal of the self-defined righteous and orthodox long since dead. The discovery of the Scrolls has helped us to see this with a clarity that was hitherto not possible.

Yet how much have we really learned? Although the evidence from the Scrolls has shown us how little we really knew before, the influx of new evidence tempts us to the conclusion that now we know much better how things really were, what the grand shape of reality was. But the nature of the new evidence—which constitutes a window onto a hitherto unimagined complexity—warns us against facile conclusions and invites us to scholarly humility and honest tentativeness about our historical conclusions. Before 1947 we were blissfully unaware that the Scrolls would blow our hypotheses about the shape of early Judaism out of the water. We need to keep a copy of the Scrolls on our desks, both because we can learn from their content and because they remind us that once we did not know that they existed.

The construction of new models of early Judaism and the circumstances of the rise of Christianity raise important questions for theologians. What happens, or should happen, when one discovers that theology is based on wrong history? It bears some serious reflection that the church has canonized documents that were written in its youth, in the heat of a polemic begotten of its identity crisis with Judaism, and that these early, highly tendentious, historically conditioned documents of the New Testament remain the yardstick for anti-Jewish and apocalyptic theologies.

These observations are not intended to undercut the uniqueness and value of these texts as theological benchmarks. The question is of a different sort. Is there sufficient elasticity in the understanding of tradition to recognize that the texts of Scripture are themselves the crystallization of moments in the tradition and to seek, cherish, and recognize the value of other moments in that tradition? Catholicism and Orthodoxy, with their understanding of the complementarity of Scripture and tradition, can perhaps more easily adopt this approach than can Protestantism, with its emphasis on *sola scriptura*.

The Scrolls press a final question upon us that is methodological in a way; it is peculiar to the age of the mass media, and its application sweeps across the academy and beyond it. How do scholars responsibly communicate their tentative, ambiguous, and complex findings and hypotheses to a public institution (the media) and a public that, comprising laypeople, have difficulty digesting this tentativeness, ambiguity, and complexity? The recent controversy about the unavailability of certain of the Scrolls, whatever its justification, was fed by misinformation, exaggerations, and half-truths uncritically repeated by media that were either unable to understand the issues or unwilling to sort them out.

## The Task and Scope of This Book

In this book I attempt to present a broad and synthetic picture of some of the results of modern scholarship on early Judaism, organized around a number of traditional topics. One can argue that the old topics are no longer valid and that one should "dismantle" and "reassemble" the structures and categories.[4] Robert Kraft and I have already sketched such a picture of the history of post–World War II research on Judaism as the introduction to a volume that is organized according to historical topics and genres of literature.[5] Here, however, it seemed profitable for pedagogical purposes to retain the scholarly and theological categories and to attempt to redefine them.

Such organization according to topics has necessitated some overlap in their treatment. However, their order unfolds a developing perspective. (1) *Scripture and tradition* are a fundamental category. (2) My discussion of *torah* expands on an aspect of Scripture that is obviously connected with the broad and basic concern of biblical and postbiblical Jewish religion that one should live a *righteous life* in accordance with God's revealed will. (3) The covenantal rewards for such conduct are sometimes construed as "salvation," but this term is often inappropriate with reference to the more general notion of divine rewards and blessings, which need not involve saving someone *from* something. As a more inclusive category, I have chosen *God's activity in behalf of humanity*. (4) In the Jewish writings of the Greco-Roman period, this divine activity in its many forms was increasingly attributed to a variety of human and transcendent agents. I have chosen the expression *"agents of God's activity"* rather than the common term "christology" in order to demonstrate that this latter term actually encompasses a range of New Testament speculation about Jesus that is based on a number of nonmessianic Jewish models. (5) *Eschatology* is less a discrete topic than a dimension or horizon on which any of the previous topics may be set at a given time. (6) Religious conceptions do not exist in a vacuum; they speak to specific *contexts* and function within concrete social and cultural *settings*. In my conclusion I summarize and synthesize my findings, indicating where issues remain unsettled, and suggest some possible directions for future study.

The chapters (except chapter 6) are organized into two main sections. The first discusses the findings of contemporary research on early Judaism. The second sketches some of the implications of this research for a possible reinterpretation of Christian origins. Since the latter is the raison d'être for this book, I have been selective in the sections on Judaism, discussing what seems profitable for a study of early Christianity. A more exhaustive treatment of the former would require a much longer book and should await detailed analyses of recently published Dead Sea Scrolls material. Both sections of the individual chapters emphasize the diversity in early Judaism and early Christianity and use this dimension in a comparative way that highlights both the continuities and the discontinuities between the two traditions.

The sources for my discussion are twofold. The first includes a mass of scholarly literature on Judaism, which I have been able to cite only selectively. In doing this I have also used the opportunity to synthesize my own research and publications.[6] The second source consists of half a century of publication on the origins of Christianity and especially its early relationship to Judaism. I have also put into print some of my own unpublished reflections and discoveries. In citing the scholarly literature on Judaism and Christianity, I kept in mind the diverse audiences for which I intend this book. Sometimes I cite technical articles and monographs. In other cases I refer to dictionary articles and commentaries that synthesize and provide responsible entrée into the mass of technical literature.

The sections of the chapters that deal with early Christianity are more suggestive than demonstrative. This reflects the fact that, in my view, a major agenda has yet to be developed and executed. It is my hope that these pages will provide some impetus in that direction.

# chapter 1

# Scripture and Tradition

Sacred tradition embodied in authoritative Scriptures is a cornerstone of both Judaism of the Greco-Roman period and early Christianity
of the first and second centuries. But what precisely did Jews and Christians consider to be authoritative Scripture, and how did they interpret it?
Three factors that have emerged in the past fifty years have immensely
complicated any attempt to answer to these questions: the manuscript
finds of the 1940s and 1950s; new insights into the nature of oral tradition;
and a developing recognition of the variety in the religious thought and
social organization in early Judaism.

## The Situation in Early Judaism

### The Extent of the Authoritative Corpus
*Manuscripts from the Caves of the Judean Desert*
The fragmentary manuscripts found in the caves at Qumran and other
locations along the rim of the Dead Sea reveal the richness of Jewish literary production during the late Persian and Greco-Roman periods and
shed new light on previously known texts that are not included in the
Hebrew Bible.[1] In addition to all the books of the Hebrew Bible except
Esther,[2] the Dead Sea caves have yielded fragmentary copies of other
texts that fall into three categories. From the Apocrypha we have Tobit in
Aramaic and in Hebrew, the Wisdom of ben Sira in Hebrew, and the Letter
of Jeremiah in Greek.[3] Representing the Pseudepigrapha[4] are *1 Enoch* in
Aramaic, *Jubilees* in Hebrew, and texts related to the *Testament of Levi* and
the *Testament of Naphtali* in Aramaic and Hebrew, respectively. A host of
other Hebrew and Aramaic texts (most of them previously unknown) in

a variety of genres fill out the complement of Dead Sea texts stemming from the last four centuries B.C.E. and the first century C.E. As a result of these discoveries, we must reassess the texts previously known to us in the Apocrypha and Pseudepigrapha, asking whence they came, when they were written, and how they relate to the writings in the Hebrew Bible. Moreover, we must place both the Hebrew Bible and these other texts into the broader context of Judaism in the Persian and Greco-Roman periods.

## The Components of the Canon

The history of the development of the Jewish biblical canon is still being written.[5] Something like the tripartite division of the Hebrew Bible (Torah, Prophets, Writings [in Hebrew: *Torah, Nebi'im, Ketubim*, known by the acronym *Tanak*]) was known already to the grandson of Joshua ben Sira, who referred to it in his prologue to his grandfather's book of wisdom (ca. 130 B.C.E.) as "the law, the prophets, and the other books of the fathers" (Sir Prol. 8-10; cf. 24-25).[6] Fifty years earlier, ben Sira himself arranged his hymn to "famous men" (chaps. 44—49) according to the contents of the Torah (44:16-26), the Former Prophets (45:1—49:7), the Latter Prophets (Isaiah, in historical context at 48:22-25; Jeremiah, 49:6-7; Ezekiel, 49:8-9; and the Twelve, 49:10), and added references to Zerubbabel, Joshua, and Nehemiah (49:11-13). Whether ben Sira knew all the Writings is uncertain; he makes no reference to Ezra, Job, or the Daniel traditions (which were finally edited after the time of ben Sira's activity). Conversely, he shows high regard for the patriarch Enoch and knows some of the traditions associated with his name and that of Noah (49:14; 44:16-17).[7]

The Qumranic evidence relating to the developing Jewish canon is ambiguous. The caves have yielded no codices to indicate an order of books,[8] nor is it clear in what sense the preserved texts of the Apocrypha and Pseudepigrapha may have been authoritative. Nonetheless, the large number of manuscripts of the *Jubilees* torah and the Astronomical Book and prophetic parts of *1 Enoch* indicate that these works had some kind of authoritative status at some point in the history of the Qumran community and its antecedents.[9] The testamentary or quasi-testamentary material written in the names of Levi, Qahat, and Amram is also of interest because it seems to provide a guarantee of the legitimacy of the priesthood and because it alleges to be revelation about the unseen world.[10] Moreover, given the absence of any manuscripts of the Diaspora story of Esther, the presence of the six manuscripts of the Diaspora story of Tobit is noteworthy.[11] That fragments of Sirach were found at Qumran and Masada is consonant with the high regard in which some rabbis later held the book,[12] but we cannot be certain that the people at Qumran and Masada considered the work to be authoritative, or at least inspired in the sense that ben Sira regarded his teaching (Sir 24:32-33).

The evidence from ben Sira and from Qumran warns us to be cautious in our views about what may have been included in the category of authoritative "Scripture" around the turn of the era and what was already excluded. More appropriate are these questions—still to be answered: What was authoritative *for whom, in what sense, and when* in the Greco-Roman period, and what were the consequences of differences of opinion in these matters?

## The Developing Text of the Hebrew Bible

The Qumran Scrolls not only suggest that the limits of the canon of Scripture were not fixed but also demonstrate a remarkable fluidity in the text of the books of Scripture.[13] Scholars long noted significant differences between the Hebrew and Greek versions of 1 and 2 Samuel and of Jeremiah; some ascribed these to scribal carelessness. The Scrolls, however, attest diversity in the Hebrew texts of a larger number of biblical books. As in the case of the canon, the history of the biblical text has yet to be written; but some facts are clear. A long and a short Hebrew text of Jeremiah existed side by side at Qumran.[14] The longer text of Samuel, previously known only in Greek, is the form of the text in the Hebrew Qumran manuscripts.[15] Textual variants in the Torah, previously attested variously in the Masoretic text, the Samaritan Pentateuch, and the Greek Bible, occur in the Qumran Hebrew manuscripts.[16] The Qumran commentary on Habakkuk (1QpHab) can quote one version of a passage and expound it by alluding to a variant text.[17] While scholars have offered a number of competing hypotheses to explain these infinitely complex data, one general fact is clear. At the turn of the era, the text of many of the biblical writings was not finally fixed, and scribal and exegetical practice allowed a great deal of interpretive freedom. This fact needs to be related to a paradox evident in both rabbinic and early Christian exegesis: a precise, word-for-word interpretation of the text went hand in hand with scribal manipulation of that text.

## Scripture in Its Interpretive Context

### The "Rewritten Bible": The Rise of Haggadah

Common among the Qumran manuscripts as well as Pseudepigrapha not found at Qumran is a type of literary work that retells narratives found in the Hebrew Bible, especially the Pentateuch. It is a precursor to rabbinic haggadic exegesis. The term "Rewritten Bible" is probably anachronistic, because we cannot always be certain that what was rewritten was considered to be "Bible" at the time it was rewritten.[18]

One of the earliest examples of this type of recast narrative occurs in *1 Enoch* 6–11, which elaborates and transforms the fragmentary story of the sons of God and the daughters of men in Gen 6:1-4.[19] Two tendencies are at work in the retold version of the story. (1) Motifs that Greek myth associated with Prometheus, the revealer of technology, are interwoven with the main narrative thread about the mating of divine beings and mortal women. (2) The story as a whole is given an eschatological twist, so that the flood becomes a prototype of the final judgment of the world, which will cure the evils brought about by the illegal mating and the revelations of forbidden secrets. Whatever the precise relationship between *1 Enoch* and Genesis 6–9, the Enoch text should be dated no later than the time of Alexander's successors (ca. 315 B.C.E.).[20]

A much longer and more complex example of rewritten narrative is represented by the book of *Jubilees,* a work that scholars have long known in an Ethiopic version and in some Greek, Latin, and Syriac fragments.[21] The Qumran caves have yielded fragments from thirteen or fourteen manuscripts of the original Hebrew form of *Jubilees,* which was the source of the aforementioned versions.[22] The author of *Jubilees,* who wrote in the first half of the second century B.C.E., recast Genesis 1—Exodus 12, deleting some parts of the pentateuchal texts, revising others, and adding substantial blocks of new material.[23] These additions include both legal material (which I deal with in chapter 2) and narrative elaborations.

Perhaps most extensive among these narrative elaborations are some of the Enochic texts described above, which *Jubilees* enhances with other traditional material about Noah and the flood (4:15-26; 5:1-12; 7:20-39; 8:1-4; 10:1-17).[24] The second major set of narrative additions elaborate on the Genesis stories about Abraham. The beginning of the cycle of stories explains why Abram left Ur of the Chaldees (11:3—12:21). The son of an idolatrous priest, he came to understand that there was only one living God, and so he set the idol's temple on fire (Hebrew *'Ur*) and fled the country. Abram's speculation about God also led him to recognize the folly of astrology (for which Chaldea was famous). Taken together, these stories recount how the conversion of an idolater led to the foundation of the chosen nation of Israel, which *Jubilees* repeatedly contrasts with idolatrous and impure Gentiles.[25] The writings of Philo and Josephus and the *Apocalypse of Abraham* attest similar stories about Abraham in the first century c.e.[26] While we cannot be certain how old the stories in *Jubilees* are, the analogy of the Enoch materials suggests that the author of *Jubilees* made use of traditional material. The antiquity of the motif of Abraham's conversion from idolatry is evident from its appearance in the recitation of Israel's history in Josh 24:2-3: "Your fathers lived of old beyond the Euphrates, Terah, the father of Abraham and of Nahor; and they served other gods. Then I took your father Abraham from beyond the River." The hints of conflict between Abraham and the other Gentiles in the *Jubilees* version may indicate that these stories originated in a Gentile context.

The second major elaborated episode in the Abraham cycle recasts the story of the sacrifice of Isaac ( *Jub.* 17:15—18:19). The author frames the testing of Abraham with a pair of scenes in heaven, where God responds to demonic accusations that Abraham obeys God only because it is in his interest. The story recalls the prologue of the book of Job (Job 1–2) and thus attests the practice of interpreting one traditional text with material from another. The same practice is attested, in reverse form, in the *Testament of Job,* where Job brings on his sufferings by seeking the true God and destroying the idolatrous temple, which is really the habitat of Satan ( *T. Job* 2–3; cf. *Jub.* 12:1-13).[27] In *Jubilees* the sacrifice of Isaac is one of ten tests that Abraham undergoes (19:7). Since the author recounts only eight of them, he appears in this case also to draw on tradition, only part of which he uses. While we do not know how old these traditions were, we must

reckon with the possibility that a process of interpreting the Genesis stories was very old. Such interpretation—originally oral—may well stem
from a time when the Genesis form of the stories was not canonical in the
sense that it came to be by the turn of the era.

The practice of retelling stories from what we now call the Bible is
documented in a wide variety of other texts found at Qumran and in the
Pseudepigrapha. The Qumran Genesis Apocryphon (1QapGen ar), written possibly in the first century B.C.E., elaborates the patriarchal narratives, recasting them into the first person singular and reshaping them to
fit his purposes.[28] The *Book of Biblical Antiquities* (Pseudo-Philo), written in
the latter half of the first century C.E., retells Genesis 1—1 Samuel with its
own set of additions, omissions, and revisions.[29] A short time later, Flavius
Josephus wrote another, much longer version of the *Antiquities of the Jews,*
again drawing on traditional interpretations of the older stories.[30] In addition to these running-narrative elaborations of biblical narrative, there
are a significant number of other texts, some demonstrably Jewish, others
perhaps Christian in their present form. In some cases, narrative elements are set in a testamentary form *(Testament of Moses, Testament of Job, Testaments of the Twelve Patriarchs, Books of Adam and Eve).*[31] A few texts convert
episodes in the Bible into independent stories *(Martyrdom of Isaiah, Joseph and
Aseneth, Paraleipomena of Jeremiah).*[32] Other texts allude to narrative elaborations that are no longer extant (cf. *1 Enoch* 8; 85–90).[33] Through all of this
one sees a tendency to interpret narrative by retelling the story.

The technique is exegetical; the storyteller elaborates on some detail
in the earlier narrative or creates an episode in the narrative on the basis
of a related text. Such elaborations or modifications are driven by a specific authorial agenda. The *Testaments of the Twelve Patriarchs* offer examples of
these techniques.[34] In elaborating Genesis 38, *Testament of Judah* 10–13
explicitly criticizes Judah's marriage to a Canaanite and warns against the
evils of wine and greed and the danger posed by women. For the author
of the *Testament of Issachar,* the episode about the mandrakes (Gen 30:14-24)
illustrates the virtue of sexual continence. The nucleus of other narrative
details in the *Testaments* can be found in references to one or the other of
the sons of Jacob in the testament of Jacob (Genesis 49) or the blessing of
Moses (Deuteronomy 33). In other cases, the author's situation may cat-

alyze the creation of an episode. The hatred that the author of *Jubilees* feels toward the Edomites—common in texts of this period—leads him to an unbiblical revision of Genesis 33: Jacob kills his brother Esau.

In summary, the texts under consideration reveal a technique of making one's theological point not by means of propositional statements but through the tendentious retelling of traditional stories preserved in the texts that came to be authoritative Scripture. It is a very old technique that has precedents within the narrative sections of the Bible itself, both in the traditional strands of the Pentateuch (Yahwist, Elohist, Deuteronomist, Priestly writers) and in the Chronicler's rewriting of the royal narratives of 1–2 Samuel and 1–2 Kings.[35] In all cases the recast narratives reflect a tension between received tradition and the author's situation, point of view, and agenda. The precise relationship between the tradition and its narrative recasting varies, and in given cases it is difficult to determine. In the case of *Jubilees,* the author presents his book as revelation; the angels who stand in God's presence dictate the patriarchal stories to Moses, interspersing them with laws that are engraved on heavenly tablets.[36] Thus the author claims divine authority for his version of the Torah. Elsewhere the relationship between ancient text and interpretation is not so clear, but in all cases older tradition is reinterpreted. What we know as the "Bible" is understood and interpreted in specific and sometimes very tendentious ways, and the base text itself includes such interpretations.

*Interpretation of the Prophetic Texts*

For many students of the New Testament and the Christian tradition, prophecy and fulfillment is the most familiar category for interpreting the Hebrew Bible. Such interpretation is explicit in the citation formulas of the Gospels (especially Matthew) and the Epistle to the Hebrews.[37] Early Christian tradition understood the biblical texts as predictions of Jesus and the events of his life. The emphasis continued in the early church fathers and was celebrated by Martin Luther, who saw the importance of the Old Testament to be in "what points to Christ" ("Was Christum treibt"). Contemporary fundamentalist Christianity interprets history as the unfolding of predictions in the Old Testament prophets (including Daniel) and the New Testament, notably Revelation, Mark 13

and its Synoptic parallels, and 1–2 Thessalonians. This manner of interpretation has precedent in Jewish practice.

Early Jewish interpretation of the prophets in terms of prediction and
fulfillment is most explicit in the Qumran *pesharim*.[38] These running commentaries on the prophets and the Psalms quote a section of biblical text
and then explain its meaning *(pesher)*. The authors of these *pesharim*
believed that the prophets and psalmists spoke about events of the imminent end time. Since, in their view, that end time had arrived, the com-
mentators were able to identify in the prophetic texts explicit references
to specific events in their own time, especially as they related to their
community. These interpretations were not simply matters of learned
opinion, in their view, but were based on divine revelation. The author of
the Habakkuk *pesher* interpreted Hab 2:1-2 as follows:

> God told Habakkuk to write down that which would happen to the
> final generation, but he did not make known to him when time
> would come to an end. . . . (But the text of Habakkuk) concerns the
> Teacher of Righteousness, *to whom God made known all the mysteries of the*
> *words of His servants the Prophets.* (1QpHab 7:1-5)[39]

The notion of prediction and fulfillment appears also in narrative writings that recast the ancient text. The *Testament of Moses* purports to be a revelation to Moses on Mount Nebo before his death.[40] In fact it is a heavily
rewritten version of the last chapters of Deuteronomy, in which the
Deuteronomic scheme of covenantal blessing-apostasy-punishment-
repentance-return of blessing is filled out in two cycles, with explicit reference to the events preceding and following the exile. The second cycle
places the author, who writes around 168 B.C.E., at the verge of the great
judgment. Other texts from this period employ the Deuteronomic
scheme to present and explain the events of the first half of the second
century B.C.E. *Jubilees* 23 is a pseudo-Mosaic prediction of events in the early
second century B.C.E. In 2 Maccabees the scheme shapes a lengthy "historical" account that reaches its climax in chapter 7, where one of the Maccabean martyrs invokes what "Moses declared in his song" as a prediction
of the martyrdom they are suffering in punishment for the sins of the
nation, and of God's promise to deliver Israel (v 6). Thus the author reuses

the tradition that is reflected in the *Testament of Moses,* but as an explanation of past events that led up to Judas Maccabeus's liberation of the temple and not as a prediction of cosmic divine intervention in the imminent future.[41]

All these writings from the Greco-Roman period accept the prophetic texts as authoritative Scripture in some sense and proceed to interpret the texts with specific reference to contemporary events. The process of interpreting the tradition is much older, however. Within the biblical texts themselves, postexilic authors interpret Deuteronomy and Jeremiah to apply to their own time. The prayers in Ezra 9 and Nehemiah 1 employ phrases from the older traditions in order to describe how the covenantal curses predicted in Deuteronomy still pertain to the postexilic Jews.[42] The speakers locate themselves within the punishment phase of the Deuteronomic scheme, and the prayers function as a ritual enactment of the repentance that will turn events from punishment to salvation, from curse to the restoration of blessing. In this case, early tradition (Deuteronomy), later to become Scripture, is being interpreted in a text that itself will become part of Scripture.

### The Servant of the Lord: A Multivalent Symbol

Probably more than any other text in the Hebrew Bible, Isa 52:13—53:12 (and, to a lesser extent, other Deutero-Isaianic texts about the Servant) has been seen by Christians as a prophecy of Christ and a key to understanding the figure of Jesus of Nazareth.[43] This is understandable since the New Testament itself quotes the passage as prophecy and employs words and phrases from the Servant texts in its descriptions of Jesus and especially his passion and death.[44]

In the past few decades some scholars have challenged the notion that the Servant passages had a pervasive influence on early Christian tradition.[45] Such reassessments of timeworn truisms need to be taken seriously by New Testament scholars and should be welcomed by them. In this case, however, close scrutiny indicates that already in pre-Christian *Jewish* texts, Second Isaiah's Servant material played an important role in explaining events in the Greco-Roman period and in developing scenarios about the eschaton.[46] Those interpretations were variegated, however, and the hermeneutical key was not always (explicitly) prophecy and fulfillment.

Second Isaiah depicts the Servant as an ambiguous figure who reinterprets older traditions.[47] He is both a personification of Israel and God's agent vis-à-vis Israel. Although he is a collective entity, he is described in personal terms. In this respect he is reminiscent of a suffering prophet like Jeremiah or Moses.[48] In other aspects he is characterized by traits and terminology that earlier applied to the Davidic king (Isa 42:1-4; 11:2-4; 49:2; cf. 11:4; 52:13-15, the Servant's exaltation). In addition, the sacrificial language that describes his death and his intercessory activity recalls priestly functions (53:10, 12).

According to one major line of early Jewish interpretation, the Servant figure is realized in the wise teachers of the Torah in the Hellenistic period. A point of departure for this interpretation is Isa 50:4: "The Lord God has given me the tongue of those who are taught, that I may know how to sustain with a word him that is weary." The opening words of 52:13 provide an additional point of contact: "My Servant will prosper" (yaśkil 'abdi). The verb śakal is interpreted in its meaning "to be wise," and the passage is seen to refer to the maskilim or wise teachers of the Torah, who served as religious leaders of the community.[49] This understanding of 52:13—53:12 was especially appropriate in the early second century B.C.E., when these leaders suffered death under the persecution of Antiochus Epiphanes.[50] Thus major aspects of the portrayal of the Servant in 50:4-9 and 52:13—53:12 spoke to the situation of the maskilim.

Second Isaiah's portrait of the Servant had a second facet, however: the Suffering Servant would be vindicated and exalted. Thus the material in Second Isaiah became a paradigm for the exaltation and vindication of the suffering spokesman of the Lord. Hence Daniel's use of Isaiah 52–53: "The wise will shine like the brightness of the firmament, and those who bring many to righteousness, like the stars forever and ever" (Dan 12:3). The author plays on the Hebrew word zhr, which can mean not only "shine" and "brightness," but also "teach" or "admonish" (cf. Sir 24:32 for the metaphor). Similarly, Dan 12:3 applies the expression "cause many to be righteous" (yaṣdiq harabbim, Isa 53:11) to the teaching activity of the maskilim that leads the community to righteous conduct (maṣdiqē harabbim).

A more extensive explication of Isaiah 52–53 in terms of the persecution and exaltation of the righteous spokesman of the Lord is laid out in

Wisdom of Solomon 2 and 5. This text from around the turn of the era paraphrases parts of Isaiah 52–53 in a literary form that draws on the stories of the persecuted and exalted courtier known from such texts as the Joseph story in Genesis 37–45 and the tales in Daniel 3 and 6.[51] The Deutero-Isaianic material is also used in 2 Maccabees 7, the story of the martyrdom of the seven brothers and their mother, who also serve as God's spokespersons, admonishing Antiochus for his opposition to God.[52]

Wisdom 2 and 5 and 2 Maccabees 7 reveal two important interpretive characteristics. First, they take words or phrases from the prophetic text and build them into narrative elements in a story. Antiochus is literally astonished at the youths' conduct (2 Macc 7:12; cf. Isa 52:14; see also Wis 5:2). The third brother refers to the tongue that God has given him, which Antiochus orders cut out (2 Macc 7:10; cf. Isa 50:4). This technique of creating a narrative incident on the basis of a detail in the original text parallels the haggadic method referred to above (p. 14). Second, both Wisdom and 2 Maccabees weave a narrative out of material derived from several different biblical passages. The first brother, though a personification of Deutero-Isaiah's Servant, describes his circumstances as a fulfillment of the Song of Moses (2 Macc 7:6; Deut 32:36), and the episode corresponds functionally to the repentance element in the Deuteronomic scheme.[53] The author of Wisdom identifies the kings who observe the Servant's exaltation in Isaiah 52–53 with the wicked royal opponent of God in Isaiah 14, and the same exegetical combination appears in 2 Maccabees, where chapter 9 describes the death of Antiochus as the fall of the mythic figure in Isaiah 14.[54] Thus, behind Wisdom of Solomon 2 and 5 and 2 Maccabees 7 and 9 stands a common exegetical tradition that weaves Deutero-Isaianic material together with material from Isaiah 14 in order to reinterpret Isaiah as a description of the suffering and vindication of the spokesmen of God and the punishment of their royal persecutors.[55] Moreover, as is clear from Wisdom and its schematic story, this manner of interpretation does not posit a single fulfillment of prophecy, but finds in the prophetic text the description of a *type* of person, whose career and fate are repeated at different times and places. In the same vein, two Qumran hymns describe their author's situation as that of the Servant of the Lord: "My tongue has been the tongue of your disciples" (1QH 15[7]:10; 16[8]:36; cf. Isa 50:4).

Finally, the variety of interpretation is noteworthy. According to 2 Macc 7:37-38 (cf. 8:5), the deaths of the brothers turn God's wrath to forgiveness. Its quasi-propitiatory function will become explicit in the rewriting of this story in 4 Maccabees (cf. 17:22),[56] and this interpretation of Isaiah 52–53 will play an important role in New Testament interpretations of the death of Jesus (see below, pp. 111–12). The Wisdom of Solomon, however, ignores this interpretive possibility and incorporates the sacrificial language in Isaiah 53:10 into a double simile: "Like gold in the furnace he tried them, and like a sacrificial burnt offering he accepted them" (Wis 3:6).

Perhaps the most remarkable of all Jewish interpretations of Deutero-Isaiah's Servant material occurs in the Parables of Enoch (1 Enoch 37–71), an apocalyptic text from the turn of the era, which will concern us in more detail in chapter 4 (see below, pp. 104–6).[57] Of interest here is the manner in which it interprets tradition. The central character does not suffer, but is a transcendent heavenly figure who acts as vindicator of the suffering righteous and chosen. As such, he personifies biblical material about Daniel's "one like a son of man" (46:1; cf. Dan 7:13-14) and the Davidic king (1 En. 49:3; 62:2; cf. Isa 11:2-4; 48:8, 10; Ps 2:2), as well as the Servant of YHWH (1 En. 48:1-6 and 49:4; cf. Isa 49:1-6; 42:1; 1 En. 62–63; cf. Isaiah 52–53). As in the previous texts, Jewish interpretation weaves together material from diverse sources, reading one source on the basis of the other: the Servant becomes the Anointed One; the Davidic king becomes a transcendent heavenly figure; the heavenly Son of Man is king and Servant. Thus each of these three sets of "biblical" texts—about the Servant, the one like a son of man, and the Davidic king—exists in an interpretive context, and the respective texts and their interpretive contexts stand in tension, or even in open conflict, with one another.

## Summary

These examples lead to some generalizations and conclusions about Jewish attitudes toward Scripture at the turn of the era. (1) What we now think of as Jewish Scripture (the thirty-nine books of the Hebrew Bible) was not fixed as authoritative Scripture for all first-century Jews in all places. A few of these works were probably not of high authority for some people. For others, works like *1 Enoch, Jubilees,* and the Qumran Temple Scroll were authoritative. The texts of all these works were not completely fixed. (2) *Scriptura* was not *sola.* A given text or set of texts was accompanied by traditional interpretation, which might have been developed in comparison with other texts and which was formulated in light of one's historical situation. (3) This interpretation was not uniform; a given text or set of texts was understood in sometimes radically different ways by different people and religious communities. (4) Such interpretations could not necessarily be separated from the text itself (as they were formally in the Qumran *pesharim*), but were understood to be *the* correct way to understand the text(s). (5) This process of interpretation was not new. It was at work not only in rewritten narratives of the Greco-Roman period, but also in the text of the Hebrew Bible itself, where one text transformed, commented on, or alluded to another text. From the start, what came to be "Scripture" was treated as tradition, to be interpreted in the context of other tradition and of one's circumstances. (6) The phenomenon of Scripture and its (authoritative) interpretation may help to explain scribal freedom in creating textual variants (where they are not mistakes) and the authority of works like *Jubilees,* the Temple Scroll, and parts of *1 Enoch.* Scribal variants are interpretation. *Jubilees* is not simply another book; it provides the authoritative interpretation of Genesis and Exodus, particularly as it pertains to right torah.

## Scripture in the Early Church

"Scripture" was obviously a major category for the Christian writers of the first and second centuries. The New Testament is saturated with quotations from the Hebrew Bible, or, more specifically, its Greek translations.[58] Often the text introduces these quotations with formulas that appeal explicitly to "Scripture," what "is written," or what God or Scripture "says," or imply Scripture with language about fulfillment.[59] In other places one senses the use of biblical idioms and style, even when there is not formal citation or extensive quotation.[60] Authors refer or allude to characters in the biblical books. In the second century and beyond, the situation becomes more complex as some authors begin to cite or treat

New Testament texts as authoritative Scripture, and the church, in response to what it considers to be its heretical opponents, develops a second part to its scriptural canon. Nonetheless, especially in response to Marcion, the Greek translation of the Hebrew Bible continues to play a major role in the argumentation, theologizing, and preaching of Christian authors.

Of early Christian authors, however, we may still ask the question: What is Scripture and in what traditional ways is it being interpreted?

## The Biblical Canon of the Early Church

According to the traditional view, the Scripture of the early church comprised the collection of thirty-nine books that we have come to know as "the Old Testament" or "the Hebrew Bible," or, to be more specific, the Greek translation of these texts, "the Septuagint." Persons in the Roman Catholic and Eastern Orthodox traditions maintain that the extra works and textual additions in this collection (called "Apocrypha" by Protestants) were also part of the Bible of the early church.

The status of the "Apocrypha" in the early church is uncertain.[61] Were these books and expansions of books part of the early church's Bible? Their inclusion in Christian codices of the Greek Old Testament suggests this. Yet it is noteworthy that, for the most part, the New Testament and the writers of the early church do not quote and refer to these books. Nonetheless, some exceptions indicate knowledge of material in the Apocrypha, whether it be the books themselves or another form of the traditions contained in them. The passion narratives in Mark and Matthew reflect material found in Wisdom 2 and 5.[62] In Romans 1, Paul's argument parallels the anti-idol polemic in Wisdom 14–15.[63]

Several facts are clear. The extraction of the Apocrypha as a separate collection was the work of Jerome, a fourth-century scholar who had a high esteem for the Hebrew Scriptures as the Bible of the Jewish people.[64] Jerome's landmark canonical decision notwithstanding, Christian scribes before and after Jerome included these texts in the codices of the Greek Bible. These books continued to be included in the codices of daughter translations of the Greek created in the Syriac, Ethiopic, Armenian, and other Eastern Christian communities.

It is not only the Apocrypha that are of concern here, however. Some works of the Pseudepigrapha were also considered to be authoritative and useful for the early church. Most notable was *1 Enoch*. Jude 14–15 formally cites *1 Enoch* 1 as something that "Enoch prophesied." The author of Luke or his tradition knew something like the last chapters of *1 Enoch*.[65] The Gospel traditions about the Son of Man interpreted Daniel 7 in light of the interpretation now preserved in the Parables of Enoch (see below, pp. 110–11).[66] Matthew's special material (M) appears especially to have utilized this material.[67] The epistle of *Barnabas* quotes part of *1 Enoch* as "Scripture." Tertullian refers to the patriarch as a prophet, quotes a passage from *1 Enoch,* and uses material from others. Other allusions to Enochic traditions appear in the writings of Justin Martyr, Irenaeus, Pseudo-Clement, Clement of Alexandria, Origen, and other authors of the second to fifth centuries.[68] While none of this justifies the conclusion that the books of Enoch were universally considered to be on a par with the books of the Hebrew Bible, it does indicate the substantial influence of these texts, and it suggests that, as in other matters, we must posit considerable variety in the early church. Moreover, lest one be provincial, the text of *1 Enoch* continues to the present time to be printed in the Bibles of the Ethiopian church, as does the book of *Jubilees*.

### The Text of Scripture

It is a well-established fact, demonstrated by more than a century of New Testament scholarship, that more often than not New Testament authors quote (and modify) the letter of the Greek translation of the Hebrew Scriptures, even in cases where it diverges from the Hebrew text.[69] Indeed, it is often to the Christian author's advantage that the Greek differs from the Hebrew because it allows the interpreter to make a point that could not be made on the basis of the Hebrew. The translation of *'almah* ("young woman") as *parthenos* ("virgin") in Isa 7:14 provides early Christians with a scriptural basis for the virginal conception of Jesus. The author of the Epistle to the Hebrews finds documentation of Jesus' incarnation in the idiosyncratic Greek translation of Ps 40:6, where "ears you have dug for me" is rendered "a body you have furnished me" (Heb 10:5-10). It is a matter of dispute, often not to be resolved, whether when a given Christian writer cites the Greek Bible to advantage, that writer or the tradition he transmits actually found the variant in a Hebrew text. The fact remains, however, that Christian writers built their exposition and apologetic on a lively and varying tradition of Jewish exposition and scribal practice, not on a fixed biblical text.

## Biblical Interpretation in the Early Church

**The Church Read Scripture within Its Traditional Interpretations**
Like their Jewish contemporaries, early Christians read the books they considered to be authoritative within the context of traditional interpretations. In the instance just cited, the Gospels might quote the *words* of Daniel 7, but the *interpretation* of the Son of Man as judge is attested in *1 Enoch*. Similarly, the book of Revelation quotes Davidic texts from Isaiah 11 and Psalm 2 (Rev 1:16; 2:27; 10:15, 18; 11:5), but it agrees with *1 Enoch* in ascribing them to a transcendent savior identified with the Son of Man and quite possibly the Servant of the Lord (5:6, 12).[70]

The Servant figure, moreover, is more pervasive in the New Testament than some recent iconoclastic interpretations have argued. As we shall see later, the early church read texts of Deutero-Isaiah within the context of Jewish interpretations that identify the Servant with the type of righteous sufferer depicted in the stories of Daniel 3 and 6, Wisdom of Solomon 2 and 5, and the Psalms (see below, pp. 106–7). In these cases, it is imperative that historical exegetes read the scriptural text (Second Isaiah) as it was read by some first-century Jews, within a tradition of interpretation that was at least two centuries old and that can be documented in pre-Christian Jewish texts.

Other examples of traditional Jewish interpretation are evident at many points in the New Testament. Both Paul and the author of Acts cite the tradition, documented in *Jubilees,* that the Torah was given by angels (Gal 3:19; Acts 7:53). The Epistle of James speaks of the "patience" of Job (Jas 5:11), certainly not evident in the canonical book, but at the heart of the *Testament of Job.*[71] In its list of heroes, Heb 11:35-38 alludes to the story of the mother and her seven sons in 2 Maccabees 7 and to legends about the deaths of Isaiah and Jeremiah, now preserved in the *Martyrdom of Isaiah* and the *Paraleipomena of Jeremiah*.[72] Many more cases could be cited, and others doubtless remain to be discovered and documented.

## The Use of Rabbinic Traditions in New Testament Exegesis

A half century ago, scholars often interpreted the New Testament in light of material drawn from the large corpus of rabbinic writings: the Talmudim, the Targumim, and the Midrashim. A major resource for such comparative work was the monumental commentary on the New Testament by Hermann Strack and Paul Billerbeck, published mostly in the 1920s.[73] For those not personally familiar with the rabbinic corpus (most New Testament scholars), this multivolume reference work offered a gold mine of parallels from the rabbinic and some other Jewish writings. However, subsequent scholarship on the rabbinic materials has warned against an uncritical use of these texts, for two reasons. First, parallels, however close, must be read in their context and not simply lifted from a compendium.[74] To do otherwise is unfair to the source being cited and to the text being interpreted. Second, careful form-critical work on the rabbinic texts during the past few decades has demonstrated that these texts consist of many layers, and that the dating of any given passage can be extremely problematic even when it is ascribed to a known and datable rabbi.[75] These caveats stand.

At the same time, the evidence presented in this chapter adds a complication for the interpreter. Narrative haggadah, well known in the rabbinic texts, has a long history dating back into the Persian period, and some of the traditions in the Talmudim, Targumim, and Midrashim are paralleled in earlier texts of the Apocrypha and Pseudepigrapha.[76] Thus, if a text in the rabbinic writings seems to shed light on a New Testament passage, one needs to ascertain whether the tradition is attested also in earlier texts. Even if one cannot find such an earlier form of the tradition, one must consider whether positing such an earlier tradition does shed light on the New Testament passage in question. Scholars have cited rabbinic tradition about the giving of the Torah at Pentecost as background for the story of the giving of the Spirit in Acts 2.[77] Others have emphasized that the tradition is unattested before the third century C.E.[78] Both groups have a point. One should not simply posit what is convenient with the claim that later texts reflected earlier tradition. At the same time, thoroughgoing skepticism is inconsonant with the facts as we know them and as new discoveries continue to reveal them: extant texts represent only a fragment of the written and oral tradition that once existed. Caution, honest scholarly tentativeness, and careful methodology remain the best approach to the data.

## Jewish Precedents for the Rise and Development of the Jesus Tradition

The lively, variegated nature of Jewish interpretation of its sacred traditions offers some precedents and models for our understanding of the rise and development of Christian traditions about Jesus of Nazareth. It should not be surprising if the first Christians—being Jews or heirs of Jewish tradition—adopted attitudes about the foundational traditions of their newly shaped religion that reflected Jewish attitudes and replicated Jewish practice.

### The Creation of Narrative Haggadah about Jesus

Many have observed that the narratives about Jesus' conception, birth, and childhood parallel Jewish stories and imitate "midrashic" technique. Models for these stories can be found in the biblical narratives about Samson and Samuel and about Moses' persecution by Pharaoh.[79] Narrative elements in the passion accounts reflect motifs in the Psalms about the suffering and restoration of the righteous one. Theological conservatives argue, however, that early Christians would not indulge in the creation of untruths about their Messiah.

The evidence presented in this chapter indicates that, when it came to narrative, Jews were quite broad-minded in their understanding of what was true. Storytellers could elaborate a biblical episode or create a whole new episode on the basis of a nonnarrative element in the text or in another text, or because they thought that their situation called for such an embellishment. Thus they could create long stories about Abraham's conversion from idolatry and they could depict Jacob killing his brother Esau (see above, pp. 13, 15). In other instances they could: (1) take a historical kernel (the death of the Maccabean martyrs); (2) read it in the light of Deutero-Isaianic motifs about the suffering and vindication of the Servant, the return of the children of Mother Zion, and the creation and redemption of Israel; and (3) narrativize those motifs into the rich and provocative story of the seven sons and their mother (2 Maccabees 7), and then repeatedly revise it to fit new circumstances (4 Maccabees, the rabbinic writings, and the history of Josippon).[80]

Such an impulse to storytelling, which is as universal as humanity, understands truth in a freer and richer way than the recounting of facts, events, and propositions. For the Jews, sacred narrative traditions spoke in new ways to new times, and nonnarrative traditions could be converted into narrative and embodied in stories about the past and present. Common to both is the notion that God's activity touches human beings in specific and concrete ways, which one can understand because they parallel one's experience, or which one can marvel at because of the disparity with one's experience. That early Christians employed such techniques in the infancy and the passion narratives about Jesus the Messiah and Righteous One should not surprise us, since it is explicable on the basis of attitudes and practices inherited from Judaism.[81]

### The Development of the Synoptic Tradition

Jewish narrative technique also illuminates the subsequent development of gospel (especially Synoptic) traditions about Jesus. It is axiomatic for critical scholarship that the respective Synoptic authors rewrote one another's texts, sometimes on the basis of oral Jesus tradition, sometimes with a view toward details in the Jewish Scriptures, and that they did so in response to the perceived needs of their communities as these were influenced by the events of their own time. In so doing, these early Christian preachers and teachers were following impulses and practices in place in the Jewish community. Even if their appeal to the authority of Jesus the risen Lord presupposed a sense of their own inspiration, as seems to have been the case, there is an analogy in some of the rewritten biblical material, for example, in the Temple Scroll, which recasts biblical law into the first person singular, and in *Jubilees,* which presents its contents as angelic revelation.[82]

## Disagreements over the Bible and Its Interpretation:
## A Cause for "Unbelief"

In Jewish practice, people could disagree as to what texts comprised authoritative sacred tradition, what was its correct text, and what constituted its correct interpretation. It followed from this that one person or one community could reject the other's teaching or practices because they did not accept the authority of a given book or textual reading, or because they considered a particular interpretation to be incorrect or implausible. We shall see specific instances of this in subsequent chapters. In the first century, specific nuances that the early church found in scriptural texts or particular christological interpretations of those texts could be rejected by some Jews on the same grounds that non-Christian Jews could disagree with one another's interpretations. For many, the books of Enoch, with their teaching about the son of man, were not authoritative. Moreover, it was inherent in the very nature of biblical interpretation that a given interpretation need not be "obvious" and that one could accept the authority of the text while disputing or rejecting a particular interpretation of the text. Claims about the "unbelief" of first- and second-century Jews are often governed by Christian apologetic with little appreciation for the variety in "canon" and text in the first century and the nature of interpretation as it was practiced then both by Christian and non-Christian Jews.

# chapter 2

# Torah and the Righteous Life

## A Theological Problem for the Church

As Israel's sacred traditions began to coalesce into a collection of Scriptures, pride of place and the highest value were accorded to the Torah, the five books of Moses. For Christians, however, this Torah, or "law," came to form the center of a cluster of crucial terms whose meaning has continued to be nuanced by polemical considerations. Other words and expressions in this group include: works, works-righteousness, legalism, Pharisees, and rabbis. Together, these terms, thus interpreted, have created a highly negative view of Judaism at the turn of the era. According to this view, Jewish religion was dominated by a nit-picking obsession with the detailed observance of commandments and prescriptions, attested in rabbinic debates about what was appropriate behavior, and when. The observant Jew was caught in a double bind, always striving for a salvation born of perfect behavior, and forever frustrated and desperate because this was unattainable. The Pharisees epitomized this piety in a special way, self-righteously despising others who could not attain their level of perfection, and hypocritical because they did not admit their failures or recognize how they put the observance of individual commandments above "the spirit of the law." This legalistic religion, born after the tragedy of the Babylonian exile, stood in stark contrast to the vital, ethical religion of the biblical prophets.[1]

This portrayal of Judaism derives from at least three sources. The first is the New Testament itself. All four Gospels depict Jesus of Nazareth in repeated controversy with the Jewish establishment, notably the Pharisees and the scribes, whose detailed concern about the Law is emphasized in *stories* about Jesus and whose hypocrisy and self-righteousness are highlighted in *sayings* attributed to him. The Gospels uniformly claim, moreover, that Jesus' death was triggered by a conspiracy among Jewish leaders, especially the chief priests, the scribes, and the elders, who rejected the authority of his teaching and were threatened by his popularity.[2] Christian views about the Jewish understanding of Torah have been influenced not only by the Gospel narratives but also by the corpus of Pauline epistles, whose interpretation has been governed by Galatians and Romans, their dichotomy of law and gospel, and their opposition of justification by faith and justification by the deeds of the Law.[3]

The second major source for Christian attitudes toward the Torah is the theology of the Protestant reformers, especially Martin Luther's writings, which drew on the Pauline formulation as a prototype for their own controversy with medieval Catholicism. The Jews of the first century became stand-ins for popes and Catholic theologians, and Paul and his opponents represented fundamentally opposed kinds of religion—one governed by faith and the other by a concern for righteousness obtained through scrupulous attention to the performance of one's religious obligations.[4] This Lutheran interpretation of the first-century documents has dominated the influential handbooks and commentaries written by Continental Protestant exegetes and historians of the nineteenth and the first half of the twentieth century and has shaped preaching, teaching, and popular views about the Jews and Judaism.[5]

Between the New Testament and the Reformation lies another, less obvious source for Christian misperceptions of Judaism, namely, the major christological controversies of the second to fifth centuries. Already in the first century, Christians sought to convince Jews of Jesus' divine nature, however they characterized or described it (see below, chapter 4). As the rift between the church and the synagogue solidified, divisions also developed within Christianity. First, the catholic church differentiated itself from Marcionites and Gnostics, and then it focused its attention on the right (orthodox) and wrong (heterodox) views of Jesus and his relationship to God. Thus, ironically, the church spawned the kind of debate and conflict that its theologians would later attribute to the rabbis and the kind of self-righteousness that they would claim was a hallmark of the Pharisees. One of the long-term results of this internal conflict has been a mind-set that identifies right and wrong *doctrine* as the touchstone of true religion. Such a field of vision often marginalizes the Hebrew Bible's emphasis on right and wrong *conduct,* and in this context one can perceive the Jewish emphasis on Torah to be alien to biblical (i.e., New Testament) religion. The situation was exacerbated, ironically, by the church's response to Marcion; the perceived need to add the New Testament to the biblical canon laid the groundwork for, in effect, considering the Old Testament to be incomplete and therefore of inferior value.[6]

The results of these complex developments are difficult to overestimate. The identity of Jesus was divisive in some circles from the beginning, and the Gospels' portrayal of the Jewish leaders' responsibility for the death of Jesus was linked to their rejection of his status as Messiah and Son of God.[7] Alongside this has been a fundamental distortion of the nature of Judaism as a legalistic perversion of biblical religion and thus incompatible with Christianity.[8] Carried to the extreme, these twin considerations created an anti-Jewish theological climate that complemented and, perhaps for some, justified the anti-Semitism that fueled pogroms and the Holocaust.[9] More immediately they continue to erect barriers to dialogue and mutual understanding. Christians wonder how Jews can deny that Jesus was the Messiah and affirm that one is saved by obedience to the Torah. Jews are puzzled at christological interpretations of their Bible and are mystified when they are characterized as legalists. Mutual understanding can develop by clarifying the record on both accounts.

In this chapter I examine the two propositions asserted in the Christian description of Judaism that I have just summarized. I argue that Jewish attitudes about the Torah derive from the Bible itself, that claims of "legalism" reflect a selective interpretation of the Jewish texts, and that a concern to live in accordance with God's will dominates the New Testament itself.

## Torah in the Hebrew Scriptures

In order to assess the character and role of Torah in Jewish religion, we must highlight two major factors in the Hebrew Scriptures' understanding of Torah—factors not always fully appreciated by Christian exegetes and theologians. First, the commandments of the Torah are not simply collections of laws; they are an integral component of a covenantal structure. Second, concern about the Torah is not limited to the Pentateuch; the Hebrew Scriptures as a whole are pervaded by the imperative to obey the divine will or its implications, whether or not one appeals explicitly to the Torah.

### The Covenantal Context of Torah

The form-critical work of George Mendenhall and Klaus Baltzer has helped to clarify within Christian scholarly circles what has been patent to Jews all along: the commandments of the Torah are an inextricable part of the larger Israelite conception of covenant.[10] The notion is widespread in the Hebrew Bible, but is most clearly explicated in Deuteronomy. The God who lays commandments and obligations upon Israel first chose Israel from among the nations and invited this people into a special relationship. Through acts of grace, God called Abraham out of Chaldea and rescued Israel from Egyptian oppression. Thus a covenantal relationship was created between God and people, symbolized variously as husband and wife and parent and child.[11] Within this relationship Israel's God presented commandments and ordinances that Israel was to observe faithfully. To the extent that Israel was faithful to its obligations, the people would experience God's blessings—long life, health and safety, and fertility in one's family and on the land (Deut 28:1-14). Disobedience, on the other hand, would bring the curses of the covenant upon the people—a shortened life, sickness, drought, famine and barrenness, invasion and captivity (28:15-29). The cause-and-effect relationship of disobedience and curse could be broken, however. If the nation repented and turned to God—that is, if they began rightly to obey the Torah—they would experience the covenantal blessings (30:1-10). Thus the commandments of the Torah lay within a broader structure and context that can be schematized as follows:

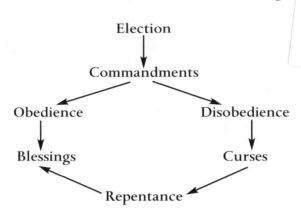

This scheme makes evident that in the *biblical* view human deeds of obedience and disobedience to the Torah are pivotal to the covenant. God rewards those who obey the commandments and punishes disobedience; the restoration of divine favor—that is, deliverance from the covenantal curses—is predicated on the return to covenantal obedience that is realized in human actions. At the same time, it is clear that the commandments, and obedience to them, are preceded by God's gracious activity.

## Torah as Instruction Rather Than Simply Law

The normal modern translation of Hebrew *torah* is "law," which, in turn, reflects the decision of the translators of the Greek Bible to use the noun *nomos* ("law") and the regular use of this same noun in the New Testament.[12] As a result, reference to the first part of the Hebrew Bible often focuses on the laws contained in it, either as customs regularly followed (when things are right) or as the embodiment of these customs in commands to do such and such. Hebrew *torah,* however, means "instruction."[13] This broad concept is more appropriate to the contents of the Pentateuch than is its description as "law," since the largest part of Genesis–Deuteronomy comprises not commandments but narrative (almost all of Genesis and Numbers, much of Exodus, and part of Deuteronomy) and instruction that is not cast in the form of individual and specific commandments and ordinances (the sermonlike addresses in Deuteronomy). For Jews, the whole of this section was divine "instruction" revealed by God and written by Moses.

## The Prevalence of Torah and Covenant in the Hebrew Scriptures

Jews of the first century certainly distinguished between the Pentateuch and the rest of the developing collection of their sacred writings, referring to them as "Torah," "Prophets," and "Other Books" (see above, p. 10). Nonetheless, the Hebrew Bible as a whole is stamped with the notion of covenant and with an emphasis on God as the giver of commandments and the judge of those who obey or disobey them. Human actions vis-à-vis the divine will are pivotal to the content of most of the Hebrew Bible.

The narrative about the first human beings revolves around a divine command, human disobedience, and God's punishment. The flood is God's judgment on human wickedness. All of this happens before God makes a covenant with Noah, calls Abraham, or instructs Israel at Mount Sinai. From the very beginning, there are right and wrong ways for human beings to act, and God is depicted as one who responds appropriately to such righteous and wicked conduct.

The narratives in Joshua, Judges, 1 and 2 Samuel, and 1 and 2 Kings—variously called "the Former Prophets" and the "Deuteronomistic History"[14]—have as their major motif Israel's response to the covenantal commandments (mainly the prohibition of idolatry) and God's reward or (primarily) punishment of this response.

Large parts of the preexilic, exilic, and postexilic prophetic books focus on the same topics, issuing "lawsuits" for disobedience of the covenant and critiques of idolatry and violations of the Torah's commands to act justly toward one's fellow human beings.[15] Additionally, one hears the appeal to return to the faithful conduct that will bring divine blessing.[16] After the exile, the writings of the Chronicler recast the Deuteronomistic History, with a focus on the covenant with David, but also with a concern for human action and divine judgment.[17] In Ezra and Nehemiah, Israel seeks to bring about the conditions that will realize the full return of God's blessing, which is still not in place despite the nation's return from exile.[18]

## The Wisdom Literature: A Special Case

The wisdom literature in the Hebrew Scriptures fits the pattern I have been describing in a special way and also stands in tension with it. Its hallmark is a kind of intellectualizing and speculation about the nature of things, not least the character of divine justice.[19] Much in the book of Proverbs is of non-Israelite origin.[20] Nonetheless, many early readers of the Hebrew Bible would have folded the linking of human action and its consequences into the dynamics of the notion of covenant.[21]

In other wisdom books, intellectual activity has a different focus. For the authors of these texts, the ineluctable connection between human action and divine response is far from clear and is not taken for granted. Although the book of Job does not mention the covenant, both the prose narrative frame and the speeches of Job's friends presume something close to the Deuteronomic notion of divine reward and punishment of human deeds; the narrative describes the reward of Job's righteousness, and the speeches interpret Job's humiliation as evidence of divine punishment for undisclosed sin. The protagonist, on the other hand, challenges God's justice and calls for his day in court.[22] A similar agonizing over the absence of divine vindication is evident in the psalms of lament, even if the psalmists anticipate ultimate reward.[23] For the author of Ecclesiastes, a fair complement of reward and punishment is not evident, and the fates of the righteous and the sinner are alike.[24] Buried in these texts are the seeds of things to come—a struggle with the straightforward notion that God is the just vindicator of the righteous and punisher of the wicked and a dawning recognition that "when bad things happen to good people," the old formulas no longer work. Theodicy—defending the justice of God against its learned detractors (including oneself)—will dominate the Jewish and Christian literature of the Greco-Roman period, notably, the apocalypses and the speculations of the Gnostics.[25]

## Divine Justice and Grace

Although the notion of justice is the very stuff of Israelite covenantal theology, this axis of action and just recompense should not obscure the biblical notion of grace that is also built into the covenantal structure and stands in tension with God's justice. God's election of Abraham and Israel is an act of grace, not based on merit.[26] Consistency may suggest that the covenantal view of reward and punishment implies the conclusion that God expels the sinner or the sinful nation from the covenantal relationship. Nonetheless, prophetic appeals to repentance, promises of return and restoration, and certain sacrificial institutions reflect a powerful consciousness of divine grace that issues in forgiveness.[27] Even major sins need not irreversibly break the covenantal relationship.[28] The undeserved divine grace that initiated the covenant invites a healing of the breach and a restoration of the covenantal blessings. Justice and grace are two sides of the covenantal coin. God rewards or punishes human actions, but in the latter case God graciously invites the renewed obedience that will be rewarded. Conversely, one must respond to God's gracious invitation through obedient action if the blessing is to return.

## Torah and the Righteous Life in Early Judaism

Against this biblical background, in which the divine Judge rewards and punishes obedience and disobedience to the Torah, it remains to be seen whether Judaism in the Greco-Roman period represents the transformation, and perversion, of this biblical religion into the kind of "legalistic" religion described at the beginning of this chapter. Historical method requires that we draw our primary evidence from contemporary Jewish texts rather than Christian polemics against Judaism.

### The Role of Torah during the Antiochan Persecution

Texts generated in response to persecution of the Jews by Antiochus Epiphanes (168–165 B.C.E.) provide some of our earliest evidence for "postbiblical" Jewish attitudes about the Torah. These texts include works contemporary to the event, like the book of Daniel and the *Testament of Moses,* as well as the later "historical" accounts in 1 and 2 Maccabees. The latter supply reasonably reliable information about events during the first third of the second century B.C.E. The former are firsthand testimony from the period.[29]

The events of the 160s were set against the background of a growing rift between Jews who adopted Greek culture and those who found such hellenization incompatible with Judaism.[30] The broader picture of Hellenistic Judaism will concern us in chapter 6. Here I focus on Jewish reactions to the decrees of Antiochus that outlawed the practice of the Torah. Jews were not permitted to observe the Sabbath and other feasts commanded in the Torah; they were forbidden to circumcise their sons; they were forced to eat food declared unclean in the Torah and to march in ritual processions of the Greek god Dionysus; altars to foreign gods were constructed around the countryside, and the Jerusalem temple was rededicated to the Syrian deity Baal Shamaim; copies of the Torah were confiscated and burned. Persons who disobeyed the decrees could be sentenced to death. In short, Antiochus forbade the observance of the Torah and commanded Jewish participation in the rites of foreign gods. The latter constituted idolatry, and other of Antiochus's commands involved the violation of the Torah through either omission or commission. At stake was a Jew's ability to practice her or his religion by living the obedient life commanded by the Torah. Faithfulness to the Torah brought the threat of death; saving one's life required disobedience of God's commands.

Many Jews chose to obey the Torah, and the slogan "We will die rather than transgress the laws of our fathers" runs through the sources (*T. Mos.* 9:6; 1 Macc 1:62-63; 2:19-22, 50; 2 Macc 6:27-28; 7:2, 9, 11, 23, 37). Daniel 11:33-35 alludes to the martyrs' deaths, and the stories in Daniel 1, 3, and 6 offer examples of people willing to be put to death rather than compromise their religion. The story of Taxo and his sons in *Testament of Moses* 9 repeats the motif, as do the legendary accounts in 2 Maccabees 6–7 and the brief allusions in 1 Macc 1:50-64; 2:29-38. The same sentiment was expressed in the militant actions of the Hasmoneans (the family of Judas Maccabeus) and their associates.

These events and the narratives that recount them are noteworthy in several respects. First, as in earlier biblical sources, the observance of the Torah is integral to the Jewish religion. Second, for substantial numbers of Jews, it follows from this fundamental point that one should be prepared to die rather than violate the Torah; *life* in obedience to the Torah may require that one *die* rather than disobey the Torah. Apart from the book of Daniel, the motif, as it applies to the passive deaths of the martyrs, does not clearly appear in the Hebrew Bible. The militancy of the Hasmoneans, on the other hand, seems to have been a case of holy warfare, which the Hebrew Bible presents as a divine institution, enacted at

God's command.[31] Third, the martyrs' deaths occur two centuries before the death of Jesus, which will become prototypical for Christian admonitions to martyrdom, and the stories of the Jewish martyrs inform the accounts of Jesus' death and the deaths of the Christian martyrs.[32]

## Faith and Obedient Action in the Jewish Texts

A dichotomy between faith and the deeds of the Law is a major theme in Paul's epistles to the Romans and the Galatians and has played a major role in some of the Reformation theologies based on these texts. In that context the Jewish texts just discussed may seem very strange. Although the term "faith" does not occur, the stories of the Maccabean heroes weld trust in God with obedience to the Torah or action in behalf of the Torah. Indeed, martyrs are people who explain their *actions* by testifying about their *trust* in the God whom they obey (Daniel 3, 6; *Testament of Moses* 10; 2 Maccabees 7). Particularly striking is the case of the three young men. They intend to obey their God even if they are not rescued from death (Dan 3:17-18): "If it be so, our God whom we serve is able to deliver us from the burning fiery furnace; and he will deliver us out of your hand, O king. But if not, be it known to you, O king, that we will not serve your gods or worship the golden image which you have set up." The speeches of several of the seven brothers and their mother in 2 Maccabees 7 tie their willingness to die for the Torah to their belief that God will vindicate this obedience by raising them from the dead (2 Macc 7:9, 11, 23, 29, 36).

Other texts also posit a close connection between action and expected reward. In his speech to his sons, the Hasmonean patriarch Mattathias recites a catalog of the patriarchs, juxtaposing their obedience and the divine reward they received; and he exhorts his sons to act firmly in behalf of the Torah, knowing that they too will be rewarded. The book of Tobit depicts its protagonist as a person whose devotion and trust in God leads him to acts of radical obedience to the Torah, which are ultimately rewarded, as Tobit claimed they would be.[33] In the spirit of the Maccabean zealots, Judith exhorts her people to trust in divine deliverance, and she exhibits this trust by risking her life for the temple and her people.[34]

All of these stories, far from attesting a dichotomy between faith and action or an external obedience to commandments, indicate an inextrica-

ble link between actions—including performance of divine ordinances—
and the trust in God that generates and enables such actions. Although
the word "faith" does not occur, the notion of trust is explicit, as is the
heroes' and heroines' faithfulness to the Torah.

The term "faith" does occur, however, in Jewish references to the
Abraham story. An idea that the Bible attaches to the patriarch's faith in
God's promise (Gen 15:6) is reinterpreted to explain the motivation for
his radical act of obedience in being ready to sacrifice the child of promise
(Genesis 22), an act that God rewards (*Jub.* 17:15—18:13; Sir 44:20-21; 1
Macc 2:52).[35] In this way the covenantal nexus of obedience and reward is
explicitly connected with, and rooted in, the faith of the obedient.

In summary, a whole complement of Jewish texts, many of them associated with the Antiochan persecution, explicate Torah observance and
the righteous life as functions of one's trust in the God who rewards the
righteous. Although the observance of certain commandments may be in
focus, there is no evidence of legalism, slavish and fearful obedience, deprecating self-righteousness, or hypocrisy. To the contrary, the righteous
are willing, exuberant, faithful servants of the covenantal God, whom
they trust to reward the potentially dangerous actions that they carry out
in obedience to God's commandments.

## Torah and the Wisdom Tradition

As I have noted, even though much of the proverbial wisdom of the book
of Proverbs originated in settings foreign to Israelite covenant theology,
the compilers and the first readers of the book interpreted this wisdom
with reference to the concepts of Torah and covenant that are widespread
in the biblical collection (see above, pp. 32–33). The tendency to identify
wisdom with the content of the Mosaic Torah is further developed in
later Jewish sapiential literature, for example, the Wisdom of ben Sira,
Baruch, and Tobit. But these authors do so with their own special
nuances. In chapter 24, ben Sira is concerned less with the giving of the
Torah on Mount Sinai as a historical event than with an ahistorical interpretation that sees the Mosaic Torah as the repository of heavenly wisdom, which is then expounded by the sages (Sir 24:23-34; cf. Baruch 4).[36]
Furthermore, in his exposition ben Sira discusses the righteous life and its

consequences at length, with only occasional references to the content of particular laws. For example, using proverbial and admonitory forms, he plays out a lengthy set of variations on the Fourth/Fifth Commandment with scarcely a reference to what specifically constitutes honoring one's parents (Sir 3:1-16). The substance of the passage is the commandment and the consequences of obeying or disobeying it. For example,

> Respect for a father atones for sins,
>> and to honor your mother is to lay up a fortune. (3:3)

The author's technique for making his point is emphasis through varied repetition from verse to verse. In Tobit the parallelism that often structures proverbs and admonitions conveys the relationship between deeds (line 1) and their consequences (line 2) that is integral to covenantal theology.

> Do not turn your face away from any poor man,
>> and the face of the Lord will not be turned away from you.
> (Tob 4:7)

The Deuteronomic pairing of "life" and "death" as expressions for divine blessing and curse may also be expressed in the wisdom imagery of the two ways.

> Walk not in the paths of evil or the paths of death;
>> approach them not, lest you perish.
> But seek and choose righteousness and an elect life;
>> and walk in the paths of peace,
>>> that you may live and prosper. (1 En. 94:3-4)

As the examples just cited from Tobit and *1 Enoch* indicate, traditional wisdom forms occur in genres other than collections of proverbs like the book of Proverbs or the Wisdom of ben Sira. In such contexts the exhortation to right conduct is enhanced by other traditional literary genres. Tobit's instruction to his son is embodied in testamentary narrative about his own life that draws on old motifs from Mesopotamian tales about persecuted and vindicated courtiers;[37] and, like the stories in Daniel 1–6, Tobit emphasizes the importance of obeying the Torah even at the risk of one's life or well-being. Other, later testamentary texts, like the *Testaments of the Twelve Patriarchs* and the *Testament of Job,* employ biblically based biographical narrative and related instruction to exemplify abstract virtues and vices.[38] Alternatively, the testamentary admonitions in the last chapters of *1 Enoch* are extrapolations from the narratives about Enoch's cosmic visions relating to the divine judgment and the reward and punishment of human deeds.[39]

An exposition of the imagery of the two ways appears in a Qumran text shaped by the biblical covenantal form (1QS 3–4),[40] which stands in the context of a document that frequently enjoins obedience to the Mosaic Torah. Intended for instruction, this text emphasizes that one's deeds along the respective paths of righteousness and wickedness receive appropriate rewards and punishments. These deeds, however, are described not as concrete actions in response to specific commandments of the Torah, but as manifestations of abstract vices and virtues, which are themselves functions of the good and evil spirits. The *Testaments of the Twelve Patriarchs* make the same connection between these vices and virtues and the activity of the two spirits.[41]

## Wisdom apart from the Mosaic Torah

Although ben Sira, Baruch, and Tobit exemplify a tendency to identify wisdom with the Mosaic Torah, there is evidence of a sapiential tradition of ethical instruction unconnected to the Torah that continued to flourish in Israel in the Hellenistic period. It is attested in two works.

The first of these is the *Musar leMevin* ("Instruction for a Student"), a text preserved in numerous copies from Qumran Cave 4.[42] Its subject matter, like that of the Wisdom of ben Sira, ranges from "secular," everyday matters to religious issues, and some of its literary forms parallel those in ben Sira.[43] These similarities notwithstanding, at no point does the author refer to the Mosaic Torah, and the text rarely employs the terminology typical of Torah instruction.[44]

The second text, *1 Enoch*, is even more striking. Material that the Bible ascribes to Moses is here attributed to Enoch.[45] There is little or no reference to the Mosaic Torah, and the notion of covenant is almost completely absent. Instead, Enoch is the primordial source of heavenly "wisdom," which is the collection's principal term for its content. In this respect, a comparison of Sirach 24 and *1 En.* 81:5—82:3 is especially instructive. Each text claims that it is the repository of heavenly wisdom. For ben Sira, this wisdom resides in the Torah. For *1 Enoch,* the wisdom contained in his book derives from the seer's journeys to heaven and through the universe. The sapiential character of *1 Enoch* is evident especially in its last major section, the "Epistle of Enoch" (chaps. 92–105), in its use of traditional sapiential literary forms and the imagery of the two ways.[46] Moreover, although the author of the epistle is interested in "the commandments of the Most High," his instruction is conveyed through the sapiential forms and not by the recitation of commandments.[47] The use of sapiential forms of ethical instruction in *1 Enoch* and its emphasis on God's judgment of human conduct undercut one of the scholarly dichotomies regarding Judaism, namely, between apocalyptic thought and a focus on Torah obedience. In this particular case, instruction regarding the right life is present, albeit in sapiential forms, and these are interwoven with apocalyptic admonitions regarding divine reward and punishment of human deeds.

In summary, this broad spectrum of texts illustrates that Jewish moral instruction had many nuances and was cast in many forms. Wisdom instruction focused on the nexus of deeds and their consequences with little attention to specific commandments and what constituted obedience in a given situation (casuistry). This fact notwithstanding, as we shall see later (pp. 44–49), the exposition of the divine law, such as one finds in the later rabbinic collections, was well under way in the Hellenistic period.

### Who Are "the Righteous" and "the Sinners"?

The reader of the New Testament, and especially of Luke and the Pauline corpus, will readily notice in the corpus of Jewish texts the frequent use of the opposed terms "the righteous/pious/godly" and "the sinners/wicked/ungodly." The substantive difference in the way that these two corpuses of literature use these terms has led many exegetes to contrast two worlds of grace and law, humility and self-righteousness.[48] Luke, for example, sees "the sinners" as the object of Jesus' ministry and "the righteous" as the objects of his criticism.[49] Jewish literature praises "the righteous" and expects that "the sinners" will be damned. This usage bears closer scrutiny.

In the Jewish texts, the word pairs are natural expressions of biblical covenantal theology. Legitimate concern about a righteous life according to the Torah, and its consequences—*fully warranted* by the biblical texts—leads naturally to a focus on righteousness and sin, the righteous one and the sinner. The one is to be celebrated and the other criticized. A significant misconception arises, however, when an exegete interprets "the righteous one" of Jewish literature to mean one who is perfect in the sense of sinless.

The texts do not support this meaning of the term. In the book of Tobit, the self-described righteous protagonist (1:1-8) admits his shortcomings and interprets his suffering as divine discipline for his sins (3:2-5). There is real ambiguity concerning the extent to which Tobit deserves what has happened to him.[50]

The *Psalms of Solomon* are more explicit in defining the terms "righteous" and "sinner." According to *Psalm* 3, the righteous one is not a person who never sins, but one who acknowledges his or her sins and God's righteous judgment of them and who atones for them by means of prescribed rituals. The sinner, by contrast, allows sins to pile up without dealing with their consequences. The deeds of the righteous reflect their covenantal fidelity, and so they are also called "the pious" (*hosioi,* probably translating Hebrew *ḥasidim*).[51] Alternatively, they are described as "those who (truly) love" the Lord[52] and "those who fear God/the Lord,"[53] both terms reflecting the Deuteronomic admonitions to "fear God" and to "love God with all your heart and all your soul and all your might."[54] In this spirit, the religion of the righteous, far from being external and limited to the mere performance of deeds of the Torah (see above, p. 38), is rooted in one's internal disposition. Moreover, *Psalm* 4 delivers a stinging critique of "the manpleasers," hypocrites who worship in the community of the pious but whose inward motivations, and sometimes whose private actions, contradict this public show of piety.

In the view of these authors, then, the righteous life according to the Torah derives from inward motivations. Sins—which are inevitable—are forgiven through the means available within the covenantal structure to which one is committed. The righteous are, by definition, people who are concerned about being such; sinners are indifferent and thus stand under the judgment of the God of the covenant.

## Summary: What the Texts Indicate and Do Not Indicate

Thus far I have criticized the stereotype that "postbiblical" Judaism was an externalized, legalistic perversion of biblical religion. The evidence of a wide variety of Jewish texts reveals significant continuity with the biblical imperative to right action and the biblical assertion that God punishes the violators of the covenant and rewards those who are faithful to the covenant and make appropriate reparation when they sin. Taken together, these texts make relatively little mention of individual commandments of the Torah and the variety of ways in which they might be interpreted and the variety of circumstances under which they might be applied or modified.

# The Development of Halakah and the Rise of Sectarianism

## A Note on Rabbinic Halakic Texts

A detailed concern with the content of the Torah's commandments is not, however, a figment of Christian imagination projected onto Judaism. Rabbinic debates and differences of opinion about halakah (the detailed and sometimes casuistic interpretation of biblical Torah, from Hebrew *halak,* "to walk" on the right path) are well attested in the Mishnah, Tosefta, and Talmudim. But in keeping with my concern to shed light on Christian origins, I shall not discuss the rabbinic texts, since they achieved their present form 150 to five hundred years after the rise of Christianity.[55] My discussion will focus on relevant texts from the Hellenistic and early Roman periods.

Nonetheless, two methodological comments about earlier and later texts may be helpful. The first concerns the Mosaic Torah itself. Briefly stated, the biblical laws and ordinances themselves are often quite detailed and circumstantial;[56] the impulse to create specifically applicable laws is very old and is not a later postbiblical rabbinic invention. The second comment relates to the genre and function of the rabbinic halakic texts. By their very nature, they are compilations of traditional interpretations of the Torah generated over centuries and organized either by topic or as commentaries on the books of the Torah. Their synchronic character, largely oblivious to their multicentury origins, and their function as archives, so to speak, can give the impression that Judaism was a religion burdened by a massive proliferation of laws and interpretations of laws.[57] The impression, however, is an illusion. As an analogy, one would not argue from the existence of a law code, or the record of the decisions of a nation's courts, that its citizens live in perpetual anxiety that, at any given moment, they might violate the law and suffer the consequences.

### The Heritage of Deuteronomic Theology: The Dynamics of Lawmaking and Legal Interpretation in the Book of Jubilees

Although the Christian attention to Jewish legal discussions has wrongly based itself on post–New Testament rabbinic texts, it is true that a concern with halakah is evident already in the texts of the Greco-Roman period. To no small degree the development of halakah was tied to interpretations of Israel's historical circumstances and was an integral part of the rise of "groups" and "sects" during the three centuries before the common era. (On my use of this terminology, see below, pp. 181–82.)

In one of its few explicit references to its author's own time, *Jubilees* 23 employs the scheme of Deuteronomy 28–31 to describe how the sins of Jews in the Hellenistic period incur the wrath of God and bring upon the nation the curses of the covenant (vv 11-15). As the situation disintegrates,

> In those days, the children will begin to search the Torah,
>> and search the commandments
>> and return to the way of righteousness. (v 26)

At that point, the covenantal curses begin to be alleviated. This author, writing in the name of Moses and in the spirit of Deuteronomy, reads Israel's history as a commentary on the people's actions. Famine, shortness of life, and oppression by the enemy are indicators of sin. The seeking and searching of the younger generation is the attempt to understand in what ways the people have disobeyed the Torah.[58] Although the book of *Jubilees* is written under the authority of Moses, it claims to be a transcript of the angels' recitation from the eternal heavenly tablets given on Mount Sinai. As such, it presents the Torah that needs to be obeyed in the real author's time if the covenantal blessings are to return to Israel. While this author reiterates pentateuchal commandments and ordinances, he

Search the scriptures

also interprets many of them in a specific and strict sense, and he derives new commandments exegetically from details in the biblical narrative.[59] Thus the book provides a window into the process and rationale for interpreting old laws and creating new ones. The catalyst is one's reading of the historical situation (as a time of covenantal curse for sins still being committed, or not yet expiated); the result is the definition of the Torah-that-must-be-obeyed if one is to be rewarded by the God of the covenant. The pseudonymous claim of revelation (HEAVENLY TABLETS → angels → Moses → *JUBILEES*) guarantees effectiveness: this Torah is the real, correct Torah; obey it and you will be blessed.

## Enochic Law

*First Enoch* also claims to transmit revealed law. In contrast to *Jubilees,* however, the Enochic account about Mount Sinai makes no reference to the giving of the Mosaic Torah (*1 En.* 89:29-35). Instead, using formulas from the last chapters of Deuteronomy, the book ascribes divine revelation to the prediluvian sage Enoch (chap. 1). His books are the repository of heavenly wisdom intended for the righteous community of the end time (chaps. 81–82; 104–5). This includes astronomical and calendrical law and information about the coming judgment. There appears also to be a critique of the Jerusalem priests, whose interpretation (and practice) of laws about sexual purity renders them unclean.[60] The admonitions in the Epistle of Enoch (chaps. 92–105), which may be roughly contemporary with the book of *Jubilees,* also contain polemics that pit the author and his colleagues against other teachers whose interpretations of the law stand at odds with his own.[61]

> Woe to you who alter the words of truth
> and pervert the eternal covenant,
> *and consider themselves without sin*
> They will be trampled upon the earth. (99:2)

The text does not refer to hardened sinners, but to people who believe that their actions are not sinful. This belief notwithstanding, these differences in the interpretation of divine law, and the deeds that follow from them, will result alternatively in damnation and salvation at the time of the great judgment.

Woe to you fools
>    for you will perish because of your folly.
You do not listen to the wise,
>    and you will not receive good things. (98:9)
Blessed are they who receive the words of wisdom,
>    and follow the commandments of the Most High
>    and walk in the path of righteous,
>    and do not sin with the sinners;
They will be saved. (99:10)

Thus the evidence from the Epistle of Enoch attests developing differences in Judaism as to what, specifically, constitutes the right interpretation and observance of divine law. Moreover, what this author considers to be right law is ascribed to Enoch, not to Moses.

### The Sectarian Torah of Qumran

The impulse to define Torah, evident in *Jubilees* and *1 Enoch,* is present also in other major Qumran Scrolls. Columns 5 and 7 of the Damascus Document (CD), interpreting Amos 9:11 and Num 21:18, describe how certain "men of discernment" and "men of wisdom" went to "Damascus," where, under the direction of "the Interpreter [lit. 'seeker'] of the Torah," they "dug the well" of the Torah (CD 6:2-4). Like the children in *Jubilees* 23, these "converts of Israel" (CD 6:4-5) saw their activity as the kind of repentance called for in Deuteronomy 30. The long collection of laws in the Damascus Document provides some of the content that resulted from their study of the Torah (columns 15–16; 9–14).[62] Other legal concerns relate to the Jerusalem priests' violation of laws about marriage and sexual purity (4:15—5:15).

A relationship between community self-understanding and Torah is explicit in the Qumran Community Rule (1QS). Column 8 describes the community's formation and their exodus to the wilderness to search (*midrash*) the Torah (8:15; cf. 5:9; 6:6-7; 8:12, 24). Here their deeds function as right sacrifices that will purify the land (8:4-10). They are the true Israel in possession of the revealed interpretation of the Mosaic Torah (5:8-9). Entrance into the community is synonymous with admission to the covenantal relationship and presupposes repentance—"return" to this Torah (5:7-9, 22; 6:14-15). The community's law also includes a wide range of regulations for the organization and functioning of the community. This document attests a full-blown sectarianism. That is, the members of the community understand themselves to be exclusively the true Israel, living apart from the rest of Israel, which is defined as wicked. Through their obedience to the true Torah, they and they alone will be saved in the coming judgment.

In the "Halakic Letter" (4QMMT), its anonymous author lays out a set of laws that, if they are obeyed, will return God's blessing to Israel (4Q398 14-17 2:4-8). The formulation is strikingly similar to the idea in *Jub.* 23:26 (see above, pp. 45–46). The Temple Scroll is also a rewriting of biblical law, set in the authoritative first person singular voice of God.

## Sect and Revealed Torah

Although all of the aforementioned documents do not derive from the same group, all of them were found among the Qumran Scrolls, and they reflect a common complex of ideas. Postexilic Israel as a whole has strayed from the true path of God's law and is suffering the curses of the covenant; certain individuals have come to understand the situation and have had the right interpretation of the law (whether that of Enoch or of Moses) revealed to them; as they repent and turn back to the path of righteousness, they can expect to survive God's judgment and receive the covenantal blessings. Thus one's status as a true Israelite, or as one of the righteous, and the receipt of God's blessings presuppose the observance of divine law, whose details have been newly revealed.

These details vary from text to text, but several cultic elements recur in the texts. The solar calendar was revealed to Enoch; *Jubilees* structures its Genesis–Exodus narratives according to this calendar; the Damascus Document emphasizes Israel's sins with regard to the observance of Sabbaths and festivals (CD 3). A concern about the sexual impurity of the Jerusalem priests appears in the Damascus Document (CD 4:15—5:15), where it is tied to specific biblical texts, and *1 Enoch* 12–16 alludes to the same issue.[63] The groups that generated these documents must have had some formal structure; observance of common laws out of tune with regular practice in Israel would have required organization and discipline. However, only in 1QS is this explicit and described.

## Halakah as the Updating of Torah

I have suggested that close study ("searching") of the Torah and the development of halakah were natural consequences of the belief that one's historical situation reflected the curses of the covenant. This should not exclude another, complementary explanation, namely, the need to accommodate or update the Torah to meet new situations. This is a natural development in the history of law codes and need not reflect a "legalistic" tendency. It is often stated that the Pharisees differed from the Sadducees in that they propounded an oral tradition with many halakot. Yet it is difficult to imagine how any group in first-century Judaism could have functioned without rules of thumb for dealing with situations not anticipated or not mentioned in the pentateuchal codes. To what extent the Pharisees represented a comparatively strict interpretation of the Torah is debatable. While much has yet to be done on the subject, investigations indicate that the halakot of *Jubilees* and the Damascus Document are stricter than known Pharisaic halakot. The Qumranic expression "Interpreters of Slippery Things" *(dorshê hahalaqot),* whether or not it refers to the Pharisees, indicates that for some of the Qumran authors, other circles provided facile interpretations of the Torah.[64]

## Summary: The Responsibility to Act Righteously

Like the biblical religion it inherited and transmitted, Judaism in the Greco-Roman period was deeply concerned about the need to act rightly. To do so was a responsibility born of the covenantal relationship, and with it came the promise that God would respond, to bless or curse his people and individuals among them.[65]

What constituted righteous behavior was spelled out first in the Mosaic Torah and in the prophets. New circumstances provided a natural impulse to create new laws and refine old ones. Reflection on an unhappy historical situation led in a similar direction. Interpretation of Torah varied considerably. In some circumstances these differing interpretations created schism through the constitution of communities or groups who saw themselves as the righteous, or the true Israel, to the exclusion of all others. Precisely how the lines fell in first-century Judaism among people with different interpretations of the Torah is no longer possible to say, because our surviving evidence is sparse and spotty. For example, *Psalms of Solomon* 2 and 8 blame Pompey's invasion of Jerusalem on the impurity of the priests, yet there is no evidence that the texts were written by colleagues of either the author of *1 Enoch* 12–16 or the Damascus Document, or for that matter by a Pharisaic opponent of Sadducean priests. As we shall see in our final chapter, the map of first-century Judaism was complex and we have only a few of its pieces.

Casuistic interpretation of divine law was only one way for first-century Jews to deal with and discuss the righteous life. Jewish literature of the period, notably the wisdom literature, reveals a variety of other approaches to the topic that do not focus on the specific what, when, and where of one's actions, but are more general admonitions to obey linked with statements about the consequences that follow from obedience or disobedience.

## Torah and Grace in Judaism

Since the nexus of deeds and divine reward and punishment found in Jewish texts is already present in the Bible, we should not presume that Judaism was characterized by a "works-righteousness" that excluded the grace integral to the structure of biblical covenantal theology. The evidence points in the opposite direction. Ben Sira's view of Torah envisions the presence of wisdom, which functions as a divine power that facilitates the obedience that the Torah requires (Sirach 24). Thus human responsibility (Sir 15:17) does not exclude divine aid.

Even the Qumran Community Rule, with its strict interpretation of the Torah and its exclusion of people of different persuasions from the real community of Israel, speaks eloquently of God's righteousness, effecting forgiveness for the sectarian. The apostle Paul might well have written:

> However, I belong to evil humankind,
>     to the assembly of unfaithful flesh;
> My failings, my iniquities, my sins, with the depravities of my heart
>     belong to the assembly of worms,
>     and of those who walk in darkness;
> As for me, if I stumble,
>     the mercies of God shall be my salvation always;

And if I fall in the sin of the flesh,
>   in the justice of God, which endures eternally, shall be my
>>       judgment;
If my distress commences,
>   he will free my soul from the pit
>   and make my steps steady on the path;
He will draw me near in his mercies,
>   and by kindnesses set in motion my judgment;
He will judge me in the justice of his truth,
>   and in his plentiful goodness always atone for my sins;
In his justice he will cleanse me
>   from the uncleanness of the human being,
>   and from the sin of the sons of man,
So that I can give God thanks for his justice,
>   and the Highest for his majesty. (1QS 11:9-15; cf. Rom 7:14-25)[66]

Nonetheless, the extreme dualism of 1QS 3–4, with its references to the promptings of the good and evil spirits and its concomitant predestinarian view, does not exclude human responsibility and the propriety of divine rewards and punishments. This is evident from the covenantal structure of the passage and the corresponding lists of good and evil deeds, and their respective rewards and punishments. In all of these respects, these ancient documents defy the consistency of later philosophical speculation about free will and much Christian theology that derives from that speculation.

## Torah and the Righteous Life in Early Christianity

This review of Jewish texts sensitizes us to elements in the New Testament that are often overlooked. Such a comparison indicates more similarity and continuity than the traditional paradigm has allowed.

### Divine Judgment on the Basis of Human Deeds

The notion that God rewards and punishes human beings on the basis of their actions is so widespread in the New Testament as to be a cliché. To label the idea "Jewish" and deny its presence in the foundational documents of the church—both the Old and New Testaments—is, in large part, an anachronistic reflection of the Reformation critique of medieval Catholicism.

The exception to the generalization has been the Epistle of James, which Luther dubbed "straw" because of its formula that one is justified by faith and works (Jas 2:14-26).[67] But there is another side. The formula of justification by faith and works is directed against people who use their "faith" as an excuse to avoid social responsibility, especially to the poor and lowly. The epistle's plea in behalf of the poor, the widow, the orphan, and the laborer resonates with overtones from the Hebrew Bible. Its appeal to the example of Abraham, which combines Gen 15:6 and Genesis 22 (Jas 2:21-23), employs the tradition in Sir 45:20; *Jub.* 17:8; and 1 Macc 2:52 (see above, p. 39). The reference to Abraham and Rahab fits the pattern of Mattathias's speech, which appeals to a list of ancients whose obedience, begotten of trust, was rewarded by God (Jas 2:21-25; 1 Macc 2:50-61).

The nexus of the righteous one's action and God's reward is not limited to James, however. Mattathias's association of faith, obedient action, and reward finds its best parallel in the catalog of heroes in Heb 11:1—12:2. According to this author, faith in God naturally and inevitably leads to daring and dangerous deeds; and in every instance, from Abel to Jesus, God rewards obedient faith—in Jesus' case through his exaltation to the right hand of God's throne. The catalog is framed by exhortations to endure persecution and by the promise of reward (10:35-39; 12:3-13). While obedience to the Torah is not the issue here, the commitment to obedient action that may be life-threatening recalls texts generated in response to the Antiochan persecution.

The eschatological judgment of human deeds is described in some detail in Matt 25:31-46, a text influenced by Jewish traditions. Specifically in focus are deeds of kindness (or the lack of them) toward Jesus' disciples. The examples are typical of Jewish catalogs. An identification between the judge (the Son of Man, the King) and the persecuted, as a touchstone for judgment, closely parallels the judgment scene in *1 Enoch* 62–63 (see pp. 104–6).[68]

My final examples derive from the Pauline corpus, indeed from Romans and Galatians. In Rom 2:1-16, a passage saturated with ideas and terminology at home in Jewish eschatological texts, Paul asserts: "God will recompense *everyone* for *what he has done.* There will be trouble and distress for *every human being who does evil* . . . but glory and honor and peace for *everyone who does good*" (2:9-10). The emphasis on human deeds as the basis of judgment and the universality of application (italics above) could not be more explicit. In Gal 5:16—6:10 Paul employs the Jewish form of two-ways instruction, describing human deeds in terms of the abstract vices and virtues that drive them, and underscoring their respective eternal consequences, namely, corruption and eternal life.[69] The formula preceding this section, "faith working in love" (5:6), could be used as an epitome of the view of ethics in the Epistle of James.

## Justification and the Righteous Life in Paul

Paul's assertion that people are judged on the basis of their actions may be seen as standing in conflict with the interpretations of his theology that have been informed by traditional Protestant thought. The topic is obviously very complex, but the discussion in this chapter suggests a few helpful points.

Discussion of right and wrong conduct dominates the extant Pauline corpus much more than do faith and justification by faith. The latter occupy Paul in Romans 1–5 and 9–11, in part of Galatians 2–3, and in Philippians 3. But these passages should be viewed in context. Galatians 5–6 balances the epistle's discussion of justification by faith with an appeal to right conduct. Romans 6–8 follows Paul's discussion of justification with a section on the dynamics of the righteous life. Chapters 12–14 continue the topic with instructions on specific ethical issues that pertain to interactions within the community of faith. In 1 Corinthians, almost from start to finish, Paul focuses his attention on ethical issues that relate to community fragmentation.[70] In 1 Thessalonians the issue is holiness as this pertains to one's sexual life, and the horizon of Paul's discussion is the coming judgment (1:10; 3:12-13; 4:3-6). In Philemon Paul admonishes the master to treat his runaway slave as a brother in Christ.

In Galatians Paul's critique of justification by the deeds of the law focuses on three areas of the Torah: circumcision, food laws, and calendar. For him, the need for the initiatory rite compromises the sufficiency of

Christ's death to effect a Gentile's entrance into the community. In Romans 12–14 his critique of the need for food laws focuses on the schism that these laws create between Jewish and Gentile Christians. In both cases, the formulaic contrast of the two justifications is related to the issues that impede the uniting of Jews and Gentiles in one community.[71]

In Galatians 5–6, having dispensed with the Torah in principle, Paul expounds his ethical instruction by means of a literary form found in no less a Jewish Torah-oriented document than the Qumran Community Rule (cf. 1QS 3:13—4:26; see above, p. 41).[72]

The Pauline discussion of the Torah in Romans 7 requires some brief comments.[73] In Romans 1–2 Paul argues that all humanity stands under God's condemnation. The solution to this problem is justification for Jews and Gentiles (chaps. 3–5). In chapters 6–8, as in Galatians 5–6, Paul draws on Jewish two-ways, two-spirits theology. Baptism is a counterpart to justification and obligates one to live the right life in Christ. Because flesh is inhabited by Sin, the equivalent of the Qumran Angel of Darkness, Torah cannot effect the righteousness it demands (contra Sirach 24). Instead it catalyzes the disobedience it prohibits. Chapter 8 provides the solution to the problem. The Spirit of Christ, the equivalent of the Qumran Angel of Light, effects the righteousness demanded by the Law and thus enables one to be rewarded in the final judgment described in chapter 2.

Thus, in no way does Paul short-circuit the requirement of a righteous life that is integral to Judaism. Rather, he argues that such righteousness is enabled through faith and through the Spirit of Christ available in baptism.

## A Spectrum of Early Christian Attitudes about the Torah

*Paul's Christian Predecessors and Contemporaries*

Early Christianity countenanced a wide spectrum of beliefs about the Torah. Paul appears not to have been the first to advocate a Christianity that was free of the Torah. His accounts of his call juxtapose his zeal for the Torah and his persecution of the church (Gal 1:13-14; Phil 3:5-6). This suggests a causal relationship; Paul the Pharisee was opposing Christians who did not believe that at least a certain kind of Torah observance was necessary and integral to one's practice of the religion of Israel. That Paul would have taken forceful action against Jewish Christians who did not observe Pharisaic halakah does not seem likely; we have no information to suggest that Pharisees adopted the exclusivist views of the Epistle of Enoch or the Qumran community. Perhaps Paul identified with the "zeal" of the Hasmoneans, who took forcible action against hellenizing Jews who abandoned major facets of Torah observance (1 Macc 2:45-48).

To some extent, Paul's firsthand account supports the picture in Acts 6–8 and its references to the Hellenists and Stephen. This account suggests, moreover, that the movement developed among Greek-speaking Diaspora Jews of Christian conviction as they did mission work among Gentiles. Because the reliability of the Acts account is dubious, we cannot be certain who, in the view of these early Christians, did not have to observe the Torah and which parts of it were dispensable. The theological support for this devaluation of the Torah I discuss in the next chapter.

At the other end of the spectrum in early Christianity were the opponents of Paul mentioned in Galatians and Philippians, who argued that Gentiles had to be circumcised in order to be members of the Abrahamic community and that Christian Israelites had to observe biblical food laws.

*Torah and Halakah in the Synoptic Jesus Tradition*
The Synoptic Gospels offer a multilayered source for early Christian attitudes about the Torah. In discussing these traditions, I shall not distinguish between words of the historical Jesus and the church's attributions to him, but treat them as expressions of attitudes in the first-century church. The spectrum of viewpoints is remarkably broad.

Certain texts in Mark advocate outright rejection of elements in the Torah or the practice of Jewish piety. The controversy story in Mark 2:18-23 suggests an end to the ritual of fasting. Although the controversy story in 7:1-13 concerns Pharisaic hand-washing rituals, vv 14-23 interpret the story as a rejection of Jewish food laws, thus espousing a position similar to that of Paul.[74] The catalog of sins in v 21 ethicizes the Jewish notion of purity and impurity and combines elements from the Decalogue with some of the internally originating vices in Paul's two-ways list in Gal 5:18-21. This internalizing of the source of human behavior is reminiscent of the catalog of human vices in 1QS 4:9-11, and finds a parallel in the *Testaments of the Twelve Patriarchs,* where the concrete deeds of the sons of Jacob exemplify abstract vices and virtues (envy, arrogance, courage and love of money, simplicity, compassion and mercy, anger and deceit, goodness, hatred, moderation, a pure mind).[75] Elsewhere in Mark we need not suppose that the traditions proposed wholesale rejection of the Torah or certain of its commandments. The point of contention may have been Pharisaic halakah. The controversies recounted in Mark 2:23—3:6 do not oppose the Sabbath observance as such, but take issue with the Pharisees' view of proper Sabbath observance. The controversy story in 7:1-13 focuses on the Pharisaic ritual of hand washing. In 2:15-17 the argument over table fellowship with sinners may attest a conflict with Pharisees who defined themselves as "the righteous." As we have seen, the authors of many Jewish texts contrast their status as "the righteous" and their expected rewards with the conduct and expected punishment of "the sinners." The positive attitude toward sinners attributed to Jesus in all strata of the Synoptic tradition is unexpected to a reader of Jewish texts of this period.

Different from the aforementioned texts is the controversy about divorce in Mark 10:2-12. Here, in his response to a Pharisaic question, Jesus rejects the Mosaic Torah about divorce in Deut 24:1-4, arguing from Gen 1:27 that divorce is forbidden in principle. In taking a stricter view of the issue than Pharisaic halakah, Jesus employs as a proof text the same passage cited in the stringent halakic polemic in CD 4:21. Thus a parallel from the Scrolls warns us against a facile stereotyping of Jesus as more lenient than the Pharisees.

Matthew and the creators of some traditions that he has preserved attribute to Jesus a more conservative attitude about the Torah than is generally evident in Mark.[76] Not a letter will pass from the Torah until all is fulfilled. The right teacher encourages the keeping of "the least of these commandments" (5:18-21). In contradistinction to Mark 2:18-23, Matt 6:16-18 presupposes the ritual of fasting, along with the parallel rituals of prayer and almsgiving (cf. Tob 12:8) and offers guidelines for their proper usage. Matthew's version of the hand-washing controversy ends by negating the ritual of hand washing, but not nullifying food laws (Matt 15:20; cf. Mark 7:19).[77] Conversely, Matthew's version of the controversy over divorce allows an exception for promiscuity, thus softening the hard line in Mark (Matt 19:9; cf. Mark 10:11-12).

In summary, the range of attitudes expressed in these texts and in the Pauline epistles (both Paul's position and those of his opponents) reflects ongoing discussion and debate in the first-century church over the issue of Torah. Only if one limits one's view to the Pauline position can one cleanly distinguish between Judaism as the religion of Torah and the first-century church's rejection of Torah in favor of gospel.

## Wisdom Instruction and the Righteous Life

Just as in ben Sira, Tobit, and other Jewish texts, the New Testament provides ethical instruction through the forms of the wisdom tradition. Moreover, as in the Jewish texts, the use of such forms need not exclude observance of the commandments of the Torah. The admonition to *seek* first the kingdom of God and his *righteousness* (Matt 6:33), found in a section of the Sermon on the Mount that speaks in the vocabulary of wisdom instruction, employs a cliché about Torah interpretation that is at home in Jewish texts from the Maccabean period (1 Macc 2:29).[78] The Synoptic Gospels' many admonitions about the proper use of wealth imply or explicitly refer to the practice of almsgiving (Luke 12:13-34; 16:1-13; Mark 8:36; 10:17-25) and also call to mind parallels in the wisdom literature.[79]

The cause-and-effect relationship between human deeds and divine reward and punishment is evident in these texts, as it is in their Jewish sapiential prototypes. Such rewards and punishments are often expressed in the eschatological traditions that will occupy us in chapter 5. The connection of deeds and their results is structured into the Beatitudes in Matthew 5 and Luke 6 and the woes in Luke 6. The command not to lay up treasures on earth is based on the promise of a heavenly treasure (Matt 6:19-21). The concluding parable in Matt 7:24-27 || Luke 6:47-49 parallels language in Wis 5:22-23 that describes the punishment of the wicked.

## Hellenistic Models for New Testament Ethical Instruction

Though it lies beyond the scope and purpose of this volume, one should note that Jewish wisdom instruction can be combined with material of Hellenistic origin (James), and that a number of New Testament writers in the Pauline tradition draw on Hellenistic models for their instruction regarding household matters. Thus the absence of reference to the Torah does not imply a lack of concern for matters also dealt with in the Torah. Writers in the Diaspora speak the idiom of the Diaspora.

## The Synoptics and Paul: Christological Models and Ethical Teaching

The Synoptic Gospels depict Jesus in primarily two roles—as a healer and as a teacher or preacher. In the latter role he speaks the dual language of the wisdom and apocalyptic traditions, announcing the coming of the kingdom, calling sinners to repentance, criticizing oppressive behavior, and exhorting trust in God. On other occasions he is embroiled in controversy about aspects of the Torah or the administration of the temple.

Paul is no less concerned about human behavior than the Jesus of the Synoptics. Rarely, however, does he cite the authority of Jesus the teacher.[80] Once he cites an eschatological word of the Lord (1 Thess 4:15). In 1 Cor 7:10-11 he cites a logion of Jesus. Other Synoptic traditions are not identified with Jesus (1 Thess 5:1-11).[81] But Paul's ethical instruction is by no means dissociated from the figure of Jesus. The connection lies not in what Jesus taught, however, but in Jesus' *actions*. Where Adam failed, Jesus obeyed (Romans 4; 7–8; Philippians 2), and Christian obedience to God is made possible through the indwelling of the Spirit of the risen Christ. The guidelines for right behavior are not the Torah as such (although he cites the Decalogue), but derive from the promptings of the Spirit (Galatians 5; Romans 8) and have love as their hallmark. Many specifics of Paul's ethical instruction derive from Hellenistic Jewish practice and find parallels in such texts as the Wisdom of Solomon.[82]

## Summary

Christian scholarship has stereotyped "postbiblical" Judaism as a religion that perverted biblical religion by advocating perfectionist observance of the Torah, emphasizing external observance to the exclusion of internal motivation, and tying divine reward and punishment to human obedience and disobedience. A close study of a wide variety of Jewish texts contradicts this stereotype. Biblical religion, in the Torah, the Prophets, and the Writings, is itself broadly concerned about living the right life; and detailed, casuistic law codes are present already in the Pentateuch. The demand for a righteous life and the notion that human deeds will be rewarded and punished are integral parts of biblical covenantal theology. Much Jewish religious thought and practice follows in this path. Observance of the Torah, however, need not be externalized, and numerous texts explicitly exhort one to fear and love God and nourish the internal virtues from which external righteous acts spring. Zeal for the Torah was not separate from faith and trust in the God of the covenant. Exhortations to Torah piety are often expressed in the vocabulary and forms of sapiential instruction without a focus on halakah and casuistry. The righteous person was not one who never sinned, but one who cared about living a godly life and made reparation for the sins that she or he inevitably committed. Halakic interpretation of the Torah developed both from the conclusion that Israel's historical situation reflected divine displeasure with disobedience of the Torah and from the need to explicate the biblical Torah for new situations. The temple, the priesthood, and the cult were a focus of legal debates. Not all Jews were satisfied with the conduct of the Jerusalem cult, and some boycotted it.

In many respects, New Testament teaching stands in continuity rather than in contrast with Judaism regarding these matters. The New Testament is replete with the notion that right conduct stands at the center of right religion and that God rewards upright conduct and punishes sinful behavior. Although Paul in principle disavows obedience to the Torah, in most of his epistles he exhorts righteous behavior and states that God will reward it and punish disobedience. However, Paul represents only one band in the broad spectrum of early Christian attitudes about the need to observe the Torah. As we shall see in the next chapter, New Testament attitudes about the temple are quite consonant with negative Jewish attitudes, though less because of criticism of the temple, priesthood, and cult than for christological reasons.

In the final analysis, with regard to the importance of a righteous life and its divine reward, there was not a black-and-white contrast between Judaism and early biblical religion, on the one hand, and early Christianity, on the other hand. In various ways, the primary difference between Judaism and Christianity on this issue was christological. For Jews, the right life was bound up with the observance of the Torah—however that might be construed—and the divine wisdom resident in the Torah enabled obedience to its commandments. For Christians, Jesus was the right teacher and the model for a right life, and the Spirit of the risen Christ was the dynamic for a righteous life.

# chapter 3

---

# God's Activity in Behalf of Humanity

As we have seen in the previous chapter, the God of the covenant responds in positive ways to right human behavior. Perhaps more than any other single word, "salvation" summarizes the essence of the Christian religion in the popular and, sometimes, the sophisticated mind. Such salvation is usually construed as deliverance from sin and its consequences— guilt and damnation. The biblical notion, however, is much broader.

The Hebrew Bible employs the verb *yasha`* ("save, rescue, deliver") to refer to a wide variety of divine activity. God rescues Israel from Pharaoh, delivers the nation and individuals from their enemies, heals the sick, and, of course, forgives sin and delivers the chosen people from its consequences.[1] Moreover, in all these instances and others, the portrait of the rescuing, vindicating God can occur quite apart from the use of a whole range of words meaning "save" or "deliver."

The New Testament, too, portrays the God who saves in different ways and circumstances and employs a number of terms (often metaphors) for "salvation," which vary according to the complex of ideas in which they fit. The rich, explicit variety in postbiblical Jewish texts, and the important transformations of biblical traditions that they attest, help us understand better the variety in early Christian thought and the similarities and differences between it and the traditions on which it draws.

## Models in Jewish Texts

### Deliverance Is a Pervasive Motif
It is a striking fact, worthy of serious consideration by historians of religion, that with few exceptions the texts of the Apocrypha, Pseudepigrapha, and

Qumran Scrolls portray hard times or deal with problematic issues. The religious sentiments that govern this literature are directed toward wrongs that need to be righted, evils from which one must be delivered, and problems that have to be solved. There are two exceptions to this generalization, but in each case the coin has a reverse side. First, texts that exhort one to live a righteous life also implicitly or explicitly direct one *away from an unrighteous life*. There are *two* ways, and where one mentions "the path of righteousness," the structure of the metaphor implies its alternative. Second, psalms of thanksgiving are occasioned by divine deliverance *from evil*.

## Two Major Developments

In the context of this general pattern, we shall view the many nuances and different concerns of the texts, both in contrast to one another and as they differ from their counterparts in the Hebrew Bible. To no small degree, the latter differences result from two changes in Israelite religious thought that occurred during the exile and postexilic period and that intensified in the Greco-Roman period. (1) Evil is often seen as the function of cosmic forces rather than as (the sum of) the deeds of human beings. (2) Decisive deliverance from evil, whether imminent or in the future, takes place in "the end time."

### The Cosmic Character of Evil

For the biblical writers in general, the evil that humans suffer is the result of their own sins or the sins and oppressive behavior of other human beings. Of course, the nations have their patron deities, but the foreign king or oppressor is generally portrayed as the responsible agent of his own actions. (The ironic exception occurs when Israel's God employs the foreigner as "a hired razor" [Isa 7:20; cf. Deut 32:19-21].) Similarly, the nation or individual that sins is wholly responsible for those deeds; speculation about a prior cause from another source is, by and large, lacking.

Behind this historical analysis of human actions, however, lies a mythic, dualistic worldview, typical of many religions in Israel's environment, a worldview that occasionally breaks through in narratives that purport to recount "historical events." Thus the reference to the chaotic waters of "the deep" (Hebrew *tehom*) in the creation story in Genesis 1 (v 2) appears to be a vestigial remain of Tiamat, the chaos dragon.[2] This primordial opponent of the high God is more evident in the mythic language of these two passages:

> Awake, awake, put on strength,
>> arm of YHWH,
> awake as in the days of old,
>> the generations of long ago.
> Was it not you that cut Rahab in pieces,
>> that pierced the dragon? (Isa 51:9)

> For God my King is of old,
>> working deliverance in the midst of the earth.
> You divided the sea by your might
>> you broke the heads of the dragons on the waters.
> You crushed the heads of Leviathan,
>> and gave him as food for the creatures of the wilderness.
> (Ps 74:12-14)

In Isaiah 14 the king of Babylon, who strives to sit in God's place and is cast down to Sheol, is depicted as an embodiment of the rebel god Athtar,[3] and Psalm 82 mentions a plethora of *'elim* ("divine beings"), who rebel against God by not defending the poor and needy.

A shift that attributes human sin to evil supernatural figures is evident in 1 Chr 21:1 (ca. 350 B.C.E.). When David decides to count the people, it is the heavenly *satan* who incites him to sin—an act quite different from that of the lying spirit who serves *God's* purpose in 1 Kgs 22:19-23. Similarly, in Job 1–2 the *satan* not only questions Job's uprightness (acts as accuser) but also sets out to prod him into sin. Thus functionaries of the heavenly court are transformed into independent demonic agents who are the (potential) source of human sin. Several myths about the cosmic origins of sin emerge in the Greco-Roman period. According to the story about Semihazah and his associates in *1 Enoch* 6–11, this heavenly chieftain led the revolt described briefly in Gen 6:1-4.[4] The giants, begotten of this forbidden union of the "sons of God" and the daughters of men, are warrior figures who appear to be symbols for the Hellenistic kings who waged war through the eastern Mediterranean area in the late fourth century B.C.E. Thus the actions of powerful and violent human beings are functions of a rebellious spirit world. According to the second strand of the myth in *1 Enoch* 6–11, certain kinds of evil result from the illegal revelations of the chieftain Asael and his associates (especially *1 Enoch* 8).[5] Two further developments of the myth appear in *1 Enoch* 12–16. (1) The rebellion of the holy ones appears to allude to the sexual sins of the Jerusalem priests.[6] (2) The giants' destruction in the deluge releases their spirits into the world, where they wreak havoc through violence, demonic possession, and other kinds of sickness. *Jubilees* 10 focuses on these spirits and adds to their repertoire the function attributed to the *satan* in Job 1–2: they are a horde of evil spirits who continually tempt human beings to sin. Thus the various developments in these traditions reflect an emerging worldview in which the sins of the mighty and the straying of the ordinary are functions of a realm of malevolent spirits who stand in continuous opposition to God. Moreover, as the *Life of Adam and Eve* 12–17 and Revelation 12 indicate, the old myth of Athtar, attested in Isaiah 14, feeds into the later tradition, identifying the serpent in the garden with "the devil," on the one hand, and seeing his embodiment in the rulers and religion of the Roman Empire, on the other.

### Locating Decisive Deliverance in the Eschaton

A second development, to which we shall return in detail in chapter 5, is the rise of eschatology. The "latter times" of the prophets become the "end time," the end of the present age, which will lead to the beginning of a new age, ushered in by a new creation or a new exodus. At this decisive, final turning point, divine judgment is located and full deliverance is anticipated for the nation and the righteous. This end-time perspective governs much of the Jewish literature's discussion and speculation about God's saving activity and is the focus of the discussion in chapter 5.

## Salvation from Sin and Its Consequences

As I have noted above (p. 61), Christian tradition most frequently construes salvation as deliverance from the results of one's sins: guilt and damnation. Here we must make an important distinction that derives from issues discussed in the previous chapter (see above, pp. 32–33). Within the covenantal framework, righteous and sinful conduct receive their just reward and punishment in the blessings and curses of the covenant. In the case of righteous conduct, however, reward and blessing are not appropriately called "salvation," because one is not being *saved* or *delivered* or *rescued from* something. Instead, one experiences the expected good consequences of good conduct.

Covenantal blessing can be construed as salvation under two circumstances. Here I deal with the first of these (see also pp. 69–71). Covenantal ethical instruction as early as Deuteronomy anticipates that the nation will sin, and some later texts focus on the sins of the individual. In both cases the receipt of the covenantal blessings reverses justly experienced curses and can take place because the divinely instituted sacrificial system facilitates the return of divine favor.

### The Sacrificial System

In various ways, depending on the particular ritual, the sacrificial system restores a broken relationship with God or, in other ways, sets right what is wrong.[7] Sacrifice may purify uncleanness, or it may make reparation for guilt that has been incurred through wrong action. In both cases it brings equilibrium and wholeness between the divine and human partners of the covenant. The Day of Atonement ritual epitomizes these functions. In the view of the prophets Isaiah, Jeremiah, Amos, and Micah, however, sacrifice must be accompanied by repentance, that is, "return" to God. Right behavior must accompany and follow appropriate ritual.[8]

### Exilic Alternatives to the Sacrificial System

The exile initiates a major change to the mechanisms of reparation. The Jerusalem temple, Israel's cultic center, has been destroyed, and sacrifices are not possible. Thus the exilic texts sound some new motifs. For Ezekiel, the divine spirit will breathe new life into the dead people (chap. 37), and God will effect a new creation of the human spirit, sprinkling the people with clean water (36:22-32). Second Isaiah presents two alternatives to the sacrificial system: through its suffering, Israel has paid double for its sins (40:2), and therefore the nation can return; the suffering of the "Servant" has functioned as a sacrifice for others (53:10-11). As Israel emerges from

Moreover, we see in place a ritual previously not attested—a
final prayer of repentance, in which a representative of the nation
acknowledges the past sins that have brought on the curses of the
covenant and begs for forgiveness and the restoration of divine favor. The
ritual is exemplified in stories about both Ezra and Nehemiah (Ezra 9 and
Nehemiah 9).[9]

## Continuations of These Developments
### Suffering as Scourging, Discipline, or Chastisement
A number of Jewish texts present an explanation for the suffering of the
righteous that builds on motifs and dynamics at work in the exile. In
the book of Tobit, the protagonist, who is the epitome of a Torah-abiding
Israelite (1:3-9), reflects on the nation's exile and on his own immense suffering and its alleviation and concludes that the righteous God of the
covenant is dealing justly with him and them, "scourging" (*mastigoō*)
them for their sins, so that they may eventually receive the "mercy"
(*eleeō*) that is at the heart of the covenant (11:15; 13:2, 5, 9).

The author of 2 Maccabees develops the notion. God deals differently
with Israel and with the nations (6:12-17). In the latter case, God with-
holds punishment, patiently allowing the Gentiles' sins to build up to the
point where they will receive severe punishment. As for Israel, God never
withdraws the covenantal mercy, but employs suffering to "discipline"
(*paideuō*), that is, to teach, the covenant people, so that they will turn
from their sins. The same contrast appears in *2 Bar.* 13:4-11 with reference
to the destruction of Jerusalem in 70 C.E. The *Psalms of Solomon* employ similar metaphors to explain the suffering of the righteous and the nation at
the time of the Roman invasion of Israel (7:8-10; 10:1-4; 13:9-10). To the
notion of discipline are added suffering's functions as "purification"
(*katharizō*) and a means to "wipe away" (*exeleiphō*) transgressions (10:1-2;
13:10); both expressions are appropriate to the sacrificial cult.[10]

### Martyrdom as Expiation and Propitiation
The unjust death of the Maccabean martyrs provides the authors of 2
Maccabees and 4 Maccabees with the opportunity to develop this pattern
in a special way. Both authors describe the events of 168–165 B.C.E. with
reference to the scheme of Deuteronomy 28–32.[11] Israel's sins have

brought punishment in the form of the foreign oppressor. The innocent deaths of the martyrs are acts of obedience that deliver Israel from the curse and restore the blessing. In the language of 2 Macc 8:5 (cf. 7:38), God's just wrath against the nation turns to mercy.[12] Fourth Maccabees 17:20-22 employs a cluster of cult-related terms: purification, ransom, and propitiation *(katharismos, antipsychon, hilasterion)*. Although the scheme and language of Deuteronomy structure and otherwise inform the idiom of both versions of the story, the version in 2 Maccabees 7 also draws on the language of Isaiah 53, and the Isaianic text's imagery of vicarious death has informed the development of the tradition here. Other considerations suggest, in addition, that this reading of Isaiah 52–53 was influenced by texts in the classical Greek tradition.[13]

The use of cult-related language in these texts was not accidental. During the Antiochan persecution, the sanctuary was considered polluted. The *Psalms of Solomon* were written in the wake of Pompey's invasion of the temple.

### Righteous Deeds as a Means of Atonement

In the texts just discussed, the extreme examples of intense suffering and the obedience of the martyrs' deaths are a means of atonement. Other acts of obedience can function in a similar way. In this respect Tobit cites almsgiving and other acts of kindness, for example, hospitality and burial of the dead (1:16-18; 2:1-8):

> For almsgiving rescues *(ryomai)* from death,
> and it will purge *(apokatharizō)* every sin.
> Those who perform deeds of charity and righteousness will have
> fullness of life;
> but those who commit sin are enemies of their own lives.
> (Tob 12:9-10)

Ben Sira employs cultic language to describe the function of Torah obedience, and he singles out the giving of alms:

> He who keeps the law makes many offerings,
> he who heeds the commandments sacrifices a peace offering.
> He who returns a kindness offers fine flour,
> and he who gives alms sacrifices a thank offering. (Sir 35 [32]:1-2)

The Qumran Community Rule, written by a group that considered the temple to be polluted, offers another example of such rhetoric. The council of twelve is described as temple and priesthood, "a house of holiness," whose deeds and suffering are the equivalent of sweet-smelling sacrifices and service to make atonement *(kipper)* for the land (1QS 8:1-10).

An extension of the idea occurs in *Ps. Sol.* 3:8 (9-10), with reference to the righteous one:

> he propitiates *(exilaskō)* for sins of ignorance through fasting and
> the humiliation of his soul;
> the Lord cleanses *(katharizō)* every pious man and his house.

In this case the self-abasing ritual of fasting is the equivalent of atoning sacrifice.

In summary, ideas about atonement that developed in the exile in the absence of the temple cult reappear in later texts. In the case of Qumran and perhaps the *Psalms of Solomon,* the idea relates to a concern about the purity of the temple (cf. *Pss. Sol.* 2:3; 8:12[13]; 17:22[25]). However, even ben Sira, a strong advocate of the viability of the temple and its priesthood, maintains that pious deeds stand alongside the sacrificial system as a means of atonement.[14]

## Prayers of Confession

Psalm 51 and the prayers in Ezra 9 and Nehemiah 1 and 9 are the earliest extant examples of prayers in which individuals or the nation formally confess their sins and request divine forgiveness. Psalm 51:10-11 employs language parallel to Ezek 36:26-27 and seems to presume the destruction of Jerusalem. The language of the prayers in Ezra, Nehemiah, and later texts is drawn from Deuteronomy and Jeremiah and depicts the speaker or the nation under the curses of the covenant.[15] The prayers articulate the repentance that Deuteronomy describes as necessary for the restoration of divine blessing (Deut 30:1-10). The precise occasion(s) on which the later exemplars of these prayers were spoken are, for the most part, uncertain. Different from Ezra and Nehemiah, they have no reliable narrative context. Baruch 1:15—3:8, Daniel 9, and the Prayer of Azariah are pseudonymously attributed to figures of the exile.[16] The Prayer of Manasseh is also pseudonymous.[17]

*Eschatological Cleansing and a Heavenly High Priest*
Some eschatologically oriented texts expect that atonement and cleansing will take place at a decisive future moment through a transcendent agent, who also has a demonic counterpart. In *1 En.* 10:20, as part of an eschatological scenario, the angel Michael will destroy Semihazah and his hosts and then cleanse the earth from impurity created by the violent acts of the giants. A similar eschatological cleansing, described in language similar to Ezekiel 36, is foreseen in 1QS 4:20-22. This final act is set in the context of a two-ways document in which the Spirit of Truth leads the righteous along the path of truth, while fending off the attacks of his counterpart, the Spirit of Perversity. 11QMelchizedek identifies the angel Michael with the ancient priest of the Most High, Melchizedek. Although the idea of a heavenly high priest is one step removed, *T. Mos.* 10:3 refers to the commissioning of the angelic agent of God's judgment in language normally used of priestly "ordination": his "hands will be filled."[18] The presence of these ideas in texts concerned about the pollution of the temple or in association with such texts (Qumran) may indicate that notions of a heavenly temple and an eschatological angelic high priest may have arisen, like some of the ideas mentioned above, in circles that considered the temple cult to be noneffective.[19] Additionally, they are integral components of a worldview in which evil has a demonic dimension.

## Salvation from One's Enemies

One typical biblical usage of Hebrew *yasha`* pertains to God's deliverance of Israel or the righteous from the just or unjust persecution, oppression, or captivity of their enemies.[20] In the latter chapters of Deuteronomy, when the people have repented in captivity, God delivers them from their captors, who are punished for their arrogant assumption that they have conquered by their own might rather than by YHWH's permission (Deut 32:1-43). Alternatively, the righteous may experience *unjust* persecution. The psalms of individual lament and individual thanksgiving document the complaints of the righteous and celebrate their vindication when they are delivered from persecution and their enemies are punished (see, e.g., Psalms 22, 27, 69). In ways that parallel the Hebrew Bible and diverge from it, the Jewish texts of the Greco-Roman period depict a variety of divine deliverance from the enemies of the nation and of the individual. Details are taken up in chapters 4 and 5. Here I note the time frames within which this deliverance occurs.

## Eschatological Judgment and Deliverance

Daniel 10–12 and the *Testament of Moses* solve the problem of the Antiochan persecution by envisioning direct divine intervention in the form of eschatological judgment that will usher in a new age.[21] For Daniel, the unjust suffering of Israel's righteous will end when Michael appears on the scene to deal with the persecutor and to participate in a judgment that involves the resurrection of righteous and unrighteous to eternal life and eternal contempt. The *Testament of Moses* employs the Deuteronomic scheme to recount the events of the Antiochan period. The oppressor is the divinely sent agent of punishment for a sinful people. But the radical act of obedient death by Taxo and his sons (chap. 9) triggers divine vengeance and ushers in the events of the eschaton, when both the high angel and the eternal God destroy the enemy and exalt Israel to the heights (chap. 10).

## Salvation within History

The books of 1 and 2 Maccabees offer alternative accounts of the Antiochan persecution that employ eschatological motifs to describe divine salvation in the historical past. As noted above (pp. 66–67), the narrative of 2 Maccabees is structured by the Deuteronomic scheme; moreover, it works with a tradition related to the *Testament of Moses*.[22] However, the innocent deaths of the righteous effect the return of divine favor not in a cosmic epiphany, but through the successful victories of Judas Maccabeus. The history of the same period recounted in 1 Maccabees uses the same traditions to a similar end, but with a different nuance. Mattathias and his sons are the counterpart of Taxo and his sons, and their victories are the historical embodiment of divine judgment against Antiochus and in behalf of Israel. These victories, however, are not catalyzed by the innocent deaths of the martyrs, and the militant ideology of the Hasmoneans is much more prominent than it is in 2 Maccabees. Indeed, 1 Maccabees presents the actions of Mattathias (especially) and his sons as a foundation myth for the legitimacy of the Hasmonean high priesthood. Mattati actions are portrayed in language drawn from the story of Phinea Numbers 25 (1 Macc 2:10-26).

## A Tension between Ideologies and Ambiguity about the Eschaton

The texts just cited—all accounts of roughly the same events employing, to some extent, the same biblical tradition—illustrate the wide variety in Jewish ideas about the character of divine judgment. For the *Testament of Moses*, the innocent, pacifist deaths of Taxo and his sons trigger direct divine intervention. The pro-Hasmonean author of 1 Maccabees describes the counterpart of Taxo and his sons' innocent deaths as ineffective and disastrous (2:29-41) and thus legitimizes the militant activity of the Hasmoneans. The stories of Eleazar and the seven brothers and their mother in 2 Maccabees 6–7, like the *Testament of Moses,* emphasize the effectiveness of martyrdom, but the author acknowledges that the historical fact of the Maccabean victories was the enactment of God's judgment. The author of Daniel 10–12 describes the activity of the Hasmoneans as "a little help" (11:34). Thus there is fundamental disagreement as to whether militant action or pacifism effects divine judgment. Does one see the hand of God in zealous action for the Torah, or does one anticipate it from no human quarter?

This disagreement is partly a function of the setting in which the texts were composed. The *Testament of Moses* and Daniel, written in the heat of persecution, await direct divine intervention, while 1 and 2 Maccabees reflect on the historical fact that Hasmonean militancy was effective. The Animal Vision of *1 Enoch* 85–90 cautions us against a simple distinction, however, for it sees Judas as the bearer of the sword of divine judgment on the brink of an eschatological denouement.[23] Thus we do not know whether, in historical fact, Judas and his associates, or the Hasidim (1 Macc 2:42-43), or any Jews witnessing this activity, understood the Hasmoneans' holy war to be a constituent part of an eschatological scenario. The Epistle of Enoch, for example, employs biblical language about holy warfare to describe the participation of the righteous in the eschatological judgment (*1 En.* 95:3; 98:12). There is no a priori reason why, at one point or another, the Hasmoneans and/or their associates might not have been governed by the ideology explicit in the Qumran War Scroll, where Israel and the angels fight side by side in an eschatological war of extermination against the Romans.[24]

## Healing and Rescue from Death

The healing of a severe illness is another form of God's saving activity in the Hebrew Bible.[25] In the Deuteronomic view, sickness is a sign of divine displeasure, and a premature death is evidence of major sin.[26] God's healing activity may indicate a reversal of covenantal curses due to repentance, or it may undo unjust suffering.[27] It may take place directly or through human agency, such as the intervention of a prophet.[28]

The later Jewish texts reflect historical changes in this respect, too. On the one hand, ben Sira attests the development of "medical science" and refers to therapeutic skills and knowledge of physicians and pharmacists. Sympathizing with the Greek world of Hippocrates and, later, Galen, he accepts these people into the realm of the healing activity of the God who created physicians and medicines (Sir 38:1-8).

*First Enoch* takes a different viewpoint. The evil spirits of the dead giants inflict illness, but "charms and the cutting of roots" are part of the forbidden knowledge revealed by the rebel chieftain Semihazah (8:1). It is unclear whether the author thinks that all pharmacy involves demonic magic and is part and parcel with the casting and removal of spells. As with other problems, God's eschatological intervention through a transcendent agent is the decisive solution. Raphael, "God's Healer," is sent to heal the earth of "plague" brought on by the rebel angels (10:7). In the later Book of Parables, Raphael heals the wounds of humanity (*1 En.* 40:9).

The book of *Jubilees* appears to be diametrically opposed to *1 Enoch* in this respect. According to *Jub.* 10:10-13, medicines are revealed by the angels of the presence, who dictate to Noah a comprehensive pharmacopeia that permits his children to deal with demonically inflicted diseases.

A similar viewpoint may be evident in the book of Tobit, although its folkloric character obscures its understanding of sickness and healing. Tobit's blindness may have been inflicted by the demon Asmodeus;[29] clearly he causes the premature deaths of Sarah's seven husbands (3:7-8). Raphael reveals both a magical fumigation apparatus to exorcise the demon from Sarah's house and life (6:1-5; 8:1-3) and a medicine to remove the film from Tobit's eyes (11:7-12). In precisely what form the author envisioned such angelic presence and how he thought such intervention and activity took place is unclear. In any case, sickness and premature death can be caused by demons, and magical cures can be the result of divine—rather than demonic—revelation.

In 1QapGen ar 20 God employs an "evil spirit" to inflict Pharaoh and his household with impotence. They are healed directly by God as a result of Abraham's intercessory prayer, although this action suggests a kind of exorcism.[30] The extant fragment of the Prayer of Nabonidus (4QPrNab) makes no reference to evil spirits as agents of that king's illness, which is divine punishment caused by his rebellion.[31] Healing ensues after seven years of futile prayer to gods of gold, silver, and the like, when Daniel, "an exorcist," forgives the sins that caused the illness. In both cases illness is a function of sin and its cure is divine healing, which follows repentance.

## Salvation as Revelation

The Hebrew Bible celebrates the activity of God's spokesmen, the prophets, and obedience to their revealed word brings deliverance from present or impending doom. However, it is in the Hellenistic period, primarily in texts usually described as "apocalyptic," that we see a full-blown salvific scheme that makes revelation an integral part of a dualistic worldview. The collection of traditions in *1 Enoch* offers the best and most explicit example.[32]

*First Enoch* posits a triple set of complementary dualisms. A spatial axis, both vertical and horizontal, separates the human world from the heavens and the outer edges of the earth, where the places, apparatus, and agents of eschatological judgment are located. A historical dualism separates the *now* of history from the *then* of the primordial angelic rebellion and the *then* of eschatological retribution. An ontological dualism distinguishes humans from God and God's heavenly entourage, and from the evil spirits, who also stand in opposition to the realm of the divine. Human existence in the present is marked by an absence of divine retribution and a separation from the places where this is in effect or being prepared. Revelation mediates these dualisms by presenting the knowledge gotten by one who has traveled to the heavens and the ends of the earth and who has seen back into the past and forward to the eschaton. This revelation is salvific in several ways. The revealer provides revealed law about the structure of the calendar and other issues.[33] The revealer also assures the faithful of the certainty of the eschatological judgment, thus encouraging them to act rightly and exhorting them to endure in the presence of injustice. The words of the revealer, which are also the presence of heavenly wisdom, have been deposited in the Enochic corpus, written of old and now available as eschatological, saving wisdom (81:5—82:3).

What is central to this scheme for our purposes is the following. Humanity in general, and Israel in particular, live in ignorance of certain facts hidden from them by the structure of the universe, the nature of history, and their present situation (injustice creates cognitive dissonance). This ignorance cuts one off from the possibility of divine blessing. The blessing and hence salvation from one's present situation require a revelation of what is hidden.

The books of Enoch represent a literary form common in the Greco-Roman period, and found in Jewish, Christian, and pagan sources. Scholars refer to the genre as "apocalypse" (from Gk. *apokalypsis*, "revelation"). In an apocalypse, a heavenly figure reveals information about the future or about the aspects of the cosmos to a human mediator, either in a dream vision or during the course of a journey through the cosmos.[34]

Enoch's apocalypticism is a complex blend of themes and literary forms at home in both the prophetic and wisdom traditions of Israel.[35] Most frequently the texts refer to it as "wisdom" (*1 En.* 37:1; 82:2-3; 93:10; 104:12—105:1), but it differs from much conventional Israel wisdom in its emphasis on revelation and in the particular form of that revelation.[36] Ben Sira, too, believes that his wisdom is revealed. Torah is the presence of heavenly wisdom, and his exposition of it has been granted by God and mediates Torah's wisdom, granting life to those who obey it (Sir 24:23-34). Enoch's apocalypticism differs from ben Sira's wisdom in four respects. (1) It stands in rivalry with the Mosaic Torah. (2) It is focused on a decisive end time. (3) Its source of authority is a pseudonymous sage who claims visionary revelation. (4) Its life-giving power is limited to the few within Israel whose righteousness is defined by its law.

Enoch's apocalyptic scheme has many contemporary parallels with many permutations.[37] Daniel's apocalypses emphasize a dualism on the historical axis and provide a revelation that the end is near. The *Testament of Moses* employs the Deuteronomic scheme to a similar end, and it parallels Daniel 9 by interpreting Scripture for eschatological purposes.

Even though the Qumran caves have yielded no apocalypses other than *1 Enoch*, Daniel, and *Jubilees*, the larger corpus of texts derived from these is remarkable for the breadth of parallels to *1 Enoch* that focus on the notion of revelation.[38] A community of the chosen has been constituted around a twofold eschatological revelation. The community has a definitive and exclusivist interpretation of the Torah. The community's place in history is understood in light of a revealed interpretation of all the eschatological secrets of the prophets. At many points in the Scrolls, salvation is construed as knowledge and revelation.[39]

## The Scope of Divine Blessing and Salvation

### A Spectrum of Biblical Attitudes

The stereotype that early Jewish views of "salvation" were relatively narrow compared to the universalism of emerging Christianity needs to be addressed in the present context.[40] From the biblical texts onward, the Israelite tradition evidences a variety of attitudes on the issue, and their development is complex. The New Testament, for all of its focus on the Gentiles, also picks up certain narrow attitudes specific to sectarian Judaism.

As early as the J stratum of the Pentateuch, the patriarch of Israel is described as one "by whom all the families of the earth shall bless themselves" (Gen 12:3; cf. 17:4). The oracles of Second Isaiah evidence a broad vision that anticipates the Servant being a light to the nations and establishing justice and law (*mishpaṭ* and *torah*) in their midst (Isa 49:6; 42:1-4). The motif recurs in the vision of the rebuilt Jerusalem in Isaiah 60, and Zech 14:9-21 modifies the idea. The books of Ruth and Jonah also reflect an openness that stands in tension with pentateuchal ideas about marriage to foreigners and prophetic oracles against Assyria. Jeremiah's and Ezekiel's oracles against the nations are especially severe (Jeremiah 46–51; Ezekiel 24–33, 38–39), although Ezekiel's vision for the land of Israel conceives of resident aliens as native-born children of Israel (47:22-23). The Deuteronomistic History (especially Joshua and Judges) describes the nations surrounding Israel as idolaters and a serious threat to the chosen people. Ezra's prohibition of intermarriage follows in this tradition (Ezra 9–10). Later Jewish attitudes fall along the broad biblical spectrum, but with some particular developments that are significant for the rise of Christianity.

## Salvation for the Nations

All the major strata of *1 Enoch* are characterized by a remarkably broad view. Although the texts divide sharply between righteous Israelites and the nation's sinners (following the cue of Third Isaiah), and although some narrow views of divine law are evident (see above, p. 46), the texts expect that "the children of all the earth" will be incorporated into the community of the end time. According to one of the earliest strata, when the earth has been cleansed,

> all the sons of men will become righteous;
>     and all the peoples will worship me;
>     and all will bless me and prostrate themselves. (10:21)

In the Animal Vision (chaps. 85–90), a figure is born who recapitulates the primordial purity of the first human being. Then all Israel and all the nations that have survived the final judgment will be transformed into one people who have the character of that eschatological figure (90:37-38). The idea is remarkably close to Paul's notion of the new Adam and the church's incorporation into Christ. The Apocalypse of Weeks (93:1-10; 91:11-17) expresses substantially the same view: after righteous law has been revealed to all the sons of the whole earth, and all wickedness has been rooted out, "all humanity will look to the paths of righteousness" (91:14). The Epistle of Enoch, in which this apocalypse has been incorporated (chaps. 92–105), asserts that the books of Enoch are the revealed wisdom that will constitute the eschatological community of the righteous and pious from among Israelites and "the sons of the earth" (100:6; 104:12—105:2). The writer of the Parables, the latest stratum of the collection, expects that some of the nations will abandon their idols and be saved in the judgment (50:1-3).

A different strain of inclusivism appears in several Hellenistic Jewish works. The *Letter of Aristeas* states that the commandments of the Torah, especially its food laws, are intended only for Jews. Gentiles need not obey them, but they are to avoid the major sins of murder, sexual promiscuity, and idolatry.[41] A similar view obtains in *Sibylline Oracles* 3. While neither text states that such righteous Gentiles are to be considered Israelites, their avoidance of idolatry, hence acknowledgment of the sovereignty of the one God, and their shunning of major sins place them within the pale of salvation.[42] The court tales of Daniel verge on a similar view (Daniel 2–6), as the respective kings acknowledge the sovereignty of the God of Israel (2:47; 3:28-30; 4:37; 6:26-27).[43] Bel and the Dragon states of Cyrus, "the king has become a Jew" (v 28), although this may express the viewpoint of the Babylonians within the story's fiction, rather than the author's own opinion. At the end of the story, however, he acknowledges the God of the Jews, as do the monarchs in the other stories (v 41). The book of Tobit shows some ambiguity. While mandating marriage within the tribe, in a hymn that draws on the ideas of Second Isaiah, the author anticipates a time when the Gentiles will bring their gifts to Jerusalem.[44]

**Israel versus the Nations**

The book of *Jubilees* represents a much narrower view.[45] Israel is the chosen people, and their obedience to the Torah (as construed by this author) distinguishes them from the nations. Abraham was chosen as patriarch and called from Chaldea because he perceived the folly of idolatry and astrology and set an idolatrous temple on fire. Israel's disobedience to the Torah is often described as following the ways of the Gentiles; marriage to a non-Israelite is strictly prohibited, not least because it may lead to idolatry. Other texts written during the Antiochan persecution (Daniel 7–12; *Testament of Moses*) also take a particularly dim view of the Gentiles and in a general way envision their wholesale condemnation in the imminent judgment.

## Interpretations of Idols and Idolatry

Jewish texts are uniform in their criticism of idolatry, although they describe the nature of idols in two different ways. The Letter of Jeremiah, for example, speaks of idols in totally materialistic terms.[46] They are nothing more than the gold, silver, wood, or stone from which they are fabricated. Since they are incapable of doing the things that a god should do, worshiping them is senseless and useless. Bel and the Dragon and the *Apocalypse of Abraham* carry the mocking polemic to ludicrous extremes.[47] A similar understanding of idols is evident in *Jubilees*. They are the fabrications of human beings and have no spirit in them (12:1-5; 20:7-9; 22:18). At the same time, the author recognizes that behind idols stands the world of evil spirits generated by the rebellion of the Watchers and the death of their progeny, the giants (11:4; cf. 10:7-11). To worship idols is to associate with these evil spirits. This latter point of view appears in the *Testament of Job,* where Job's destruction of the idol temple that serves as Satan's sanctuary triggers Satan's persecution of him (*T. Job* 1–4).[48] A short passage in the Epistle of Enoch manages to combine both views (*1 En.* 99:6-9), as does the apostle Paul.[49]

## Sectarian Judaism

As noted, the Enochic texts combine a kind of sectarianism with an openness to the Gentiles. The righteous are distinguished from sinful Israelites, who oppress the righteous and do not interpret and observe God's law properly. At the same time, the Enochic authors anticipate the inclusion of righteous Gentiles, who convert to Enochic law. *Jubilees* also draws a line between Israelites who obey the Mosaic Torah as it is expounded in that book and others who follow the way of the Gentiles and will be damned. Many of the Qumranic texts take a different tack. Their sectarianism based on revealed exclusivist interpretation of the Torah is pronounced and explicitly structured.[50] Different from *1 Enoch,* however, the Qumran texts evidence little openness to Gentiles. The Habakkuk Commentary (1QpHab) is particularly severe in its condemnation of the Romans, who are described under the code word "Kittim."

In summary, Jewish attitudes about the salvation of the Gentiles vary widely, from exclusivity to inclusivity. To some extent, these attitudes seem to have been governed by experience. Gentile persecution generated sharply condemnatory attitudes (Daniel, *Testament of Moses*). Close association with Gentiles may result in strong warnings, for example, against intermarriage (*Jubilees*, Tobit). Texts with a more universalistic viewpoint probably reflect better relationships with non-Israelites *(Aristeas)*.

## God's Interaction with Humanity according to Early Christianity

All the major points about Jewish views of God's interaction with humanity that have been discussed above have counterparts in early Christianity. Some of them are taken up here, while others are treated in chapters 4 and 5. Chapter 4 provides a detailed comparison of the *agents* of divine deliverance in Jewish texts and New Testament speculation about Jesus. Chapter 5 focuses on Jewish eschatological transformations of traditional ideas and their carryover in the New Testament.

### Salvation from Sin
*Jesus' Death for Others*
For the New Testament as a whole, the sacrificial system of the Jerusalem temple is no longer viable because its function has been permanently replaced by Jesus' death. The idea has roots in the martyrdom accounts in 2 Maccabees 6–7 and 4 Maccabees, and New Testament formulations of the idea reflect the language of Isaiah 52–53.[51] The New Testament's particular nuance is an emphasis on the unique character of Jesus' death and its permanent significance and applicability. This emphasis results from the convergence of many lines of speculation about Jesus, which are discussed in chapters 4 and 5.

This interpretation of the crucifixion as sacrifice, propitiation, or death for others appears in some of the earliest strata of the New Testament. Paul cites such a tradition in Rom 3:25.[52] Another formulation occurs in Rom 4:24-25, in the context of a creedal formula based on Isaiah 52–53.[53] Paul quotes received tradition about Jesus' death "for our sins" in 1 Cor 15:3 as part of a death/resurrection formula. As 1 Cor 11:23-25 indicates, the eucharistic formula was an early locus for this interpretation of Jesus' death, and the motif recurs in Mark 14:22-24 and Matt 26:27-28.

The only other locus for this idea in the Synoptic Gospels is in connection with Jesus' third prediction of his passion in Mark 10:45 and its parallel in Matt 20:28. Nonetheless, the idea is so powerful that it occurs in three contexts in the Fourth Gospel (John 10:11, 15, 17-18; 11:51; 15:13), a text whose soteriology is thoroughly governed by the idea of salvation as revelation (see below, p. 84).

The uniqueness of Jesus' sacrifice is indicated by another factor. The Synoptic Gospels, Paul, Hebrews, and 1 Peter all transmit traditions in which Jesus' obedient suffering and death offer the paradigm that Christians are to follow.[54] In no case, however, is such a death efficacious as sacrifice for oneself or others.[55]

### Attitudes about the Temple

Although a few texts in the book of Acts indicate some early Christian appreciation for the Jerusalem temple (2:46; 3–4; 21:26), for the most part the devaluation of the temple is a corollary of Jesus' efficacious death for others. To some extent this is expressed in ways that are reminiscent of a similar devaluation in Jewish texts.[56] The Epistle to the Hebrews is most explicit in its devaluation of temple and priesthood (especially chaps. 5, 7–9). This point of view appears to be catalyzed more by a high view of Jesus' death than by a presupposition that temple and priesthood are corrupt or malfunctioning.[57] All four Gospels tie the conspiracy leading to Jesus' death to his critique of the temple. That is, the devaluation of the temple serves as a foil to the high estimate of Jesus' death. Whether here or elsewhere in the New Testament there may be an implicit critique of the priesthood and cult, as such, is uncertain.[58] Without any explicit critique of the temple or priesthood, the church is depicted as the true temple, in language, however, that is reminiscent of 1QS 8:5-10 (Eph 2:19-22; 1 Pet 2:4-10; and possibly Matt 16:13-19). In the last two instances, this notion is tied to the figure of Peter. Finally, we should note the book of Revelation. John's vision of the new Jerusalem (21:1—22:5), while this idea has a long history in Jewish texts, may be an allusion to the destruction of the temple.[59]

### Salvation through Repentance

The Gospel according to Luke strikes a different note. Although this evangelist has retained the notion of death for others in his account of the

Last Supper (22:19[-20]), he has expunged the formula from the context of the third passion prediction (18:31-33) and replaced it with a reference to Jesus' preaching activity among sinners: "the Son of Man came to seek and save the lost" (19:10). Indeed, throughout the Gospel, Luke depicts Jesus primarily as one who called sinners and outsiders to repentance, and he emphasizes that salvation for sinners requires repentance. His use of the verb *sōzō* in this respect is noteworthy, as is the word pair "lost/found."[60]

However, this emphasis on salvation through repentance runs through all the strata of the Synoptic tradition. The traditions about John the Baptist's preaching (Mark 1:48; Matt 3:2-12 | | Luke 3:2-18) and material about Jesus in Mark (2:13-17), Q (Matt 18:12-14 | | Luke 15:1-7), M (Matt 20:1-6; 21:28-32), and L (passim) make mention of the repentance that leads "sinners" to salvation. Concrete deeds of obedience are sometimes in focus, for example: confession of sin (Mark 1:5 | | Matt 3:6; Luke 15:21), giving alms and other forms of generosity (Luke 3:11-13; 16:1-9; 19:1-10; contrast 12:16-21), obeying the father's command (Matt 21:28-32; cf. Luke 15:11-32). Almsgiving as a form of reparation picks up on one of the aforementioned Jewish substitutes for sacrifice.

Paul reflects on how the Thessalonians "turned to God from idols" and were awaiting the coming of Jesus, who has "delivered us from the wrath to come" (1 Thess 1:9-10). In all these instances, salvation means that one is transferred from God's disfavor to the realm of divine blessing (cf. the covenantal paradigm discussed above, pp. 32–33) and that one is rescued from the divine wrath that will be executed at the final judgment.

### *The Humanity of the Son of God and the Transcendence of His Spirit: A Solution for the Anthropological Problem of Sin*

While the sacrificial character of Jesus' death is fundamental for Paul's soteriology, his understanding of the nature of sin requires a broader solution (Romans 7–8).[61] Following in part the theology of the two ways and two spirits, attested in the Qumran Community Rule (see above, p. 41), Paul sees sin as a universal human condition. Flesh qua flesh is inhabited by Sin (Rom 7:17-20), which is the functional equivalent of the evil spirit. All human beings are "under sin" (3:9), that is, "slaves of sin" (6:16-19; 7:14). Even the Torah cannot catalyze the obedience it demands of Jews (7:9-12). "All flesh" is under God's indictment and liable to condemnation at the final judgment (1:18; 2:1-2; 3:19-20) because of the generic human inability to obey God's commands, whether in the Torah or as attested by the human conscience. God solves the problem by sending his Son "in the likeness of sinful flesh," as a new, obedient Adam who founds a new human race (8:3).[62] The resurrection of Jesus unleashes the spirit of Christ, the functional equivalent of the good angel, which is appropriated through baptism and catalyzes the obedience on the basis of which one can be "saved" at the judgment. Thus an anthropologically nuanced understanding of the demonic cause of sin is balanced by a soteriology that ties the notion of a transcendent agent of salvation to the humanity of the historical figure of Jesus.

Justification is another metaphor for the process and is tied to the efficacy of Jesus' death. Nonetheless, the notion of *being* righteous is also associated with the new human condition in which righteous conduct is facilitated by the Spirit of Christ. I touch on the eschatological dimension of this soteriology in chapter 5.

### Rescue from One's Enemies

The wars of the successors of Alexander the Great, the Antiochan persecution, the Roman conquest of Palestine, and the destruction of Jerusalem in 70 C.E. were responsible for the frequent occurrence of this motif in the texts that have been preserved from these four critical moments in Jewish history. In this context, the infrequency of the motif in the New Testament is noteworthy.

Most often, the motif occurs in connection with Jesus' death. The Gospels are structured as accounts of the conflicts that lead to the persecution, death, and vindication of Jesus the Righteous One (see chapter 4). Secondarily, and less frequently, Christian suffering is construed as the imitation of Jesus, and disciples are promised the just reward for their obedience unto death. The motif occurs in the Synoptics especially (Mark 8:34-36; 13:9-10 par.), but also in Heb 10:32-39; 12:1-4; and 1 Pet 2:18-25, with reference to the example of Jesus' suffering. The story of Stephen's death and its aftermath (Acts 6:8—9:21) is modeled after the account of Jesus' passion.[63] Other occasional references to the persecution of Christians occur in all four Gospels, but the pattern of persecution and vindication is less evident.[64]

Not surprisingly, the best parallel to Jewish apocalyptic notions about God as vindicator of the righteous and punisher of their enemies occurs in the Johannine apocalypse, where persecution under Roman rule is focal and endurance is the appropriate response.[65] The text is saturated with language and ideas at home in *1 Enoch* and Daniel in particular, and it is easy to identify imagery drawn from the traditions of militant messianism.[66]

## Salvation as Healing

In addition to the overarching paradigm of Jesus as the persecuted and vindicated Righteous One (see chapter 4), the portrayal of Jesus as the divinely empowered healer is one of two other models of salvation in the Gospels. As in *1 Enoch* and *Jubilees,* sickness and demon possession are difficult to distinguish in the Synoptic Gospels, and healing is an act of divine deliverance from demonic evil. In Mark, for example, Jesus, endowed by the Spirit (1:10), opposes Satan in the wilderness (1:12-13), and then repeatedly opposes and neutralizes the unclean and evil spirits that inhabit humans and cause illness (1:23-26, 34; 3:11-12, 22-26; 5:1-13; 6:7-13).[67] Precisely how Jesus' healing activity related to non-Jewish, as opposed to Jewish, practice is a widely discussed topic. Here I highlight the fact that Jewish texts antecedent to the Gospels tie together demons, sickness, and divinely sent healing.

One passage in Paul may be enlightened by the Jewish texts. The apostle refers to his "thorn in the flesh" as a "messenger of Satan" sent to prevent him from becoming too elated by his visions (2 Cor 12:7). That God can use evil spirits to inflict disease is attested in the Genesis Apocryphon (1QapGen ar 20). That the "thorn" effects God's purpose suggests an interpretation related to this viewpoint.

## Salvation as Revelation

This paradigm promises to shed new light on the study of Christian origins, because it has not had the substantial influence it deserves among New Testament scholars. I can only be suggestive.

The book of Revelation, of course, is a splendid example of the apocalyptic worldview and of the genre "apocalypse" and its classical function. The closest parallel to Revelation is probably the Parables of Enoch. Like Enoch, John has been transported to heaven (*1 En.* 39:3; Rev 4:1), where he sees the heavenly throne room and events taking place that are related to the imminent final judgment.[68] John's claim to reveal an imminent judgment that will be enacted by mechanisms already established in hidden places again parallels *1 Enoch* as a whole. His repeated appeals to endure, based on this revelation, also fit the paradigm.

The Fourth Gospel develops its portrait of Jesus, the Word, on the basis of a Wisdom-related model discussed in chapter 4 (below, p. 113). The text is striking in the present context because, in spite of occasional formulas about the efficacy of Jesus' death and a few references to a future resurrection, it construes salvation in terms of an eschatological revelation that is the property of the elect community. The revelation is brought by Jesus the revealer, and the faith that it generates grants the gift of eternal life here and now (see below, pp. 140–41). Other motifs at home in apocalyptic literature (not least the Son of Man as judge) can be multiplied,[69] and often-perceived parallels to the Qumran corpus are also significant in this respect.[70] The salvific model of Jesus as revealer appears, strikingly, in the eucharistic prayers in *Didache* 9, where one would expect references to other paradigms of salvation.

The Synoptic Gospels are also relevant. We may focus on the Q tradition, which embodies the notion of Jesus as teacher and revealer.[71] Although the model of Jesus as Wisdom or Wisdom's spokesman is relevant (see chapter 4), the blend of "wisdom" motifs and forms with others usually construed as "apocalyptic" is also noteworthy. While some scholars argue that this blend is secondary in Q, one should note that the Enochic corpus provides a pre-Christian model for blending forms and content at home in the prophetic and wisdom traditions.[72] This Enochic revelation goes by the name of "wisdom," and the function of this revealed wisdom is salvific (above, pp. 73–75). As one example, the message is cast in admonitions to heed nature as a parable of divine activity and a paradigm of obedience to God, and these admonitions are blended with warnings of an imminent eschatological judgment that will wreak havoc on those who do not heed the apocalypticist's revealed, eschatological message.[73]

Central to much of Jewish apocalypticism is the claim that one is transmitting a revelation that is constitutive of the eschatological community of the chosen. In *1 Enoch* the message comprises and presumes a c beliefs, ethical teaching, astronomical and calendrical law, and eschatological promises and warnings, which circulate in the community of those transmitting this tradition. The extant Enochic corpus begins with the superscription, "The words of the blessing of Enoch with which he blessed the chosen righteous who will be present on the day of tribulation." The title suggests that we might appropriately think of this collection as the "Gospel according to Enoch."

This analysis offers an important model for the Christian gospel, as articulated (according to the Gospels) by John the Baptist, Jesus of Nazareth, and the disciples of Jesus, and as construed by Paul the apostle. It is the revealed message—proclaimed by God's messengers and comprising wisdom and prophetic strains, ethical teaching and warnings about the judgment—that constitutes the eschatological community of the chosen. Scholars of Christian origins are thus directed to the Enochic corpus and the writings of Qumran for significant predecessors to the shape of early Christian preaching and community organization.[74]

## The Scope of Salvation

The Enochic corpus, with its claim to be a revelation intended also for "all the sons of the whole earth," provides a functional antecedent to the Christian gospel, which is to be preached to "all the nations," according to the Synoptic Gospels as well as Paul (Mark 13:10; Matt 28:19; Luke 24:47; Gal 1:16).

The content of Paul's gospel has important precedents in such Hellenistic Jewish literature as the *Letter to Aristeas* and the *Sibylline Oracles*.[75] Gentiles who avoid the great sins, turning from idolatry (1 Thess 1:9; 1 Corinthians 10) and avoiding promiscuity (1 Thess 4:3-7; 1 Cor 6:9-20), will be saved. Circumcision and food laws are not necessary. Where Paul differs from these texts is in his claim that these Gentiles are the descendants of Abraham. However, his lengthy exposition on Abraham in Galatians 3–4, which presumes that his readers know the biblical story of Abraham, may indicate that Paul employed Jewish traditions about the conversion of Abraham from idolatry, such as those preserved in *Jubilees* and the *Apocalypse of Abraham*.[76]

The salvation of the Jews is a real problem for the writers of the New Testament. In Romans 9–11 Paul expresses profound anxiety over the fact that the majority of Israel has not come to faith in Christ. Nonetheless, the apostle is confident that "all Israel will be saved" (11:26). How this will come about is the topic of considerable debate among New Testament scholars.[77] Must they come to faith in Christ, or will God provide another way to salvation? In my view, the former option is correct, for this reason: According to Paul's anthropology, sin, which resides in all humanity, has neutralized the Torah's ability to catalyze the obedience that leads to blessing; and therefore for Jews, as well as Gentiles, faith in Christ and the indwelling of the Spirit are the only means to salvation from the human predicament.[78] Thus we are to take Paul quite literally when he makes the condition of the salvation of Israel that they "do not remain in their unbelief" (11:23). The thrust of his doxology in 11:33-36 is that, contrary to present evidence, this eschatological turnabout will take place.

The evangelists take a dimmer view of the possibility of Israel's salvation. According to Matthew, the nation by and large has rejected Jesus' message and mission. The disciples, first sent to the "lost sheep of the house of Israel" (10:6), are commissioned after Jesus' resurrection to make disciples of all the nations (28:16-20). While this does not exclude some Jews, the plotline of the Gospel points in the direction of a chosen people that will be largely a Gentile community.[79] A similar pattern of rejection by Israel characterizes the other three Gospels and, especially, Luke-Acts and John. After Luke has emphasized the Jewish rejection of Jesus, especially in his passion narrative, he describes the continuation of this rejection in Acts in his account of Stephen's stoning and Paul's ministry, and he ends with Paul in Rome, preaching with little effect among the Jews, whose fate is emphasized in his citation of an Isaianic text about the hardened hearts of Israel.[80] For John, the story of Jesus recounts the descent of the divine Logos, whose message in Jesus is accepted by a few but rejected, by and large, by "the Jews."[81] Thus, as the church moved into the second century, the anguish and the hope that Paul the Jew expressed about his fellow Jews gave way to the conviction that God's salvation would be received by believing Gentiles but, by and large, not by the Jews.

## Sectarianism in the Context of Universalism

Herein lies a paradox, though one for which we can find a precedent in Judaism. The Enochic Jews adopted a sectarian viewpoint. They were the eschatological community of the chosen, constituted by a revelation that could bring salvation. Nonetheless, they anticipated that while many of their fellow Jews would be damned, Gentiles who observed Enochic law would be saved. Early Christianity followed the broader, inclusivist strains of Judaism, but adopted the sectarian viewpoint that salvation was only for those who accepted *their* gospel. For Christianity, there was a special, ironic paradox. By the middle of the second century, the church that claimed to be the chosen of Abraham's God was increasingly composed of Gentiles.[82] To some extent this resulted from their rejection of the Mosaic Torah as a common base for Jews and Gentiles. More importantly, it derived from the primary touchstone of their proclamation, namely, the uniqueness of Jesus of Nazareth. This "christological" focus, also derivative from Judaism, is the topic of chapter 4.

## Summary

Like the Hebrew Bible, Jewish texts of the Greco-Roman period construe God's activity in behalf of humanity in a variety of ways, although circumstances modified how this activity was construed. The causes of evil and sin were increasingly ascribed to a demonic realm, and divine deliverance was often projected into the eschaton. Exile and the destruction of the temple led to substitutes for the sacrificial system, which continued into the postexilic period. These means of atonement were especially important among people who denied the efficacy of the temple cult, though this use was by no means limited to them. During the difficult times of the Greco-Roman period, old paradigms were reshaped to promise vindication for the righteous who stood fast in persecution. In part, such assurances were embodied in apocalyptic texts, which claimed to present revealed knowledge about the hidden divine and demonic realms and God's judgment in the imminent eschaton. In that this knowledge constituted the community of the chosen and righteous, it was salvific in its function. Jewish texts varied widely in their understanding of who was the recipient of divine blessing—Israel, or a small number of the righteous in Israel, or, in addition, those Gentiles who obeyed divine law.

The New Testament adopts most of the aforementioned Jewish paradigms. Divine/demonic dualism is regular fare, and eschatology is the air that early Christianity breathed (see chapter 5). Salvation from sin is mediated through the death of Jesus, not through the temple. For Paul, sin has so infected the human race that the problem can be solved only through the appearance of a new Adam. Repentance can effect salvation from sin, and almsgiving, as in Judaism, is one means of atonement. The paradigm of the vindication of the persecuted righteous is applied mainly to the death and resurrection of Jesus, which, however, can also be a model for Christian suffering and salvation. Salvation in the form of revelation is important, and the primary source of revelation is, of course, Jesus, construed as the personification of the Logos, or the bringer of Wisdom. The healing of sickness is an important facet of God's activity through Jesus, according to the Gospels. Although emerging Christianity develops a broad and significant mission to the Gentiles, thus reflecting the inclusivist side of Judaism, paradoxically, in tying salvation exclusively to belief in Jesus as God's agent, it carries with it the earmarks of a radical sectarianism that anticipates the salvation of few Jews. In all these respects, the principal factor that differentiates Christianity from its Jewish matrix is the centrality and indispensability of Jesus of Nazareth, the unique agent of God's activity in behalf of humanity.

# chapter 4

# Agents of God's Activity

The identity of Jesus of Nazareth was central to the early church's self-understanding and its appropriation of its Jewish heritage. The language, imagery, literary forms, and theological conceptions through which the church expressed itself and its view of reality were traditional—a heritage from its culture and environment. The uniqueness of the early church lay in the church's appropriation of this heritage to the figure of Jesus, whom it perceived to be the unique agent of God's activity, and in the modifications of that heritage that resulted from this process of appropriation.

Exegetical and theological exposition of the figure of Jesus over the centuries has focused on the title *christos* or its Hebrew counterpart *mashiah*, and thus we continue to speak of *Christology* and of Jesus as "the Christ." The nomenclature is understandable, given the New Testament's frequent use of "Christ" as a surname for Jesus, which is, in turn, a reflection of very early practice in the church.

This early tendency to speak of "Jesus Christ" notwithstanding, the New Testament applies a wide range of titles and terminology to Jesus, and many modern treatises on New Testament christology are organized according to "christological titles": Son of God, Son of Man, Lord, Messiah or Christ, prophet, and the like. The method and terminology are problematic, however. First, the expression "christological titles" attaches undue weight to a single title among the many that the early church ascribed to Jesus as it sought to identify him with the various divine agents in Jewish belief and expectation. Second, categorization according to titles ignores the fact that different titles may attribute the same functions or roles to Jesus, and a single title may have a variety of meanings or nuances.[1] We need an approach to the subject that better suits the data.

"Narrative christology" is an innovative approach that has been informed by the methods of literary criticism.[2] The method rightly recognizes that Jesus is a character in a story with a plot that began in the past and continues into the future. Who or what Jesus was, or is, or will be becomes evident as the plot unfolds and his roles develop.

This chapter will modify the titular approach to christology and use some of the insights of narrative christology. While convenience suggests that my discussion be organized in part according to titles, I focus that discussion on the functional diversity and seek the similarities that transcend titles. Since functions and roles imply story and plot, my approach parallels that of narrative christology.

## God's Agents in Early Judaism

The diverse functions served by divine agents fit a number of overlapping categories: God's activity as creator; God's reign or royal authority; related to this, God's rule as judge—the vindicator and rewarder of the righteous and the punisher of the wicked; God's activity as savior or deliverer in the variety of senses discussed in chapter 3.[3]

Although some of the agents of these divine functions are described or anticipated in the Hebrew Bible, texts from the fourth century B.C.E. onward reveal a developing tendency to proliferate such agents and emphasize their activity.

### When God Acts Alone

Despite this tendency to emphasize agents and intermediaries, Jewish texts sometimes assert God's direct activity, or at least mention God's activity without reference to an agent. The eschatological scenarios in the hymn in Tobit 13 and in *Psalms of Solomon* 11 anticipate the restoration of Jerusalem and the return of the dispersion without any indication that God will accomplish this through a divine or a human agent. A related prayer in Sir 36:1-17 appeals to God to destroy Israel's enemies, gather all the tribes of Israel, and have pity on Jerusalem. All three texts follow Third Isaiah in its silence about a future king. It is a tendency to which we shall return.

*First Enoch* 1:1-8 and *T. Mos.* 10:1-10 draw their imagery about God's future appearance as judge primarily from Deuteronomy 33 and Micah 1. In both cases God is the primary actor in the epiphany, although *1 En.* 1:1-4 mentions the heavenly entourage, which is described in Deut 33:2, and *T. Mos.* 10:2 mentions the preliminary activity of a high angel (see p. 101).

## Human Agents

Agents of divine activity may be either human beings or figures from the heavenly realm. Our discussion begins with human agents, because they abound in the Hebrew Bible, while transcendent agents proliferate in later Jewish speculation.

### The King

"King" is one of the Bible's primary metaphors for YHWH, and the celebration of YHWH's royal status is prominent especially in the Psalms and in the prophecies of Isaiah and Second Isaiah, which emphasize YHWH's functions as ruler, judge, and warrior. YHWH's kingship is crucial to the ideology of the preexilic monarchy, which sees the Israelite king as the executor of YHWH's rule over Israel and over the nations and their kings (Psalm 2).

Two sets of texts focus on the relationship between the Israelite king and God: royal psalms such as Psalms 2, 45, and 72; and royal oracles in 2 Samuel (7:4-17), Isaiah (9:1-7; 11:1-9), Jeremiah (23:1-8), and Ezekiel (34). This relationship is sometimes expressed by the term "YHWH's anointed one" *(mashiah yahweh)*. The act of anointing with oil denotes YHWH's selection of the king and delegation of divine authority on him. While the expression is a technical term and thus a kind of title, one should note that it originally referred to the reigning monarch of Israel and that in order to show the continuity between biblical and postbiblical texts, it is best translated ("Anointed One") and not transliterated ("Messiah").

The privilege of being the anointed bearer of YHWH's rule brings with it the responsibility to uphold the justice and righteousness. The king's role as shepherd of his people, as defender and vindicator of the weak, as executor of divine justice, and as opponent of foreign kings and rulers runs like a thread through the royal psalms and oracles (Ps 45:4, 7; 72:3-4, 12-14; Isa 9:7; 11:2-9; Jer 23:5-6; Ezekiel 34).[4]

Attitudes about the king varied in the exilic and postexilic periods, not least because there was no reigning Israelite monarch. Opinions differed as to whether there would again be such a monarch. On the one hand, the royal psalms and oracles were preserved. Psalm 89 enshrines a belief in the eternal viability of the Davidic covenant and enters an impassioned plea for the restoration of the Davidic dynasty and the enthronement of God's chosen and anointed one. On the other hand, Second Isaiah refers to the *Persian* king Cyrus as YHWH's "anointed one" (chap. 45), demotes David to a "witness, leader, and commander" and democratizes the Davidic covenant (55:3-4), and applies royal functions to the "Servant of YHWH" (see below, p. 105). This absence of a Davidic king continues in the oracles of Third Isaiah, who applies the metaphor of anointing with the spirit (Isa 11:3) to the prophet's commissioning as a preacher to the lowly, grieving, and disenfranchised (61:13). By contrast, Haggai expects that the Davidide Zerubbabel, who was governor of Judah, will assume royal status.

Our most detailed source for postexilic speculation about a future Davidic king is *Psalms of Solomon* 17. A text not unlike Psalm 89 in its tone and in the direction of its argument, this psalm was composed in the first century in the wake of Pompey's invasion of Jerusalem and annexation of Palestine. According to this author, Israel's plight is due to the Lord's punishment of either the Hasmoneans or Herod the Great, both of whom usurped the Davidic throne (vv 5-12).[5] The situation will be reversed when God raises up Israel's king, the son of David (v 23). This king is described in language drawn from Ps 2:9 (vv 23-24); Isa 11:2, 4 (vv 37, 24); and Ezekiel 34 (v 40).

> God will gird him with strength . . .
>> in righteous wisdom to cast out sinners from the
>>> inheritance,
> To shatter the arrogance of the sinner as a potter's vessel,
>> with a rod of iron to crush all their substance;
> to destroy transgressing Gentiles with the word of his mouth.
> (vv 22-24[24-27])
> He will not grow weak in his days because of his God;
>> for God will make him mighty by (his) holy spirit,
>>> and wise in the counsel of understanding, with strength and
>>>> righteousness. (v 37[42])

> He will be strong in his days, and mighty in the fear of God,
> shepherding the flock of the Lord in faithfulness and
> righteousness. (v 40[45])

By means of this imagery and the title "the anointed of the Lord" (v 32[36]), the author applies to a future monarch traditional ideas and terminology that the biblical texts employed of a reigning or imminently expected monarch. This son of David will destroy the enemies of Israel and their rulers. Especially striking are the priestly functions ascribed to him (v 30[33]; cf. vv 36[41], 43[48-49]). The concern with the defilement of Jerusalem is consonant with criticism of the Jerusalem priests elsewhere in the *Psalms of Solomon* (2:3; 8:11-12[12-13]), but it is unclear whether this author expects that the king will function regularly as a high priest.[6]

Other fragmentary texts from the Qumran corpus also attest belief in a future Davidic king, and some of them see him as a victorious warrior over Israel's enemies and their rulers.[7] Around 100 C.E., in response to the Roman victory in the Jewish war of 70 C.E., belief in a militant Davidic Anointed One appears again in two Jewish apocalypses, *4 Ezra* and *2 Baruch*.[8] In both instances, the king is a larger-than-life figure, who is interpreted in light of Jewish speculation about the son of man (see below, pp. 104–6).[9]

### The High Priest and Cult

As intermediaries between God and Israel, the priests, especially the high priest, removed impurity, mediated God's forgiveness and blessing through the cult, and interceded for the people. The high priest, who was anointed by God as the king was (Lev 8:1-13), pronounced the Aaronic benediction at temple services[10] and presided over the great Day of Atonement. In another role, priests executed God's wrath against idolaters and others who brought impurity into Israel, and in some cases won their credentials in this way. Levi (along with Simeon) exterminated the Shechemites after the rape of Dinah (Genesis 34). The sons of Levi killed the idolaters at Mount Sinai (Exod 32:25-29). Phineas stayed the wrath of God that had been caused by idolatry and sexual immorality (Numbers 25). Elijah led an attack on the prophets of Baal after he had offered sacrifice on Mount Carmel (1 Kings 18). Mattathias, following the example of Phineas, killed an idolatrous Israelite (1 Macc 2:23-26).

In postexilic Judah, the high priest assumed greater prominence. The prophet Zechariah, like Haggai, expected that Zerubbabel would serve as king, and he referred to Zerubbabel and Joshua the high priest as God's two anointed ones ("sons of oil," 4:14). When the Davidic dynasty was not restored, however, the high priest eventually became political head of Judah.

Postbiblical texts express a variety of ideas about the high priest, which reflect differing appraisals of the cult and priesthood. Ben Sira strongly supports the Jerusalem cult and the priesthood and utters lavish praises over the high priest Simon (chap. 50). Writing almost a century later, the pro-Hasmonean author of 1 Maccabees defends the legitimacy of his patrons by recounting the story of Mattathias's zeal with an explicit reference to the Phineas incident (1 Macc 2:23-26; cf. Num 25:6-8). Thus Mattathias, along with Judas and his high-priestly brothers, Jonathan and Simon, become God's agents for the purification and deliverance of Israel (1 Macc 3:1; 5:61-62; 9:23-31; 13:8-9).

Other texts take a dim view of the present state of the high priesthood and look for a future resolution of the situation. I have already noted that the *Psalms of Solomon* ascribe priestly functions to the anointed one, the son of David (see pp. 92–93). Other texts circle in the orbit of the Qumran community. Although the *Testament of Levi* in its Greek form is part of a Christian collection of twelve testaments ascribed to the sons of Jacob, it draws on Jewish Aramaic traditions that were preserved among the manuscripts of Qumran and in the medieval collection from the Cairo Geniza.[11] While we must use material from the Greek Testament cautiously, some interesting elements emerge when we compare it with the Aramaic evidence. A historical apocalypse chronicling the progressive disintegration of the priesthood climaxes with a description of an ideal future priest (chaps. 14–18). Chapter 18 makes no reference to this priest's sacrificial activity, but describes him as the revealer of God's will, the executor of God's righteousness, and the one who grants access to Eden and the tree of life. Especially noteworthy is the application of language from the Davidic oracle in Isaiah 11 to the Levitic priest (*T. Levi* 18:2, 5, 7).[12] There is no evidence that the author of the *Testament of Levi* expected a Davidic king, although the notion appears elsewhere in the *Testaments of the Twelve Patriarchs* (*T. Jud.* 24).

The reasons for positing an ideal future high priest vary from place to place. Like the *Testament of Levi,* the *Psalms of Solomon* (2:3; 8:11-12[12-13]) and the Damascus Document (CD 4:17-18; 5:6-7) claim that the cult has been polluted through forbidden sexual contacts (in part, due to wrong inter-pretations of the Torah). The Qumran Habakkuk Commentary criticizes the Hasmonean high priests for accumulating wealth and oppressing the righteous and lowly (1QpHab 8:3—10:12). It is uncertain to what extent criticism of the priestly leadership may also have involved a rejection of the credentials of the Hasmonean high priests. This may lie behind the aetiological legend in 1 Macc 2:23-26 supporting Mattathias's priestly action and may be suggested in the hymn to Simon 1 Macc 14:4-15.[13] However, clear references to such criticism seem to be lacking in the Qumran manuscripts. Nonetheless, the *Testament of Levi* and the Qumran fragments of Aramaic texts ascribed to Levi's son and grandson, Qahat and Amram, provide some tantalizing hints of a concern about high-priestly genealogy.[14] What is curious about this literature is its connection with the broader Levitic, rather than narrower Aaronic, origins of the priest-hood. Levi's line is traced to Amram and stops short of mentioning Aaron (*T. Levi* 12), and Qahat instructs Amram to pass the tradition on to his sons (plural) rather than simply to his one son (Aaron). A similar tendency appears in *Jubilees* 32, which recounts Levi's inaugural vision (cf. 30:17-19). It is astonishing that this fifty-chapter text ascribed to Moses nowhere mentions his brother, the first high priest. What is especially curious about all this is that the Levi- rather than Aaron-oriented material is pre-sent in the collection of Qumran Scrolls, where "sons of Aaron" is a cliché for "priests."[15]

The idea of dual anointed leaders in Israel, explicitly expressed first by Zechariah, may appear in the Wisdom of Joshua ben Sira. In his hymn in praise of the fathers, in the context of a reference to the covenant with the high priest Phineas, he also mentions the covenant with David (45:23-26), although a lengthy treatment of David will follow at the appropriate chronological place in the hymn (47:1-11).[16] The expectation of two future anointed heads of Israel, attested in the Christian version of the *Testaments of the Twelve Patriarchs,* is present in various forms in the Qumran texts, which refer to "the anointed one(s) of Aaron and Israel" (1QS 9:11; CD 20:1) and to "the anointed one of Israel" and "the priest" (1QSa 2:11-21).[17]

*Prophets and Revealer Figures*

The prophets of the Hebrew Bible were understood to be divine agents par excellence. But according to a common scholarly cliché, prophecy was thought to have ceased during the Persian period (with Malachi), and it was commonly believed that prophecy and the spirit of God would return only at the eschaton.[18] The idea that prophecy has ceased is attested in Josephus, who sees the time of Artaxerxes as the cutoff point (*Ag. Ap.* 1.40). A similar notion appears twice in 1 Maccabees (4:46; 14:41). This latter expression of the idea, however, should be interpreted in its context. It was in the Hasmoneans' best interest to defer a decision about the high-priestly line until some time in the future when a "trustworthy" prophet would arise. It is uncertain whether these two passages in 1 Maccabees imply that there were self-proclaimed prophets whose trustworthiness the Hasmoneans rejected. Josephus's accounts of the first century C.E. record instances of "prophets" whom he views as false prophets.[19]

Other evidence from the Greco-Roman period attests a plethora of claims to revelation or inspiration.[20] Within the wisdom tradition, ben Sira the "scribe" claims to be an inspired interpreter of the Torah and the prophetic tradition (Sir 24:32-34; 39:1-11). The corpus of pseudepigraphic apocalypses, which also stand in the wisdom tradition, makes a variety of claims to revelation. The authors of *1 Enoch* employ traditional prophetic forms: a theophanic oracle (chap. 1), a commissioning story (chaps. 12–16), woes (chaps. 94–103).[21] In addition, "the wise," who know the true and saving interpretation of God's commandments, stand in opposition to those "who lead many astray with their lies" (98:9—99:10). The book of Daniel depicts sages to whom God grants visions about the future and inspired interpretations of the dreams of others. In the real world of the apocalypticist, "the wise" *(maskilim),* like their counterparts in *1 Enoch,* "cause many to be righteous" through their teaching of the Torah. Many argue that pseudepigraphic composition was necessary in a time when people did not accept claims of prophecy. However, the direction of the argument can be reversed; the very writing of these texts reflects their authors' claims to prophetlike inspiration. Moreover, terms like "scribe" and *maskil* and the hints about their teaching activity and claims to revelation attest a social reality that corresponds, in some respects, to that of the prophets. Remarkable in this respect is the description of the righteous spokesman of the Lord in Wisdom of Solomon 2 and 5. His principal activity is to criticize his opponents for their transgressions of the Torah, and his career and fate are portrayed in a traditional reformulation of the last Servant poem of Second Isaiah.[22]

The Qumran literature provides complementary evidence.[23] This community claimed to have a revealed interpretation of the Torah (1QS 5:9) and believed that God had "made known" (hodi'o) to the Teacher of Righteousness all the mysteries of the prophets (1QpHab 7:4-5). The author of one of the Qumran hymns contrasts his own theophany with the claims of lying interpreters and deceitful seers (1QH 12[4]:22). The language indicates a competing set of revelatory claims and a conflict between opposing self-defined seers.

Nothing that has been cited here contradicts the fact that for some a resurgence of prophecy and the spirit of God would be major features of the end time. Two Qumran texts anticipate an eschatological prophet along with the anointed priest and king (1QS 9:11; 4QTestimonia). Nonetheless, ben Sira, the apocalypses, and the Qumran texts also indicate that people in Greco-Roman Israel made claims to revelation and inspiration. This evidence must be sifted carefully to see what historical conclusions we can draw from it.[24] What did these people call themselves? What public and private roles did they play? With whom did they associate? To what extent were they accepted or rejected by others? Were their claims of prophecy tied to a belief that they were living in the end time? In interpreting and evaluating this evidence, we must not move too quickly from ancient tendentious rejections of the "prophecies" and "visions" of others to the judgment that there were no prophets, or prophetlike figures, on the religious landscape. The story of Michaiah and Zedekiah (1 Kgs 22:1-40) reminds us that opposing claims about true and false prophecy are as old as monarchical Israel. Moreover, Christian presuppositions about the uniqueness of Jesus (and John the Baptist) should not compromise one's attempt to determine what the historical situation was in pre-Christian Israel.

## Transcendent Agents

One of the significant features of Jewish religious thought in the Persian and Greco-Roman periods is the proliferation and delineation of an array of transcendent divine agents and intermediaries. It was a very old idea that heaven was inhabited by a host of divine beings, known by terms that denote their divinity ("sons of God," "holy ones," and "gods" [*'elim*]) and sometimes identified with the stars (cf. Gen 6:1-4; Deut 32:8; 33:2; Judg 5:20; 1 Kgs 22:19-23; Psalm 82). In addition, one reads in the Pentateuch and elsewhere of the "messenger of YHWH" or "my messenger"—whatever precisely the expression denotes.[25]

The texts of the later Second Temple period attest several new developments, however. Major figures are defined and given proper names. They take on clearly delineated roles as agents of divine activity and intermediaries between God and humanity. Some of these roles were previously attributed to human beings. In some cases a single figure combines roles. Rarely are these beings called "angels," since that denotes the particular function of messenger. More often we find the older generic terms "sons of God" and "holy ones."

### The Holy Watchers: Attendants and Agents of the Heavenly King

Among the myriads of holy ones who form the heavenly entourage (Deut 33:2; *1 En.* 14:22; Dan 7:10), texts of the fourth to first centuries B.C.E. identify a smaller group, who are given proper names and specific functions. Etymology is a problem; the original meaning of the Aramaic `ir waqaddish` is uncertain.[26] Does `ir` denote that they are constantly "awake" (from `ur`, "to arouse oneself, to be awake")? Some texts suggest that meaning (*1 En.* 14:23; 39:12; 71:8). In any event, the functions of these heavenly beings are explicit, diverse, and related to particular ways of understanding and describing God.

The elaborate description of Enoch's heavenly ascent and prophetic commissioning offers a good starting point for understanding the nature and role of these heavenly beings (*1 Enoch* 12–16). Within the construal of God as the heavenly king, one thinks of God enthroned in a palace surrounded by myriad courtiers. Because the king is the Deity, the palace is the heavenly temple, and the courtiers of "the Great Holy One" are the "holy ones." In addition to serving as priests in the heavenly temple, they perform all the tasks typical of an earthly court. They praise the greatness of the king; they advise the king of what is happening in the realm; they receive and relay petitions from the sovereign's subjects; they serve as messengers.

### The Four or Seven Holy Watchers

From among the attendants of the Great Holy One, an inner group of four or seven holy watchers (the texts differ) is singled out for special attention and given names. The four correspond to the four living beings in Ezek 1:5-14. In our earliest text, *1 Enoch* 10, the four are named Sariel, Raphael, Gabriel, and Michael (cf. 1QM 9:15-16). A tendency to favor the number seven expands the list, already in *1 Enoch* 20–36, to include Uriel, Re'uel, and Remiel. The group of seven is known also in the book of Tobit (12:15). Later lists of four replace Sariel with Uriel. As we shall see, the traditions that build on these names and their meanings differ considerably from one another, sometimes even in the same document (notably *1 Enoch*).[27]

### Witnesses, Scribes, Intercessors

The idea that the righteous one has a heavenly patron is as old as the book of Job (16:19; cf. 19:25). The notion is expanded, or at least explicated, in *1 Enoch* (chaps. 9–10; 89–90; 97–104).[28] The holy watchers carefully observe human actions and write them in heavenly books, which will serve as evidence at the great judgment. When human wickedness increases and the wicked prosper in their unjust oppression of the righteous, these heavenly witnesses intercede in behalf of the righteous, calling on the heavenly king to initiate judgment. Additionally, they receive the petitions of the righteous, who request vindication or deliverance; and again acting as intercessors, they relay them to the divine throne room like memoranda in an earthly court. All of this activity is an expansion of the biblical notion that God sees human actions (Gen 6:5; cf. *1 En.* 9:1), hears the plea of the righteous (Gen 4:10), and acts accordingly.

The holy watchers involved in this heavenly activity vary according to the texts. *1 Enoch* 9–10 names four. Chapters 89–90 refer to seven, but single out one as a scribe (89:61-64, 76-77). Chapters 97–104 give no indication that witnessing and scribal functions are limited to four or seven. Daniel 12:1 identifies Michael as the patron of the whole nation and associates him with the book that contains the names of the righteous; in the *Testament of Abraham* two unnamed angels are in charge of the books of righteous and wicked deeds, respectively (chaps. 11–12, rec. A; in chaps. 10–11, rec. B, their counterpart is Enoch).

### Executors of God's Judgment

In addition to these activities that prepare for the judgment, the holy ones can also execute the judgment. In *1 Enoch* 10 God sends the four holy ones to enact on earth the judgment they had advocated in heaven (chap. 9). They are to protect the righteous, consign the rebellious watchers to the places of punishment, and restore the earth as a place of blessing for the righteous. According to *En.* 1:4, 9; and 100:4, a larger number of holy ones will actively participate in the judgment that will accompany the theophany. In Dan 12:1 Michael, Israel's patron, will defend the righteous at the coming judgment. His opponent in court, not explicitly mentioned in this context but evident in the tradition, is the satanic figure, the accuser of the heavenly court. The obstructor of justice and the opponent of God, he is also the demonic power behind Israel's earthly opponent, Antiochus Epiphanes (see below).[29]

### General of the Army

God's judgment is frequently construed in terms of warfare. In *1 En.* 10:8 Gabriel, the bearer of God's power (*gabra*), prods the giants (*gibborim*) into a war of mutual extermination. In Dan 10:13, 21 Michael is named *haśśar haggadol* ("the great chieftain, general, prince"); his judicial activity includes leading the heavenly armies against the prince of Greece, the heavenly patron of Antiochus Epiphanes. Michael's name ("who is like God?") is a challenge to Antiochus's pretensions to storm the place of God and be like God (8:11; cf. Isa 14:13-14).[30] The Qumran War Scroll ascribes military functions to all four principal holy ones and to the hosts that support them (1QM 9:15-16; cf. 17:6-8). *1 Enoch* depicts God's entourage as an army (1:4, 9).[31]

### God's High Priest

As noted, the holy ones in *1 Enoch* serve as priests in the heavenly sanctuary, although their precise priestly functions are not detailed. An exten-

sion of this notion occurs, however, in 10:20-22, where Michael is assigned
the priestly responsibility to "cleanse" the earth of impurity and defilement. The nameless great angel in *T. Mos.* 10:2, though his task is explicitly judicial, is ordained like the high priest; his "hands are filled" (see
above, p. 91). In later Jewish literature, Michael is explicitly the heavenly
high priest.[32]

### Melchizedek

A special instance relating to all three of the previous categories is found
in the Qumran text about Melchizedek (11QMelchizedek).[33] The central
figure in this text, identified with the mysterious king and priest of Genesis 14, is a heavenly being who serves as chieftain of the heavenly armies,
opponent of Belial the archdemon, agent of divine justice in an eschatological setting, and executor of high-priestly functions. Perhaps he is to be
identified with Michael. On the other hand, it is possible that the collocation of functions that are ascribed to Michael in a variety of texts are here
bestowed on a figure known as Melchizedek.

### Raphael: God's Healer

A very different image occurs in the case of Raphael, "God's healer." To
heal the earth of the plague of the watchers is his responsibility in *1 En.*
10:4-5. According to the Book of Parables, Raphael "is in charge of all the
diseases and all the wounds of humanity" (*1 En.* 40:9). In Tobit he displays
an array of functions. Having heard and transmitted Tobit's and Sarah's
prayers, he is sent to heal both of them, curing blindness and exorcising
the demon Asmodeus. Accompanying Tobias across Mesopotamia,
Raphael reveals and explains a magical cure and thus plays the role of the
accompanying and interpreting angel that is typical of apocalyptic
visions.[34] Preeminently, however, through his healing activity, he is the
agent of God's salvation (deliverance from Asmodeus) and God's judgment (the reward of the righteous).

### Messengers and Interpreters

Following the old biblical tradition of the *mal'ak yahweh,* some texts ascribe
the role of heavenly messenger to individuals among the holy ones. In *1
En.* 10:1-3 Sariel, much like an eschatological prophet, is sent to Noah to

warn him of the coming judgment. The passage, like *1 En.* 9:1, is a significant reinterpretation of the divine–human contact described in Genesis 6. Functions that the Bible ascribes to God are here ascribed to one or several holy ones (Gen 6:5; cf. *1 En.* 9:1 [seeing sin and violence]; Gen 6:13; cf. *1 En.* 10:1-3 [speaking to Noah]). In Dan 8:16 and 9:21-27 Gabriel is the interpreter of Daniel's vision and Jeremiah's prophecy. In the journeys of Enoch (*1 Enoch* 21–32), various holy ones accompany Enoch and explicate what he sees.

### Facilitators of Righteousness

Preserving an old tradition, *Jub.* 4:25 describes how, after the fall and before the corruption that led to the flood, God sent angels *(mal'akim)* to instruct humanity in righteousness. One sees here an extension of the notion that salvation occurs through revelation, and in *1 Enoch* the rebellion of 'Asael and his associates, which leads to disaster, seems to have been a perverted extension of this mission.[35]

The role of heavenly beings as revealers and facilitators of righteousness is developed in the Jewish two-ways literature, where "the Prince of Light," God's "Angel of Truth," leads the children of light on the right path and struggles with the Angel of Darkness, the Spirit of Falsehood (1QS 3–4).[36] The opposition of the two spirits relates to the judicial imagery associated with the eschatological antagonism between Michael and his satanic opponent, and the idea of angels as guides is reminiscent of the visionary accounts in *1 Enoch* 20–36.

### Guardians and Governors of the Cosmos

The account of the second cosmic journey of Enoch (*1 Enoch* 21–32) illustrates beautifully the multiple functions of the holy watchers. Described in chapters 9–10 as heavenly witnesses and intercessors and as executors of God's judgment, they are here portrayed as the overseers of various places of eschatological significance. As such, they accompany Enoch and explain the significance of their areas of responsibility. Uriel, who is in charge of all the luminaries according to chapters 72–82, is the overseer of the abyss in which certain disobedient luminaries have been cast (chap. 21). Raphael attends to the mountain of the dead, where their shades

*(reph'aim)* reside (chap. 22), while Michael, the patron of the righteous of
Israel, oversees the tree of life, which will be food for the righteous (24:2—
25:7). In their roles as guardians of the cosmos, all of these holy ones—to
say nothing of the many other subordinates mentioned in the Book of the
Luminaries (chaps. 72–82)—are agents of the creator and sustainer of the
universe.

*God's Vice-Regent: "One Like a Son of Man"*
In Daniel 7 God and the court of holy ones pronounce and execute
judgment on the last of the four empires and its final king. When that judgment is concluded, a heavenly being, described as "one like a son of man"
(i.e., human being) (in distinction from the beasts, who represent the
empires), arrives in the heavenly court and is given "dominion, glory, and
kingship" over all the nations on earth. The demonic forces of chaos
embodied in the Gentile kingdoms that have dominated Israel have been
judged and destroyed; a heavenly being has been enthroned, and this
enthronement promises that Israel ("the people of the holy ones of the
Most High") will dominate the nations.[37] The text transforms an old
Semitic myth about the enthronement of a young god into an Israelite
myth in which the kingly authority of Israel's God is received, borne, and
executed by a member of the heavenly court.[38] The crossover of functions
evident in the many texts surveyed here warns against an easy identification of this heavenly figure. While Michael is a candidate, especially in
view of 12:1, the presence of the unnamed heavenly figure in chapter 10
suggests caution in this respect. In any case, the significance of the text lies
in its notion that divine sovereignty will be held forever not by an earthly
Israelite monarch—the Davidic covenant notwithstanding—God has
delegated it to a heavenly vice-regent.

## Two Major Transcendent Figures
*Wisdom*
Proverbs 8, Sirach 24, the Wisdom of Solomon, and *1 Enoch* 42 attest a
developing tendency to hypostatize and concretize God's wisdom and
eventually to "embody" it in a heavenly figure. Depicted as a female figure
in the heavenly court, she is an active agent at creation, and she sustains

and upholds the universe. In Sir 24:3 she is identified as the divine creative word and as the mist that covered the primordial earth (cf. Gen 2:6). Later she took up her dwelling in Israel, where she functions as a divine power in the Torah and in its exposition by the sages (cf. Baruch 3–4). For the Wisdom of Solomon she is the spirit of God, the witness of human activities (1:1-8), and (especially for monarchs) the enabler of the righteousness that passes muster in God's judgment. She is especially present in the activity of the righteous spokesman of God (chaps. 2, 5). In the latter chapters of Wisdom, the Word of God (the Logos) has taken her place as the agent of God's deliverance and judgment.

The little poem in *1 Enoch* 42 reads like a parody on most of the previous texts, especially Sirach 24.

> Wisdom found no place to dwell,
>> her dwelling was in heaven;
> Wisdom went out in order to dwell among the sons of men,
>> but did not find a dwelling .
> Wisdom returned to her place,
>> and took her seat in the midst of the angels.
> Iniquity came out of her chambers;
>>> those whom she did not seek she found
>>> and dwelt among them
> Like rain in the desert,
>> and like dew on parched ground.

*First En.* 94:5 alludes to the same myth. Wisdom, present in the righteous sages, has been maltreated by the wicked (cf. the story in Wisdom 2 and 5).

This complex of texts reflects a tendency to cluster around one major heavenly figure a group of functions that elsewhere are distributed to a number and variety of divine agents.

### The Enochic Son of Man/Chosen One/Righteous One

The transcendent heavenly figure who dominates the narrative in *1 Enoch* 37–71 represents the most remarkable of all Jewish syntheses of speculation about the agents of divine activity.[39] Four streams of tradition influenced the portrayal of this figure. (1) The first appears in a modification of the presentation scene from Daniel 7 (*1 En.* 46:1-3; cf. chap. 47). (2) The account of his "naming" (chap. 48), however, is built on the call of the Servant of YHWH in Isaiah 49, and the titles "Chosen One" and "Righteous One" are consonant with that stream of tradition (Isa 42:1; 53:11). In a major scene that is dependent on Isaiah 52–53, the Chosen One is seated on the throne of God's glory and empowered as vindicator of the righteous and the judge of their enemies and oppressors, the kings and the mighty (chaps. 62–63). This is a major departure from Daniel 7, where the heavenly figure appears and is enthroned only after the court has judged and destroyed the fourth kingdom. (3) Closely related to this judicial function of the Chosen One is the use of a Davidic royal tradition, specifically language from Psalm 2 and Isaiah 11. He is the Lord's Anointed One (*1 En.* 48:8-10) and, as such, the executor of God's justice against the rebel kings of the earth. His wise judgment is informed by the Spirit of God (*1 En.* 49:3-4; 62:2-3). (4) This element of wisdom, combined with assertions that the Son of Man existed before creation (48:3), suggests that this transcendent figure embodies also characteristics of divine Wisdom.

Thus the Parables of Enoch bring together major elements in Jewish attempts to attribute divine activity to human and transcendent agents. The hopes that were pinned on the Davidic dynasty are now attached to a heavenly figure, who is identified as the Danielic "one like a son of man" and Second Isaiah's Servant of YHWH. Conversely, the enthroned Danielic figure is explicitly seen as the culmination of Israelite royal ideology. The Servant of Second Isaiah was already a synthesis of royal, prophetic, and, in a way, priestly strains of the tradition.[40]

The functions of the Son of Man/Chosen One are primarily judicial, building on the notion that the king is responsible for justice and especially for maintaining and vindicating the rights of the oppressed. The judgment envisioned here, however, is eschatological. The destruction of Israel's powerful and royal opponents is final, as are the blessings that await the righteous (*1 En.* 62:13-16).

Finally, and perhaps most remarkable, is the tension between the Parables' portrait of the Chosen and Righteous One and its source in Second Isaiah. Noteworthy in the latter are the aspects of the Servant's career that have been informed by the portrait of the suffering prophet (Isa 50:4-9; 52–53), eventually exalted and vindicated by God. Here it is the righteous and chosen who suffer, while the Righteous and Chosen One is a preexistent exalted heavenly figure who serves as their vindicator. As we shall see in the next section, however, there is a final twist in the tradition. Wisdom of Solomon 2 and 5 retains the Deutero-Isaianic notion of the Servant's humanity and suffering, but envisions the heavenly exaltation of the suffering righteous one as judge over his own enemies.

## The Lord's Persecuted and Exalted Spokesman:
## A Synthesis and Transition

The story of the persecuted and vindicated righteous one in Wisdom 2 and 5 is governed by two different but complementary traditions.[41] In its theme, plot, and literary form it resembles the court stories in Genesis 37–45, Esther, and Daniel 3 and 6. A wise (and righteous) man is the victim of a conspiracy and is condemned to death, but he is rescued, vindicated of charges against him, and exalted to a high position in the royal court, where his enemies are condemned for their opposition to him. The version in Wisdom differs from these stories in two major respects. The story is not set in a specific time and geographical location; the protagonist is a type rather than an identifiable individual. His vindication and exaltation take place not in an earthly court but in the heavenly court, after he dies. There, in the midst of the sons of God, the holy ones, he condemns his enemies. Many of these differences from the earlier tradition are attributable to, or at least expressed in, the language and form of the last Deutero-Isaianic Servant passage (Isa 52:13—53:12), which describes how an unnamed prophetlike figure (50:4-9) is persecuted and condemned as an evildoer, and how he dies but is exalted in the presence of the astonished and kings and nations.[42]

Central to the portrait of the righteous one in Wisdom is his criticism of the lawless actions of his opponents (Wis 2:12-15). Like the heroes in Daniel 3 and 6 and the parallel story in 2 Maccabees 7, action and testimony are inseparable. In his wisdom and his speech he stands in the line of the prophets. Pivotal for the story are the veracity of his claims and self-understanding. By condemning him to death, his enemies test his claims to be a son of God, in order to see whether his alleged divine Father will protect him (2:17-20). Thus, in a real sense, the story turns on the notion of the sage's credentials. Exaltation in heaven vindicates the truth of his claims and the actuality of his authority as God's mouthpiece and the bearer of divine wisdom (chap. 5).

The locus and nature of the righteous one's exaltation are of special importance. His claims are vindicated in the heavenly court, where the one who said he was a son of God stands among the heavenly sons of God, condemning his opponents (5:3-5). While it is not said explicitly that he is transformed into a heavenly being, the notion is very close at hand, for he exercises the authority of the court depicted in Daniel 7. Moreover, a comparison of Wisdom 5 and *1 Enoch* 62–63 indicates that the scene of the Chosen One's exaltation and judgment of the kings and the mighty and the scene of the righteous one's exaltation and condemnation of his enemies are cut out of the same Deutero-Isaianic cloth. They are variations of a common traditional exposition of Isaiah 52–53. They differ from one another in that the Wisdom of Solomon depicts the Servant figure himself as the heavenly judge of his enemies, while *1 Enoch* portrays the heavenly judge as vindicator of the persecuted righteous of the earth.

Their common usage of royal imagery and, specifically, the language of Psalm 2 strengthen the link between the Wisdom of Solomon and the Parables of Enoch. Wisdom 1:1—6:11 is framed by a pair of addresses to the kings and rulers of the earth, which resonate with the admonition of Ps 2:10, and God's scorn for them (Wis 4:18) recalls Ps 2:4. The status of the righteous one as God's son is compatible with the oracle in Ps 2:7.

This is especially remarkable. Although the book of Wisdom is ascribed to David's son, Solomon, there is no hint that the author, who writes around the turn of the era, anticipates a restoration of the Davidic dynasty. The functions and attributes of the king, as ruler (3:8) and righteous judge, are the prerogative of the righteous one, as they are of the Servant in Second Isaiah. Like Second Isaiah and various other expositors of the Deutero-Isaianic tradition, this author finds no place for an earthly Israelite monarch from David's line.[43] The king has been replaced by the righteous one, whose earthly career is that of the persecuted prophet and whose vindication is associated with his exaltation as a heavenly judge. This portrait and its complementary but substantially different variation in *1 Enoch* 37–71 place us one step away from the formulations of early Christian speculation about Jesus of Nazareth.

King replaced by righteous one

## Summary

Our survey of Jewish texts has revealed a gamut of speculation about the agents of God's activity as creator, ruler, judge, and savior. Judaism in the Greco-Roman period greatly expanded the notion that God operates through agents and emphasized especially the roles played by transcendent agents. The tradition is marked by duplication (various agents serving the same function), combination (one agent playing several roles), and the attribution of traditionally human functions to divine figures. While Davidic ideology is alive and well in this period, it is simplistic and wrong to reduce Jewish speculation in this period to "messianism," much less Davidic messianism. In addition to an anointed king, speculation about an anointed priest and an anointed prophet and traditions associated with the Davidic king were interpreted with reference to the heavenly anointed Chosen One/Son of Man, as well as the suffering and vindicated righteous spokesman of God.

If the early church quickly identified Jesus of Nazareth as "the anointed one" (i.e., *christos*), this is in itself remarkable in the context of the variety of Jewish speculation. However, this variety, and especially its diverse use of royal traditions, warns us to be sensitive and careful as we step into the realm of "christology."

## Early Christian Speculation about Jesus

### Jesus as God's Unique Agent

Although some Jewish texts describe or seem to presume God's unmediated activity, the early church appears not to have thought of God acting as savior or judge apart from an agent. Moreover, with a few exceptions, that agent is either the earthly Jesus or the exalted Jesus by whatever title he might be called. These exceptions include: Michael in Revelation 12 and occasionally another angel; the Holy Spirit in some texts; the son of man in an early form of a few Synoptic texts; the apostles or the Twelve acting in the name or authority of Jesus. These last do not really constitute an exception, since Jesus remains the primary agent of God. Thus we must begin our inquiry recognizing that, by and large, the early church structures its theology around the belief that the earthly or exalted Jesus was and is the unique agent of God's activity as savior and judge.

## New Testament Models of the Messiah

As I have noted, there is persuasive evidence that "Christ" was a title applied to Jesus very early in the history of the church. But what were the connotations of the term?

### Davidic King

That the title *christos* implied Davidic descent in some cases cannot be disputed. Paul quotes an early creed that refers to Jesus' Davidic ancestry (Rom 1:3). The nativity stories in Matthew 1–2 and Luke 1–2, the account of the entrance into Jerusalem, and some other pericopes also attest the belief.[44] To what extent Jesus' kingship may have been tied to notions of earthly rule is unclear. Texts like Matt 19:28-30 | | Luke 22:30 and Acts 1:6 may reflect such an expectation. Nonetheless, the variety of expressions that we have observed in Judaism leads us to ask whether early Christians may have understood the term *christos* in ways other than as a reference to the Davidic king.

### Anointed Priest

Jesus' role as high priest is a well-known feature of the description of Jesus in the Epistle to the Hebrews. One aspect of this high priesthood is associated with Jesus' offering of himself as a onetime sacrifice for sin (2:17; 9:11-14; 10:5-12). However, another aspect of this priesthood is explicitly associated with Jesus' exaltation and is tied to the citation of Ps 110:1. Jesus' realization of his status as a priest forever after the order of Melchizedek (Ps 110:4) is his exaltation to God's right hand (Heb 1:3; 5:10; 7:26; 8:1; 9:24). Jesus' activity as heavenly high priest, moreover, is explicated especially in terms of his intercession for those for whom he made high-priestly sacrifice (4:16; 7:25; 9:24). This role parallels the functions ascribed to the holy ones in *1 Enoch* 9 and 97–104. Indeed, Hebrews' emphasis on Jesus' humanity (2:14-17), expressed in the form of a double negative (4:14-16), may even be a rejection of the very model of angelic priesthood on which Jesus' heavenly high priesthood appears to be based.

Other New Testament allusions to Psalm 110 may indicate that this passage was used early to refer to Jesus' role as high priest. Paul alludes to Ps 110:1 in Rom 8:34 with reference to Jesus' heavenly intercession. In Mark 12:35-37 Jesus quotes the passage in a dispute that takes place in the

Jerusalem temple. The confrontation with the high priest in Mark 14:60-64 includes the question, "Are you the Christ?" as well as Jesus' answer that the high priest will see "the son of man seated at the right hand of power." This is a reference to his own future exaltation, which will confirm his present confession to be the Christ and the high priest's rejection of the claim. Although the Synoptic account of Jesus' baptism makes no allusion to Psalm 110, second- and third-century Christian tradition read the story as a reference to Jesus' anointing as high priest,[45] and the present form of *T. Levi* 18:6-7 may well be a similar interpretation of that story.

These texts in the New Testament and later sources, and the New Testament use of Psalm 110 aside from Hebrews, suggest that the Epistle to the Hebrews was not innovative in identifying Jesus as God's anointed high priest, and that early tradition may have tied his status as the anointed one to his exaltation in heaven.

## Son of Man

The son of man in *1 Enoch* presents another model for interpreting the "Anointed One" with reference to an exalted heavenly figure.[46] Although New Testament passages about the son of man sometimes employ the wording of Dan 7:13-14 (Mark 13:26; 14:62; Rev 1:7), many of them reflect the interpretation of the Danielic passage attested in *1 Enoch*. In Q, Mark, Matthew, and Luke and their special material, and the Fourth Gospel, the son of man has judicial functions that he does not have in Daniel 7 but that the Parables of Enoch attribute to him.[47] Moreover, in both Mark 13:21-22 and 14:61-62, reference to the exalted son of man follows immediately after a reference to *ho christos* and as an interpretation of the title. Similarly, the judgment scene in Matt 25:31-46 also conflates the titles "son of man" and "king." Thus New Testament references to Jesus the exalted and/or coming son of man point once again to a Jewish source that takes the notion of the "Anointed One" in a direction other than speculation about a Davidic king.

Although the apostle Paul never uses the term "son of man" (the term would have been meaningless to his Gentile audience), a number of Pauline texts indicate that he was aware of Synoptic traditions about the coming son of man preserved in both Mark 13 and Q (1 Thess 4:15-17; cf.

Mark 13:26-27; 1 Thess 5:2; cf. Matt 24:42-44||Luke 12:37-40; cf. also 1 Thess 5:3-17 with Luke 21:34-36).[48] Moreover, his references to Jesus' function as judge in God's behalf may well derive from this son of man tradition, although his operative title in these contexts is "Lord."[49]

### The Righteous One and Servant of the Lord

Another source of early Christian language about Jesus is Jewish speculation about the suffering spokesman of God, depicted as the persecuted, vindicated, and exalted righteous one, and derived from an exegesis of Second Isaiah's Servant theology, diversely interpreted. In 2 Maccabees 7 the story of the Maccabean martyrs employs the paradigm of persecution and vindication through resurrection and interprets the deaths of the brothers as expiation for the sins of the nation. The Wisdom of Solomon omits any reference to expiatory death, focuses on the paradigm of persecution and vindication through heavenly exaltation, and conflates the Deutero-Isaianic material with Davidic royal tradition (Psalm 2), albeit without identifying the protagonist as a son of David.

New Testament usage of Servant material is broad and diverse. In some cases it focuses on Jesus' expiatory death (Rom 4:24; Mark 10:45; 1 Pet 2:21-25; see above, pp. 79–80). Other creedal formulas interpret Jesus' death and resurrection in terms of persecution and vindication or exaltation, but without the motif of vicarious death.[50] In Mark's Gospel three predictions of Jesus' death and resurrection employ the paradigm of persecution and vindication and reflect the language of Isaiah 53 (Mark 8:31; 9:31; 10:33-34).[51] Moreover, the passion narrative itself is shaped after the genre found in Genesis 34–45, Esther, Daniel 3 and 6, 2 Maccabees 7, and Wisdom of Solomon 2 and 5;[52] and it is enhanced by details that reflect haggadic exegesis of the canonical Psalms about the persecution and vindication of the righteous one.[53] The other Gospels follow suit, though with many variations.[54]

Although the Gospels devote little attention to the notion of Jesus' death in behalf of others, the story of his passion and resurrection fits perfectly with the bulk of the Gospel narratives, which depict him as the persecuted spokesman of God in the tradition of the Wisdom of Solomon. Possibly this paradigm was associated with Jesus' messianic identity. The story in Wisdom conflates the portrayal of the Servant qua wise teacher with material drawn from Psalm 2. The exalted one of the Davidic psalm is here not a Davidic king but the Servant of the Lord. Is it possible that early speculation about Jesus simply went one step further and used the title *christos,* taken from the Davidic tradition, to refer to the exalted one of the Deutero-Isaianic tradition?

## God's Spokesman, the Mouthpiece of Wisdom

A major aspect of Jesus' ministry in the four Gospels is his preaching and teaching. To what extent the portrayal of him depends on any one of a variety of Jewish and Gentile models is a point of considerable dispute.[55] Our discussion of the Jewish texts, however, suggests some possibilities that need to be investigated. Since the Gospels interpret Jesus' death with reference to the tradition of the persecuted spokesman of God, it is plausible that some of their descriptions of Jesus' preaching have also derived from the tradition. The accounts of Jesus' baptism are noteworthy in this respect, because the wording of the heavenly voice uses language from the Servant passage in Isa 42:1-2, and the stories serve as prologue to Jesus' Spirit-prompted ministry.[56]

> Behold my Servant whom I uphold,
>> my chosen one, in whom my soul delights;
> I have put my spirit upon him;
>> he will bring forth judgment to the Gentiles. (Isa 42:1)

Luke makes the point explicit by having Jesus quote Isa 61:1 with its reference to the anointing of the prophet shortly after his baptism (see above, p. 106).[57]

It has frequently been observed that the Q traditions make no reference to the death and resurrection of Jesus, who is portrayed, rather, as Wisdom's spokesman or as the voice of Wisdom herself. The issue is more complicated, however. As the Wisdom of Solomon indicates, Wisdom's spokesman can be, precisely, the persecuted prophet, and thus the former notion can imply the latter.[58] In addition, the variants of the son of man saying in Luke 12:8-9||Matt 10:32-33 correspond to the respective variants of the tradition in the Parables of Enoch (the son of man vindicates the righteous) and the Wisdom of Solomon (the righteous one resp in kind to his enemies).

## The Incarnation of Preexistent Wisdom and Logos

That Jesus was thought to be the earthly presence of heavenly Wisdom is attested in several New Testament texts. Most briefly it is stated in the hymns in Col 1:15-20 and Heb 1:1-4, both of which emphasize his role in creation.[59] John 1:1-18, probably quoting a Jewish exposition of Gen 1:1-5, makes the same point, identifying Jesus as the preexistent Word *(Logos/Memra)* at the very beginning of the Gospel.[60] Of importance in both Hebrews and John, however, is the combination of the motif of the sending of Wisdom/the Word in God's spokesman with the pattern of the suffering and exalted one. What results is a pattern of heavenly preexistence—descent—death—exaltation. Hebrews and John also parallel one another in two other important respects. Both employ "Son of God" as the primary title for the heavenly figure. Additionally, both texts work with ideas that recall the activity of angels: Hebrews describes Jesus' intercessory activity; John employs the formula used by Raphael in Tobit: "Behold I ascend to him who sent me" (John 16:5; Tob 12:20).

## Philippians 2:6-11: A Problematic Text

Philippians 2:6-11 has generally been considered a hymn about the descent, death, and exaltation of Jesus, God's preexistent son, now Lord.[61] This interpretation has its difficulties, however. Different from Hebrews, Colossians, and the Fourth Gospel, this text nowhere identifies its central figure as divine Wisdom or God's Logos, or refers to his function as an agent of creation. Moreover, a number of scholars have focused on the hymn's assertion of Jesus' humanity and have argued that the hymn's christology depicts him as the second Adam, whose death is essentially an act of obedience.[62] Although he bears the image (here *morphē*) of God, he chooses not to presume on that fact (contrast Gen 3:5).[63] In addition, as has often been noted, he appears to be in some sense an embodiment of Deutero-Isaiah's Servant of YHWH.[64] This is indicated by the noun *doulos* (rather than *pais,* as in the Greek of Second Isaiah's Servant passages), the pattern of death and exaltation, and the expression "he emptied himself," which can translate the Hebrew of Isa 53:12.[65] The motifs of second Adam and Servant may be linked through the traditional counterposition of the Servant, who humbles himself and is exalted, and the demonic figure in Isa 14:14, who seeks to exalt himself and be like God.[66] Although "the case" for expunging Jesus' preexistence from this text "has not been closed,"[67] the recent discussion's emphasis on Jesus' humanity, which is central to the text, fits well with Pauline soteriology (see above, pp. 81–82). It may also fit with traditions that interpret Jesus' death as in some sense a demonic temptation.[68]

## The Gospel according to Mark: Son of Man and Son of God

Mark's understanding of Jesus reflects a double tension.[69] The term "son of man" indicates both his identity as a human being and his future status as the exalted, transcendent "one like a son of man" of Jewish expectation. The term also stands in tension with his preeminent identity as "Son of *God*," a term evoked at key points in the narrative: by God at the baptism (1:11) and the transfiguration (9:7), and by the centurion in counterposition to the high priest (15:39; cf. 14:61). While the centurion's "confession" suggests a meaning less exalted than Christian usage of the word, other indicators in the text reveal Jesus to be a unique divine figure, acknowledged as such by God and the unclean spirits  (1:24, 34; 3:11; 5:7), and exercising divine functions (forgiveness, 2:7; authority over the Sabbath, 2:28; control of creation, 4:41). Thus Mark presents an understanding of Jesus close to that of the Fourth Gospel, although the precise nature of Jesus' divinity is less than clear. The term "son of God" is used of the corps of heavenly beings (as is "holy one," Mark 1:24). The story of the baptism suggests that the man Jesus becomes Son of God at the moment that God's Spirit (a term used of Wisdom in Wis 1:4-5) descends on him. In any case, the Son of God/son of man axis in Mark suggests a conflation of Enoch's view of the son of man and the notion of the descent—death—exaltation pattern noted above. Enoch speaks of the son of man's preexistence and eschatological exaltation. The descent—death—exaltation pattern allows one to identify the historical Jesus with both the preexistent and the eschatologically exalted one.[70]

## Jesus as Healer

Jesus' activity as a healer suggests many parallels and models in the Greco-Roman world.[71] The previous analysis of the Gospel of Mark suggests another possibility.[72] We may compare the descent of the Son of God, his ministry of healing, and his disappearance from the tomb with the descent of Raphael, his healing of Sarah and Tobit, and his disappearance and ascent to "him who sent me" (Tob 12:20).[73]

## The Exaltation of Jesus: The Foundation of Christology

Given the ubiquity of the pattern of death and vindication in the New Testament, one can argue that belief in Jesus' resurrection is an extrapolation from his death. He fit the pattern of the persecuted spokesman of the Lord, and the Wisdom of Solomon, to cite one text, offered a rationale for postulating his resurrection or direct exaltation in heaven. At the same time, however, Paul's language in Galatians 1 is couched in the traditional form of a prophetic call account with Jesus playing the role of the exalted one.[74] Almost all the Gospel accounts of Jesus' resurrection appearances also fit the commissioning genre, even if the portrayal of his exaltation is one step removed (but note the son of man language in Matt 28:18-20).[75] Thus one can plausibly argue that christophany gave rise to christology. The precise nuances of early speculation about Jesus appear to have been diverse, to the extreme, but the focus appears to have been on the notion that the risen one was the exalted one. To the extent that the exalted one was thought to be the "Anointed One," it would have been in the Enochic sense of this term or with reference to the parallel exaltation tradition attested in the Wisdom of Solomon.

## Jewish "Unbelief"

As I have noted (above, p. 31), much is made of the failure of most first-century Jews to accept the early church's claims that Jesus was the Messiah. We should place this historical fact in the context of the breadth of the Jewish beliefs cataloged in the first part of this chapter. Only for some would the Messiah be an exalted, heavenly figure. For others, he would fit the description of *Psalms of Solomon* 17 and some of the Qumran texts. In other schemes there was no expectation of a messiah. In short, early

Christian claims about Jesus' status as the Christ, or some other figure, would not have been universally taken for granted even among pious, eschatologically oriented Jews.

### Jesus' "Messianic Consciousness"

Before one dismisses the notion of Jesus' "messianic consciousness," one must place the concept in the spectrum of Jewish belief. First, given this spectrum, the historical Jesus could have had a high understanding of his place in God's scheme of things without having claimed to be the "Anointed One." Certainly the prophets did. Indeed, Jesus' activity seems to fall into the category of the righteous spokesman of the Lord in the Wisdom of Solomon. Second, in that context, he certainly could have anticipated his violent demise and believed in his eventual exaltation. Other Jewish ideas about the expiation of the martyrs, attested in the *Testament of Moses* and 2 Maccabees 7, allow that Jesus might have taken such a view of his own death.[76] In any case, the notion that Jesus could not have thought of himself as the "Anointed One" presumes a set of loaded categories that need to be dismantled and reassembled in the light of the whole range of Jewish texts and a careful study of relevant New Testament passages.

### Summary

Israelite religious thought, attested in the Bible, asserted that God interacted with humanity through a variety of agents, both human and divine. Jewish texts from the Greco-Roman period reflect continuity in this matter, but also attest some significant transformations and a great deal of variety. With the Davidic monarch a thing of the past, some awaited a new Davidide, while others transferred royal characteristics and hopes to a heavenly figure. Although the priesthood continued to function in a postexilic temple and was accepted by many as efficacious, some considered the priesthood to be polluted and the temple cult defunct. Some solved this problem by positing a future high priest or an angelic high priest who would cleanse the earth. Although some scholars dispute that "prophets" flourished in Judah in the Greco-Roman period, sages and apocalypticists presented themselves as inspired spokesmen of God and of heavenly Wisdom. The Greco-Roman period saw an increasing tendency to posit the existence of divine agents of God's activity, some of them assuming functions previously attributed to human beings. To some extent this may respond to the corresponding tendency to attribute evil to a demonic realm. "Anointed One" is a multivalent term that can refer to a future Davidic king, to the high priest, to a prophet, or to a transcendent heavenly figure such as the son of man.

The first Christians interpreted the person and activity of Jesus in light of this whole range of figures, or conversely, Christian beliefs about any or several of these figures were almost uniformly tied to Jesus of Nazareth. Constitutive was the belief that he was raised from the dead and exalted in heaven. Both his career as a preacher and his death and resurrection/exaltation revealed him to be the suffering and exalted righteous spokesman of God and of divine Wisdom, the Servant of the Lord. "High" christologies saw in him the embodiment of a heavenly figure, either the Logos, Wisdom, or "the Son of God" (which may have been a sobriquet for Wisdom). The term *christos* as a title for Jesus is early, but it is uncertain precisely how, or in how many different ways, early Christians applied this multivalent term to him. Several possibilities present themselves: descendant of David, anointed priest, anointed prophet, exalted son of man, exalted righteous one. Christian beliefs about Jesus diverged from their pre-Christian Jewish counterparts in their perception that the eschaton had arrived and that Jesus was God's final agent and presence in a world that faced the new age. This eschatological consciousness is the subject of the next chapter.

# chapter 5

# Eschatology

Eschatology, a theological catchword that has come to dominate the exegetical and historical study of biblical texts, provides the horizon on which to orient much of the content of our previous chapters. Traditionally, the topic was discussed last in theological treatises and treated the woes of the last days, the resurrection of the dead, the final judgment, and eternal salvation and damnation. Its biblical moorings were located in the prophets and in certain New Testament texts, primarily the Synoptic apocalypses, a few Pauline texts (1 Thessalonians 4–5; 2 Thessalonians 2; 1 Corinthians 15), and the book of Revelation. To the extent that eternal life was seen as the culmination of "salvation," eschatology was a logical conclusion to a comprehensive theological system.

The nineteenth-century discovery and publication of Jewish eschatological works, such as *1 Enoch, 2 Baruch,* and the *Testament of Moses,* hitherto unknown in the West, and the rise of historical criticism gave a new focus to the discussion of eschatology. Scholars like Johannes Weiss argued that Jesus himself was an eschatological prophet and that the early church's understanding of itself and its times was thoroughly eschatological.[1] This approach was given widespread circulation in Albert Schweitzer's *The Quest of the Historical Jesus,* and Schweitzer himself used the Jewish apocalypses *2 Baruch* and *4 Ezra* as context for his discussion of *The Mysticism of Paul the Apostle.*[2] The publication of the Qumran Scrolls has provided additional, primary manuscript data from an eschatologically dominated wing of first-century Judaism.

Scholarly discussion during the past century has moved back and forth over the chaos of the ancient texts,[3] disputing what the historical Jesus may have said and what that may have meant, discussing to what extent he and his disciples may have agreed or disagreed with the eschatological sentiments of their Jewish contemporaries, and arguing in what ways "apocalyptic was the mother of all Christian theology."[4] Yet one fact remains constant: Christianity arose in the context of a sector of Judaism that was conscious of living in the last times. From a historical point of view, "eschatology" should not be used to describe the doctrine of "things to come"; it denotes, rather, the early church's pervasive perspective on its present situation.

The fact that first-century Christians believed that they were living in the end time has some obvious theological difficulties; those end times have strung out over almost twenty centuries of history. Exegetes and theologians have responded to the problem in a variety of ways. Rudolf Bultmann, for example, demythologized first-century eschatology and cosmology. The importance of Jesus' eschatological message was (and is) its existential claim on its hearers, not the first-century worldview in which it was cast.[5] C. H. Dodd argued that Jesus and the early church propounded the notion of a realized eschatology; the parables of Jesus and the Fourth Gospel, in particular, proclaimed that the end had come.[6] Both of these scholars agreed, however, that an eschatological viewpoint characterized the ancient texts and their thought world.

In this chapter I affirm that "the last days" and "the end" were increasingly important ideas in the Hebrew Bible and postbiblical texts, and that they governed the worldview of the early church. As in previous chapters, however, I emphasize the varied nuances in the expression of these ideas. Finally, as the overlaps with previous chapters will make clear, "eschatology" and "eschatological" are terms that define and qualify much in early Judaism and early Christianity that has been discussed in previous chapters.

## The Bible's Developing Eschatological Tendency

### Jeremiah and Ezekiel

Although an orientation toward God's action in the future is present already in the promises to the patriarchs and the eighth-century prophetic oracles about "those days" or "the latter days," the exilic and postexilic prophets intensify this concern by describing what we may reasonably refer to as *an end,* or indeed, *the end.*[7] The notion is implied in references to a *new beginning,* specifically the repetition of Israel's foundational events, the exodus and the establishment of the covenant. For Jeremiah, the God of the exodus will be known as the God who has returned the dispersion (23:7-8). Moreover, that same God will make a new covenant with Israel that is *qualitatively superior* to the covenant made at the time of the exodus from Egypt (31:31-34). Ezekiel strikes a similar note in chapters 34–37. The sheep of Israel will pasture again on the mountains under a new covenant of peace (chap. 34). In addition, he intensifies his appeal to the beginnings by describing the restoration as *a new creation* (36:22-36), and as the nation's *resurrection* from the death of exile to a new life in the Holy Land (chap. 37).

## Second and Third Isaiah
The exilic oracles of Second Isaiah repeat the motifs of new exodus and new creation, with the use of language that details this qualitative difference between the present and the future. The new exodus led by God (52:11-12; 40:3-5, 9-11) is set in a new creation in which the old chaos dragon is conquered (51:9-11), the world is reshaped (40:4; 45:2), and the wilderness is made fertile like Eden (51:3). Israel's vindication through the return from exile is the Suffering Servant's resurrection from the dead and exaltation in the presence of the kings and the nations (52:13—53:12; cf. Ezekiel 37). Summarizing the whole notion, Second Isaiah asserts that the "new things" that God "creates" far surpass the former things (49:3-7). Second Isaiah surpasses his colleagues, moreover, by identifying God's great act of deliverance with a historical event, the rise of Cyrus, king of Persia (chap. 45). The future has broken into the present.

The author of the oracles in Isaiah 56–66 expresses deep disappointment with the realities of life in the Holy Land after the return, but he places in the future—evidently the imminent future—the new creation that Second Isaiah believed was in the process of taking place (chaps. 63–66). First there must be a sharp break with the present. In a new theophany God will execute judgment on all humanity (66:15-16), and then God will create "new heavens and a new earth" and a new

Jerusalem, where all the woes and sorrows associated with life in the present time will be eliminated, and the world will return to its primordial bliss, with human beings living extraordinarily long lives and existing in harmony with the rest of creation as they did at the beginning (chaps. 65–66).

Herein lie the seeds for what will emerge in the Greco-Roman period as full-grown and explicit eschatology: a decisive break between the present troubled time—an end to that time—and the beginning of a new age in which God's intentions at creation will be realized and God's sovereignty will extend over all humanity finally and forever. Paul D. Hanson argues that the eschatology of Third Isaiah (and Deutero-Zechariah) is "apocalyptic eschatology," because it does not differ qualitatively from the eschatology of the apocalypses of the third to first centuries B.C.E.[8] However, these prophetic oracles are not cast in the literary form of the apocalypses that are found in *1 Enoch* and Daniel 7–12, nor are they integral parts of such an apocalyptic worldview (see above, pp. 73–74). Thus it seems more appropriate to define the eschatologized portions of Third Isaiah, and, indeed Second Isaiah, with reference to what does characterize them, namely, their use of primordial *myth* and its projection into the future and, perhaps, a *dualism* that qualitatively contrasts present and future.

### The Legacy of Prophecy

The high hopes of the exilic and postexilic prophets (including Haggai and Zechariah) went, by and large, unfulfilled.[9] There was a return, though not a full gathering, of the dispersion. A second temple was built, but not on the scale expected, nor did Jerusalem see the inflow of the Gentiles and the worship of YHWH by all humanity. The heavens and the earth were not re-created, nor did the world return to primordial bliss. This dismal state of affairs is reflected in different ways in the book of Malachi and the Ezra-Nehemiah corpus. At the same time, the prophetic oracles were collected and formed a basis for hopes yet to be realized. It was from this material that the writers of the Jewish apocalypses of the Greco-Roman period constructed their varied eschatologies.[10]

## Jewish Writings of the Greco-Roman Period

### The Apocalypses in *1 Enoch* and Daniel

The materials collected in *1 Enoch* were composed and edited over the three and a half centuries before the turn of the era; the earliest of them was composed within a century after the time of Ezra.[11] Running through these texts is the belief in an imminent great judgment that will terminate the present age dominated by the evil spirits generated by the rebel angels, and that will usher in a new creation and new age marked by God's final and universal sovereignty. The texts clearly make use of prophetic tradition.[12] The introduction to the corpus (chaps. 1–5) describes the coming theophany, using the form of a judgment-salvation oracle like those in Third Isaiah[13] and language akin to Deuteronomy 33, Micah 1, and the oracles of Balaam. In chapter 5 and elsewhere in the collection, the authors employ the idiom of Isaiah 65–66 to describe conditions in the new age and the new Jerusalem. Especially important are *1 Enoch* 24–27, which cast Third Isaiah's description of the new Jerusalem into the form of an apocalypse (vision/seer's question/angel's interpretation). In spite of these specific parallels and the other uses of biblical motifs and language throughout the corpus, *1 Enoch* does not attribute them to a corpus of received prophetic scripture. Rather, it presents itself as the written deposit of special revelation that Enoch received in antiquity by means of dream visions and angelically interpreted journeys to heaven and through the cosmos. Thus, while the eschatology is dualistic and mythic in the same sense as in Second and Third Isaiah, it is also a constitutive part of an apocalyptic worldview (see above, pp. 73–74). Therefore the term "apocalyptic eschatology" is appropriately used to distinguish it from its biblical counterparts.

The latter chapters of Daniel also posit a decisive break between the present time, which is dominated by the demonic forces of chaos, and a new age that will be ushered in by the great judgment, when God's sovereignty will prevail universally and permanently. Allusions to the prophetic tradition are not frequent, although Dan 12:2-3 suggests the language of Isaiah 65–66 and the motif of the exaltation of the Suffering Servant.[14] As in *1 Enoch*, interpreted dream visions are the source of this information about the coming judgment and the new age.

An explicit belief in a resurrection of the dead is integral to the eschatology of *1 Enoch* and Daniel and an expression of its finality and its mythic character.[15] Life in the new Jerusalem (Isa 65:17-25) and destruction in the Valley of Hinnom (Isa 66:24) are facilitated by this resurrection of the righteous and the wicked. The exaltation of the Suffering Servant, in the context of Second Isaiah a symbol for the restoration of the nation, is interpreted individually to refer to the glorification of the *maskilim*, the teachers of the Torah who gave their lives in the effort to "make many righteous" (Dan 12:3).

## Teleology and the Fulfillment of Prophecy

If the apocalypses transmit the beliefs and hopes of the prophetic tradition in the form of "new revelation," other literature from the Greco-Roman period attests the belief that there was an end, a telos, toward which the unfulfilled prophecies pointed and in which they would find their fulfillment. One locus for this viewpoint is in the wisdom tradition. The book of Tobit (third century B.C.E.) is explicit. God's future salvation has been predicted by the prophets, whose word awaits fulfillment in their time:

> Then they will all return from their captivity
>     and rebuild Jerusalem gloriously;
> Then indeed the house will be built in her
>     as the prophets of Israel foretold. (14:5; cf. v 4)

The unfolding of that fulfillment is spelled out in the succession of events in 14:4-7, and one aspect of it is celebrated in the hymn of return and restoration in chapter 13, with its heavy use of Deutero- and Trito-Isaianic imagery about Jerusalem.

For Joshua ben Sira, the prophets uttered predictions that proved to be trustworthy (Sir 46:15; 49:6). His summary of Second and Third Isaiah, however, indicates that he also believed that the prophets forecast hidden events that still lie in the future (48:24-25). Following a prayer for deliverance that laments Israel's subjugation by the nations, the dispersion, and the present humiliation of Zion (36:1-7), ben Sira appeals to God to fulfill the ancient prophecies and thus reward those who wait for God to vindicate the trustworthiness of the prophets (36:15-16). He awaits the reappearance of Elijah, who will calm God's wrath, bring repentance to Israel, and return the dispersion (48:10), and perhaps he expects the restoration of the Davidic dynasty in keeping with God's eternal covenant with David (47:11, 22).[16]

The Apocryphal book of Baruch appeals to Israel to repent of its sins (1:1—3:8), obey the Torah, in which is found divine Wisdom (3:9—4:4), and thus receive the blessings of the covenant, which he spells out in language drawn from (though not explicitly attributed to) Deuteronomy and the oracles of Jeremiah and Second and Third Isaiah (4:5—5:9).[17]

*Psalms of Solomon* 11 and 17 take a similar tack. *Psalm* 11 embodies a Deutero- and Trito-Isaianic tradition related to Baruch 4–5, while *Psalm* 17 appeals to the Davidic covenant and describes the future king in language drawn from Psalm 2, Isaiah 11, and Ezekiel 34 (see above, pp. 92–93).

Through all these nonapocalyptic texts runs the motif that the prophetic oracles await their fulfillment at a time when Israel repents, and the chastisement of its sins is completed. The end is less an end to the present time than a goal, a time of fulfillment toward which the prophetic predictions point.

## Pseudepigraphic Apocalypses and the Fulfillment of Prophecy

Two texts from the second century B.C.E. blur the distinction between the claim of new revelation and the interpretation of traditional (prophetic) texts. Both employ the genre of pseudepigraphic revelation to embody the notion of the fulfillment of prophecy. The *Testament of Moses* claims to be God's revelation to Moses before his death (see above, p. 16). In it the last chapters of Deuteronomy are recast in detail so as to place the final time of blessing in the author's own time, when the great judgment will occur and Israel will be exalted to the heavens. Thus the goal of Moses' prophecy coincides with the end of the old age and the beginning of the new, and the authority for placing this in the author's time is attributed to Moses himself as the recipient of divine revelation. A similar combination of motifs occurs in Daniel 9, which reinterprets Jeremiah's prophecy of seventy years to refer to seventy weeks of years (vv 2, 24-27). The source for this interpretation is the angel Gabriel, who provides the revelation in answer to the prayer of Daniel in exile. The fulfillment of prophecy coincides with the turn of the ages described in three different apocalypses in Daniel 7–12. Both texts posit divine revelation as authority for their interpretation of traditional texts.

## Qumran: An Eclectic, Eschatologically Oriented Community

The manuscript collections found in the caves around Qumran offer rich and diverse testimony to a community with a thoroughgoing eschatological perspective. Combined with archaeological evidence that indicates time and geographic setting, these manuscripts help the historian and exegete to gain some perspective on the social and physical realities that attended an eschatological mind-set. As study of them has emphasized, especially in the past decade, the Qumran manuscripts are of diverse origin, some originating before the formation of the group, some imported from the outside, some written within the community over the course of two centuries.[18] For this reason one should not systematize their content. Nonetheless, some common motifs run across documents and provide a few indices of the worldview and religious thought of the community. I have discussed their sectarian outlook above (pp. 47–48). Here I focus on their eschatology, which reflects the diversity indicated in the previous paragraphs.

The collection includes fragments of all the major parts of the apocalypse of *1 Enoch* except the Parables, as well as the pseudo-Mosaic revelation, the book of *Jubilees*. Neither of these texts was authored at Qumran, and there appears to be no evidence that any pseudepigraphic apocalypse was written at Qumran. Nonetheless, both 1QS 11:3-9 and 1QH 9(1):24 employ language traditional in the apocalypses, referring to specific realia in the heavenly throne room.[19] Thus explicit and implicit claims of revelation with eschatological implications are put forth that parallel those in the descriptions of heavenly journeys in *1 Enoch*.

The *pesharim* (commentaries) on the prophets and the Psalms express an eschatological understanding of the community's situation in history that places them at the end of the age and the telos of the ancient prophecies.[20] Different from the texts cited in the previous section, this communal self-understanding is expressed in the form of detailed commentary on Scripture. Moreover, according to the Habakkuk *pesher,* this self-understanding is the result of a special divine revelation to the Teacher of Righteousness.

> God told Habakkuk to write down that which would happen to the final generation, but He did not make known to him when time would come to an end. . . . [But the text of Habakkuk] concerns the Teacher of Righteousness, to whom God made known all the mysteries of the words of His servants the Prophets. (1QpHab 7:1-5)[21]

The text does not state in what form the Teacher received this insight; however, the claim brings together, with reference to a historical though unnamed person, many of the motifs discussed above. The founder, or at least prime leader, of the community called his followers to "believe" his claim to the insight that this group was the chosen of the end time. Thus the Qumran community, which is heir to an apocalyptic eschatological viewpoint that reaches back to the late fourth century, complements this apocalyptic tradition with the claim to possess a revealed interpretation of the prophetic Scriptures. Quite possibly, this emphasis on the prophets reflects the waning of Enochic authority and the increasing authority of texts that would become part of the Hebrew Scriptures.[22]

Several Qumran texts indicate a close connection between (the repentance that leads to) Torah obedience and the sense that one is living in the last times. The Damascus Document (CD 6:2-11) describes a group gathering at "Damascus" to study the Torah as they await "the one who will teach righteousness *at the end of the last days.*" Similarly, 1QS 8–9 portrays the community as a remnant living righteously in order to atone for the land and studying the Torah *until the coming of the anointed ones and the prophet.* "Torah" is the community's revealed interpretation of the Torah (5:8-9), and entrance to the community involves a conversion to the new covenant embodied in the community (5:7-8). This complex of ideas closely parallels the viewpoint of the authors of *Jubilees* (see above, p. 45) and some of the strata of *1 Enoch*[23]—texts found in numerous copies in the Qumran collection.

The eschatological view that places the community on the threshold of a new age just beyond "the end of days" is intensified in some of the Qumran Hymns, which employ traditional eschatological conceptions like new creation, resurrection from the dead, and standing in the presence of the holy ones, to describe the individual's conversion and present situation in the community (1QH 11[3]:19-23; 19[11]:3-14).[24] What the apocalypses ascribe to the future, the Qumran sectarians experience in the present because of the conversion that has brought them into the community of the saved. One has been reshaped from the dust and has passed from death to life; one is rescued from Sheol and stands on the heavenly heights, singing praises in chorus with the holy ones. In these texts physical death is not an operative category; the important salvific event has already occurred.

There is a certain tension between the present salvation and its future consummation, and this is spelled out in both individual and cosmic terms in the teaching of the two ways in 1 QS 3–4. Moreover, other texts anticipate future events that include the coming of the anointed ones of Aaron and Israel and the prophet like Moses.[25]

## The Eschatology of Some Heavily Hellenized Jewish Texts

Several Greek texts, possibly written in Egypt, present a form of eschatological expression similar to that in the Qumran Hymns. Most explicit is *Joseph and Aseneth,* a document whose origin is disputed (Jewish or Christian?).[26] Aseneth's conversion involves her eating the bread of immortality and drinking the cup of incorruption (15:5[4]). Her resulting physical transformation attests that she has passed from the realm of death that attended her participation in idolatrous worship to eternal life and immortality (18:9[7]). The story attests a realized eschatology similar to the Qumran Hymns, but clothed in Greek conceptions like immortality and incorruption.

The Wisdom of Solomon expresses a similar viewpoint, although the language of Greek philosophy is much more explicit.[27] Death and immortality are the spheres in which the wicked and righteous exist in their earthly lives. The righteous one does not die; the souls of the righteous are in the hands of God, and what appears to be their death involves their ascent to God's presence.

The *Testament of Job* seems to be working with traditions based on Isaiah 52–53 that are related to Wisdom of Solomon 2 and 5.[28] Its dualistic world-view, which is more explicit than in the book of Wisdom, has things in common with both Jewish apocalypticism and Platonic philosophy. Although Job, king of Egypt, has been toppled from his throne and sits in degradation, his real throne is in heaven, the realm of incorruption. His revealed insight into this fact and his mystic ability to commune with the angels are the source of his present ability to endure suffering. When he dies, his soul ascends to God.

All these texts express a timeless eschatology, which has little or no concern about a future point in time when God's purpose is consummated and focused, and which is interested rather in one's present immortality or communion with the realm of immortality. The axis of salvation is vertical—between earth and heaven—rather than horizontal—between now and the future. The emphasis is on the individual rather than the community.[29]

## Eschatology: A Common Horizon Seen from Many Points of View

As I suggested at the beginning of this chapter, it is appropriate to think of eschatology not as a particular set of teachings, but as a horizon on which to place the aspects of Jewish religious thought and practice discussed in the previous chapters. *Scripture and tradition* can be interpreted with reference to the end time. Obedience to the *Torah* can have an eschatological function, preparing one for the final judgment. *God's activity* may occur at the end time through the instrumentality of *a variety of divine agents.*

Texts with an eschatological emphasis have several points in common. One sees one's present situation in need of change, and a belief in divine justice impels one to posit such a change. Oppression, persecution, suffering, and premature or unjust death cry out for divine vindication, and the prosperity and success of the wicked call for God's condemnation. If the general situation is sufficiently severe, one posits a qualitative break between the present evil age and a new age, between troubled existence here and heavenly bliss. Part of the driving force for such a viewpoint is a belief in the faithfulness of God, whose promises for such a change, spoken through the prophets, have yet to be fulfilled. On a larger scale, one perceives a creation that is not at all in keeping with the creator's intention, a world in which God's will is not done on earth as it is in heaven. Thus the eschaton is portrayed as a return to paradise, and heaven is seen as the place of intimate communion between humanity and God.

In general, it is appropriate to see in the exilic and postexilic biblical texts, and in the "postbiblical" texts of the late Persian and the Greco-Roman periods, the attestation of a developing eschatological consciousness and emphasis, although there are some exceptions. By and large, however, the centuries before the turn of the era appear to have been marked by wide and considerable eschatological ferment, and this, in its many forms, constituted a significant context for the rise of Christianity.

## Variations on a Common Theme

The eschatological theme and its individual components are played with many variations, and this variety is important if one is to appreciate aspects in early Christianity and features in the New Testament. In several cases my summary is a reprise of topics discussed in previous chapters.

### Messianism

Messianism is an inappropriate synonym for eschatology and an inappropriate way to describe ideas about the appearance of a future agent of divine deliverance.[30] A "messiah" is not a regular and fixed figure in eschatological scenarios, and where he is present, he need not be a Davidic king. To cite one specific example, texts that transmit traditions from Second and Third Isaiah follow their sources in that they almost never mention a restored Davidic dynasty. Ironically, the restored and glorified Jerusalem tends not to include the king whose throne has been located on Zion.

### The Kingdom of God

The eschatological use of this term is relatively rare in the texts of the Greco-Roman period,[31] and its usage may or may not indicate the presence of a Davidic king. In *Psalms of Solomon* 17 a restored Davidic king will be the agent of God's reign on earth (vv 1-3[4], 46[51]). In Daniel 7 the heavenly "one like a son of man" is the guarantor of the earthly proliferation of God's reign (7:14). According to *Testament of Moses* 10, God's reign will be universal (v 1), but earth itself will be turned into a place of punishment (vv 9-10). The Qumran *Songs of the Sabbath Sacrifice* refer frequently to God's "kingdom" or "kingship" and provide present cultic access to the heavenly counterpart to the eschatological kingdom.[32]

### Resurrection, Immortality, and Eternal Life

Oscar Cullmann's notion of a uniformity in Jewish belief about the resurrection of the dead is not borne out in the texts.[33] Resurrection of the body is not the standard, mainline Jewish formulation among those who believed that God's power entailed a transcendence of death. Variety in Jewish texts included resurrection of the body, of course (2 Maccabees 7), but also a resurrection of one's spirit (*1 Enoch* 102–104), immortality of the soul (Wisdom of Solomon 2 and 5; 4 Maccabees), and assumption of the spirit to heaven (*Jub.* 23:31). As anthropologies differed, so did their eschatological formulations in this respect. Positing a difference between a Hebrew conception of bodily resurrection and a Greek notion of immortality of the soul begs the question by overlooking the fact that Judaism in this period was hellenized. It also does not account for the possibility that early formulations may not have focused sharply on how one transcended death.

### The Locus of the New Age

Anthropology tends to be related to one's views about the locus of eschatological salvation, but one must be cautious. A text like the *Testament of Moses* consigns earth to the role of hell, with heaven as the realm to which righteous Israel is exalted. Dualistic texts like the Wisdom of Solomon and the *Testament of Job* move in the same direction. With *Jubilees* 23 and the last chapters of *1 Enoch* the situation is less clear. Does the ascent of the spirits of the righteous to God's presence mean that earth will be obliterated in the future? Both *Jubilees* 1 and the Apocalypse of Weeks (*1 En.* 93:1-10; 91:11-17) speak of the creation of new heavens *and a new earth*.

This paradigm of a new earth, which draws on the language of Isaiah 65 and 66, is far more common than is usually supposed. In *1 Enoch*, chapters 6–11, 24, 26–27, the Animal Vision (chaps. 85–90), and the Parables (chaps. 37–71) envision a renewed earth. For all of its cosmic dualism, with visions of the heavenly throne room and heavenly preparations for the coming judgment, the Book of Parables asserts that the righteous and chosen will possess the earth (or the Land).[34] The cosmic and historical dualism of apocalyptic texts need not imply that heaven is the locus of eschatological salvation. For other, nonapocalyptic eschatological texts, like *Psalms of Solomon* 11 and Tobit 13–14, the Deutero- and Trito-Isaianic texts anticipate a renewal of Jerusalem and a return to the Holy Land.[35]

## The Distinction between Eschatology and Apocalypticism

The use of the terms "apocalyptic" and "apocalypticism" among contemporary biblical scholars represents something of a paradox. On the one hand, scholars of Judaism have engaged in seemingly endless attempts to provide meaningful definitions.[36] On the other hand, scholars of the Hebrew Bible and the New Testament continue to use the terms in ways that hardly take account of the complexities of the definitional problem. The issue is complex. Discussions of apocalyptic should take into account the issue of *apokalysis,* that is, revelation (see above, pp. 73–74). At the same time, one should recognize that not all apocalypses focus on, or at least limit their revelations to, eschatology.[37]

One way of making the distinction is to limit the use of the term "apocalyptic" to texts that are formally apocalypses.[38] While this is an appropriate point of departure, usage in the Qumran Scrolls suggests that an eschatology can have its moorings in revelation, even revelation like that of the apocalypses, and yet be embodied in texts that are not formally apocalypses.[39]

The problem is further complicated by what appears to be a variety in the understanding of revelation. Not only does much of Judaism of the Greco-Roman period have a strong eschatological orientation, but eschatological consciousness is often governed by the conviction that the nearness of the end is something that has been revealed. Sometimes, however, the manner in which revelation was believed to have been received eludes the modern historian. Did study of Scripture lead one to conclude that one lives in the last times, or did one's assessment and experience of the times lead one to an eschatological consciousness that may or may not have been born of one's study of Scripture? Did the experience of a vision create eschatological consciousness, or was the form of a revelation a fictional, literary expression that legitimated one's eschatological consciousness? In any case, what might have been the connection to one's study of Scripture? The texts offer evidence that can point in any one of these directions.

## Eschatological Timetables

It is sometimes assumed that speculation about the time of the end is a peculiar function of apocalyptic texts.[40] Clearly there are connections. Daniel and *1 Enoch* contain detailed historical apocalypses and, to some extent, a strict periodizing of history (Daniel 2, 7–12; *1 Enoch* 85–90; 93:1-10; 91:11-17). The later, post-70 apocalypses, *4 Ezra* and *2 Baruch,* follow in that tradition. However, the historical summary in Tob 14:4-7, which bears some resemblances to the Enochic Apocalypse of Weeks, suggests that speculation about a fixed eschatological time scheme was not limited to circles that produced apocalypses.[41] How any of this is related to notions of determinism and the existence of heavenly tablets is something that must be studied in individual cases, and sometimes it is obscure.

A corollary of eschatological speculation, and a knot in the cord of deterministic theories, is the problem of the perceived delay of the eschaton. The problem is explicitly attested in Dan 12:12, where an editor has revised the calculations of his predecessor. In *Testament of Moses* 6 an editor has interpolated material in order to move the time of the eschatological scenario from the persecution by Antiochus to the Herodian period. The Animal Vision in *1 Enoch* 85–90 may indicate a similar editorial addition.[42] The Habakkuk *pesher* (1QpHab 7:7-13) also alludes to a delay, although there is no indication on what basis the first calculation was made.

## Realized Eschatology

The belief that one is living in a situation in which the end has already begun has a long history and many variations. For Second Isaiah, God's kingly power had already begun to break in with the accession of God's "anointed," Cyrus (Isaiah 45). There may well be political overtones associated with that notion. Explicitly political is the claim in 1 Macc 14:4-15 that the reign of Simon the Hasmonean brought conditions that realized biblical prophecies that might be considered messianic or eschatological in a broader sense.[43] More radical is the language of the Qumran Hymns that see entrance into the community as tantamount to resurrection from the dead (see above, p. 128). These specific instances aside, the term "realized eschatology" might be appropriately applied to any situation thought to be associated with the end (e.g., the woes). The term is slippery, however, and is often used carelessly. It should be employed with careful nuancing and explanation, and with attention to its individual historical circumstances.

## The Lack of Explicit Eschatology

One final caution is in order. Although Judaism in the Greco-Roman period was marked by widespread eschatological consciousness, it is wrong to assume that anticipation of the end was foremost in the minds of all Jews. Some of the *Psalms of Solomon* see God's judgment in historical events that are not described as eschatological (*Psalms* 2, 5, 8, 9, 16). In other of these psalms a belief in resurrection is not tied to an imminent expectation of the end (*Psalms* 3, 13, 14, 15). The book of Judith seems to anticipate a final judgment (16:17), but it focuses on God's recent judgment in history, that is, the Hasmonean defeat of the Syrian armies. Different from 1 Maccabees 14, this particular interpretation of these events does not suggest the fulfillment of prophecy.[44]

## Summary

The discovery of new texts in the nineteenth century generated a good deal of discussion about eschatology. Major monographs appeared that either were devoted to that topic or contained major sections on it. The names of Emil Schürer, Wilhelm Bousset, R. H. Charles, and Paul Volz are prominent in this respect.[45] Nonetheless, while we remain in the debt of these pioneers in the field, it is doubtful that any such systematic treatises will be successfully written in the near future. The discovery of the Qumran Scrolls and the subsequent reassessment of other texts previously known make abundantly clear that Jewish thought in this period was not uniform or systematic. Moreover, the patterns that did exist and their relationship to the historical circumstances and social organization of given groups involve questions that remain to be probed—questions that were rarely raised in the systematic treatises of the late nineteenth and early twentieth centuries. I discuss some of these issues briefly in chapter 6.

## The Eschatological Orientation of Early Christianity

The New Testament sections of the previous four chapters have discussed a number of issues that have an eschatological dimension: the interpretation of Scripture as prophecy and fulfillment, God's judgment and deliverance as eschatological phenomena, Jesus as an eschatological agent of judgment and salvation. Here I focus on a few points where the issue is explicitly related to the end.

### John the Baptist—Herald of the End Time

New Testament testimonies about John identify him almost uniformly as a herald of the eschatological judgment.[46] Allusions to John's identification as the awaited Elijah redivivus are clear (cf. Mal 4:1; Sir 48:10),[47] and the Gospels enhance this identification by drawing a John-Antipas-Herodias triangle in analogy to that of Elijah-Ahab-Jezebel.[48] The Q logion in Matt 11:7-15 and Luke 7:24-28 may point in the same direction with its contrast between John the prophet and those in kings' houses.

We have no hint as to the source of John's eschatological consciousness, and therefore we should be cautious of using the term "apocalyptic." Nonetheless, his message is reminiscent of Jewish apocalyptic writings and, especially, of the Qumran texts. The judgment and the eschaton are at hand; radical repentance is necessary; one's identity as a Jew ("a son of Abraham") is irrelevant. This last motif suggests that John's preaching was not directed to "sinners"—people whose concern with covenantal relationship and obedience was minimal or nonexistent—but more broadly to those who relied on their Jewish identity vis-à-vis the Gentiles (cf. Rom 2:17-28) or the sinners in their own nation. Like the Qumranites he redefines election and ties it to repentance and its fruits in a righteous life. Whether his ritual of ablution was related to that at Qumran (or other "baptizing sects in the Jordan") is debated; however, the description of the coming purification with fire and the sprinkling of the Spirit has a close parallel in 1QS 4:20-21.[49] It is sometimes noted that John calls people simply to repentance and not into a community, as in Qumran. It is unclear whether this reflects the paucity or narrow focus of our sources, or John's high eschatology, which did not allow time for community formation, or John's aversion to creating a community.

### When the End Is Not Yet the End

We have noted that in the Qumran Scrolls a high eschatological consciousness leads to the double proposition that resurrection has happened, but that the consummation of salvation is yet to come (see above, p. 128). Like the Qumran community, the early church found itself living between the initiation and consummation of the end. The tension between these two poles is a noteworthy feature of many New Testament writings and is expressed in different ways, with different emphases, and for different reasons.[50]

*The Tension between Present and Future in the Early Jesus Tradition*

I cannot here discuss criteria for determining the genuine sayings of Jesus, but what I do note are elements of both fulfillment and expectation in the early Synoptic tradition. Although "kingdom of God" does not appear frequently in Jewish eschatological literature, it is attested as an eschatological expression in Daniel, *Testament of Moses,* and *Psalms of Solomon.* That the kingdom was central to the message of Jesus is stated in all strata of the Synoptic tradition. Whether that kingdom was thought to be present, future, or some combination of the two has been vigorously debated.[51] The example of the Qumran Hymns adds plausibility to the notion that the teaching of Jesus could have been marked by some form of eschatological tension between present and future.

Is it possible that Jesus could have proclaimed the presence of the kingdom while anticipating the coming of the son of man? Or is Vielhauer correct that these ideas are contradictory and mutually exclusive?[52] To begin with, their coexistence in Daniel 7 indicates that the terms are not mutually exclusive. One can also suggest the following analogy with the Qumran texts:

The individual repents and enters the kingdom now,
a cosmic judgment by the son of man lies in the future.

The individual repents and enters the community of the chosen now,
a cosmic purification will take place in the future.

In order to make this work, one would want to demonstrate that the kingdom teaching ascribed to Jesus included a functional parallel to the notion of repentance in the Qumran texts. Such a notion is explicit in Mark 10:17-31, which is directed to one who observed the commandments from his youth, as well as in the Q text about the lost sheep (Matt 18:12-14||Luke 15:3-7) and to Luke's stories about the dishonest steward and Zacchaeus (16:1-9; 19:1-10), all of which refer to the repentance of sinners. One should also note that in some of the kingdom parables it is difficult to sort out the present-future issue because they focus on one's present response to the proclamation, not on the future implications and dimensions of this decision. Nonetheless, this focus on the individual's present decision need not exclude the future element, specifically, the notion of a great final judgment. Methodologically, it is important to acknowledge the circumscribed scope and function of a particular formulation before suggesting that it could not be part of a larger configuration—especially when there are Jewish analogies for such configurations.

Leaving aside the alleged logical tension between present kingdom and future son of man, it is problematic in my mind to eliminate the possibility that Jesus spoke about a future son of man just because all four evangelists identify the son of man with Jesus. At least one of the son of man sayings in Q seems to refer to that figure as someone distinct from Jesus.[53] Moreover, the writings of Paul know a number of Synoptic son of man traditions (see above, p. 110–11). While this does not demonstrate the authenticity of sayings, it attests an earlier date for them that we can determine on the basis only of Mark and Q.

### Fulfillment and Expectation in the Epistles of Paul

Like the Qumranites, Paul places himself in the end time, between decisive eschatological events. For the apostle, the Christ event marks the beginning of the end. God sent his Son at "the consummation of the time" (Gal 4:4).[54] Not only does Paul use an eschatological technical term here, but the whole of his argument in Gal 3:6—4:7 has a temporal, eschatological drive. Similarly, according to 1 Cor 10:11-13, Christians live at the "the ends of the ages," the telos toward which Scripture's admonitions pointed and during which demonic temptation is intensified. At the other pole is Paul's expectation of the parousia, mentioned at the very beginning of 1 Corinthians (1:7), as a point of reference for the Corinthians' self-understanding and an explanation of their possession of *charismata*. The same point of reference appears near the end of the epistle in Paul's detailed discussion of the events of the end (chap. 15): Christ's death and resurrection, his exaltation and battle with the demonic forces, his victory culminating in the defeat of death at the time of his parousia and the resurrection of the righteous. That Paul expected the parousia in his own lifetime is evident in the distinction between "they" and "we" in 1 Cor 15:51 and 1 Thess 4:16-17.

The Epistle to the Romans provides its own set of conceptions to describe the tensions between present accomplishment and future fulfillment. The individual's justification by faith corresponds to the Qumranites' entrance into the community. In a different formulation that draws on two-ways imagery and is closely associated with the conceptual complex in the Qumran Hymns, Paul encourages his readers to consider themselves dead to sin and alive to God (chap. 6, especially v 11). In that situation their bodies are vivified by the Spirit of the risen Christ, through which they long for ultimate redemption at the time of the transformation of the cosmos (chap. 8). A component of this future element is the coming judgment of all humanity (2:1-11), which is the complement to the notion of justification. Those now justified will be "saved" from God's wrath at that judgment. In 2 Corinthians Paul focuses less on the parousia and more on the Christian's present state. While one waits to be clothed with a new body, one is already being inwardly transformed (4:16—5:10). Indeed, to be in Christ is to be "a new creation" (5:16-21). This individual application of the eschatological notion is consonant with the individual character of justification and with the Qumranic parallelism between the accomplished resurrection and new creation of the individual.

*The Presence of Eschatological Realities in the Post-Pauline Tradition*

Both Colossians and Ephesians emphasize the present reality of crucial eschatological events almost to the exclusion of the future and without even mentioning the parousia. Colossians 1:3—3:4 speaks of the Christian's death (to the demonic realm) and resurrection as past events. Similar language runs through Ephesians 1–2, according to which one is already seated with Christ in heaven (2:6). The author acknowledges that one still has to contend with demonic forces and must be prepared for "the evil day." However, both Colossians and Ephesians emphasize the accomplished fact of one's resurrection, and in this respect they are reminiscent of the Qumran Hymns. In both Colossians and Ephesians, the emphasis provides a basis for a string of ethical exhortations: act in accordance with one's new status.[55]

*Fulfillment and Postponement in Luke*

Although the Gospel according to Luke may be considered the least Jewish and most Gentile-oriented of the four Gospels, its viewpoint is heavily influenced by Jewish eschatology. The major components of this eschatology are twofold. Luke believes that scriptural prophecies about the eschaton have been fulfilled and other eschatological events are presently taking place; he also looks forward to the coming of the Son of Man, a notion rooted in the apocalyptic books of Daniel and *1 Enoch*. For Luke these two components complement one another; a postponement of Mark's immediate expectation of the consummation is compensated for by an emphasis on fulfillment.

A postponement of "the end" and the parousia is evident from a comparison of Luke 21:7-36 with Mark 13:4-37. At 21:8-9 Luke adds "the time has drawn near" as a sentence of the false teachers and refutes it with the comment that "the end is not yet." Then, through the addition of "but before all this" (v 12), he places the time of persecution before the cosmic woes (vv 10-11). In vv 20-24 he eliminates the eschatological catchword "desolating sacrilege" and the connected reference to Daniel, describes the siege and desolation of Jerusalem in a straightforward way, and posits its occupation "until the times of the Gentiles are fulfilled." Only at that point does he move into the great cosmic woes and the parousia of the Son of Man (vv 25-28), which will bring redemption to the chosen, because they are able to "stand before" the judgment throne of the Son of Man (v 36). This explicit reference to the Son of Man, added to Luke's Markan prototype, is one of numerous Lukan additions focusing on this figure's juridical function.[56] Thus Luke both underscores his belief in the parousia and places it at some undefined distance.

Compensating for this postponement is Luke's emphasis on fulfillment. He strikes the note programmatically in his prologue with reference to the whole Jesus story ("the things that were fulfilled among us," 1:1) and again at 4:21 in Jesus' inaugural sermon, where he describes his activity as the fulfillment of Scripture. Here and elsewhere in the Gospel, Luke portrays this activity as a reprise of events in the Hebrew Bible. In addition, the infancy narratives, and especially the canticles, employ biblical prophetic terminology to define John and Jesus and the character of their activity.[57] Thus Luke compensates for his perceived postponement of the end by focusing on the accomplished fact of other scriptural prophecies of the end.

Another complementary aspect of Luke's eschatology is his focus on immediate postmortem rewards and punishments. Drawing on Jewish apocalyptic traditions, he envisions Lazarus already enjoying nourishment at Abraham's bosom and the rich man suffering in the fires of Hades (16:22-31).[58] Jesus, too, assures the penitent thief that "today" they will be together in paradise (23:39-43). In the debate with the Sadducees, he adds that the righteous "live to" God, a phrase to be found in two-ways and immortality texts (20:38).[59] Thus, although the parousia, the resurrection, and the judgment are in the future and not as near as some had supposed, the rewards and punishments associated with resurrection and judgment are already in effect for those who have died.

The tension between fulfillment and expectation evident in Luke's Gospel is carried through in the book of Acts. The day of judgment has been fixed (17:31), and the one appointed to be judge is exalted at God's right hand (7:56). When the disciples pose the eschatological question, however, Jesus directs them away from apocalyptic speculation to their responsibility to proclaim the gospel (1:6-8).

### The Presence of Judgment and Eternal Life in the Fourth Gospel

More than any other New Testament book, the Fourth Gospel presents what may justifiably be called realized eschatology. The descent, ministry, death, and ascent of the Logos/Son of God is an eschatological event, and belief that this is the case transfers one from death to life (5:24), granting eternal life to the believer in the present time (3:16, 36). The resurrection as a future event is not significant, because Jesus is "the resurrection and the life," and the person who believes in him "will never die" (11:23-27).[60] Conversely, rejection of Jesus immediately effects condemnation (3:18; 5:24-25). Other passages, probably of later provenance, do refer to a final resurrection and judgment (5:28-29; 6:44, 54).[61] However, the Gospel emphasizes the present realization of eschatological events, and the conception and the language are strikingly close to the formulations of the Qumran Hymns.[62]

Complementing this emphasis is the understanding of Jesus' death and parousia expressed especially in the farewell discourses. Jesus' death is his glorification and ascent to the Father, and his return takes place in the gift of the Spirit (e.g., 13:31; cf. 3:14). The traditional story of the empty tomb does stand in tension with this formulation, but once again the death/exaltation emphasis of the discourses has an important prototype in the Wisdom of Solomon.[63] While many argue that John's realized eschatology is a function of "the delay of the parousia," the issue needs to be studied carefully. The notion that Jesus returns in the form of the Spirit may indeed spring from such reflection; however, language about death as exaltation and about the presence of eternal life, with their parallels in Jewish literature, may be expressions of a high eschatology in its own right and of an anthropology that does not envision a resurrection of the body.

## Resurrection, Immortality, and Eternal Life

If any element in the New Testament is clearly eschatological, it is the widespread belief in resurrection, immortality, and eternal life.

### The Resurrection and Exaltation of Jesus

From the earliest creeds and formulas embodied in the Pauline epistles to the book of Revelation, decisive divine salvation is tied to belief in Jesus' triumph over death and his exaltation in heaven. The formula "the God who raised Jesus from the dead" appears to have been developed in parallel to the biblical formula "the God who brought Israel out of Egypt."[64] Thus the God of the exodus is redefined as the God of the resurrection. Jesus' resurrection is, on the one hand, his own vindication vis-à-vis those who condemned him and put him to death.[65] But it is also an eschatological event of universal salvific significance.

These implications are spelled out in several ways. The Spirit of the risen Christ vivifies those who are "in Christ," enabling righteousness and guaranteeing their future resurrection and eternal life (Rom 8:11). Thus Christ is the "first fruits of them that sleep," and his parousia will accompany the great resurrection (1 Corinthians 15). Jesus' resurrection is functionally synonymous with his exaltation to the rank of Lord (Rom 10:9). His present lordship over creation and his future appearance as exalted Son of Man have universal implications (1 Cor 15:24-28; Phil 2:10).

## Modes of Resurrection and Eternal Life

The variety in expression that Cullmann failed to see in Judaism is present also in the New Testament, his denials notwithstanding. The stories about Jesus' resurrection appearances are ambiguous as to the form of the risen Christ and have much in common with biblical accounts of angelophanies. He appears to the Emmaus disciples out of nowhere, remains unknown to them, and disappears as soon as his presence is recognized in a eucharistic action (24:13-32).[66] In the commissioning story in Luke 24, the protests about his corporeality notwithstanding, he is first mistaken for an angel or ghost (v 37). The parallel in John 20:19-29 has the same tension: although he is recognized as the Crucified One, he has materialized through closed doors. In the empty tomb story in John 20:11-18, Mary mistakes Jesus for the gardener. The persistent motifs of sudden appearance and disappearance and of lack of recognition or mistaken identity run like a thread through the stories and suggest that, despite their juxtaposition to accounts of the empty tomb and despite the emphasis on corporeality in some of them, these stories are crystallizations of traditions in which the form of the risen Christ was much more ambiguous.[67] The commissioning story in Matt 28:16-20, where the exalted Christ has the authority of the exalted son of man, the Lukan accounts about the christophany on the Damascus Road (Acts 9:1-9; 22:3-11; 26:10-19), Paul's own statements and hints about the glorified Christ (1 Cor 9:1; 15:8, 49; 2 Cor 4:6; Phil 3:20-21), and the commissioning christophany in Revelation 1–2 all suggest that the commissioning stories in Luke 24 and John 20 and 21 stem from a common tradition that assumes and implies that the Risen One was perceived as a divine being with authority to call apostles, just as the Deity did in the case of the biblical prophets. Both the angelophanic overtones of the Emmaus appearance and the story's motif of presence at the moment of eucharistic action suggest a *Sitz im Leben* with a loaded theological function rather than a straightforward account about the Jesus who has disappeared from the tomb.

Death and exaltation are two sides of the same coin in the Johannine discourses, as we have seen, and there is a Jewish model for this idea. However, this idea is complicated by the Gospel's christology, which is closely paralleled by the descent and ascent of Raphael in the book of Tobit.[68] As Ernst Käsemann has argued, John, in spite of his statements to the contrary (1:14; 19:34), presents a Jesus whose quasi humanity does not fit well with the idea of mortality.[69]

The Epistle to the Hebrews has it both ways. The author explicitly asserts the incarnation and real suffering and death of the wisdom figure, suggesting at least some opposition to some sort of docetic, angelic christology (4:14-15; 5:7-10). At the same time, he speaks of death and exaltation with no explicit reference to resurrection (1:3, 2:9; 12:2, etc.).[70]

New Testament formulations about the great resurrection also vary, and few if any posit a straightforward resuscitation of dead bodies. The texts are sketchy, but ultimate glorification is a common motif. In Mark 12:18-27 the result of resurrection is the Jewish notion of angel-like existence (cf. Dan 12:3; *1 En.* 104:2-4; *2 Baruch* 49–51). For Paul in 1 Cor 15:48-50 and Phil 3:21, the model of glory is the glorified Christ.

New Testament ideas about an "intermediate state" are not consistent. As already noted, the Gospel of Luke is clear. In Rev 6:9-11 the souls of the martyrs weep beneath the altar. In 1 Thess 4:13-17 Paul envisions a resurrection that will bring the dead up to meet the descending Lord, while in Phil 1:21-24 he anticipates that in death he will be "with the Lord." In general, his expectation of the parousia in the near future seems to make speculation about these matters superfluous. Overall it is important to note that the New Testament contains no detailed apocalyptic visions on these matters; with a few exceptions, it is best to recognize that early Christian views might have been as varied as those of contemporary Judaism.

## The Locus of Final Salvation

The prevailing supposition among most New Testament readers is probably that heaven is the locus of final salvation. The idea is borne out at many points. Paul expects that Christians will meet Christ in the air (1 Thess 4:17), for heaven is our homeland (Phil 3:20). This is consonant with his belief in an immortal, Christ-like resurrection body (1 Cor 15:49-54; Phil 3:21). John's Jesus speaks of returning to the Father to "prepare a place," so that believers may be with him (John 14:1-3). This, too, is consonant with his understanding of death and probably with his christology. Synoptic texts about the angelic existence of Christians fit the same pattern (Mark 12:25 par.).

Nonetheless, a few texts strain against this notion and hint at a variety that parallels the situation in contemporary Judaism. Revelation draws on the rich tradition stemming from Trito-Isaiah and envisions "a new heaven and a new earth," and a new Jerusalem descending from heaven (21:1—22:5). Paul's universal vision of the redemption of the whole creation (Rom 8:18-25) fits better with the Trito-Isaianic idea than with a notion of heavenly salvation. Finally, in contrast to the Johannine Jesus, the speaker of the Synoptic beatitudes promises that "the meek will inherit the earth" (or "land," Matt 5:5). The formulation is reminiscent of the Parables of Enoch and their vision of a resurrection and a restored and perfected earth (*1 Enoch* 51).

## Jewish Responses to the Gospel: A Noneschatological Horizon

Although the first century was a time of eschatological ferment among Jews, not all Jews had an eschatological perspective. Not only might they disagree as to what kind of messianic figure was expected; some saw no need for such a figure. The worldview of some posited no need for radical change of the ages, no judgment and resurrection of the dead. To such persons the message of Jesus and the Christian gospel might well have seemed superfluous. The issue is not unbelief or "hardness of heart" with respect to these particular proclamations. The problem is, more radically, a language not understood, a worldview not shared.

## Summary

Jewish religious texts from the exilic and postexilic periods increasingly attest the rise of eschatology, the belief that things are moving toward an end. This end was construed in two ways. First, the present time was coming to a close, and a new age would begin, accompanied by a reprise of ancient or primordial events—a new exodus, a new covenant, or, more radically, a new creation. Second, prophecies were directed toward an end, a telos, when they would find their fulfillment.

Many texts of the Greco-Roman period reflect this heightened eschatological perspective. As suffering, persecution, and a sense of evil and injustice increased, there was a concomitant belief that a just God would bring the present evil age to an end, execute judgment, and initiate the new age. A belief in resurrection, immortality, or eternal life was often a major component in the eschatological worldview, especially if suffering and persecution led to unjust death and the wicked prospered.

Eschatological claims were naturally bound up with the issue of authority. How do you know? Who says so? Apocalypticists asserted their authority by claiming, pseudonymously, that their works were the products of ancient worthies who had ascended to heaven and brought revelation to earth, or who had seen into the future by means of dream visions. Others, also claiming to be inspired, asserted that they were living in the time when the predictions of the prophets were being fulfilled.

The specifics of eschatology varied widely. When would the end come? Perhaps the crucial events were already happening. In what form would salvation from evil take place? Who might be the agents of God's deliverance? What would be the form and locus of life after death? Would one's body or spirit be resurrected on a last day? Would one's spirit or soul be assumed to heaven at the time of death? Had one already passed from death to life? Would there be a renewed earth?

Christianity arose in Jewish circles with a high eschatological con-sciousness. Most of the wide spectrum of eschatological belief in the New Testament can be attested in contemporary Jewish writings, and con-versely, the New Testament attests most forms of eschatological belief found in these writings. The defining characteristic of Christian eschatol-ogy was its connection with Jesus of Nazareth. It was in his death that final atonement was made for sin. Jesus' resurrection had unleashed the Spirit of God into the Christian community, and this Spirit was the promise of an imminent resurrection of the dead, when the now exalted Lord would return from heaven to judge the living and the dead and to bring God's reign to its final and full consummation.

# chapter 6

## Contexts and Settings

Because of the topical and synthetic nature of this book, I have focused thus far on the religious conceptions and phenomena under consideration and have not digressed into the diverse contexts and settings that generated, nourished, and transformed these conceptions. This approach, which runs contrary to my normal way of treating these issues, has left undiscussed an essential aspect of the ancient sources. In order to fill this gap, I sketch in this chapter some of the ways in which contemporary biblical scholarship has complicated matters both by shedding new light on the concrete contexts and settings of the ancient texts, and by refuting or at least casting serious doubt on much of the accepted wisdom about these issues.

### Ancient Texts as Historical Artifacts

Both the development of archaeological science and the use of new historical and social scientific methods have emphasized the need to read the ancient religious texts historically and not simply to treat them as pieces of literature or theological compendia. They are artifacts that were created in time and place. As with fossilized footprints, we should ask: What sort of creature made this imprint; where was it coming from, where was it going, and why? Along with the theological conceptions and ideologies that these texts express and the religious intuitions and issues that they embody, these texts arose in response to concrete historical circumstances and functioned in particular geographic and social locations. To be fair to the texts and their authors, we must try to identify these times, circumstances, and locations.

This is easier said than done, however. As we read these texts, we must be conscious of the fact that we are a third party interjecting ourselves into communications that took for granted much that their authors and first readers knew firsthand, but to which we have not been privy. Thus historical exegesis requires careful extrapolation and self-conscious tentativeness about the results of its study. (In the case of material, nontextual archaeological remains, the problem is even more difficult, both because they were not intended to communicate information and because of the fragmentary nature of the evidence.)[1]

Yet if we cannot always place texts in precise time and place, with careful reading we can learn something about the *kind of* situation to which they respond, and this, in turn, enables us better to appreciate how the content of the texts may have functioned in their concrete settings. Much theological exegesis has ignored these axioms and has distorted into timeless truths formulations that were conditioned by time and place.

Historical exegesis must consider not only time and place, but also social location and function. To what kind of a recipient or community was the text addressed? What was the author's religious and social identity, and what kind of role did the author play with respect to the audience? What institutions are presumed, or described, or alluded to? What kind of function is served by the text and the religious formulations and claims that it expresses? All these questions are further complicated by the fact that the texts are often the product of recasting, redaction, and rewriting over a long period of time.[2]

As we shall see, the contemporary study of Judaism has shed much light on these matters. This light, however, is mixed with many shadows, and thus the complex social and religious map of early Judaism is difficult to draw. The complexity of the map and the difficulty in drawing it raise, in turn, some important questions for the study of Christian origins. For all of these reasons, in this chapter I honor my own call for historical tentativeness and punctuate my discussion with more qualifiers and question marks than in the previous chapters.

## Responses to Troubled Times

As we look at the Jewish literature from the Greco-Roman period through a historical lens, we discover that virtually every text clearly reflects or arguably implies bad times or problematic circumstances: religious persecution and martyrdom; social oppression; the occupation or destruction of Jerusalem or the Holy Land; social, cultural, and religious conflict; and the like. Thus the worldviews and the ideas expressed in these texts, in effect, present explanations of difficulties and offer solutions to existential problems. Suffering and persecution led people to ponder received traditions about divine justice and to posit apocalyptic eschatologies that articulated the conviction that a just God would vindicate the chosen people in spite of present evidence to the contrary. A heightened sense of evil might be expressed in the portrayal of a dualistic universe whose demonic inhabitants required the intervention of transcendent agents of divine deliverance and executors of God's judgment.

Conversely, if one's circumstances were reasonably comfortable or one had adapted to them, angelic intervention, apocalyptic eschatology, and promises of resurrection and eternal life, which were not part of the old received traditions (the biblical texts), might not seem necessary. To the contrary, the notion that God rewards people here and now, articulated especially in the Deuteronomic traditions of the Bible, vindicated the status of those who were reasonably well-to-do.[3]

A historical approach is crucial also for the theologian as he or she considers how to appropriate the religious conceptions found in ancient religious texts. One must read the texts empathically in the contexts in which they were generated and then honestly ask the theological questions. For example, is an emphasis on demons and eschatological catastrophe and the vision of a heavenly home appropriate in circumstances over which one has some reasonable control? Conversely, does it resonate in conditions of deep distress? Is the depth of radical evil obscured when one eliminates the notion of the demonic and reduces evil to the accumulation of human misdeeds? What care must one take in citing Deuteronomic notions of retribution to explain one's own misfortunes or those of one's enemies?

## Geographic Location

Part of a text's historical setting is its geographic location. As has long been noted, life in the Diaspora brought its own set of problems and challenges.[4] What tensions did one experience while living as a minority community? How, in those circumstances, did one maintain one's Jewish identity and that of one's family? What compromises did one make? Where did one draw the line? To what extent might one couch traditional religion and culture in the language and thought world of the Gentiles?

Geography also played a role in Palestinian Jewish religion. Jerusalem and the temple were sacred space. How do we imagine that kind of worldview and how it functioned? The area around Mount Hermon was also sacred space, to judge from a range of biblical texts and from some of the Enochic writings.[5] How was one's religion affected by these land forms and the mythology associated with them?[6] For the Qumranites, the wilderness of Judea was an integral part of their religious self-understanding as the repentant, chosen remnant and the temple of God.[7]

The wilderness setting of Qumran is suggestive for an interpretation of John the Baptist's ministry, though it need not indicate that there was a connection between him and that group (see below, pp. 180–81). The account of Peter's commissioning near Caesarea Philippi stands in a long tradition that esteems the area around Mount Hermon as sacred space and that places the accounts of the commissioning of Enoch and Levi in the environs of Dan and Hermon.[8] The many references to agriculture in the Jesus tradition bid us to pay more heed to the rural setting of Jesus' ministry and the function of the logia and parables attributed to him.[9]

## Judaism and Hellenism

A sharp dichotomy between Palestinian and Hellenistic Judaism—the latter largely equated with Diaspora Judaism—was a leitmotif in many of the handbooks that dominated the study of early Judaism in the pre-1950 period.[10] The discovery of the Dead Sea Scrolls and the scholarship of the past half century, however, have shown this dichotomy to be scholarly fiction. The arrival of Alexander the Great in Palestine and the area's governance by Ptolemaic and Seleucid rulers ensured that not only the lan-

guage but also the culture of Greek civilization would make their presence felt in many ways.[11] Both in Palestine and in the Diaspora, Judaism
interacted with its Hellenistic environment, albeit in different ways and to
different degrees.

On the positive side, Diaspora writers like Philo of Alexandria and the
author of the Wisdom of Solomon employ the rhetoric and conceptions
of Greek philosophy in order to communicate their message to audiences
that are at home in this thought world, and the author of 4 Maccabees
equates Torah obedience with a kind of syncretistic Stoicism.[12] The pseudonymous author of the *Letter of Aristeas* writes like a Hellenistic allego-
rizer as he seeks rapprochement between Torah-observant Judaism and
Hellenistic notions of kingship and enlightened moral conduct that were
not based on the Torah.[13] Earlier scholarship, of course, cited precisely
these Diaspora examples to support its dichotomy.[14] But the marks of
Hellenism can also be found in Palestinian religious texts. While Joshua
ben Sira, writing in Hebrew, draws some lines between Jewish religion and
Hellenistic religion and culture, he can also sound like a Hellenistic
philosopher.[15] Similarly, a Palestinian Aramaic text like *1 Enoch* employs
elements from Greek myth to express its critique of the actions of Hellenistic kings.[16] Some forms of Jewish eschatology in both Palestinian and
Diaspora texts envision resurrection or assumption of *the spirit* and immortality of *the soul*.[17] The two-ways instruction of the Qumran Rule of the
Community (1QS 3–4) describes human conduct in terms of abstract
vices and virtues, which is reminiscent of Greek moral instruction.[18]

Jewish literature of this period, from both Palestine and the Diaspora, is
also marked by severe criticism of Hellenistic rulers and Hellenistic civilization. Most obvious, in the first case, are the texts that describe or
reflect the Hellenistic reforms of Antiochus IV Epiphanes, or the religious
persecution that he enacted—for example, Daniel, *Jubilees,* an early form
of the *Testament of Moses,* and 1 and 2 Maccabees.[19] Criticisms of idolatry and
warnings against it offer ambiguous evidence. The critiques are clear, but
their frequency suggests that the phenomenon was a clear and present
danger for Jews.[20]

The issue is complex, however. First, hellenization comes in many
forms, ranging from idolatry to philosophical formulations to the use
of Greek literary genres, and it is employed with various degrees of

significance. Even if we find an author working with a Hellenistic genre or speaking in Hellenistic idiom, we should ask, Does this voice substantially change what we might call the Israelite substance of what the author is saying? For example, if an author recasts a biblical text in a Hellenistic genre, does the transformation express something that is non-Jewish and substantially different from the original?[21] Second, an author can be at the same time Jewish, anti-Hellenistic, and Hellenistic. Although 2 Maccabees opposes the hellenization of the Jerusalem priests and propounds a materialistic notion of resurrection of the body, it recounts its story in the idiom of Hellenistic historiography.[22] Similarly, as noted above, *1 Enoch* employs imagery from Greek myth to criticize Hellenistic kings, and ben Sira speaks with two voices.

Thus we must use the term "hellenization" with caution, and we should define precisely what we mean. Judaism interacted with its Hellenistic environment in complex, ambiguous, and ambivalent ways. This should not surprise biblical scholars, who have long noted the complex positive and negative ways in which pre-Hellenistic Israelite religion interacted with its Near Eastern environment.[23] In trying to understand the phenomena that I have been describing, it might be useful for biblical scholars to enter into dialog with cultural anthropologists and interpreters of modern cultural and religious syncretism. The conversation might be enlightening for the interpreters of both ancient and modern cultures.

Much of the literature on early Christianity has been governed by a distinction between Palestinian and Hellenistic Christianity, or Jewish and Hellenistic Christianity.[24] Early New Testament creeds and hymns have been pressed into these dichotomous molds.[25] Oscar Cullmann argued for a distinction between the Jewish belief in resurrection of the body and the Greek notion of immortality of the soul and applied it to the New Testament.[26] Adolf von Harnack saw Pauline Christianity as the hellenization of the Palestinian Jewish religion preached by Jesus of Nazareth.[27] The collapse of the scholarly paradigms related to Judaism requires that we rethink the implications that New Testament exegesis has drawn from these paradigms.

## Temple, Cult, and Priesthood

It has always been recognized that the Jerusalem temple was a major Jewish religious institution. Here God's praise was sung, the Torah was expounded, and sacrifices were offered for the atonement and purification of the people.[28] This truism notwithstanding, recent scholarship has emphasized that the situation was more complicated. In the six hundred years from the early postexilic period to the temple's destruction in 70 C.E., a significant number of dissenters criticized and even denied the efficacy of the Jerusalem cult and sought alternatives for purification and atonement. Here, as in other cases, the discovery of the Qumran Scrolls and the resultant recognition of the religious and social diversity in postexilic Israel have required and allowed us to reassess old data and integrate it with new information. Texts that have long been known take on new significance when we view them in the light of newly discovered works. Critiques of the temple, the priesthood, and the cult in Third Isaiah, Zechariah, and Malachi seem to be less a matter of episodic aberration than an indication of the early roots of some later religious division.[29] Evidence for a critique of the temple, cult, and priesthood appears in several layers of *1 Enoch,* in *Psalms of Solomon,* and in various Qumran Scrolls (see above, pp. 46, 68, 95). Among the writings composed after 70 C.E., *2 Baruch* explicitly criticizes the priesthood, and the *Apocalypse of Abraham* ties the temple's destruction to cultic aberrations that are likened to the idolatry of Manasseh.[30] This evidence need not indicate a continuous anti-temple movement over time, or a single anti-temple party at any given time. Nor do the polemics necessarily stem from a single concern or kind of criticism. Nonetheless, taken together they falsify the notion that all Jews in the postexilic period held the temple in high regard. This requires, in turn, that we rethink how we portray the significance and traumatic effect of such events as the pollution of the temple by Antiochus Epiphanes, the rise of the Hasmonean high priesthood, and the destruction of the temple in 70 C.E. For some people the temple was problematic apart from these individual events.

Archaeological excavations in the past fifty years have enhanced our knowledge of Israelite temples. Excavations on the Temple Mount in

Jerusalem have significantly improved earlier reconstructions of the Herodian Temple and give us a clearer and more accurate picture of the sanctuaries of Zerubbabel and Herod, in which events of early Jewish and Christian history were played out.[31] Excavations on Mount Gerizim have raised questions about the nature of the Samaritan sanctuary at that location.[32] Although no trace has been found of the Jewish sanctuaries at Elephantine and Leontopolis in Upper and Lower Egypt, it might be worth considering how their existence fit into the broader spectrum of Jewish temple theologies.[33]

These new data and the questions that they pose impinge on our interpretation of early Christian attitudes about the Jerusalem temple. The New Testament's generally negative view of the temple and its cult is explicitly connected in some texts with the interpretation of Jesus' crucifixion as death in behalf of others (see above, pp. 79–80). Nonetheless, New Testament language about the community as the temple has precedents in similar formulations in the Qumran Scrolls. How, we may ask, do New Testament formulations about the high priesthood of Jesus fit this picture? Does any of this indicate a historical connection between elements in the early church and Jewish counterparts of a similar disposition? As one example, does Revelation 21 reflect a tradition like *1 Enoch* 90, where God dwells with God's people in a new Jerusalem that has no temple, and how might this fit with the traditions in the Qumran document on the new Jerusalem?[34]

## The Synagogue

That the synagogue developed as a major religious and social institution during the Greco-Roman period was taken for granted by nineteenth- and twentieth-century scholars of Judaism and early Christianity.[35] This supposition notwithstanding, these scholars have debated many specific issues relating to the institution. When and where did the institution originate? When and where did Jews begin to construct buildings for the specific purpose of housing their religious assemblies? What was the relationship between synagogue buildings and the Jerusalem temple, and how common were such buildings in Palestine before the destruction of the temple in 70 c.e.? What kinds of activity took place in synagogues, and who officiated at these assemblies? Do the New Testament accounts of Jesus and the apostles frequenting synagogues accurately reflect the historical situation in the first century?

Although "the state of synagogue studies" is still very much "in flux,"[36] some significant answers have been forthcoming. Recent decades have seen numerous archaeological excavations, and the resultant material remains and epigraphic evidence, supplemented by evidence from the Qumran Scrolls and the rereading of long-known literary sources (especially Josephus and Philo), have shed considerable light on the history of this institution as it evolved from Hellenistic times to the Byzantine period.[37]

Not surprisingly, the question of origins remains the most difficult to answer. When did Jews in Palestine and the Diaspora begin to assemble in some formal way in order to carry out nonsacrificial forms of worship? Three suggestions are prominent in the discussion: the late First Temple period, as a result of Josiah's reforms; the Babylonian exile, after the Jews had lost their temple and when they sought to maintain their identity while they lived as a minority in a foreign land; the early postexilic period in conjunction with the activities of Ezra and Nehemiah. Perhaps the question is wrongly put. The biblical passages that support these various possibilities seem to indicate a long and variegated history of such religious assemblies. As is often the case, it is difficult, and perhaps an oversimplification, to seek a single historical starting point for the institution.[38]

In tracing the history of "the synagogue," it is important to recognize the ambiguity of the noun. Septuagintal usage suggests that the term *synagōgē* in our Greek sources corresponds to the Hebrew *qahal* or *'ēdah* (or their Aramaic equivalent, *kenishta*).[39] In the Hebrew Bible *qahal* and *'ēdah,* and in the Septuagint *synagōgē,* can denote an assembly, gathering, or group as such, without implying the place or building where the assembly or group is gathered.[40]

The earliest evidence for the existence of buildings constructed for, or converted to, the use of Jewish religious assemblies comes from the Diaspora, in two inscriptions from Egypt, dating to the reign of Ptolemy III

Euegertes (246–221 B.C.E.) and his wife Berenice.[41] References to synagogues (most often designated as *proseuchē,* "[house of] prayer") appear in thirteen other Egyptian documents dating from the late third century B.C.E. to the second century C.E.[42] Philo of Alexandria provides further information from the early first century C.E.[43] Other Diaspora synagogues from the Second Temple period, known mainly from inscriptions and literary references, include Berenice in Cyrenaica (end of the first century B.C.E.);[44] Rome and Ostia (first century C.E.);[45] the Island of Delos, where there may have been both a Samaritan and a Jewish synagogue from around the turn of the era;[46] Acmonia in Phrygia (first century C.E.);[47] Gorgippia in the Bosporus (mid-first century C.E.);[48] evidently Halicarnassus (first century C.E.);[49] and in Syria almost certainly Antioch and Damascus.[50]

Evidence for the existence of synagogues in Palestine in the Second Temple period is scarce, but it has increased over the past several decades. The presence of religious assemblies or congregations is attested occasionally in first-century B.C.E. Palestinian literature, where the term denotes groups of like-minded people, who saw themselves as "pious" and, in some cases, as exclusively the chosen of God. Thus we find the expression "assembly of the pious" in 1 Maccabees (2:42, *synagōgē Asidaiōn*), *Psalms of Solomon* (17:16 [18], *synagōgē tōn hosiōn*; cf. 4:1, *synedrion hosiōn*), and one of the Qumran apocryphal psalms (11QPs[a] 18:10, *qahal ḥasidîm*).[51] A similar set of expressions occurs in the Parables of *1 Enoch.* The kings and the mighty persecute "the houses of his assemblies," a reference to a plurality of congregations of the righteous or chosen (46:8). Other references in the Parables apply the term to the eschatological community yet to be revealed—"the assembly of the righteous" (38:1), "the house of his assembly" (53:6), "the assembly of the chosen and the holy" (62:8).

Excavations in Palestine have uncovered a few structures from the last century of the Second Temple period that were constructed for or converted to the purpose of housing Jewish religious assemblies: Gamla (late first century B.C.E.),[52] Masada and the Herodium (beginning of the Jewish War, ca. 66 C.E.),[53] Qumran,[54] and perhaps Capernaum (early first century C.E.).[55] The discovery in 1918 of the Theodotus inscription on Mount Ophel substantiates the presence of a synagogue in Jerusalem and lends some credence to New Testament claims that there were a number of synagogues in the city (Acts 6:1-9; 24:12).[56] Finally, Josephus attests the presence of synagogues in Dor, Caesarea Maritima, and Tiberias in the first century c.e.[57] Scholars discuss whether other structures now uncovered may have been synagogues as well.[58] Taken together, this evidence suggests that synagogue buildings were more widespread on the landscape of first-century Palestine than had previously been thought to be the case.

Earlier descriptions of the activities that took place in late Second Temple period synagogues relied heavily on talmudic sources and the New Testament.[59] A closer look at the *contemporary* literary evidence—including now the Qumran Scrolls—together with the study of new epigraphic data and the remains of synagogues excavated in the past several decades considerably enhances our knowledge and enables us better to envision life in the material environment of the synagogue. The presence of ritual baths *(mikvaot)* and the location of synagogues near natural bodies of water complement allusions in Philo, Josephus, the *Letter of Aristeas,* and Acts and suggest that water purification was customary before one entered a synagogue.[60] Readings from the Torah and the Prophets and the exposition of Scripture were perhaps the central element of synagogue services,[61] and the recitation of a Targum or vernacular translation in Aramaic (and perhaps Greek in the Diaspora) seems also to have been common.[62] That communal prayer played a role in pre-70 synagogue assemblies seems likely,[63] although the point is disputed.[64] The frequent term *proseuchē* ("[house of] prayer") indicates that this activity took place in synagogues of the Diaspora.[65]

In Palestine the situation is more complicated.[66] The rich collection of prayer texts among the Qumran Scrolls (more than two hundred of them) indicates that the practice was at home in that community, evidently as a substitute for sacrificial worship in Jerusalem.[67] But what of nonsectarian synagogues? Some of the prayers in the Qumran corpus almost certainly originated outside that community and show remarkable parallels to prayers from the post-70 period.[68] In addition, we need to look for a context for the composition and ongoing use of the Palestinian collection known as the *Psalms of Solomon,* as well as other penitential and petitionary prayers, such as 1 Bar 1:15—2:5 and Sir 36:1-17.[69] Continued study of all these texts promises to increase our knowledge of late Second Temple synagogue liturgies. That sacred assemblies were held on the Sabbath in many places seems certain,[70] and other religious festivals were most likely celebrated in the synagogues, perhaps with communal meals, when appropriate.[71]

In addition to these occasional, religious functions, the synagogue was at its heart a communal institution.[72] As such it served in some cases as the communal treasury, archive, and school,[73] as the locus for legal and civic proceedings and meetings,[74] and as a hostel for people from other lands.[75]

The precise relationship between the Jerusalem temple and the synagogues of the Diaspora and pre-70 Palestine is still in need of clarification and is doubtless complex. After 70 C.E. the synagogue helped to fill the gap in Jewish religious life left by the destruction of the Jerusalem sanctuary. But what of the pre-70 period? Inscriptional and literary evidence indicates that synagogues were called by names appropriate to temples (*hieron, temenos*), and in the Diaspora pagan rulers treated them as sacred precincts. Some of the functions typical of the synagogue paralleled those of the temple, and some the synagogue functionaries mirrored those in the temple.[76] Whether all of this adds up to the conclusion that the synagogues functioned as the distant precincts of the central cultic site in Jerusalem is a matter that will be debated.[77] Some complicated issues and alternatives need to be considered. Qumran is a radical example, where the community functions as *the* temple, offering its own forms of sacrifice (see above, p. 68). What do we make of other alternative forms of atonement, which seem to be substitutes for temple sacrifice (see above, pp. 66–69)? Is there an implied association with Jerusalem? And what of other Jewish sanctuaries (see above, pp. 153–54)? In short, how do we construe the sense of sacred space as it applies to the Jerusalem temple and to other locations that support religious functions? In certain respects we return to the issue of sacred geography discussed above (p. 150).

In conclusion, new archaeological, epigraphic, and literary evidence about the synagogue, and the light it sheds on other evidence long known, nicely exemplify the topic of our study. We have learned a great deal in the past fifty years, not least about the material aspects of Jewish life in the first century. But what we have learned raises more questions than it answers—though it points in new directions. We should also note, however, that the archaeological and epigraphic evidence promises to illuminate the life and activity of the Jewish synagogue in the late Roman and Byzantine period much more than it does the pre-70 period with which we are here concerned. Archaeologists have uncovered many later ruins and inscriptions and have a massive rabbinic corpus with which to correlate this material.[78]

Data about the first-century synagogue are both suggestive and complicating for the student of the New Testament and early church. First, the data confirm the verisimilitude of a number of the narratives in the Gospels and Acts, if not their historical accuracy. Whether these accounts tell us much about the activity of Jesus of Nazareth remains uncertain, but they demonstrate that these authors were familiar with aspects of Jewish life in the synagogue. Jews gathered in the synagogues on the Sabbath.[79] Scripture was read and expounded.[80] Synagogues were sometimes located by bodies of water.[81] Second, they offer us comparative data that raise questions for the study of early Christian religions, institutions, and praxis, which, in turn, need to be compared with non-Jewish religions, institutions, and praxis. What do we make of the term *ekklesia*? Does it draw on the Jewish notion of a gathered community while distinguishing it from a *synagōgē*?[82] What is the relationship between regular Christian worship on the first day of the week and Jewish worship on the Sabbath? Does it both imitate the Jewish practice and self-consciously differentiate itself from it?[83] To what extent do the Christian practice of the Eucharist and the communal meals mentioned in Acts and 1 Corinthians relate to Jewish practice and specifically to the Qumran sacred meals?[84] Looking to the second century, does Justin's account of Christian weekly Sunday worship and its reading of the Gospels or the Prophets indicate both continuity and discontinuity with the Jewish synagogue practice of reading the Scriptures?[85] These questions and others like them constitute part of a larger picture in which we can see the early church as both a child of its Jewish mother and "an individual," whose uniqueness was partly a function of its non-Jewish environment.

# Religious Groups

## Sources

Scholars of early Judaism have universally recognized that the Jewish religious landscape in the Greco-Roman period comprised a variety of distinguishable groups. All handbooks on Judaism or the "background" of the New Testament treat the subject, and the primary sources themselves justify this emphasis. Three times Flavius Josephus interpolates his narratives in the *Jewish Antiquities* and *The Jewish War* with excursuses on the beliefs, practices, and influence of the Pharisees, Sadducees, and Essenes; and he refers, as well, to a fourth philosophy and to the Zealots and the Sicarii.[86] Philo of Alexandria discusses the Essenes of Palestine twice and devotes a treatise to the Egyptian Therapeutae, who bear some resemblance to his Essenes.[87] The four Gospels and Acts take note of the Pharisees, the Sadducees, and the Herodians.[88] In his *Refutation of All Heresies,* the second/third-century church father Hippolytus describes the Essenes, drawing on a source known also to Josephus.[89] Other scattered Christian and Jewish evidence attests the existence of a number of other baptizing groups.[90] Various strata of the Talmud make numerous references to the Pharisees *(perushim)* and to the *Sadoqim(n)*.[91] One other group, the Asideans, appears in early Jewish sources (1 Macc 7:12-13; 2 Macc 14:6). The term "congregation of the Hasidim" appears to be presumed in the *Psalms of Solomon* and in a noncanonical composition in the large Qumran Psalms scroll (see below, pp. 176–78). In addition to using these primary historical sources as a basis for their discussions of these named groups, scholars have attributed many of the Apocrypha, Pseudepigrapha, and Dead Sea Scrolls to various members of these groups.[92] Moreover, they have inferred from these anonymous and pseudonymous texts the existence of yet other unnamed groups.[93]

Drawing on the sources cited above, scholars of the nineteenth and the first half of the twentieth centuries sketched portraits and maps of the social structure of early Judaism that proposed all manner of variations and their opposites. With the discovery of the Qumran Scrolls and the intensive new scrutiny of the old sources, new variations made their appearance and compounded the confusion.[94] Indeed, while we now know much more about early Jewish groups than we did in the late 1940s, we know much less than we *thought* we knew a half century ago.

The reasons for this situation are the same that we have seen throughout the previous chapters. While the Scrolls have provided an immense new database of contemporary evidence, the ambiguity of their contents (caused not least by the fragmentary condition of the manuscripts) has mitigated their value, and the order in which they were published has permitted a less than full and accurate picture of the complex historical contexts in which they were created. Moreover, the Qumran corpus as a whole reveals a religious sociology in Judaism that was much more complex than Josephus's Pharisee-Sadducee-Essene triad. Finally, the quantum leaps in the methods employed by scholars and the resultant increased methodological consciousness raise new questions for the old sources.

## Methodology

New methods of literary criticism have generated new insights. The source-critical methods that were in vogue in the late nineteenth and early twentieth centuries and that sometimes led scholars to ascribe parts of texts to particular groups engender less certainty than they previously did.[95] Redaction criticism and other forms of holistic literary analysis help to identify the tendencies and biases of ancient historians, and hence affirm or call into question the historical reliability of some of their claims.[96] Form-critical and redaction-critical work on the rabbinic corpuses has drastically reduced the amount of certain knowledge that we possess from the pre-70 period.[97] The sociology of knowledge and a "hermeneutic of suspicion" focus the spotlight on the presuppositions, biases, agendas, and propensities of the modern students of these ancient texts, and this in turn requires closer scrutiny of judgments and conclusions that we have drawn from the texts. The history of scholarship on the Pharisees and Rabbinic Judaism has been colored by Christian anti-Judaic theological presuppositions and prejudices, Jewish projections of the sociology of modern Judaism, and Christian post-Holocaust apologetics.[98] Other methods from the social sciences remind us that the history of ideas provides only part of the picture. The theological interests of many of the scholars who have probed these texts have often obscured the broader life contexts of the people who wrote the texts and were their first readers.[99] Christian scholars have been much more interested in religious beliefs than in praxis.

Now we must ask broader questions. What can we learn about social roles, class, status, and power?[100] How do ideas and ideologies function, and where can we discover social and religious conflict and its consequences?[101] What do we mean by the terms "sect" and "group"? What variations might we find among them?[102] By what criteria do we decide whether a text implies the existence of simply its author or of a group, and if so, what kind of a group?[103] To what extent can we begin to understand how such entities were constituted, what the criteria were for membership, what purposes the groups served, and how they changed over time, and perhaps why they dissolved?[104]

Finally, there is the scholar's great idol and nemesis: in our desire to draw the big picture and create the grand synthesis, we have harmonized and conflated texts whose differences and individuality should be honored.[105] Moreover, we have failed to acknowledge the fragmentary character of our evidence, speaking and writing as if some of the pieces constituted the whole.

## The Pharisees

The heart of the Pharisees' religion was the scrupulous observance of the Torah according to the interpretive traditions they claimed to have received from their ancestors.[106] To judge from early rabbinic tradition and concurring contemporary accounts in the Gospels, this observance emphasized the proper sanctifying of the Sabbath, full tithing, and the application of the priestly laws of ritual purity to the preparation and consumption of the ordinary food that they ate each day, apart from the temple.[107] These latter two concerns—that one eat only properly tithed food in a state of priestly purity—were reflected in the exclusiveness of their communal table fellowship. This may have given rise to the name *perushim* ("separatists"), although it is uncertain whether this was a self-designation or a deprecating nickname assigned by others.[108]

In tension with the exclusiveness of the Pharisees' table fellowship was the fact that they lived their workaday life in priestly holiness in the midst of their fellow Jews, who did not think that God required them to do so and consequently did not observe Pharisaic halakah. Thus, in order to maintain the level of purity to which Torah called them, the Pharisees found it necessary to observe the relevant precepts of the Torah in every setting in which they found themselves. This "imposed perpetual ritualization of daily life, and constant, inner awareness of the communal order of being."[109] Life as a Pharisee was self-consciously, from start to finish, life according to God's will as expressed in the Torah as they understood it. According to this understanding, though they were laity, they saw themselves called to the higher holiness that was appropriate to the temple and its priesthood.

We know of other aspects of the profile of the Pharisees besides those portrayed by the later rabbinic halakah. In his two comparative accounts of the Pharisees, Sadducees, and Essenes, Josephus correctly notes the Pharisees' central concern with the right interpretation and observance of the Law, but he does not dwell on its details. Instead, describing these groups like Greek philosophical schools, he focuses his comparison on their beliefs regarding certain speculative issues. In the case of the Pharisees, he claims that they attribute everything to fate and God, but allow human responsibility. Thus the good and evil are rewarded or punished after death, with the soul of the virtuous passing on to a new body and a new life.[110] What sounds like a description of the transmigration of the soul is Josephus's hellenization of the Pharisaic belief in the resurrection of the body, which is attested also in the New Testament.[111] Whether this Pharisaic belief in resurrection was set in the context of an apocalyptic theology is uncertain, however. By the first century, the resurrection topos is attested apart from its apocalyptic matrix.[112]

In their interaction with the populace, the Pharisees sought to reform Jewish society so that it would conform better to their understanding of divine law.[113] This involvement is evident in their political activity during the Hasmonean period, when the Pharisees as a named group first appear in our historical sources. To judge from Josephus, they wielded considerable influence on John Hyrcanus (134–104 B.C.E.), then fell out of favor with him, came into conflict with his son, Alexander Jannaeus (103–76), and then returned to power during the reign of Jannaeus's widow, Alexandra Salome (76–67).[114] During the reign of Herod the Great, the

Pharisees remained active in public life, and some of them were held in favor by the king, but there is no certain indication that as a party they exercised significant political influence.[115]

During the Jewish War (66–70 c.e.), the Pharisees opposed armed resistance to Rome. After the war they emerged in time as the religious leaders of Palestinian Judaism and the founders of the rabbinical tradition that would become codified in the Mishnah and Tosefta.[116]

With these facts reasonably certain, much about the Pharisees in the first century remains uncertain. We know little about how the Pharisaic movement was organized and how the group recruited new members.[117] Their social status and roles in society are not altogether certain. Although there may well have been scribes among the Pharisees, they were a religious group, not a "lay scribal movement," that is, a profession of religious scholars and intellectuals.[118] Conversely, it is improbable that they belonged to the ranks of the artisans, who were poor and uneducated.[119] Instead they seem to have filled a variety of "professional" roles among the ranks of those who served as "retainers of the governing class."[120]

Scholars debate the extent and nature of Pharisaic influence on Palestinian Jewish society during the first century. Josephus tends to emphasize their influence on the masses and their political role, while the rabbinical traditions see them as a nonpolitical group with a religious agenda. The Gospels also focus on their religious practices.[121] Gospel accounts that highlight controversies between Jesus and the Pharisees need not indicate that these interactions were a microcosm of widespread Pharisaic presence in Palestinian society, whether in Judea or Galilee.[122]

Especially problematic is the extent to which these stories reflect the history of the church in the mid-first century and the extent to which they provide a window into the career of Jesus of Nazareth. Even if they do reflect historical events in both respects, what was the issue: opposition to the Torah as such or, more specifically, to Pharisaic halakah? In most cases the evidence appears to point to the latter. Although Mark's controversy story about hand washing includes Jesus' wholesale dismissal of biblical food laws, it is a story about the Pharisaic ritual of hand washing, as Matthew recognized.[123] The tradition is complex. Above all, we must distinguish between Gospel stories about Jesus (and his disciples) disputing Pharisaic interpretations of the Torah, which often focus on known Pharisaic concerns (Sabbath observance, tithing, and purity regulations as they relate to table fellowship), and other logia or comments by the evangelists that are broadsides against the Pharisees' religion and religious intentions.[124] Hypocrisy and "self-righteousness" can be the dark underbelly of any religion that is deeply concerned with right conduct. In apologetic and polemical documents, however, such accusations against one's opponents and enemies are suspicious at the very least, and they do not constitute a sure foundation for a historical description of these opponents and enemies.[125]

Finally, it is important to note that we possess no primary text that unquestionably comes from the hand of a Pharisee. To cite one example, although the *Psalms of Solomon* espouse some tenets of Pharisaic belief (some tension between predestination and free will and a number of references to resurrection, albeit not explicitly of the body), the frequent identification of this text as a Pharisaic document has presupposed that there were only three main Jewish groups in the first century B.C.E. to which one can attribute a given text.[126] A Pharisaic ascription for *4 Ezra* and *2 Baruch* (both post-70 documents) may be more likely, but even in this case one should exercise caution in using this material to inform a historical reconstruction of first-century Pharisaism and its interrelations with early Christianity.[127]

In short, while we know quite a bit about the first-century Pharisees, the bodies of data that do not always fit well together do not allow anything close to a full systematic account. Careful form-critical study of the Gospel pericopes may shed some light on the interactions between the Pharisees and the historical Jesus. More certainly, these texts reflect events in the life of the early church as it cuts its own path away from its Jewish matrix, asserting its superiority and its legitimacy as the true Israel through the rhetoric of apologetic and polemical differentiation from the inferior and illegitimate "other."[128] That this "other" is so often and so bitterly personified as the Pharisees rather than the Jews almost certainly reflects the particulars of the Jewish-Christian religious entanglements from the middle to the end of the first century.[129]

## The Sadducees

According to accepted wisdom, the Sadducees were conservative priestly aristocrats of the ruling class who denied the validity of Pharisaic oral law, as well as Pharisaic belief in the resurrection and related matters. While this characterization draws on material in Josephus, the New Testament, and the rabbinic writings and contains elements of truth, it oversimplifies the matter and overinterprets the sources.[130]

As to the Sadducees' social status, Josephus is far from clear. He names two Sadducees: Jonathan, who was "one of Hyrcanus's closest friends" (*Ant.* 13.293 [§10.6]); and Ananus, a high priest, "who followed the school of the Sadducees" (*Ant.* 20.197-203 [§9.1]) and had the support of the wealthy and prominent in society (*Ant.* 13.297 [§10.6]; 20.17 [§1.4]). Although this evidence indicates that some priestly aristocrats were Sadducees and that some of the wealthy felt comfortable with Sadducean doctrine, it does not prove that all priestly aristocrats were Sadducees, or that all Sadducees were priestly aristocrats.[131] Nonetheless, some relationship between the high priesthood and the Sadducees, at least in their origin, seems to be indicated by the name "Sadducee," which scholars generally connect with the Zadokite high-priestly line that was in power until the Hasmoneans assumed the office.[132] Acts 4:1 and 5:17, which associate the Sadducees with the priests and temple captain and with the high priest, are consonant with this, but do not indicate what the relationship was. The evidence is tantalizing, but skimpy and vague.

Antagonism between the Pharisees and the Sadducees is a thread that runs through all the sources. It is at the heart of the Josephus's story about the transfer of Hyrcanus's allegiance from the Pharisees to the Sadducees (*Ant.* 10.288-98 [§10.5-6]), in his contrasting accounts of the beliefs of the Pharisees, Sadducees, and Essenes (*J. W.* 2.162-66 [§8.14]), in Acts' account of Paul's hearing before the Sanhedrin (23:1-10), and perhaps in a number of rabbinic passages.[133] Their differences appear to have been both in their beliefs and in their practice. The Sadducees' denial of an afterlife and post-mortem judgment is attested in Josephus (*J. W.* 2.163-65 [§8.14]; *Ant.* 18.14, 16 [§1.3-4]), the Synoptic Gospels (Mark 12:18-27 par.), Acts (23:6-8), and the rabbinical writings (*Abot Rab. N.* A.5; *b. Sanh.* 90b). The Sadducees' denial of the existence of angels, which is consonant with denial of an afterlife, is attested only in Acts (23:8), although Mark 12:25 may contain an ironic allusion to it. Josephus also contrasts Pharisaic and Sadducean views of fate and human responsibility (*J.W.* 2.162-65 [§14]). According to some rabbinic texts, they disagreed with the Pharisees on matters of purity and the observance of the Sabbath.[134]

Much has been made of Josephus's statement that the Sadducees did not accept the laws promulgated by the Pharisees (*Ant.* 13.297 [§9.6]). That they were biblical literalists who had no tradition of interpretation is doubtful, since any law code requires interpretation in light of situations not envisioned in the code.[135] Claims that the Sadducees were gross hellenizers are not supported by the evidence.[136]

In summary, we know relatively little about the Sadducees. They first appear in the historical account at the time of John Hyrcanus, in a story that also offers us our first glimpse of the Pharisees (*Ant.* 13.288-98 [§8.5-6]). At least some of them were, in ways that are not clear, related to the priestly aristocracy and the ruling class. Their denial of an afterlife seems to indicate a theological conservatism, which *may be* consonant with their relationship to the political establishment.[137] They and the Pharisees represented two differing and often antagonistic views of Jewish religious belief and practice. How this worked out in detail is, on the whole, uncertain.[138] This sketchy picture, which leaves much to be desired, warns exegetes not to overinterpret what we have in the New Testament, and above all, not simply to equate mention of the Sadducees with a reference to the high-priestly establishment.[139] While the pairing of Pharisees and Sadducees in the Gospels lends some verisimilitude to the narrative, in any given instance it may simply reflect cliché or general historical memory.

### The Essenes and the Qumran Community

Of Josephus's four religious parties, it is the Essenes about whom we have heard the most in the last fifty years. The scrolls and scroll fragments found in the caves near Khirbet Qumran by the northwest edge of the Dead Sea were the property of the community that resided at Qumran from about 100 B.C.E. to 68 C.E.[140] Among these scrolls is a core group of texts that were composed either in the Qumran community or

in a community closely related to it.[141] Of these texts the Community
Rule (or the Manual of Discipline), the Damascus Document, and the
Halakic Letter in particular present the theological undergirding and
many of the rules and laws governing the community. Many of the procedural details in the Community Rule are strikingly similar to those
described in the accounts of the community life of the Essenes in Philo
and in the common source employed by Josephus and Hippolytus.[142] Evidence corroborating the location of an Essene community in this general
area appears in the *Natural History* of Pliny the Elder (23–79 C.E.).[143]
Although there were always some dissenters, a scholarly consensus arose
rather quickly after the publication of the first Scrolls that the authors of
the nonbiblical texts among these Scrolls were the Essenes described by
the aforementioned ancient authors.[144]

This consensus is still largely intact; however, in recent years the ranks
of the skeptics have increased somewhat. They cite three reasons for their
doubt. (1) Some argue that previously unpublished Qumran texts point
in another direction. Especially prominent has been the claim that the
Scrolls reflect Sadducean halakah.[145] The data for this claim are ambiguous, however. It is doubtful that they demonstrate anything more than a
common Zadokite origin for both the Sadducees and the priests at Qumran.[146] An additional problem with the claim is found in the points at
which Josephus's description of the Sadducees conflicts sharply with elements in the Scrolls, notably their beliefs about determinism and spirits,
angels, and the afterlife.[147] (2) Some continue to emphasize that not all
the details in Philo, Josephus, and Hippolytus coincide with those in the
Community Rule.[148] (3) Most important has been the recognition that
the map of the religious landscape of early Judaism was more complex
than Josephus's listing of four groups suggests.[149] That is, we need not
identify the Qumran community with *any* of Josephus's four groups if
other Jewish religious groups existed in first-century Palestine. While the
detailed parallels in procedure and practice mandated by the Community
Rule and cited by Philo, Josephus, and Hippolytus require an explanation,
one must also look closely at the differences, especially, I suggest, those
that are not the focus of the literature on the subject. It is useful to begin
such a comparison with a summary description of the community that is
presupposed and, to some extent, portrayed in the core group of Scrolls.

This community was a tightly knit group who understood themselves to have entered a new covenant (1QS 5:7-8, 21) that constituted them as the true Israel, the eschatological community of God's people, whose life of purity and holiness would prepare them to pass muster at the imminent final judgment. The basis of their lifestyle was an interpretation of the Mosaic Torah that had been revealed to their priestly leadership, the sons of Zadok (1QS 5:9), and especially to their founder, "the Teacher of Righteousness."[150] Because they, and they alone, had the correct interpretation of the Torah that enabled them to live according to God's will, the rest of Israel and the Gentiles, of course, were bound for damnation.[151] They had retired to the wilderness, separate from their doomed compatriots, where they "prepared the way of the Lord" through the ongoing study and practice of the Torah and its interpretation in the Prophets (1QS 8:12-16; cf. 5:10-20).[152]

The Torah as rightly interpreted comprised: the observance of festivals on the basis of a solar calendar;[153] halakot that tended to be stricter than those, for example, of the Pharisees;[154] daily ritual ablutions;[155] and the maintaining of a strict discipline that respected the sense of community and the status of those who ranked higher in the community either because of their more perfect understanding and practice of the Torah, or because of their positions of authority. The breaking of communal discipline led to sanctions that ranged from reduced rations to expulsion.[156]

The priestly character of Qumranic faith and piety was one of their most notable aspects. The communal leaders were "the sons of Zadok" and "the sons of Aaron,"[157] and "an anointed priest" would be the future leader of the community (1QS 9:11; 1QSa 2:11-22).[158] Priestly purity in the community was essential.[159] Believing that the cult of the Jerusalem temple was defiled, the Qumranites understood their community to be the temple of God, where they offered sacrifice and effected atonement for the Holy Land through their prayers and observance of the Torah (1QS 9:3-7; cf. 1QH 14[6]:22-29).[160]

Undergirding Qumranic theology was a dualistic worldview that divided humanity into two groups: the children of light, who were under the tutelage of the Spirit of Truth, the Angel of Light; and the children of darkness, who were shepherded by the Spirit of Falsehood, the Angel of Darkness (1QS 3:13—4:26; cf. 1QM).[161] Because they were the children of light in possession of divine truth, of necessity they separated themselves from all others and kept the secrets of their theology from outsiders (1QS 5:14-20; 10:24-25). Those who interpreted the Torah differently were "searchers of slippery things," that is, facile interpreters, whose exegesis was filled with lies and deceit and led many astray (4QpNah 2:2; 3:6-7; CD 1:13—2:1). This polarized worldview allowed no compromise. Things were black and white with no shades of gray.

Qumranic dualism also had a temporal dimension. The world stood on the threshold of a new age that would be ushered in by the great judgment. The ancient prophets looked toward the end time, and therefore their oracles spoke of present events and, specifically, of the interaction between the community of the chosen and the children of darkness.[162] More radically, the Qumranites believed that their entrance into the community had transferred them from the sphere of death into communion with the heavenly realm of eternal life, where they already participated in the blessings of the eschaton (1QH 11[3]:19-24; 19[11]:3-14).[163] In one view, the consummation of the end would be preceded by a fierce battle between the children of light and those of the children of darkness who comprised the Gentiles (1QM).[164]

A powerful notion of revelation governed and gave authority to the theology and worldview of the Qumran community and assured them of their identity as the chosen of the end time.[165] This notion is indicated by the multiple copies of apocalyptic texts found among the scrolls that are ascribed to Enoch, Levi, Qahat, Amram, and Moses.[166] It is also evident in the Qumranites' confidence that the end was now at hand. Complementary to this was their belief that their interpretation of the Torah and their exegesis of the prophets had been mediated through divine revelation, in part through the Teacher of Righteousness.[167]

Thus the Qumranites lived in a closed, self-validating world, in which belief, practice, and the continual return to the sources of their sacred tradition both bound them together and separated them from the rest of humanity.

As noted above, the accounts of Philo, Josephus, and Hippolytus overlap and agree with the contents of the Scrolls at many points. Josephus refers to their strong deterministic view (*Ant.* 13.171-73 [§5.9]) and to their belief in the immortality of the soul ( *J. W.* 2.154-58 [§8.11]).[168] All three authors emphasize the Essenes' strong sense of community. Moreover, their detailed accounts of Essene communal practice, ritual, and discipline echo many of the specifics in the Community Rule.[169]

Yet, as my summary above indicates, the essential elements of Qumran theology are totally lacking in the accounts of Philo, Josephus, and Hippolytus. We hear not a word about their exclusivistic dualistic worldview, their thoroughgoing eschatological outlook,[170] their strong sense of revelation, or the desert existence of the Qumran community. Moreover, while Josephus and Hippolytus refer to the priest speaking a blessing before the meal ( *J. W.* 2.131 [§8.7]), this scarcely suggests to the reader the dominating priestly character of the community indicated by the Community Rule[171] and the priestly orientation of the purificatory practices it describes. In short, the accounts of Philo, Josephus, and Hippolytus omit any reference to the rationale and worldview that provide the basis for Qumran theology and practice.

From these observations we may draw one of two conclusions, either of which is pertinent to the topic of this book. (1) The mainline view: the Qumran community was a branch of the Essenes, and the differences in practice indicated by a comparison of the Scrolls and the other sources reflect actual differences among Essene communities (or misinformation in the secondary sources).[172] In this case the accounts in Philo and the source of Josephus and Hippolytus were substantially affected by the authors' interests, biases, and agendas, including the desire to communicate to an audience that was schooled in the categories of Hellenistic philosophy and religious practice.[173] As a result, without the Scrolls one could never have inferred from these Hellenistic sources the dualistic, exclusivistic, eschatological, and priestly character of Essene theology. Thus the Scrolls have transformed our understanding of the Essenes, and they immensely enrich our knowledge of apocalyptic Judaism in the two centuries around the turn of the era. (2) The minority view: the Qumran community was not demonstrably Essene. Instead, the Scrolls may well illustrate that Judaism in the two centuries around the turn of the era was much more diverse in its religious expression and social organization than the source of Josephus and Hippolytus would lead us to believe. In this case, however, one should acknowledge that the detailed parallels in practice attested in the Scrolls and Philo, Josephus, and Hippolytus are so close and so many that they indicate some sort a substantial relationship between the Essenes and the Qumran community.

A choice between these two options depends on one's hermeneutic for reading Philo and Josephus/Hippolytus. Does one read these texts as more or less full and accurate accounts? Or, recognizing authorial tendency, does one use the Scrolls to tease out of the Hellenistic sources information that appears to be implied in light of the Scrolls: a priestly presence, a heavy emphasis on purity, a closed community?

In my view, although I argue below for religious and social diversity in early Judaism, it seems best to give full weight to the considerable array of detailed procedural parallels and to identify the Qumran community as Essene. At the same time, following the cue of Josephus and Hippolytus, we can imagine a broad Essene movement ( J. W. 2.160-61 [§.13]; Haer. 9.23), whose diversity is attested by the differences between the sources. In the final analysis, what is most important for a historian of this period is the recognition of this diversity—whether it be within the Essene movement, or between the Essenes and other groups. In the interest of clarity, however, rather than use the term "Essene" broadly and generically, it might be helpful to distinguish between Qumran belief and practice, as attested by the Scrolls, and Essene belief and practice, as attested by the secondary sources.[174]

The discovery of the Qumran Scrolls has produced a mass of literature over the past half century. Rarely, if ever, has a discovery bearing on humanistic learning spawned such concentrated, sustained, and diverse scholarly activity with such significant and wide-ranging implications.[175] While the scholarship has, in part, been driven by the data, it has also been informed and shaped by broader aspects of "the state of the discipline" and by agendas and methodologies and the complex social settings of the academy and the scholars that populate it.[176] This mix of hard data and subjective judgment has led to both consensus and controversy, probably more of the former than is usually supposed. Part of the controversy has swirled about the long delays in the publication of many of the fragmentary texts. However, with the publication of the monumental, forty-volume *Discover-*

*ies in the Judaean Desert* now on the verge of completion (twenty volumes in ten years!),[177] this particular problem is now a thing of the past, and hopefully the experience will help us to avoid similar situations in the future.[178]

The full publication of the Scrolls offers a new platform on which to construct another generation of scholarship, with its consensuses and controversies, its revision of old theories, its solutions to old problems, and its posing of new questions. Halakic, exegetical, and sapiential works, which were only sparsely represented among the texts that informed the first half century of scholarship, now abound in the public domain in exemplary editions, and they are already at the center of the discussion. New technologies and new methods, especially those imported from the social scientific disciplines, provide new avenues into the data.[179]

In touching on some of these open questions, I focus not on the texts as such (where problems and questions are legion), but on the topic of this chapter, and specifically on the history, the social location, and the life and practice of the Qumran community. Considerable debate still swirls around the origins of the community. The older, widely accepted hypothesis that the Essenes and Pharisees derived from the Hasidim was based on an oversimplified religious and social map of second-century Judaism (see below, pp. 178–81).[180] The presence of multiple copies of such works as the Enochic corpus, the book of Daniel, and *Jubilees* indicates either that the communities that spawned these works were ancestral to the Qumran community, or that persons from those groups joined the ranks of the Qumranites.[181]

Another open question concerns the source of the anti-temple polemics in the Scrolls. Such polemics exist in texts that are considerably older than the split between the Qumran community (or its ancestor) and the Hasmonean high priesthood.[182] Debate will continue on the relationship between Qumran and Sadducean halakah. Connected to this are the relationships between the Qumran community and the Pharisees. The latter are very likely to be identified with the Scrolls' "seekers after smooth things," facile interpreters of the Torah, but this identification is an inference.[183] Even granting these polemics, can we establish any connection between the observance of priestly halakah among the Pharisees (see above, pp. 162–63) and among the Essenes?

It will be useful to think imaginatively about the meaning and function of the desert setting of the Qumran community. What might we learn about the community's social psychology? What was it like to be a Qumranite living in isolation in the Judean desert?[184]

Another debated topic is the presence or absence of women in the Qumran community. Philo, Josephus, and Hippolytus emphasize that the Essenes were a celibate group (Philo, *Hypoth.* 11.14-17; Josephus, *J. W.* 2.120-21 [§7.2]; Hippolytus, *Haer.* 9.13), although the last two mention an order of Essenes that permitted marriage ( *J. W.* 2.160-61 [§7.13]; *Haer.* 9.23). The evidence from the Scrolls and archaeological excavations at Qumran is ambiguous, and doubtless the discussion will continue.[185]

Finally, debate will continue regarding the name "Essene" itself. Does it derive from Aramaic *ḥasen, ḥasayya* ("the pious"), or *'asayya* ("healers"),[186] or Hebrew *'ośim* ("doers" [of the Torah])[187] or from Greek *essenēs,* which designates a cultic official?[188]

Soon after the Scrolls' appearance in the public arena, scholars perceived that they had far-reaching implications for the study of the New Testament and Christian origins.[189] Indeed, articles, monographs, and parts of books that relate the Scrolls to the New Testament have constituted a large part of the Scroll bibliography over the last half century.[190] In a real sense the topic has provided the rationale for writing this book. The precipitate of this wide-ranging discussion is as follows: In the Qumran community and in the Scrolls that attest it, we find a first-century Jewish religious community whose worldview and many of whose institutions, theological ideas, and rhetoric anticipate the early church, its institutions, and its theology.[191] I have treated many of the theological parallels in chapters 1–5. Here I focus holistically on the communities, also taking into consideration one of the predecessors of the Qumran community, the group that authored the various sections of *1 Enoch.*[192]

Like the Qumran community and the Enochic group, the early Christian communities saw themselves as the true Israel, the unique, exclusive eschatological community of the chosen, constituted by divine revelation. They were informed, in large part, by a dualistic worldview that envisioned a cosmic conflict between the powers of good and evil and that expected an imminent final judgment that would separate themselves from nonbe-

lievers and would usher in the new age. Like the Qumran comm
the early Christians held in precious memory the person of a po
charismatic founder and leader, they treasured the sacred traditions of
Israel, and they were governed by many of the same institutions and
social structures. They had many of the same beliefs, hopes, and expecta-
tions.

Three major issues distinguished the early Christian movement from
the Qumran community. (1) The church was Christian. It believed that
the crucified and exalted Jesus was God's transforming eschatological
agent, the sine qua non of their identity. Thus the risen and exalted Christ
was granted a status and functions that vastly exceeded those the Teacher
of Righteousness and that stretched from the recent past—and in the
view of some, from eternity—into the imminent consummation of the
new age.[193] (2) The tightly knit Christian communities, while claiming
exclusive uniqueness for their status as God's people, nevertheless had an
open door and vigorously pursued a mission among the Gentiles. This parallel with the vision of the Enochic writers constituted a major difference
from the Qumran community.[194] (3) In keeping with this Gentile mission
and the church's increasing Gentile membership, the largest part of the
church set aside most of the Mosaic Torah as the criterion for right human
conduct before God and drew much of its ethical rhetoric from Greco-
Roman religion and philosophy. The last point must be qualified, however. Although Torah observance—to do or not to do—was not a major
issue in some Christian communities during the early days and years of
the church's existence, for over a century Torah observance of various
sorts was an important institution in some Christian communities.[195]

In other respects these generalizations are subject to qualifications and
nuances that are evident in the variegated and developing social and theological history of first- and second-century Christianity. But overall the
stated parallels and differences sum up the historical implications that
the Scrolls have had on our understanding of Christian origins. The
matrix of the early church was an apocalyptic wing, or wings, of Judaism,
exemplified by the communities attested by the Enochic writings and the
Qumran Scrolls. The situation becomes more complex, however, as we
survey further the multiplicity of groups in early Judaism.

## The Hasidim

How we have come to understand the identity of the Hasidim illustrates how perceptions about Jewish religious history in the later Second Temple period have changed in the last fifty years, and how some of the issues have become much more uncertain.[196] Generally accepted wisdom from the 1950s through much of the 1970s depicted the Hasidim as a more or less unified group of (pacifist) pious Jews who opposed the hellenizers' reforms around and during the time of Antiochus IV Epiphanes (175–163 B.C.E.),[197] and who were the religious roots of the Pharisees and the Essenes. Three passages in 1 and 2 Maccabees were the basis for this interpretation. According to 1 Macc 2:42, a "company of the Asideans" *(synagōgē Asidaiōn)*, who were especially devoted to the Torah, made common cause with Mattathias the Hasmonean, as he made war against the lawless in Israel. First Macc 7:12-13 recounts how a "group of scribes" *(synagōgē grammateōn)*, connected in the text with the Asideans, made peace with the Seleucids and were slaughtered for their effort. In 2 Macc 14:6 Demetrius, the Seleucid general, claims that the Asideans have been making war against the Seleucids under the leadership of Judas Maccabeus, the son of Mattathias.

First Macc 2:42, which describes this group as "mighty warriors" *(ischyroi dynamei)*,[198] and 2 Macc 14:6, if it is not intended to depict a Seleucid misrepresentation,[199] would appear to cast some doubt on the pacifist image of the Asideans. The issue is more complicated, however, because the strongest textual evidence for 1 Macc 2:42 reads "company of Jews" *(synagōgē Ioudaiōn)* rather than "company of Asideans."[200] Thus the connection with Mattathias and the inception of the Hasmonean revolt is uncertain at best.

As we shall see in the next section, it is now evident that the Hasidim of the second century B.C.E. were only one component in a larger, complex religious sociology, of which we can catch only a few glimpses. What we may conclude is the following. Although *hasidim* can be construed as a generic term for pious and faithful Jews (see below), the transliteration of the word in 1 Maccabees 7 and 2 Maccabees 14 suggests that they were a formally constituted group with that name.[201] Their association with his son Judas Maccabeus is less certain (2 Macc 14:6).[202] The textual association

of scribes with the Asideans (1 Macc 7:12-18) may indicate that some of
them were scribes, but it does not prove that the group as a whole was
more or less made up of people from this profession. Whether the origins
of the Pharisees are to be found among the Hasidim is uncertain, and the
evidence does not support the claim that the Hasidim were a parent
group of the Essenes.[203]

The term "company [or 'assembly'] of the Hasidim" is attested in two
works from the last centuries before the common era. Column 18 of the
large Qumran Psalms scroll (11QPs[a]) includes a noncanonical psalm that
celebrates the piety of the *qahal ḥasidim* (line 10).[204] Noteworthy for our
purposes are the psalm's many references to a communal cultic setting
where the pious recount and praise God's deeds, apparently eat and drink
in community (line 11), and meditate on "the Torah of the Most High"
(line 12). There is no clear indication that "assembly of the *hasidim*"
denotes a formally constituted social group. Quite likely, it refers to a
worshiping assembly of persons who understand themselves to be variously "upright, faithful, good, perfect, pious, and righteous." The lack of
typical Qumranic theological terminology indicates that the psalm is not
a product of the Qumran community, but its presence in a Qumran manuscript suggests that it derived from a provenance that was either ancestral to the Qumran community or that was the prior religious home of
some member(s) of the community.[205] Other references to *hasidim* appear
in two other noncanonical compositions in the Psalms scroll (19:8; 22:3,
6), and the former is also sprinkled with language related to worship.

Two other occurrences of the term "council/assemblies of the pious"
appear in the *Psalms of Solomon* (4:1, *synedrion hosiōn*; 17:16[18], *synagōgai hosiōn*;
cf. 10:6[7]). The Greek reflects a Hebrew expression like that in 11QPs[a]
18:10.[206] In addition, the noun *hosios* appears frequently throughout the
*Psalms,* with reference to those who are devoted to God and the observance of the Torah, and who are the object of divine mercy and blessing.[207]
References to praise and worship are also frequent in the corpus.
Although the *Psalms* have traditionally been ascribed to the Pharisees, this
attribution has been based on Josephus's Pharisee-Sadducee-Essene triad.
The plural "assemblies of the pious" (17:16[18]) seems to denote local wor-
shiping communities that consider themselves to be the pious. While this

term implies a contrast with others who are sinners, and the dichotomy of "the pious" or "the righteous" with "sinners" runs like a thread through the *Psalms,* the term may be generic rather than a proper noun.

Thus the texts in the Qumran Psalms scroll and the *Psalms of Solomon* are noteworthy for a usage that parallels the minority textual evidence for 1 Macc 2:42, and they should not be cited as evidence of the ongoing life of a group that was formally named and known as Hasidim. They point to communities rather than individuals, but concerning the name and shape of these communities we learn little.

## Other Groups, Communities, and Sects

Throughout this chapter I have maintained that the religious map of late Second Temple Judaism was more complex than Josephus's scheme suggests, even when one takes into consideration the Zealots, the "Fourth Philosophy," and the Sicarii, whom he mentions but whom I have not discussed.[208] Four kinds of evidence support this contention, although my discussion here can only suggest some possibilities. First, to Josephus's list we should add the Hasidim (Asideans). Second, the Qumran Scrolls include multiple copies of a number of texts that derive from circles ancestral to or contemporary with the Qumran community. Third, other texts from this period derive from circles whose identity remains obscure. Finally, some scattered historical evidence attests the existence of still other groups.

Before treating the second and third categories, I should define my term "circles." I use it in two ways. First, it refers to actual established and organized communities. Of this type we have detailed knowledge only of the Essenes. This knowledge is based on the fortuitous discovery of a Qumran community manual and on a source (behind Josephus and Hippolytus) that appears to have had firsthand knowledge of such a text, or of the Essene community itself. Second, I use "circles" to refer to more or less loosely associated groups or numbers of people, about whose social structure and common life we know relatively little. Among these I include the Pharisees, Sadducees, and Hasidim. Finally, I use the term cautiously to denote aggregations of people whose existence we can reasonably infer. As the example of Philo of Alexandria and Josephus would seem to indicate, the diverse religious mix of Second Temple Judaism included "isolated" individuals who wrote from their own theological, ideological, and political points of view. It is uncertain how many works of the Apocrypha, Pseudepigrapha, and scrolls found at Qumran but not written there were written by people who had no religious companions or support systems.

Some texts found in the Scrolls collection, but not authored at Qumran, provide our best data for imagining some of the diverse social aspects of Second Temple Judaism. As we have seen, (some of) the noncanonical Psalms from 11QPs^a were authored apart from and prior to Qumran by those who designated themselves as (the assembly of) the pious. The Enochic corpus and its ongoing life provide a window into the social diversity of apocalyptic Judaism. The various Enochic treatises represented among the Scrolls were composed over the course of three hundred years. This developing tradition, each stage dependent on the previous ones, presupposes an ongoing context in which the traditions were transmitted.[209] Unfortunately, we know almost nothing about the specific identity, structure, and daily life of this Enochic community. Thus, for example, both the Animal Vision (*1 Enoch* 85–90) and the Apocalypse of Weeks (*1 En.* 93:1-10; 91:11-17) attest a group or groups of people who constituted a reform movement or reform movements in the early second century B.C.E., and the Epistle of Enoch (*1 Enoch* 92–105) employs the term *hoi hosioi* ("the pious"). But these works do not demonstrably derive from known groups, or specifically from the Hasidim.[210]

While, for the most part, we cannot specify names or clearly define communities, we can trace continuities in the theological and intellectual traditions that funneled into the Enochic group and out of it, and we know that the contexts that transmitted this material split in various directions. Among those who received the Enochic books were the circles that authored *Jubilees*.[211] That there was an organized group that created and received the peculiar halakah of this work is suggested in the eschatological scenario depicted in 23:16-29, particularly its description of a communal study of the Torah (v 26) that is reminiscent of 1QS 6:6-8. Although this group stood in the Enochic chain of transmission, it went in its own direction, emphasizing the importance of the Mosaic Torah, which the Enochic writers had de-emphasized or simply ignored.[212] This community should be distinguished, in turn, from the Qumran community, although *Jubilees* became an important document for the Qumranites.[213] The Aramaic Levi text, preserved in seven fragmentary Qumran manuscripts, provides a hint of a priestly provenance that was in some sense ancestral to the author of *Jubilees,* as well as to the Qumran community.[214] "The wise" (*maśkîlîm*), who authored the final form of the book of Daniel, are to be distinguished from the Hasidim, but they stand in historical continuity with the authors of some of the early Enochic texts, and with (the members of) the Qumran community, among whose scrolls nine fragmentary copies of the work have been preserved.[215] As we have seen, the Qumran community cherished the early Enochic texts, but there is no evidence that the author(s) of the Enochic Book of Parables (*1 Enoch 37–71*)—who reshaped these traditions and conflated them with Danielic traditions—was associated with the Qumran community. Finally, some first-century Christian community or communities received the Enochic Book of Parables and identified the risen Jesus as the Son of Man who would function as the eschatological judge.[216]

In addition to these interrelated groups, which we can infer from the Enochic texts, we may presume some ill-defined groups or circles that produced works like the *Testament of Moses,* composed in its original form around the time of the book of Daniel,[217] and the *Martyrdom of Isaiah,* a text of the second century B.C.E. that describes a desert band of the righteous gathered around a prophetlike leader.[218]

Taken together, these texts indicate the existence of a number of Jewish religious groups or circles, some more clearly discernible than others, some associated with others. While we know little about the shape and organization of these groups, the general outline of the picture reflects a religious social diversity that should be more closely scrutinized.

Finally, "historical" sources provide additional hints of the religious diversity in early Judaism. According to the Gospels, John the Baptist was an eschatological preacher in the region near Qumran who announced an imminent judgment and set the terms for who was or was not a true Israelite.[219] However, the parallels between John and the Scrolls provide no conclusive evidence that he was or remained an Essene or a member of the Qumran community,[220] nor do the sources (either the Gospels or Josephus [*Ant.* 18.116-19 (§5.20)]) indicate to what extent his disciples constituted a formally organized community.[221] Josephus mentions another religious leader in the desert named Bannus, with whom Josephus claims to have had a relationship and whose daily ablutions seem more like those at Qumran than John's; however, Josephus's sketchy reference allows no conclusion about the nature of his retinue (*Life* 11). Two centuries earlier, according to 1 Macc 2:29-38, a group described as "many who were seeking righteousness" *(polloi zētountes dikaiosynēn)* opposed the hellenizing decrees of Antiochus IV and went into the desert, where they died in caves when they would not defend themselves on the Sabbath. Although they have often been identified with the Hasidim, this is not substantiated by the text.[222] Whether they might have been an organized group, perhaps known as "the seekers of righteousness," is uncertain.[223] In all these cases the evidence is skimpy, but it does point to numbers of people, in two cases gathered around a leader (John and Bannus), pursuing God's will in an environment that they perceive to be adverse to such activity.

## Summary

### Variety among Jewish Groups and Sects

Scholarship on the social aspects of early Judaism has shown that there was considerable variety in the beliefs, practices, rationales, and strategies of Jewish religious groups in the centuries around the turn of the era, although many of the specifics are uncertain. Employing a widely accepted sociological typology of religious protest groups,[224] we can distinguish between "reformist" groups, which seek to change a world that they see in need of changing, and "introversionist" groups, which give up on the world and turn in on themselves.[225] An example of the former was the Pharisees, while the latter were represented by the Qumran community and perhaps the desert dwellers of 1 Maccabees 2. Focusing more on beliefs, we can also identify groups that I find it useful to distinguish by the term "sects": communities "whose religious worldview portrays one's group as the sole and exclusive arena of salvation and thus sees those who are not members of that community as cut off from God's favor and bound for damnation."[226] Among these we may include the Qumran community as well as the authors of many of the Enochic texts and *Jubilees*.

The causes for the formation of religious groups and sects were doubtless varied and, in some cases, are difficult to determine.[227] In general, however, it was perceived threats in the religious environment, the culture in general, or one's political and social circumstances that caused people to pull the wagons into a circle. That is, in addition to formulating theological responses to one's (unhappy) circumstances, people sometimes gathered into groups. In these contexts the making of common cause, the pooling of intellectual, theological, and physical resources, and mutual encouragement and reinforcement helped these people maintain their identity, practice their religion, formulate strategies to cope with the situation, and perhaps protect themselves from the perceived or real threat. Reformist groups ventured out beyond the wagons and tried to change the alien or threatening environment. Strategies for change include the following: study of the sacred tradition, both to ascertain what is God's will (*Jubilees* and Qumran) and to discern the times (Qumran); the practice of mantic visionary skills for the same purpose (parts of *1 Enoch* and Daniel); liturgical activity and other practices carried out in communal assembly (Qumran and perhaps the Epistle of Enoch with its Woes and Exhortations); and, among reformist groups, public exercises of piety or preaching (*1 Enoch* 92–105, at least in its rhetoric).[228]

### Early Christianity and Its Relationship to Sectarian Judaism

The explosion of literature on the Scrolls and the New Testament revealed an astonishing number of parallels between the two corpuses of literature, and this literature often gave the impression and sometimes made the assertion that a direct relationship existed between the early church and the Qumran community. I have identified three major similarities and differences above (p. 175). As the intervening paragraphs have indicated, however, we should exercise caution in asserting direct connections. The religious map of first-century Judaism was complex, and our knowledge of it is skimpy. What tentative conclusions might we draw?

I would call the early church a Jewish "sect," a group with a strong sense of its Israelite identity, which saw itself as the exclusive arena of God's blessing, defining its identity around Jesus of Nazareth rather than the Torah, and excluding from the pale of salvation all who did not acknowledge Jesus as God's eschatological agent. That is, christology rather than Torah was determinative of one's status as a true Israelite. Thus, although the church offered an open door to Gentiles, it was also characterized by an exclusivism that gradually came to deny the covenantal status of the majority of ethnic Jews.

Like the Qumran community and the Enochic group, the church considered itself to be the eschatological community of the chosen constituted by divine revelation. That revelation was the epiphany of the risen Christ, which became the core of the gospel that its apostles and teachers now proclaimed among the Gentiles. In its openness to the Gentiles, it was much more like the Enochic Jews than those of Qumran. Moreover, the similarity to Enochic Judaism may have involved some sort of historical connection. Early Son of Man christology drew on a tradition that is attested in the Parables of Enoch.[229] Other parallels between Enochic and Petrine traditions are striking.[230] Later affinities for the Enochic tradition in the second- to fourth-century church are also noteworthy, although they are hardly appreciated in the historical literature.[231]

Having said this, we must acknowledge the unique parallels between the New Testament and the theology and practice attested in the Qumran Scrolls. Moreover, we should note this fact: although the Gospels mention both the Pharisees and the Sadducees, they make no reference to Josephus's third group, the Essenes, nor can we demonstrate that they refer to the Qumran community. Perhaps, in their eschatological proclivities, the early Christians were too close to the Essenes or to the Qumran community for the evangelists to depict them as enemies of Jesus and his followers. This does not mean that Jesus or his first followers were Essenes or Qumranites. At best, we can say that early Christianity arose in a wing of apocalyptic Judaism that was also inhabited by later Enochic Judaism, John the Baptist, and the Qumran community. The precise connections and interrelationships remain obscure, however. On the one hand, we must acknowledge that nascent Christianity was conceived in the matrix of first-century apocalyptic Judaism. On the other hand, we must recognize how little we know of the particulars of that conception and birth. This knowledge and this ignorance—for better and for worse—are the gift of the Scrolls and of the subsequent resurgence of Jewish and Christian research into the whole corpus of Jewish literature, inscriptions, and material evidence from the centuries that precede and follow the turn of the era.[232]

# chapter 7

## Conclusions and Implications

### Diversity within Early Judaism and Early Christianity: A Comparison

Christian descriptions of Judaism written in the nineteenth and the first half of the twentieth century emphasized the differences between early Judaism and early Christianity. Scholarship in the last half century has shown that both Second Temple Judaism and first-century Christianity were remarkably diverse in their religious expression,[1] and comparative study of early Jewish texts and the New Testament indicates many more points of continuity between the two than the previous paradigms allowed.

### Scripture and Tradition

Although the Jews recognized no formal biblical canon in the Hellenistic and early Roman periods, by the turn of the era most sectors of Judaism considered almost all the books of the Tanak to be authoritative. Some groups also recognized the authority of works like the books of Enoch, *Jubilees,* and the Temple Scroll. The text of some books of the Tanak was in flux in this period, and different text forms could be found in a single location, such as Qumran. The Torah, the Prophets, and the Writings did not exist in isolation, but were inextricably associated with interpretive traditions. Some of these traditions conflicted with or even contradicted one another and were authoritative for some persons and groups and not for others.

While the New Testament quotes from, or alludes to, almost all the books of the Tanak, it also draws on material attested in other Jewish works such as the Wisdom of Solomon and the Parables of Enoch. In both instances it employs traditional Jewish interpretations of biblical material (Wisdom's interpretation of Isaiah 52–53 and the Parables' interpretation of Isaiah 52–53, the Davidic oracles, and Daniel 7). In many other ways, the New Testament reflects specific and sometimes idiosyncratic traditional interpretations of the Tanak. Following Jewish practice, it can also build its exegesis and argumentation on textual variants, derived from the Hebrew text or its Greek translation. The Christian use of interpretive traditions, at home and acceptable to some Jews but not others, helps to explain why the church's claims were acceptable to some Jews and not others.

The Jewish complementarity of Scripture and traditional interpretation is paralleled in the Gospels, both in the creation of stories about Jesus that involve haggadic interpretation of the Bible and in the evangelists' reshaping of their source material about Jesus. The conflict and contradiction between the various crystallizations of the Jesus tradition are also consonant with Jewish interpretive practice.

## Torah and the Righteous Life

In emphasizing the divine imperative to live according to God's will, and in asserting that God would reward the righteous and punish evildoers, Judaism of the Greco-Roman period followed biblical covenantal theology, articulated in the Torah and the Prophets. What precisely constituted God's will was a matter of debate, however. The Pharisees developed their own halakot, particularly regarding cult and purity regulations and legal procedures, which were sometimes a matter of debate even in their own circles and often conflicted with the legal interpretations of the Sadducees and the Essenes. For the authors of the Enochic books, the authority of "Enoch" preceded and superseded that of Moses. The authors of the Enochic books, *Jubilees,* and some of the Qumran writings believed that differences of opinion on legal issues could be a matter of salvation and damnation, and this inevitably led to sectarian divisions. The Enochic books and other works of a sapiential character attest a form of ethical teaching quite different from that in the biblical law codes and the halakic collections. Instead of explicating detailed, casuistic descriptions of right and wrong behavior, one exhorted right behavior and emphasized the relationship between conduct and its consequences.

These considerations contradict the Christian stereotype that Judaism in this period was a legalistic perversion of biblical (prophetic) religion. The Bible itself affirms the nexus of human act and divine recompense. Jewish instruction about the right life was much more diverse than halakic texts and later accounts of rabbinic disagreements and debates. In addition, the notion of divine grace is by no means lacking in Jewish texts concerned with instruction about the Torah.

Early Christian attitudes about the Torah were much more diverse than Paul's systematic dismissal of the ongoing validity of the Law. The Synoptic Gospels run the gamut—sometimes approximating Paul, sometimes dismissing Pharisaic halakah, occasionally adopting a more strict position, and in the case of Matthew embracing the Torah in principle. Paul's emphasis on justification by faith in three epistles should not obscure the fact that the apostle spends far more space in his epistles exhorting his congregations to live the right life than he does calling on them to affirm their faith in Jesus. In adopting sapiential forms of ethical instruction, Paul, the Synoptics, and James follow Jewish precedent, although the influence of non-Jewish Hellenistic moral instruction is also evident and sometimes blends with material of Jewish origin. The nexus between human conduct and divine reward and punishment, present in the Hebrew Bible and in Jewish texts, appears in most books of the New Testament, including the Pauline epistles and the Jesus tradition. Apart from whether New Testament texts affirm or dismiss the Torah, in part or in its totality, the specifically Christian nuance lies in the association with Jesus, either as the embodiment or exponent of Wisdom or as the resurrected one whose Spirit facilitates a God-pleasing life.

## God's Activity in Behalf of Humanity

Salvation is an inadequate term to describe God's activity in behalf of humanity, because not all of this activity involves saving people *from something*. The blessings of the covenant can be bestowed apart from a situation that requires deliverance from some sort of evil. Even in the proper sense of the term, however, salvation comprises a variety of activities. One can be cleansed from impurity or find atonement from the guilt of sin. Although forgiveness or atonement takes place through the sacrificial system, in postexilic Judaism it can also be effected through repentance that is realized in penitential prayers, acts of self-abasement, and charitable deeds in behalf of others. Salvation also occurs when God rescues the righteous from their enemies and heals those who are sick or in danger of death.

Revelation is another mode of God's activity. Speaking in the name of God the righteous judge, a prophet or apocalypticist or teacher calls one to repentance, exhorts one to remain faithful, or explains how to do this. The apocalyptic worldview that develops in the Greco-Roman world posits revelation in part as the solution to a dualistic universe in which one is bereft of divine judgment. Jewish writers in this period differ on the scope of salvation and divine blessing. Some include all or almost all of Israel, others envision the salvation of a righteous few within Israel and/or those Gentiles who turn to the worship of the God of Israel.

For Christian theology at least since Augustine, God's salvific activity has been epitomized in Jesus' sacrificial death for others. *The* human problem is sin, and forgiveness through the death of Jesus is God's primary act of salvation. While some early Christian creedal formulas and the Pauline epistles emphasize Jesus' death for others, our study of Judaism enables us better to see other forms of God's actions in behalf of humanity in the New Testament books. The four Gospels spend relatively little time discussing Jesus' vicarious death. Mainly, they depict him as God's healer and as the spokesman or the embodiment of divine Wisdom or Logos, critiquing the establishment, expounding God's will, and calling sinners to repentance. For Paul, the human dilemma is more radical than the fact that humans sin and need forgiveness. Taking up a two-ways, two-spirits theology, similar to that in the Qumran Community Rule, and focusing on its anthropological aspect, he claims that sin's universal domination over humanity negates the Law's ability to engender the obedience it requires. This situation requires incorporation into Christ, the new Adam, who has overcome humanity's slavery to sin. This negative assessment of the Torah has a corollary: in order to be saved, Jews must turn to faith in Christ. Paul is confident that the majority will do this. His own mission, however, is to the Gentiles. The Synoptic evangelists also assert that the gospel is to be preached to all the Gentiles, but they are much less optimistic about the salvation of the Jews than Paul is.

## Agents of God's Activity

It is reductionistic to identify God's agent in the world as "the messiah." God operates through a variety of human and transcendent agents, which are appropriate to the situation and the type of divine activity under consideration. Sometimes one anticipates an anointed Davidic king, usually when the enemy or opponent is a royal figure or some other ruler. The term "anointed" is multivalent, however. In addition to the king, it can apply to a prophet, who speaks in God's behalf, or to the high priest, who intercedes for the people and presides over the cult, effecting forgiveness or purification. Prophets, apocalypticists, sages, and interpreters of the Law mediate revelation in various ways. A prophet or a physician heals illness in God's behalf. As people come to perceive the universe in increasingly dualistic terms, they construe divine agents as heavenly, transcendent figures. An angel may function as a revealer or messenger, as God's healer, as the eschatological high priest, or as an agent of judgment—whether as mediator or intercessor for the oppressed and persecuted, or the leader or a member of the heavenly army. There are, in addition, two transcendent agents par excellence. Wisdom dwells in books of revealed wisdom received and transmitted by the apocalypticist and speaks through the sage. The Enochic son of man is the heavenly "Chosen One" or "Anointed One" of God, the vindicator and protector of the righteous and chosen, who executes judgment on their oppressors, the kings and the mighty.

As long as the discussion of Jesus' identity has been construed in terms of "christology," this discussion has been bound to emphasize the differences between early Judaism and early Christianity. Of course, the church separates from contemporary Jewish religion in that it identifies Jesus as God's final and superlative agent in the world. Beyond this, however, the diversity of Jewish thought suggests a number of points of continuity with the New Testament's multiform profile of Jesus. As an early title of Jesus, *christos* probably had a number of connotations, all consonant with Jewish usage. In some cases it identified him as the Davidic king, though not demonstrably as a political or military figure. Alternatively, citations of Psalm 110 suggest that Jesus was seen as the eschatological high priest, in which capacity he could have been called *christos*. This title may also have denoted his identity as the eschatological, exalted son of man, God's chosen and anointed one according to the Parables of Enoch. The application of Isaiah 52–53 to Jesus appears to reflect the paradigm of the persecuted, vindicated, and exalted spokesman of the Lord, though not always implying a sacrificial death. It is worth considering whether any of the New Testament authors, or their received traditions, connected this paradigm of suffering and exaltation with Davidic traditions (as did the author of the Wisdom of Solomon), and whether they may have seen this as a connotation of the title *christos* (as the author of Wisdom did not).

## Eschatology

As the present time is increasingly perceived to be difficult, problematic, or downright evil, one looks to an end time when God will act in behalf of humanity. Thus eschatology is not a category in its own right, but the horizon on which one interprets Scripture, sees the need to live a righteous life, or anticipates God's activity as revealer, deliverer, judge, and healer. Diversity is abundantly evident in texts with an eschatological perspective. When will the end come, or has it begun to happen? In what form will one transcend death; might one already be participating in eternal life? Will one live eternally in heaven, or will God create a new earth along with a new heaven?

This consciousness of the end is the horizon on which the New Testament plays out the events of Jesus' life, death, and resurrection, as well as the history of the early church. The many variations on the theme reflect the diversity of the early Jewish texts: imminent end and realized eschatology; the perceived delay of the time of the end; vacillation regarding the mode of Jesus' resurrection and eternal life for Christians. The uniqueness of the early church's eschatological proclamation lies in its association of the end time with the person and career of Jesus of Nazareth.

## Contexts and Settings

Ancient religious texts are historical artifacts, created in time and place. Their conceptions and ideologies responded to specific historical circumstances and functioned in particular social locations. If our interpretation is to do these texts justice, we must try to identify their time, circumstances, and locations to the extent that this is possible.

Most of the Jewish texts that provide such information reflect troubled times and difficult situations: religious persecution and martyrdom; social oppression, the occupation of the Holy Land, or the destruction of Jerusalem; social, cultural, and religious conflict. These circumstances provided the context for the eschatology and apocalypticism that characterized much of Judaism and Christianity around the turn of the era.

Geographic location played a more important role in religion and culture than is generally recognized. Life in the Diaspora brought its own problems and challenges to those who sought to maintain a Jewish identity while living as a minority community. Geography also played a role in Palestinian Jewish religion. Jerusalem and its temple were sacred space, more for the Jews than for the early church. The area in the north around Mount Hermon and Dan had special significance in the early Enoch tradition and was the locus for traditions associated with the apostle Peter. For the Qumranites, as for John the Baptist and his followers, the wilderness of Judea was integral to their religious self-understanding as repentant, chosen remnants.

The political and cultural triumph of Alexander the Great was a major component in the environment of later Second Temple Judaism, both in Palestine and in the Diaspora. Jews interacted with this Hellenistic environment in positive and negative ways and to different degrees. The collapse of the Palestinian-Hellenistic scholarly dichotomy has important ramifications for New Testament theologies and histories of early Christianity that have employed it in order to distinguish between Palestinian and Hellenistic Christianity.

The Jerusalem temple was a major Jewish religious institution. Nonetheless, dissenters from the early postexilic period to the temple's destruction in 70 C.E. criticized the temple and its priesthood, and some denied the efficacy of its cult. In part this provided the context for alternatives for purification and atonement. The New Testament's generally negative view of the temple and its cult reflects, in part, its interpretation of Jesus' crucifixion as death in behalf of others. It also suggests some association between the early church and Jewish circles that were critical of the temple and its cult.

Archaeological excavations and epigraphic and literary evidence have begun to shed light on the development of the synagogue as a major Jewish religious and social institution in the Second Temple period, both in the Diaspora and in Palestine. Precisely how synagogues related to the Jerusalem temple, as sacred space, is an open question. These findings lend verisimilitude to New Testament accounts about activities of Jesus and the apostles in synagogues, though not necessarily to the accuracy of individual stories. Study of religious and communal activities in first-century synagogues may shed light on the origins and character of early Christian worship.

The religious and social map of Palestine in the centuries around the turn of the era was more complex than we might suppose on the basis of Josephus's descriptions of the triad Pharisees-Sadducees-Essenes and his references to a few others. Concerning his major parties, we may note the following. As the rabbinical writings and the Christian Gospels attest, the Pharisees were devoted to a life of priestly purity, fasting, observance of agricultural laws, and special Sabbath halakot, which they lived out in their workaday world, seeking to set an example for all Israel. The claim that such a life in itself constituted self-righteous and hypocritical religion derives from first-century Christian polemics that were directed against them for reasons that are not altogether clear. The Sadducees appear to have derived their name from Zadok the high priest, and some of them, though demonstrably not all of them, were associated with the wealthy class and the high-priestly rulers. They differed from the Pharisees in matters of law and eschatology. The community at Qumran appears to have been a branch of the Essenes, who understood themselves to be the exclusive eschatological community of the chosen, constituted by revelation, awaiting the end time. Their isolated existence enabled them to live in the purity appropriate to their Zadokite priestly leaders.

Although we know little about them, the existence of other religious groups is attested by Jewish and Christian literary sources. What we do know warns us against a facile identification of any given text as deriving from the Pharisees, Sadducees, Essenes, or Hasidim. Not surprisingly, as our sources have multiplied, we have come to see that Second Temple Judaism was more complex than we had previously thought.

The Qumran community, as described in the Scrolls, and the Enochic writings provide a Jewish prototype for the early church. It was an eschatological Jewish sect, constituted by revelation, claiming to be exclusively the chosen of the end time. The church's uniqueness lay in its identification of Jesus of Nazareth as God's transforming eschatological agent, its pursuit of a Gentile mission, and, increasingly, as a corollary of this, its dismissal of most of the Mosaic Torah. While we cannot demonstrate a *direct* connection with the aforementioned prototype, it is evident that the church was conceived in an apocalyptic environment that was also inhabited by John the Baptist, the Qumran community, and the circles that produced the Enochic literature. The discovery of the Scrolls and the subsequent study of the broader range of Judaism contemporary to the Qumran community enables us to see aspects of this environment with a clarity previously not possible.

## Judaism and Early Christianity: Where They Differed and Why They Parted

The early church was a child of Jewish religion and culture. The child, like the mother, was a complex creature. In substantial ways many aspects of early Christian life and religion were derivative from and similar to their counterparts in Judaism. Jews and Christians worshiped a common God, attested in a common set of authoritative Scriptures. They believed that this God called them to live in accordance with the divine will, and they expected that this God would recompense them according to their deeds. They also believed that in a variety of ways this God acted in their behalf, forgiving their sins and delivering them from evil.

Yet the child broke away from its mother because the two viewed and valued some things very differently. For the early church the identity of

Jesus of Nazareth made all the difference in the world. In spite of his disastrous death at the hands of the Roman government, they believed that he was God's agent to effect the change from the present evil age to the new age. All the components of this belief can be found in Jewish belief prior to the appearance of Jesus and the church. The first Christians were good eschatological Jews.

So why did the majority of their Jewish coreligionists in the first and second century reject them as apostates? Why did *they* not believe that Jesus was God's last word to the chosen people? Like all major historical questions, the answer is complex. Our study provides a few pointers, however.

Judaism was a diverse religious and cultural phenomenon. Not every Jew was of an eschatological inclination, and many of those who were differed in how they thought the end time would be played out, and what the character of God's final deliverer might be. Yet it is not likely that noneschatological Jews would disown other Jews because of their eschatology, though many surely raised their eyebrows.

There was another factor. As Christianity moved into what we call the second century, it increasingly rejected in principle what most Jews considered to be the cornerstone of divine revelation, namely, the Mosaic Torah. Thus, when Rabbinic Judaism and the early church went their separate ways, each was drawing on a different element in its Jewish heritage. Each maintained that its impulse was the sine qua non for true Judaism. From the viewpoint of the history of religions and historical criticism, it would appear that the rabbinic Jews had the better side of the argument. Historically, Mosaic Torah and not eschatology stood at the center of Jewish religion—unless one was an Enochic Jew.

Once again, the diversity of Judaism sheds further light on the question. The early church arose in an eschatological wing of Judaism that also had sectarian proclivities. Both the Enochic Jews and the Qumran community offer us a model for this religious mentality. Each claimed to be the community of the chosen, constituted by a special eschatological revelation. As a corollary of this, they believed that those who did not accept their version of the truth were doomed to damnation. The issues, of course, were different. The Enochic Jews devalued the Mosaic Torah in favor of a new revelation that they claimed was a revelation more ancient than that of Moses. The Qumranites claimed that they exclusively had the correct interpretation of the Mosaic Torah. For Christians, the exclusive eschatological revelation concerned the identity and activity of Jesus of Nazareth.

The various books of the New Testament explicate their claims in different ways, but the religious impulse is the same. For Paul the human condition required a radical solution: incorporation into the new Adam and participation in his Spirit, which facilitated the godly life necessary for salvation. This was possible through faith in the gospel and baptism into Christ's death and resurrection. For John this issue was faith in Jesus the incarnation of the divine Logos and the revealer of the Father. Those who rejected this revelation were damned. The dim view that the Synoptic evangelists take of the Jews seems to turn on the same issue—rejection of Jesus, God's divinely sent messenger. The paradigm is very old: when Israel rejected the prophets, the nation was doomed. In the Wisdom of Solomon those who rejected the righteous man's credentials as "son of God" met their fate after their death.

## The Consequences of These Events

### The Curious Irony of Gentile Christian Exclusivism

Having begun as an eschatological sect within Judaism, the church claimed to be the heir of the promises given to Israel. As the church's membership became increasingly Gentile, it disavowed the Mosaic Torah as the hallmark for a righteous life, and it claimed that salvation and God's blessing were possible only through faith in Jesus. In time, the more or less exclusively Gentile church claimed to be the true Israel, and it excommunicated the native children of Israel who maintained the traditional criterion of Israelite identity, adherence to the Mosaic Torah.

### The Triumph of Christianity without the Torah

The gradual ascendancy of Pauline Christianity was a major factor in these developments. Christian writings of the early second century show relatively little influence from the writings of the apostle Paul. Justin Martyr knew Romans but had to rely on Matthew to do what Paul himself would not do, namely, disenfranchise the Jews.[2] The decisive figure, however, was Marcion. Although he would be excommunicated as a heretic, his canonization of the Pauline epistles forced the "orthodox" church to follow suit. Thus the course was set. Mainline Christianity would be substantially Pauline Christianity. The dismissal of the authority of the Mosaic Torah would become a constitutive part of orthodoxy, though different from Marcion: the catholic church would canonize both Old Testament and New Testament. In an eerie way the antithesis of law and gospel, celebrated by Marcion, would echo in the reformers, and its new context in Protestant-Catholic polemics set the stage for a typology that devalued Judaism as an inferior religion.

## A Denigrating Comparison of Judaism and Christianity

Two kinds of consequences have followed from this chain of events. First, even honest and sophisticated New Testament exegetes and historians continued to depict Judaism in contrast to prophetic religion on the one side and New Testament Christianity on the other. The situation has changed in the past fifty years, but much needs to be done to revise the old paradigms that govern New Testament scholarship and Christian theology and preaching. Standard textbooks on Christian origins and New Testament "backgrounds" continue to be republished without critical revision of their outdated contents. The old comparisons continue to echo in the Gospel pericopes that are read each Sunday in services of worship. To the extent that this is not in some way accompanied by critical comment, the old stereotypes are reinforced.

## The Backwash of Christian Apocalyptic Eschatology

Apocalyptic eschatology propounds the belief that history is moving toward its consummation in a new age and a new world, and it reinforces this belief in a worldview that dualistically divides between heaven, the place of the divine, and earth, the human habitat. The notion that the "here and now" are marked by the absence of the salvation that will be effected "then and there" has had a tremendous impact on Christian theology, piety, and practice. Although catholic Christianity rejected the Gnostic synthesis of apocalyptic and Platonic thought, Christian theology has tended to side with the Jesus of the Fourth Gospel ("I go to prepare a place for you") rather than with the Jesus of the Beatitudes ("The meek will inherit the earth"). The millennialism of Irenaeus, whose exegetical instincts were sometimes more correct than those of many of his contemporaries and successors, was severely criticized.

Human history and experience have provided an understandable rationale for siding with apocalyptic and eschatological thought. These theologies have worked as well for persecuted, oppressed, and suffering Christians as they did for their Jewish forebears. There is, however, another side to the issue, which is related to the nature of religious formulations. The eschatology of the apocalypticists was generated as an effective way to affirm faith in a God whose justice was not apparent in the empirical world. It fostered endurance and made life livable in difficult times. When the New Testament writings that enshrined this theology were canonized, however, what was once specific became general, mainline, and universally applicable. The process repeated itself in the piety of the church. Hymns composed as expressions of faith by people on their deathbeds or in the midst of plague and war were incorporated into the church's hymnals, to be used as regular complements to the canonized apocalyptic theology. As heaven became increasingly one's home, life and this world were regularly perceived as a desert drear. The rest is commentary: exploitation of the earth, environmental disaster, and brinkmanship by "Christian" nations. The tradition was seen to provide a theological justification for this behavior.

This theological rationale has sometimes served another, wrongheaded purpose. Formulations created by the persecuted and the oppressed, as a means of coping with life and maintaining faith when they were unable to change their situation, have been employed by rich and powerful oppressors in order to maintain and justify the status quo to their own advantage when they could have changed the situation. This adds up to bad theology, as well as opportunism.

## Looking to the Future: Some Possibilities

Our study suggests some possibilities for an agenda that has exegetical and historical aspects, theological implications, and practical consequences.

## Three Axioms for Exegetical and Historical Study

I propose three exegetical rules of thumb.

*Scholarly humility and tentativeness:* The revolution that has occurred in the study of Judaism and its relation to Christian origins reminds us that scholarship is an ongoing process, in which accepted truths are questioned and sometimes undercut by new data, insights, and methods. It will be healthy to present our findings in this spirit.

*Awareness of the social construction of knowledge:* The falsification of the stereotype that early Judaism was legalistic warns us that our approach to the texts and the history behind them is governed by our own presuppositions, which in circular fashion can easily become our conclusions. We find what we are looking for. At the very least we need to be aware of our presuppositions and prejudices.

*Diversity in early Judaism and early Christianity:* By its very nature, however, the fact of this diversity is not likely to be falsified by new data. Theories of normative Judaism were created from a tendentious comparison with Christianity, and the myth of an early monolithic orthodox Christianity was a historical retrojection. As we study the texts, we need to be sensitive to manifestations of diversity, and we would do well to eschew constructing simple schematizations in order to tidy up the chaos of developing religions.

## Exegetical and Historical Possibilities

Many questions remain concerning the shape of early Judaism and its relationship to the rise of Christianity. Answers to them require serious study of both the Jewish and the Christian primary sources. In addition to the issues mentioned above ("Contexts and Settings"), here are several more.

First, what more can we learn about the varied nature of revelation and authority in Judaism of the Greco-Roman period? What was the spectrum of revealer figures? What kind of authority lay in the various sorts of scriptural interpretation? What kind of framework does this provide for understanding how John the Baptist, Jesus, and the apostles were perceived?

Second, most of the layers of the Gospel tradition depict Jesus of Nazareth attending to the sinners rather than the righteous. This stands on its head the normal formulation in Jewish texts, which celebrates the righteous and denigrates the sinners. How do we interpret this anomaly without falling back into the old Judaism versus Christianity stereotype?

Third, what paradigms can we find—apart from Paul's theology—for the Christian devaluation of the Mosaic Torah? To what extent do the Jewish sapiential literature and the Enochic corpus help us to understand this phenomenon?

Fourth, can we probe further into the rise of "high" christologies and into the Jewish/Christian split over christology? How far did Jews go in espousing the notion that heavenly Wisdom dwelt in the righteous spokesman of the Lord? In what ways did early Christian formulations go beyond this and why?

## Theological and Practical Consequences

If our exercise reminds us of one thing, it is the inherent historicality of good theology. It works well because it speaks relevantly to the issues. Its afterlife is viable and valid, however, only to the extent that it is sensitive to the historical situation and to the extent that theologians are prepared to make responsible shifts and transformations in the tradition that are appropriate to new situations and new worlds. Theologians and preachers need to keep this in mind as they deal with the two issues mentioned above (pp. 196–97). (1) It has been almost two thousand years since the expected time of the parousia. How can eschatology be reformulated to avoid the problematic consequences that have traditionally followed from excessive literalism in the matter? (2) How do Christians deal responsibly with Paul's expectation that all Israel will be saved? How might Paul have handled the matter had he lived for another fifty or seventy-five years? Was he right in his intuition that the almighty and faithful God of the covenant would see to it that "all Israel will be saved," and wrong in his solution that faith in Christ was the sole means of salvation, or vice versa? Genuine theological honesty is required here.

Theological dialog between Christians and Jews needs to proceed on the basis of historical honesty. Outmoded, historically falsified theological stereotypes need to be acknowledged as such and taken off the table. While dialog engages people who are who they are here and now, clarification of the historical issues that created the Jewish/Christian schism need to be studied with honesty and on the basis of the best available data.

Finally, what can we learn from early Jewish and early Christian attitudes about diversity? Can we take seriously the remarkable flexibility with which both Jews and Christians approached the texts of Scripture, and the degree to which those texts begat differing interpretations? Exclusivism and sectarianism in both Judaism and Christianity had ugly consequences in both communities and between them, consequences that were inconsonant with the heart of both religions. How does one balance a genuine concern for the truth with respect and tolerance for those who disagree with us? In the final analysis, is theology about grasping the truth, or is it the unending process of searching for what we humans can know only in part? If it is the latter, can we admit it and learn to live with it?

# Notes

## Introduction

1. Thomas S. Kuhn, *The Structure of Scientific Revolutions* (2d ed.; Chicago: Univ. of Chicago Press, 1970). Although the book has been criticized in some scientific circles, his description of the scholarly process has resonated with many humanists.

2. See Dwight W. Swanson's comment on the *Festschrift* for Heinz-Wolfgang Kuhn: "Once again it seems, in spite of Kuhn's life-long 'Qumranproject' to map the comparative worlds of the NT and the Scrolls, that NT scholarship makes a compulsory nod to the existence of the Scrolls, then goes on without further attempt to assimilate the extensive Scroll work which is now readily available," review of Michael Becker and Wolfgang Fenske, eds., *Das Ende der Tage und die Gegenwart des Heils: Bewegungen mit dem Neuen Testament und seiner Umwelt, Festschrift für Heinz-Wolfgang Kuhn zum 65. Geburtstag* (AGJU 44; Leiden: Brill, 1999), in *DSD* 9 (2002) 106.

3. The classical expression of this is Walter Bauer, *Orthodoxy and Heresy in Earliest Christianity* (2d ed. by Georg Strecker; trans. and ed. Robert A. Kraft and Gerhard Krodel; Philadelphia: Fortress Press, 1971). For the first century see the essays by James M. Robinson and Helmut Koester, *Trajectories through Early Christianity* (Philadelphia: Fortress Press, 1971).

4. Drawing on the imagery of Robinson and Koester, *Trajectories,* 4.

5. Robert A. Kraft and George W. E. Nickelsburg, eds., *Early Judaism and Its Modern Interpreters* (Philadelphia: Fortress Press, 1986) 1–30.

6. Ibid., for a starter. In much greater detail see Andreas Lehnardt, *Bibliographie zu den jüdischen Schriften aus hellenistische-römischer Zeit* (*JSHRZ* 6/2; Gütersloh: Gütersloher Verlagshaus, 1999); Lorenza DiTommaso, *A Bibliography of Pseudepigrapha Research 1850–1999* (JSPSup 39; Sheffield: Sheffield Academic Press, 2001); the bibliographies on the Dead Sea Scrolls, cited below, p. 237, n. 141; and the bibliographies on Josephus cited below, p. 204, n. 30.

## 1. Scripture and Tradition

1. For general bibliography on Qumran and the Scrolls, see chapter 6, n. 141. For variously organized catalogs of all the Scrolls, see DJD 39:29–114, 115–64, 204–28.

2. For a catalog of the biblical texts and their specific content, see Emanuel Tov, DJD 39:165–201. On the problem of a text that may relate to a source of Esther, see Sidnie White Crawford, "The Book of Esther," *NIB* 3:862–66.

3. "Apocrypha" denotes books or parts of books included in the Greek Bible but not in the Hebrew Bible; see Charles T. Fritsch, "Apocrypha," *IDB* 1:161–66; and George W. E. Nickelsburg, "Introduction to the Apocrypha," in Bernhard W. Anderson, ed., *The Books of the Bible* (2 vols.; New York: Scribner's, 1989) 2:3–11.

4. "Pseudepigrapha" are, technically, texts written under a spurious name (pseudonym), though the term is problematic; see George W. E. Nickelsburg, *Jewish Literature between the Bible and the Mishnah* (Philadelphia: Fortress Press, 1981) 6.

5. On the history of the canon see Lee McDonald and James Sanders, eds., *The Canon Debate* (Peabody, Mass.: Hendrickson, 2002); J.-M. Auwers and H. J. de Jonge, eds., *The Biblical Canons* (Colloquium Biblicum Lovaniense; BETL 163; Louvain: Louvain Univ. Press and Peeters, 2002).

6. For the triad, the "book (law) of Moses," "the prophets," and "David (the Psalms)," cf. 4QMMT$^d$ 7 10; Luke 24:44.

7. On these texts see Randal A. Argall, *1 Enoch and Sirach: A Comparative Literary and Conceptual Analysis of the Themes of Revelation, Creation, and Judgment* (SBLEJL 8; Atlanta: Scholars Press, 1995) 9–13.

8. A few MSS contain fragments of two books of the Pentateuch (Genesis–Exodus, Exodus–Leviticus, Leviticus–Numbers); see DJD 39:167–69.

9. On the *Enoch* MSS see George W. E. Nickelsburg, *1 Enoch 1: A Commentary on the Book of 1 Enoch, Chapters 1–36; 81–108* (Hermeneia; Minneapolis: Fortress Press, 2001) 9–10; for the Cave 4 copies of *Jubilees* see James C. VanderKam, DJD 13:1–185. That these texts had some sort of canonical status seems indicated by the commentaries on the story of the watchers (4Q180–181) and perhaps the Apocalypse of Weeks (4Q247); for citations of the texts see VanderKam, DJD 13:77. See also CD 16:2-4, which cites *Jubilees* as authoritative.

10. For the fragments of the Aramaic Levi document, see Michael E. Stone and Jonas C. Greenfield, DJD 22:1–72; for a discussion see idem, "Levi, Aramaic," in Lawrence H. Schiffman and James C. VanderKam, eds., *Encyclopedia of the Dead Sea Scrolls* (2 vols.; New York: Oxford Univ. Press, 2000) 1:486–88.

11. For the Tobit MSS see Joseph A. Fitzmyer, DJD 19:1–76.

12. On ben Sira and the rabbis see Patrick W. Skehan and Alexander A. Di Lella, *The Wisdom of Ben Sira* (AB 39; New York: Doubleday, 1987) 20.

13. For two comprehensive treatments of the text of the Hebrew Bible in light of the Qumran Scrolls, see Eugene C. Ulrich, *The Dead Sea Scrolls and the Origins of the Bible* (Studies in the Dead Sea Scrolls and Related Literature 2; Grand Rapids: Eerdmans, 1999); Emanuel Tov, *Textual Criticism of the Hebrew Bible* (2d rev. ed.; Minneapolis: Fortress Press, 2001). For a summary see Eugene Ulrich, "The Dead Sea Scrolls and the Biblical Text," in Peter W. Flint and James C. VanderKam, eds., *The Dead Sea Scrolls after Fifty Years: A Comprehensive Assessment* (2 vols.; Leiden: Brill, 1998) 1:79–100; Leonard J. Greenspoon, "The Dead Sea Scrolls and the Greek Bible," in ibid., 101–27.

14. For the Jeremiah texts with bibliographies of the scholarship, see Emanuel Tov, DJD 15:145–207.

15. For the Samuel texts see Frank M. Cross and Donald Parry, DJD 17 (forthcoming). For a discussion see Ulrich, *Dead Sea Scrolls,* 184–201.

16. On the Pentateuch at Qumran see Ulrich, "Dead Sea Scrolls," 86–89.

17. William H. Brownlee, *The Text of Habakkuk in the Ancient Commentary from Qumran* (SBLMS 11; Philadelphia: Society of Biblical Literature and Exegesis, 1959) 118–23. On the document see Maurya P. Horgan, *Pesharim: Qumran Interpretations of Biblical Books* (CBQMS 8; Washington, D.C.: Catholic Biblical Association, 1979) 10–55.

18. The notion of rewriting the Bible appears in its classical form in the seminal article by Renée Bloch, "Midrash," *DBSup* 5:1263–81; and it is pursued systematically by Geza Vermes, *Scripture and Tradition in Judaism* (SPB 4; Leiden: Brill, 1961), esp. 7–10 (sources provided by Daniel J. Harrington, private communication 7/12/02). Although I myself have used the term, and, as this section indicates, believe the traditions of the Greco-Roman period are rooted in the texts we call the Bible, it is less clear that the earliest of these were self-consciously interpretation of authoritative tradition.

19. For *1 Enoch* 6–11 as a rewritten form of Genesis, see Nickelsburg, *1 Enoch 1,* 166.

20. For a date in the fourth century B.C.E. see ibid., 169–71.

21. For an English translation of *Jubilees* see Orville S. Wintermute, *OTP* 2:52–142; for a critical text and translation see James C. VanderKam, *The Book of Jubilees* (2 vols.; CSCO 510-11; Louvain: Peeters, 1989). For studies on the work see James C. VanderKam, *Textual and Historical Studies in the Book of Jubilees* (HSM 14; Missoula, Mont.: Scholars Press, 1977); Nickelsburg, *Jewish Literature,* 73–80; idem, "The Bible Rewritten and Expanded," in Michael E. Stone, ed., *Jewish Writings of the Second Temple Period* (CRINT 2/2; Philadelphia: Fortress Press, 1984) 97–104.

22. For the Hebrew texts see VanderKam, DJD 13:1–185. On the versions see idem, *Textual and Historical Studies,* 1–18; idem, *Book of Jubilees,* 1:ix–xvi.

23. On these revisions and their rationale see Nickelsburg, "Bible Rewritten," 97–102.

24. Idem, *1 Enoch 1,* 71–76.

25. For polemics against the Gentiles see Nickelsburg, *Jewish Literature,* 78–79.

26. Philo, *Migr.* 1.176-86; *Abr.* 66-68; Josephus, *Ant.* 1.154-57 (§7:1); *LAB* 4.16—7:5; *Apoc. Abr.* 1–8; see George W. E. Nickelsburg, "Abraham the Convert: A Jewish Tradition and Its Use by the Apostle Paul," in Michael E. Stone and Theodore A. Bergren, eds., *Biblical Figures outside the Bible* (Harrisburg: Trinity Press International, 1998) 160–65.

27. The date of the *Testament of Job* is problematic; see John J. Collins, "Testaments," in Stone, *Jewish Writings,* 353.

28. For an introduction, text, translation, and commentary on 1QapGen ar see Joseph A. Fitzmyer, *The Genesis Apocryphon of Qumran Cave 1* (2d ed.; BibOr 18a; Rome: Biblical Institute Press, 1971). For an extensive rereading of previously indecipherable lines, see Matthew Morgenstern, Elisha Qimron, and Daniel Sivan, "The Hitherto Unpublished Columns of the Genesis Apocryphon," *AbrN* 33 (1995) 30–54. On some of its interpretive tendencies see Nickelsburg, *Jewish Literature,* 263–65; idem, "Patriarchs Who Worry about

Their Wives: A Haggadic Tendency in the Genesis Apocryphon," in Michael E. Stone and Esther G. Chazon, eds., *Biblical Perspectives: Early Use and Interpretation of the Bible in Light of the Dead Sea Scrolls; Proceedings of the First International Symposium of the Orion Center for the Study of the Dead Sea Scrolls and Associated Literature, 12–14 May, 1996* (STDJ 28; Leiden: Brill, 1998) 137–58; see also James C. VanderKam, "The Granddaughters and Grandsons of Noah," *RevQ* 16 (1994) 457–61.

29. For a translation of Pseudo-Philo see Daniel J. Harrington, *OTP* 2:297–377; for an introduction, critical text with French translation, commentary, and extensive bibliography see Daniel J. Harrington, Jacques Cazeaux, Charles Perrot, and Pierre-Maurice Bogaert, eds., *Pseudo-Philon: Les Antiquités Bibliques* (SC 229, 230; Paris: Cerf, 1976). On Pseudo-Philo's interpretation of the Bible see George W. E. Nickelsburg, "Good and Bad Leaders in Pseudo-Philo's *Liber Antiquitatum Biblicarum*," in John J. Collins and George W. E. Nickelsburg, eds., *Ideal Figures in Early Judaism* (SBLSCS 12; Chico, Calif.: Scholars Press, 1980) 49–65; Richard J. Murphy, *Pseudo-Philo* (New York: Oxford Univ. Press, 1993); Betsy Halpern-Amaru, "Portraits of Women in Pseudo-Philo's *Biblical Antiquities*," in Amy-Jill Levine, ed., *"Women Like This": New Perspectives on Jewish Women in the Greco-Roman World* (SBLEJL 1; Atlanta: Scholars Press, 1991) 83–106.

30. For bibliography on Josephus see the massive compilations of Louis H. Feldman, *Josephus and Modern Scholarship (1937–1980)* (Berlin: de Gruyter, 1984); idem, *Josephus: A Supplementary Bibliography* (New York: Garland, 1986). On interpretive tendencies in the *Antiquities* see idem, *Josephus and Modern Scholarship,* 120–91; Naomi G. Cohen, "Josephus and Scripture: Is Josephus' Treatment of the Scriptural Narrative Similar throughout the *Antiquities* I–XI?" *JQR* 54 (1963–64) 311–32; Harold W. Attridge, *The Interpretation of Biblical History in the Antiquitates Judaicae of Flavius Josephus* (HDR 7; Missoula, Mont.: Scholars Press, 1976); Shaye J. D. Cohen, *Josephus in Galilee and Rome: His Vita and Development as a Historian* (Columbia Studies in the Classical Tradition 8; Leiden: Brill, 1979) 232–42; Louis H. Feldman, *Studies in Josephus' Rewritten Bible* (JSJSup 58; Leiden: Brill, 1998).

31. For translations of the *Testament of Moses* see John Priest, *OTP* 1:919–34; and R. H. Charles and J. P. M. Sweet, *AOT,* 601–16; for a discussion see Nickelsburg, *Jewish Literature,* 80–83. For translations of the *Testament of Job* see Russell P. Spittler, *OTP* 2:839–68; and R. Thornhill, *AOT,* 617–48; for a text see Sebastian P. Brock, *Testamentum Iobi* (PVTG 2; Leiden: Brill, 1967); and for a text and translation see Robert A. Kraft, *The Testament of Job* (SBLTT 5, Pseudepigrapha Series 4; Missoula, Mont.; Scholars Press, 1974). For discussion see Spittler, *OTP* 2:829–38; Nickelsburg, *Jewish Literature,* 241–48; Collins, "Testaments," 349–55. On the *Testaments XII Patriarchs,* for a critical text see M. de Jonge, *The Testaments of the Twelve Patriarchs: A Critical Edition of the Greek Text* (PVTG 1.2; Leiden: Brill, 1978); for a commentary see H. W. Hollander and M. de Jonge, *The Testaments of the Twelve Patriarchs: A Commentary* (SVTP 8; Leiden: Brill, 1985). See also Robert Kugler, *The Testaments of the Twelve Patriarchs* (Sheffield: Sheffield Academic Press, 2001). On the *Books of Adam and Eve,* for a synopsis of the major texts see Gary A. Anderson and Michael E. Stone, eds., *A Synopsis of the Books of Adam and Eve* (2d ed.; SBLEJL 5; Atlanta: Scholars Press, 1999); for discussions see Nickelsburg, *Jewish Lit-*

*erature,* 253–57; idem, "Bible Rewritten," 110–18; Michael E. Stone, *A History of the Literature of Adam and Eve* (SBLEJL 3; Atlanta: Scholars Press, 1992).

32. On the *Martyrdom of Isaiah,* for translations of the *Ascension of Isaiah,* in which it is embedded, see Michael E. Knibb, *OTP* 2:156–76; and R. H. Charles and J. M. T. Barton, *AOT,* 775–812; for discussions see Knibb, *OTP* 2:143–55; Nickelsburg, *Jewish Literature,* 142–45. On *Joseph and Aseneth,* for translations of two different text forms see Christoph Burchard, *OTP* 2:177–47; and D. Cook, *AOT,* 468–508; for a detailed discussion that reflects previous scholarship see Ross Kraemer, *When Joseph Met Aseneth* (New York: Oxford Univ. Press, 1998). On the *Paraleipomena of Jeremiah,* for a translation see S. E. Robinson, *OTP* 2:414–25; for a text and translation see Robert A. Kraft and Ann-Elisabeth Purintun, *Para-leipomena Jeremiou* (SBLTT 1, Pseudepigrapha Series 1; Missoula, Mont.: Society of Biblical Literature, 1972). For discussions see Gerhard Delling, *Jüdische Lehre und Frömmigkeit in den Paraleipomena Jeremiae* (BZAW 100; Berlin: Töpelmann, 1967); Nickelsburg, *Jewish Literature,* 313–18; Jens Herzer, *Die Paralipomena Jeremiae: Studien zu Tradition und Redaktion einer Haggada des frühen Judentums* (TSAJ 43; Tübingen: Mohr/Siebeck, 1994).

33. Nickelsburg, *1 Enoch 1,* 195–96, 358–60.

34. That the compiler of the *Testaments of XII Patriarchs* employed older Jewish tradi-tions was recognized by R. H. Charles, *APOT* 2:290; see also James Kugel, *In Potiphar's House: The Interpretive Life of Biblical Texts* (San Francisco: HarperSan Francisco, 1990) 82–83. This fact is now borne out by some Qumran documents relating to Naphtali and Levi, although the relationship between these texts and the *Testaments* is far from clear. For these texts and bibliography see Stone and Greenfield, DJD 22:1–72; Michael E. Stone, DJD 22:73–82.

35. For the roots of "midrash" in the Bible itself, see Bloch, "Midrash," 1267–75. See also Michael Fishbane, "Inner Biblical Exegesis: Types and Strategies of Interpretation in Ancient Israel," in Geoffrey H. Hartman and Sanford Budick, eds., *Midrash and Literature* (New Haven: Yale Univ. Press, 1986) 20–37.

36. See George W. E. Nickelsburg, "The Nature and Function of Revelation in 1 Enoch, Jubilees, and Some Qumranic Documents," in Esther G. Chazon and Michael E. Stone, eds., *Pseudepigraphical Perspectives: The Apocrypha and Pseudepigrapha in Light of the Dead Sea Scrolls; Proceedings of the International Symposium of the Orion Center for the Study of the Dead Sea Scrolls and Associated Literature, 12–14 January, 1997* (STDJ 31; Leiden: Brill, 1999) 104.

37. For the quotations in Matthew see F. van Segbroeck, "Les citations d'accomplisse-ment dans l'Évangile selon saint Matthieu d'après trois ouvrages récents," in M. Didier, ed., *L'Évangile selon Matthieu: Rédaction et théologie* (BETL 29; Gembloux: Duculot, 1972) 107–30. On Hebrews see F. C. Synge, *Hebrews and the Scriptures* (London: SPCK, 1959).

38. On the *pesharim* see Horgan, *Pesharim*; Timothy H. Lim, *Pesharim* (Sheffield: Sheffield Academic Press, 2002).

39. Geza Vermes, *The Dead Sea Scrolls in English* (4th ed.; Sheffield: Sheffield Academic Press, 1995) 343, italics mine.

40. Nickelsburg, *Jewish Literature,* 80–81.

. George W. E. Nickelsburg, *Resurrection, Immortality, and Eternal Life in Intertestamental ism* (HTS 26; Cambridge: Harvard Univ. Press, 1972) 97–102.

42. Rodney A. Werline, *Penitential Prayer in Second Temple Judaism: The Development of a Religious Institution* (SBLEJL 13; Atlanta: Scholars Press, 1998) 45–59.

43. The literature on the Servant of the Lord is voluminous. For bibliography see Klaus Baltzer, *Deutero-Isaiah* (Hermeneia; Minneapolis: Fortress Press, 2001) 19, n. 105.

44. For the Servant in the NT see Joachim Jeremias, *"pais theou," TDNT* 5 (1967) 677–717; Morna D. Hooker, *Jesus and the Servant: The Influence of the Servant Concept of Deutero-Isaiah in the New Testament* (London: SPCK, 1959) 1–24.

45. See, e.g., Hooker (*Jesus and the Servant,* 154–59), who concludes that the Servant is absent from early Christian thought.

46. Hooker, however, does not discuss these passages in her book.

47. Christopher R. North, *The Suffering Servant in Deutero-Isaiah* (2d ed.; London: Oxford Univ. Press, 1956).

48. For Moses see Baltzer, *Deutero-Isaiah,* 20–22, 42–44, 396–98.

49. On the verb *śakal* see ibid., 394.

50. On the persecution by Antiochus Epiphanes and the Jewish responses to it, see Nickelsburg, *Jewish Literature,* 71–95.

51. On Wisdom 2 and 5 and its relationship to Isaiah 52–53, see Nickelsburg, *Resurrection,* 62–65.

52. On 2 Maccabees 7 and Isaiah 52–53 see ibid., 103–6.

53. Ibid., 118–20.

54. Ibid., 79–80.

55. Ibid., 76–78.

56. For the difficulties in interpreting notions of substitutionary death in 2 Maccabees 7 and 4 Maccabees as they possibly relate to Isaiah 53 or to Greco-Roman ideas, see Sam K. Williams, *Jesus' Death as Saving Event: The Background and Origin of a Concept* (HDR 2; Missoula, Mont.: Scholars Press, 1975) 96–202. See also David R. Seeley, *The Noble Death: Graeco-Roman Martyrology and Paul's Concept of Salvation* (JSOTSup 28; Sheffield: JSOT Press, 1990), esp. 87–99. The use of language found in Greco-Roman sources does not exclude Isaiah 52–53 as a trigger for this language, especially when other traces of Isaianic influence are evident in the text.

57. On the date of the parables see Nickelsburg, *Jewish Literature,* 221–23; for more detail on my judgment about the Son of Man traditions, see Nickelsburg, "Son of Man," *ABD* 6:138–49.

58. See the list of passages in Erwin Nestle and Kurt Aland, eds., *Novum Testamentum Graece* (26th ed.; Stuttgart: Deutsche Bibelgesellschaft, 1979) 739–73.

59. For examples, cf. Matt 1:22; 2:6, 15, 17-18, 23; 3:3||Mark 1:2-3||Luke 3:4-6; Matt 4:14-16; Matt 11:10||Luke 7:27; Matt 15:8-9||Mark 7:6-7; Matt 21:4-5; 21:13||Mark 11:17||Luke 19:46; Matt 21:42||Mark 12:10-11||Luke 20:17-18; Matt 22:43-44||Mark 12:36||Luke 20:42-43; Matt 26:31||Mark 14:27; John 12:38-40; 19:24, 36-37; Acts 1:20; 2:16-21, 25-28, 34-35; 4:35-36; 7:42-43, 48-50; 13:33-35, 41, 47; 15:15-18; 28:26-27; Rom 3:4, 10-18;

8:36; 9:25-26, 29, 33; 10:19-20; 11:8-10, 26-27; 14:11; 15:9-12, 21; 1 Cor 1:19; 2:9; 10:7; 2 Cor 6:2, 10-12; 9:9; Heb 1:5-12; 2:6-8, 12-13; 3:7-11, 15; 4:3, 5:5-6; 7:17, 21; 8:8-12; 10:16-17, 37-38.

60. As an example cf. Luke 1–2, whose infancy narratives plunge one into the world of biblical stories about special or miraculous births. See below, p. 208, n. 79.

61. See Bruce M. Metzger, *An Introduction to the Apocrypha* (New York: Oxford Univ. Press, 1957) 175–80. On the Wisdom of Solomon, however, see C. Larcher, *Études sur le livre de la Sagesse* (EBib; Paris: Gabalda, 1969) 11–63.

62. On the influence of Wisdom in the passion narratives, see Larcher, *Sagesse,* 11; George W. E. Nickelsburg, "The Genre and Function of the Markan Passion Narrative," *HTR* 73 (1980) 167–82; idem, "Passion Narratives," *ABD* 5:174.

63. On the Wisdom of Solomon and Paul see Larcher, *Sagesse,* 14–20.

64. Metzger, *Introduction,* 179–80.

65. George W. E. Nickelsburg, "Riches, the Rich, and God's Judgment in 1 Enoch 92–105 and the Gospel according to Luke," *NTS* 25 (1979) 324–44; idem, "Revisiting the Rich and the Poor in 1 Enoch 92–105 and the Gospel according to Luke," *SBLSP, 1998* (2 vols.; Atlanta: Scholars Press, 1998) 2:579–605.

66. Nickelsburg, "Son of Man," 142–46.

67. Johannes Theisohn, *Der Auserwählte Richter* (SUNT 12; Göttingen: Vandenhoeck & Ruprecht, 1975) 161–200.

68. Nickelsburg, *1 Enoch 1,* 87–100.

69. Hans Hübner, "New Testament, OT Quotations in the," *ABD* 4:1096–1104; Karen Jobes and Moises Silva, *Invitation to the Septuagint* (Grand Rapids: Baker, 2000) 189–93.

70. Nickelsburg, "Son of Man," 148.

71. On this motif in the *Testament of Job* see Collins, "Testaments," 350–51.

72. Cf. *Asc. Isa.* 5:1; *Par. Jer.* 9:22.

73. Hermann L. Strack and Paul Billerbeck, *Kommentar zum Neuen Testament aus Talmud und Midrasch* (5 vols.; Munich: Beck, 1922–28).

74. For an essay that was wise before its time, see Samuel Sandmel, "Parallelomania," *JBL* 81 (1962) 1–13. Interestingly, he cites an 1830 critique of parallels between Romans 1 and the Wisdom of Solomon, on which, however, see above, n. 63.

75. On Jacob Neusner's pioneering work in this regard see Anthony J. Saldarini, "Reconstructions of Rabbinic Judaism," in Robert A. Kraft and George W. E. Nickels- burg, eds., *Early Judaism and Its Modern Interpreters* (Philadelphia: Fortress Press; Atlanta: Scholars Press, 1986) 459.

76. For example, see above, n. 34.

77. Strack and Billerbeck, *Kommentar,* 2:604–5; F. J. Foakes Jackson and Kirsopp Lake, *The Beginnings of Christianity: Part 1, The Acts of the Apostles* (5 vols.; reprint Grand Rapids: Baker, 1979) 4:17; 5:115–16; Ernst Haenchen, *The Acts of the Apostles: A Commentary,* trans. B. Noble, G. Shinn, and R. McL. Wilson (Philadelphia: Westminster, 1971) 174.

78. C. K. Barrett, *A Critical and Exegetical Commentary on the Acts of the Apostles* (2 vols.; ICC; Edinburgh: T & T Clark, 1994) 1:111; Luke T. Johnson, *The Acts of the Apostles* (SP 5; Col- legeville, Minn.: Liturgical Press, 1992) 46.

79. See Raymond E. Brown, *The Birth of the Messiah* (Garden City, N.Y.: Doubleday, 1977); George M. Soares Prabhu, *The Formula Quotations in the Infancy Narrative of Matthew: An Inquiry into Tradition History of Mt 1–2* (AnBib 63; Rome: Biblical Institute Press, 1976) 288–92; Beverly A. Bow, "The Story of Jesus' Birth: A Pagan and Jewish Affair" (Ph.D. diss., University of Iowa, 1995) 143–65, 193–393.

80. Moses Hadas, *The Third and Fourth Books of Maccabees* (JAL; New York: Harper, 1953) 127–35.

81. Compare the infancy narratives and the passion narratives with their Jewish predecessors; see above, p. 207, nn. 60, 62.

82. On the Temple Scroll see Florentino García Martínez, "Temple Scroll," in Schiffman and VanderKam, eds., *Encyclopedia,* 2:927–33; on *Jubilees* see above, p. 205, n. 36.

## 2. Torah and the Righteous Life

1. See Charlotte Klein, *Anti-Judaism in Christian Theology* (Philadelphia: Fortress Press, 1978) 16, 41–43.

2. For the ongoing emphasis on this tradition, see ibid., 92–106. A striking exception to this appears in Bach's *St. Matthew Passion,* where the interpolations into the biblical narrative focus on humanity's (and especially the Christian's) responsibility for Jesus' death and leave without comment or emphasis the Gospel's references to the Jews and their leaders.

3. For two landmark protests against using Romans and Galatians as the hermeneutical key to Paul's thought, see Albert Schweitzer, *The Mysticism of Paul the Apostle* (New York: Macmillan, 1931); Krister Stendahl, *Paul among Jews and Gentiles and Other Essays* (Philadelphia: Fortress Press, 1976).

4. See the discussion by Klein, *Anti-Judaism,* and the review article by George W. E. Nickelsburg, *RelSRev* 4 (1978) 161–68. For an example of Luther's easy transition from the historical Galatian Judaizers to the papists, see Jaroslav Pelikan and Helmut T. Lehmann, eds., *Luther's Works,* 55 vols. (Philadelphia: Fortress Press; St. Louis: Concordia, 1955–86) 26:23–26.

5. Klein, *Anti-Judaism,* 39–66. For some modern examples of the theological aspects of this anti-Judaism, see the comments of Hermann Lichtenberger, in Jacob Neusner and Alan J. Avery-Peck, eds., *George W. E. Nickelsburg in Perspective: An Ongoing Dialogue of Learning* (JSJSup 80:2; Leiden: Brill, 2003) 714–20.

6. Adolf von Harnack, *The Origin of the New Testament and the Most Important Consequences of the New Creation* (London: Williams & Norgate, 1925) 125–30.

7. This tendency runs through the passion narratives of the four Gospels. It is especially evident in John 18–19. The Synoptic Gospels focus more on the responsibility of the Jewish leaders, but cf. Matt 27:25, on which see below, p. 218, n. 79.

8. George Foot Moore, "Christian Writers on Judaism," *HTR* 14 (1921) 197–54; Klein, *Anti-Judaism,* 39–66.

9. This is not to say that theological anti-Judaism was synonymous with racist anti-Semitism, or that such anti-Judaism caused the Holocaust, only that its portrayal of

Judaism as an inferior religion may have helped to create a climate in which broader assaults against Jews were tolerated.

10. George E. Mendenhall, *Law and Covenant in Israel and the Ancient Near East* (Pittsburgh: Biblical Colloquium, 1955). Reprinted from *BA* 17 (1954) 26–46, 49–76; Klaus Baltzer, *The Covenant Formulary in Old Testament, Jewish, and Early Christian Writings* (Philadelphia: Fortress Press, 1971) 19–38. Thus also E. P. Sanders, *Paul and Palestinian Judaism* (Philadelphia: Fortress Press, 1977), though I believe that his scheme of "covenantal nomism" oversimplified the complex evidence. The connection between God's act and the covenant obligations is especially clear and pithy in Exod 20:2-17.

11. Cf., e.g., Jeremiah 3; Ezekiel 16; Hosea 2; 11:1.

12. C. H. Dodd, *The Bible and the Greeks* (London: Dodder & Stoughton, 1954) 25–41.

13. Ludwig Koehler, Walter Baumgartner, Johann Jakob Stamm, and M. E. J. Richardson, *The Hebrew and Aramaic Lexicon of the Old Testament* (5 vols.; Leiden: Brill, 1994–2000) 4:1710–12.

14. "Former prophets" is the Jewish designation for the first part of the second section of the tripartite canon; see Nahum Sarna, "Bible: The Canon, Texts, Editions," *EncJud* 4:820–22. "Deuteronomistic History" is a modern scholarly term designating Deuteronomy through 2 Kings; see Steven L. McKenzie, "Deuteronomistic History," *ABD* 2:160–68.

15. See G. Ernest Wright, "The Lawsuit of God: A Form-Critical Study of Deuteronomy 32," in Bernard W. Anderson and Walter Harrelson, eds., *Israel's Prophetic Heritage: Essays in Honor of James Muilenburg* (New York: Harper, 1962) 26–67. On social justice see especially Amos and Micah. On Moses in Jeremiah see William Holladay, *Jeremiah 2: A Commentary on the Book of the Prophet Jeremiah Chapters 26–52* (Hermeneia; Minneapolis: Fortress Press, 1989) 38–39. On the Torah and Moses in Second Isaiah see Klaus Baltzer, *Deutero-Isaiah: A Commentary on Isaiah 40–55* (Hermeneia; Minneapolis: Fortress Press, 2001) 42–44. Explicit reference to the "Torah" is relatively rare in the prophets. The situation is perhaps analogous to Paul's rare reference to the sayings of Jesus; see below, p. 212, n. 80.

16. Cf., e.g., Isa 44:22; Jer 3:1, 12, 22; 4:1; Hos 14:1; Mal 3:7.

17. Ralph W. Klein, "Chronicles, Books of 1-2," *ABD* 1:999–1001.

18. Rodney A. Werline, *Penitential Prayer in Second Temple Judaism: The Development of a Religious Institution* (SBLEJL 13; Atlanta: Scholars Press, 1998) 45–59.

19. Note the chapter headings in James L. Crenshaw, *Old Testament Wisdom: An Introduction* (rev. ed.; Louisville: Westminster John Knox, 1998): "The Pursuit of Knowledge," "The Search for Divine Presence," "The Chasing after Meaning," "The Quest for Survival," "The Widening Hunt."

20. See ibid., 205–26. See also the essays collected in idem, ed., *Studies in Ancient Israelite Wisdom* (New York: KTAV, 1976) 63–171. For a summary see Roland E. Murphy, "Wisdom in the Old Testament," *ABD* 6:928–30.

21. Sirach 24 and Bar 3:9—4:4 attest the identification of Wisdom with Mosaic Torah in the second century B.C.E. Cf. also Tobit, which is a bit earlier. However, the Qumran *Musar leMevin* indicates that this identification was not universal (see p. 41).

22. Marvin Pope, *Job* (AB 15; Garden City, N.Y.: Doubleday, 1965) lxxiii–lxxxiv.

23. Cf., e.g., Psalms 22 and 69.

24. On Ecclesiastes see Michael V. Fox, *Qohelet and His Contradictions* (JSOTSup 71; Sheffield: Almond Press, 1989) 123–50.

25. *1 Enoch,* Daniel, *2 Baruch, 3 Baruch, 4 Ezra, Apocalypse of Abraham,* Revelation, *Apocryphon of John.*

26. This interpretation is based on the abrupt appearance of Abraham's call in Gen 12:1-3. By contrast, cf. *Jubilees* 11–12; *LAB* 6; *Apocalypse of Abraham* 1–9.

27. On grace in the Hebrew Bible see John S. Kselman, "Grace: Old Testament," *ABD* 2:1084–86.

28. This is the case, for example, with David. Conversely, the guilt of Manasseh's sin remains, perhaps because one looked for a specific explanation for the destruction of Jerusalem and the exile. The Prayer of Manasseh in the Apocrypha is an exception to an otherwise uniform tradition. On this text see George W. E. Nickelsburg in John Barton and John Muddiman, eds., *The Oxford Bible Commentary* (Oxford: Oxford Univ. Press, 2001) 770–73.

29. George W. E. Nickelsburg, *Jewish Literature between the Bible and the Mishnah* (Philadelphia: Fortress Press, 1981) 80–94 (*Testament of Moses* and Daniel), 114–23 (1–2 Maccabees).

30. On the events of this period and the presence of Hellenism in Palestine see Victor Tcherikover, *Hellenistic Civilization and the Jews* (Philadelphia: Jewish Publication Society, 1971) 90–174; Martin Hengel, *Judaism and Hellenism* (2 vols.; Philadelphia: Fortress Press, 1974) 1:1–106.

31. Norman Gottwald, "War, Holy," *IDBSup,* 942–44.

32. Cf. 2 Maccabees 7; *Martyrdom of Isaiah;* 4 Maccabees.

33. Nickelsburg, *Jewish Literature,* 30–34.

34. Ibid., 105–8. In the story of *Joseph and Aseneth* (chap. 12), the Egyptian priest's daughter utters a long prayer of repentance that expresses her trust that the God of Israel will reward her radical action of abandoning her idols and unclean food. The date and origin (Jewish or Christian) of this story are disputed, but the motif is noteworthy.

35. According to *Jub.* 17:17-18, faith(fulness) is reflected in all of Abraham's actions. See also at Qumran, where faith in the Teacher of Righteousness is tied to Torah obedience (1QpHab 7:16—8:3).

36. On Sirach 24 see briefly Nickelsburg, *Jewish Literature,* 59–62. On Baruch 4 see ibid., 111–12.

37. On Tobit as a testament see ibid., 31–32.

38. On *Testaments XII Patriarchs* see H. W. Hollander and M. de Jonge, *The Testaments of the Twelve Patriarchs: A Commentary* (SVTP 8; Leiden: Brill, 1985) 41–47. The classic work is R. Eppel, *Le piétisme juif dans les Testaments des Douze Patriarchs* (Paris: Imprimerie Alsacienne, 1930). On *Testament of Job* see Collins, "Testaments," in Michael E. Stone, ed., *Jewish Writings of the Second Temple Period* (CRINT 2/2; Assen: Van Gorcum; Philadelphia: Fortress Press, 1984) 350–51. On both texts see Nickelsburg, *Jewish Literature,* 232–47.

39. For the testamentary aspects of *1 Enoch* see George W. E. Nickelsburg, *1 Enoch 1: A Commentary on the Book of 1 Enoch Chapters 1–36; 81–108* (Hermeneia: Minneapolis: Fortress Press, 2001) 25–26. On the relationship between the epistle and Enoch's journeys, see ibid., 422–23. For explicit examples of Enoch's testamentary ethical instruction, see 81:1—82:3; 91; 94:1-2.

40. George W. E. Nickelsburg, *Resurrection, Immortality, and Eternal Life in Intertestamental Judaism* (HTS 26; Cambridge: Harvard Univ. Press, 1972) 156–59.

41. Ibid., 61–62.

42. For the text and a translation, with a substantial introduction, copious notes, and a bibliography, see John Strugnell and Daniel J. Harrington, DJD 34:1–495.

43. Ibid., 34–35.

44. Ibid., 27.

45. Nickelsburg, *1 Enoch 1,* 58–59.

46. Ibid., 454–56.

47. Ibid., 50–51, 58–59.

48. See, e.g., Joachim Jeremias, *The Parables of Jesus* (rev. ed.; New York: Scribner's, 1963) 139.

49. In Luke cf. 5:29-32; 7:34-50; 14:15-24; 15:1-32; 18:9-14; 19:1-10.

50. Nickelsburg, *Jewish Literature,* 31–32.

51. *Pss. Sol.* 2:36(40); 3:8(10); 4:6(7), 8(9); 8:23(28), 34(40); 9:3(6); 12:4(5), 6(7); 13:10(9), 12(11); 14:3(2), 10(7); 15:3(5), 7(9).

52. *Pss. Sol.* 4:25(28); 6:5(9); 10:3(4); 14:1.

53. *Pss. Sol.* 2:33(37); 3:12(16); 4:21(24), 23(25); 5:18(21); 12:4; 13:12(11); 15:13(15).

54. Deut 6:2, 5; 10:20, 11:1; 13:3-4; 30:6.

55. On the problems of dating the rabbinic texts see Anthony J. Saldarini, "Reconstructions of Rabbinic Judaism," in Robert A. Kraft and George W. E. Nickelsburg, eds., *Early Judaism and Its Modern Interpreters* (Philadelphia: Fortress Press, 1986) 438–51.

56. For some examples see Exodus 21–23.

57. Klein, *Anti-Judaism,* 39–66.

58. On the Hebrew verb *darash* to denote the careful study of texts, see Werline, *Penitential Prayer,* 111–12.

59. For examples see Nickelsburg, *Jewish Literature,* 74–75; idem, "The Bible Rewritten and Expanded," in Michael E. Stone, ed., *Jewish Writings of the Second Temple Period* (CRINT 2/2; Assen: Van Gorcum; Philadelphia: Fortress Press, 1984) 97–98.

60. Nickelsburg, *1 Enoch 1,* 230–31, 271–72.

61. *1 En.* 98:9—99:10; see ibid., 486–89.

62. On the laws in the Damascus Document see Joseph M. Baumgarten, DJD 18:11–22, and the bibliography on pp. 16–18. For other halakic material in the Scrolls, see DJD 10 and 35. See also the discussion by Hannah K. Harrington, "Biblical Law at Qumran," in Peter W. Flint and James C. VanderKam, eds., *The Dead Sea Scrolls after Fifty Years: A Comprehensive Assessment* (2 vols.; Leiden: Brill, 1998) 1:160–85; Sarianna Metso, "Constitutional Rules at Qumran," in ibid., 1:186–210.

63. See *Pss. Sol.* 2:3; 8:11-12(12-13).

64. For this term see, e.g., 4QpIsa<sup>c</sup> 2:10-11; 4QpNah 2:2, 4-5; 3:6-7; CD 1:18, which interprets Isa 30:10.

65. This same scheme of human action and divine recompense appears in *1 Enoch* 92–105, even though this text does not focus on the notion of covenant; see Nickelsburg, *1 Enoch 1,* 50.

66. Translation by Florentino García Martínez and Eibert J. C. Tigchelaar, eds., *The Dead Sea Scrolls: Study Edition* (2 vols.; Leiden: Brill, 1997) 97, 99. The poetic format is my own.

67. See Theodore Bachmann, ed., *Luther's Works,* 55 vols. (Philadelphia: Fortress Press; St. Louis: Concordia, 1955–86) 35:362, 395–97.

68. David R. Catchpole, "The Poor on Earth and the Son of Man in Heaven: A Reappraisal of Matthew xxv.31-46," *BJRL* 61 (1979) 378–83.

69. George W. E. Nickelsburg, "The Incarnation: Paul's Solution to the Universal Human Predicament," in Birger A. Pearson, ed., *The Future of Early Christianity: Essays in Honor of Helmut Koester* (Minneapolis: Fortress Press, 1991) 349–51.

70. For Paul's halakah, especially in 1 Corinthians, see Peter J. Tomson, *Paul and the Jewish Law* (CRINT 3/1; Assen: Van Gorcum; Philadelphia: Fortress Press, 1990) 55–281.

71. Stendahl, *Paul,* 27–30.

72. Nickelsburg, "Incarnation," 349–51.

73. Ibid., 351–54.

74. Charles E. Carlston, "The Things That Defile (Mark VI.14) and the Law in Matthew and Mark," *NTS* 15 (1968–69) 91–96. Jesper Svartik, *Mark and Mission: Mk 7:1-23 in Its Narrative and Historical Context* (Lund: Almqvist & Wiksell, 2000).

75. Hollander and de Jonge, *Testaments,* 41–47; Nickelsburg, *Jewish Literature,* 232–41; cf. also *Testament of Job,* on which see Collins, "Testaments," 350–51.

76. See the discussion of "Matthew's Torah" by Anthony J. Saldarini, *Matthew's Christian-Jewish Community* (Chicago: Univ. of Chicago Press, 1994) 124–64.

77. Carlston, "Things that Defile," 75–90.

78. On the verb "seek, search," see Werline, *Penitential Prayer,* 111–12. Cf. 1 Macc 2:29.

79. Cf., e.g., Tob 4:7-11; 12:8-10; Sir 11:18-20; 13:24—14:10. See also George W. E. Nickelsburg, "Riches, the Rich, and God's Judgment in 1 Enoch 92–105 and the Gospel according to Luke," *NTS* 25 (1979) 324–44; and the response to this article by John S. Kloppenborg in Neusner and Avery-Peck, eds., *Perspective,* 2:572–85.

80. See David L. Dungan, *The Sayings of Jesus in the Churches of Paul* (Philadelphia: Fortress Press, 1971). See above, p. 209, n. 15.

81. For parallels to 1 Thess 5:1-11, cf. Mark 13:17, 32-37; Luke 12:35-40; 21:34-36.

82. On Paul and the Wisdom of Solomon see C. Larcher, *Études sur le livre de la Sagesse* (EBib; Paris: Gabalda, 1969) 14–20.

## 3. God's Activity in Behalf of Humanity

1. For occurrences of the root *yasha',* cf., e.g., Exod 14:13; 15:2; Ps 74:12 (the exodus); Judg 15:18; 1 Sam 14:45; 2 Sam 15:10; Ps 3:8; 69:1 (deliverance from other enemies); Isa

38:20 (healing from sickness); Ps 51:12 (sin). In much greater detail see Georg Fohrer, "*sōzō*, etc.," *TDNT* 8 (1971) 970–80.

2. Gerhard von Rad, *Genesis: A Commentary* (rev. ed.; OTL; Philadelphia: Westminster, 1972) 50.

3. George W. E. Nickelsburg, *Resurrection, Immortality, and Eternal Life in Intertestamental Judaism* (HTS 26; Cambridge: Harvard Univ. Press, 1972) 15.

4. Idem, *1 Enoch 1: A Commentary on the Book of 1 Enoch Chapters 1–36; 81–108* (Hermeneia; Minneapolis: Fortress Press, 2001) 165–68.

5. Ibid., 171–72, 190–93.

6. Ibid., 271–72.

7. Gary A. Anderson, "Sacrifice and Sacrificial Offerings," *ABD* 5:878–81.

8. On the prophetic critique of the cult, see ibid., 881–82. For specific passages that juxtapose this critique with a call for social justice, cf. 1 Sam 15:22-23; Isa 1:11-14; Amos 5:21-23; Mic 6:6-9; cf. also Jer 7:21-23. On prophetic notions of repentance as "return," see E. Würthwein, "*metanoieō, metanoia*," *TDNT* 4 (1967) 980–89.

9. Rodney A. Werline, *Penitential Prayer in Second Temple Judaism: The Development of a Religious Institution* (SBLEJL 13; Atlanta: Scholars Press, 1998) 45–59.

10. Friedrich Hauck and Rudolf Meyer, "*katharos, katharizō*," *TDNT* 3 (1965) 414, 416–22. For *exaleiphō, apaleiphō/machah* with sin or wrongdoing as its object, cf. Ps 51:3 (50:3 Gk.); 51:9 (50:11 Gk.); Isa 43:25; 44:22; Sir 40:12; 46:20.

11. On 2 Maccabees see George W. E. Nickelsburg, *Jewish Literature between the Bible and the Mishnah* (Philadelphia: Fortress Press, 1981) 118–20. The Deuteronomic scheme is less explicit in 4 Maccabees, but beginning with chap. 4, the story line is roughly the same as in 2 Maccabees.

12. Ibid., 119–20.

13. See above, p. 206, n. 56.

14. On ben Sira and the priesthood and temple, see H. Stadelmann, *Ben Sira als Schrift-gelehrter: Eine Untersuchung zum Berufsbild des vor-makkabäischen Sofer unter Berücksichtigung seines Ver-hältnisses zu Priester-, Propheten-, und Weisheitslehrtum* (WUNT 2/6; Tübingen: Mohr/Siebeck, 1980); Saul Olyan, "Ben Sira's Relationship to the Priesthood," *HTR* 80 (1987) 261–86; Benjamin G. Wright III, "Putting the Puzzle Together: Some Suggestions concerning the Social Location of the Wisdom of ben Sira," *SBLSP* 35 (1996) 144–46. For specific passages, see Sir 7:29-31; 35:4-11 (32:6-13 Gk.); 45:16 on priest and cult; and 3:3, 30; 34:18—35:3 (31:21—32:5) on deeds of charity as atonement. For a later text that employs this theology with respect to the destruction of the Second Temple, see the story about Rabban Yohanan ben Zakkai in *Abot Rab. N.* 4.5:2.

15. Werline, *Penitential Prayer*, 51–58.

16. On these prayers see ibid., 65–108, 168–79.

17. On the Prayer of Manasseh and its narrative context, see George W. E. Nickelsburg in John Barton and John Muddiman, eds., *The Oxford Bible Commentary* (Oxford: Oxford Univ. Press, 2001) 770–71.

18. On this expression see Nickelsburg, *Resurrection*, 29.

19. John Kampen, "The Significance of the Temple in the Manuscripts of the Damascus Document," in Robert A. Kugler and Eileen M. Schuller, eds., *The Dead Sea Scrolls at Fifty* (SBLEJL 15; Atlanta: Scholars Press, 1999) 185–97. On the possible association of ideas about a heavenly temple and angelic priests with a concern about a defunct temple cult in Jerusalem, see John Strugnell, "The Angelic Liturgy at Qumran," *Congress Volume, Oxford, 1959* (VTSup 7; Leiden: Brill, 1960) 335.

20. See above, p. 212, n. 1.

21. Nickelsburg, *Jewish Literature,* 80–83, 87–90.

22. Ibid., 119–20; and in more detail, idem, *Resurrection,* 97–102.

23. Idem, *1 Enoch 1,* 400–401.

24. On this text see Philip R. Davies, "War of the Sons of Light against the Sons of Darkness," in Lawrence H. Schiffman and James C. VanderKam, eds., *Encyclopedia of the Dead Sea Scrolls* (2 vols.; Oxford: Oxford Univ. Press, 2000) 2:965–68. See also Lester L. Grabbe, "Eschatological Warfare," in ibid., 2:963–65.

25. Isa 38:20.

26. Deut 28:59-60; 29:22-28.

27. The former is presumed in Psalm 38. The classic example of the latter is the book of Job.

28. 2 Kings 5, or, more radically, 1 Kings 17; 2 Kings 4. See also Isa 38:21.

29. See my suggestion in George W. E. Nickelsburg, "Tobit," in James L. Mays, ed., *The HarperCollins Bible Commentary* (San Francisco: HarperSan Francisco, 2000) 722.

30. Suggested to me by Norman Petersen in a comment on my manuscript.

31. For parallels to other healing stories see the edition of John J. Collins, DJD 22:83–93, esp. 90–91.

32. See Nickelsburg, *1 Enoch 1,* 37–42.

33. Ibid., 50–51.

34. On the genre "apocalypse" see John J. Collins, "The Jewish Apocalypses," in idem, ed., *Apocalypses: The Morphology of a Genre* (Semeia 14; Missoula, Mont.: Scholars Press, 1979) 21–59.

35. Nickelsburg, *1 Enoch 1,* 59–60.

36. For a comparison of *1 Enoch* with the Wisdom of Joshua ben Sira, see Randal A. Argall, *1 Enoch and Sirach: A Comparative Literary and Conceptual Analysis of the Themes of Revelation, Creation, and Judgment* (SBLEJL 8; Atlanta: Scholars Press, 1995).

37. Nickelsburg, *1 Enoch 1,* 68–70.

38. Idem, "The Nature and Function of Revelation in 1 Enoch, Jubilees, and Some Qumranic Documents," in Esther G. Chazon and Michael E. Stone, eds., *Pseudepigraphical Perspectives: The Apocrypha and Pseudepigrapha in Light of the Dead Sea Scrolls, Proceedings of the International Symposium of the Orion Center for the Study of the Dead Sea Scrolls and Associated Literature, 12–14 January 1997* (STDJ 31; Leiden: Brill, 1999) 107–14. See also idem, "Religious Exclusivism: A Worldview Governing Some Texts Found at Qumran," in Michael Becker and Wolfgang Fenske, eds., *Das Ende der Tage und die Gegenwart des Heils: Begegnungen mit dem Neuen*

*Testament und seiner Umwelt: Festschrift für Heinz-Wolfgang Kuhn zum 65. Geburtstag* (Leiden: Brill, 1999) 45–67.

39. This was first noted by W. D. Davies, "Knowledge in the Dead Sea Scrolls and Matthew 11:25-30," *HTR* 46 (1953) 113–39, reprinted in idem, *Christian Origins and Judaism* (Philadelphia: Westminster, 1962); and Jacob Licht, "The Doctrine of the Thanksgiving Scroll, 1 and 2," *IEJ* 6 (1956) 1–13, 89–101.

40. See, e.g., Wilhelm Bousset and Hugo Gressmann, *Die Religion des Judentums im späthellenistischen Zeitalter* (3d ed.; Tübingen: Mohr/Siebeck, 1926) 304–7.

41. See Nickelsburg, *Jewish Literature,* 165–69.

42. John J. Collins, "A Symbol of Otherness: Circumcision and Salvation in the First Century," in Jacob Neusner and Ernest D. Frerichs, eds., *"To See Ourselves as Others See Us": Christians, Jews, "Others" in Late Antiquity* (Scholars Press Studies in the Humanities; Chico, Calif.: Scholars Press, 1985) 164–70.

43. This notion is built into the structure of these tales; see George W. E. Nickelsburg, "Stories of Biblical and Early Post-Biblical Times," in Michael E. Stone, ed., *Jewish Writings of the Second Temple Period* (CRINT 2/2; Assen: Van Gorcum; Philadelphia: Fortress Press, 1984) 33–37.

44. Nickelsburg, *Jewish Literature,* 30–38. Cf. also *Joseph and Aseneth,* a text whose Jewish or Christian provenance is disputed; see Ross Kraemer, *When Joseph Met Aseneth* (New York: Oxford Univ. Press, 1998). If it is Jewish, it has special significance for our topic. In effect, it offers an explanation for Joseph's marriage to the daughter of an Egyptian priest. Aseneth, perceiving that Joseph is "a son of God," converts from idolatry and is transformed from death to immortality. In imagery remarkably close to the Abraham stories, she is described as the matriarch of all future proselytes.

45. See George W. E. Nickelsburg, "The Bible Rewritten and Expanded," in Stone, ed., *Jewish Writings,* 103.

46. Nickelsburg, *Jewish Literature,* 35–38.

47. Ibid., 26–28, 294–99.

48. See also *Joseph and Aseneth,* where the heroine expects that her conversion from idolatry will cause her to be pursued by the devil, who is the power behind her idols (12:9-10).

49. Rejection of idols and idolatry is standard fare in the Pauline corpus. Like the authors of the Jewish texts, he adopts two conflicting lines of reasoning. In justifying the Christian freedom to eat food sacrificed to idols, he claims that they are nothing (1 Cor 8:4), an assertion paralleled in the Letter of Jeremiah, Bel and the Dragon, and the *Apocalypse of Abraham.* A few chapters later, he warns that association with an idolatrous cult brings one into dangerous proximity to a demonic force field (1 Cor 10:20-22). This assertion parallels the narrative in the *Testament of Job.* The contradiction between the two positions should not be taken too seriously since both appear in a single passage in *1 En.* 99:6-9. According to 1 Thess 1:9-10, Paul warned the Thessalonians that idolatry would bring on God's wrath at the final judgment.

50. Nickelsburg, "Exclusivism," 46–59.

51. As examples of the influence of Isaiah 52–53 in the NT, I cite Mark 8:31; 9:31; 10:45; Phil 2:6-11; 1 Pet 2:21-25, in addition to Rom 4:24-25, listed below. In keeping with some Jewish usage of the Isaianic passage, several of these texts posit not the idea of substitutionary death but the scheme of persecution and vindication/exaltation. On the Markan passion predictions see Nickelsburg, "Son of Man." See above, however, p. 206, n. 44.

52. For a detailed discussion see Sam K. Williams, *Jesus' Death as Saving Event: The Background and Origin of a Concept* (HDR 2; Missoula, Mont.: Scholars Press, 1975) 5–56.

53. I see Isaiah 53 behind this text because of the text's pattern of persecution and vindication, its use of Isaianic verbs (the verb *paradidōmi* and the *dikai*- root), and the reference to death in behalf of the sins of others.

54. Cf. Mark 8:31-34; Phil 2:5; Heb 12:1-5; 1 Pet 2:21.

55. Note, however, how the motif is used in Col 1:24.

56. For a survey of these passages, with translation and notes, see George W. E. Nickelsburg and Michael E. Stone, *Faith and Piety in Early Judaism* (Philadelphia: Fortress Press, 1983) 65–73, 77–84.

57. Hebrews' critique of the priesthood relates to its temporary character and not to some flaw in its execution of its biblically ordained functions.

58. For some possibilities see George W. E. Nickelsburg, "The Genre and Function of the Markan Passion Narrative," *HTR* 73 (1980) 153–84; idem, "Enoch, Levi, and Peter: Recipients of Revelation in Upper Galilee," *JBL* 100 (1981) 575–600.

59. See, e.g., *1 En.* 90:28-30 (on which see Nickelsburg, *1 Enoch 1*, 404–5); the Qumran "New Jerusalem Text"; and the Qumran Temple Scroll. While all of the aforementioned NT texts date in their present form from after the destruction of the temple in 70 C.E., and some of them reflect that event, their devaluation of the temple is less than explicit.

60. For Lukan occurrences of *sōzō* without Synoptic parallels, cf. Luke 7:50; 8:12, 36, 50; 13:23; 17:19; 19:10; cf. also Acts 2:21, 40, 47; 4:9, 12; 11:14; 15:1, 11; 16:30, 31; 19:9; 27:20, 31. On the lost and found without Synoptic parallels, cf. Luke 15:6, 8, 9, 24, 32.

61. George W. E. Nickelsburg, "The Incarnation: Paul's Solution to the Universal Human Predicament," in Birger A. Pearson, ed., *The Future of Early Christianity: Essays in Honor of Helmut Koester* (Minneapolis: Fortress Press, 1991) 348–57. Paul's pessimism about the Law's effectiveness to catalyze obedience is also shared by the author of *4 Ezra* 3:20-22.

62. Cf. Gal 4:4-5 and Phil 2:7, where "slave" designates the human condition; see Norman R. Petersen, *Rediscovering Paul: Philemon and the Sociology of Paul's Narrative World* (Philadelphia: Fortress Press, 1985) 24.

63. On the genre of the passion narrative see Nickelsburg, "Genre"; idem, "Passion Narratives," *ABD* 5:172–77. The story of Stephen's martyrdom contains all the major generic components: cause and conspiracy (6:8-11); trial 6:12—7:53); condemnation (7:54); vindication and exaltation (of Jesus) (6:15 [7:55-56]); confession that Jesus is the Son of God (9:20); cf. also 9:20-21 with Wis 5:4-5.

64. See Nickelsburg, "Passion Narratives."

65. A number of Jewish apocalypses are set in a time of persecution or oppression (parts of *1 Enoch,* Daniel) or suffering (*2 Baruch, 3 Baruch, 4 Ezra, Apocalypse of Abraham*). The motif of endurance (Rev 1:9; 2:2, 3, 19; 3:10; 13:10; 14:12), however, also occurs in Hellenistic Jewish literature, where it describes a quality of the "spiritual athlete"; cf., e.g., 4 Maccabees and *Testament of Job*; see Nickelsburg, *Jewish Literature,* 223–24, 247–48. For further diversity, cf. *Jub.* 17:15—19:8, on which see Nickelsburg, *Jewish Literature,* 75–76. Cf. further the *Testament of Joseph* (ibid., 240) and Heb 11:1—12:2.

66. See the margin of Erwin Nestle and Kurt Aland, eds., *Novum Testamentum Graece* (26th ed.; Stuttgart: Deutsche Bibelgesellschaft, 1979) ad loc. See also Nickelsburg, "Son of Man."

67. For the pervasiveness of satanic activity in Mark see James M. Robinson, *The Problem of History in Mark* (SBT 1/21; London: SCM, 1957) 26–53. Norman Petersen notes (in a comment on the manuscript) that in Matthew and Luke the healings are fulfillments of prophecy and in John are related to his claim to being a prophet like Moses and are signs of who he is. See also Heinz Joachim Held, "Matthew as Interpreter of the Miracle Stories," in Günther Bornkamm, Gerhard Barth, and Heinz Joachim Held, *Tradition and Interpretation in Matthew* (NTL; Philadelphia: Westminster, 1963) 165–299. In all cases, whatever the evangelist's particular emphasis, the healings remain actions of divine deliverance from evil.

68. Revelation, passim. In *1 Enoch* see especially 39:6—40:10; 46:1—49:4; 61–63; 69:26-29.

69. Nickelsburg, "Son of Man," 146–47.

70. Raymond E. Brown, "The Qumran Scrolls and John: A Comparison in Thought and Expression," in Michael J. Taylor, ed., *Companion to John: Readings in Johannine Theology* (New York: Alba, 1977) 69–90; and the papers collected in James H. Charlesworth, ed., *John and the Dead Sea Scrolls* (New York: Crossroad, 1990).

71. James M. Robinson, "*LOGOI SOPHON:* On the Gattung of Q," in James M. Robinson and Helmut Koester, *Trajectories through Early Christianity* (Philadelphia: Fortress Press, 1971) 71–113; John S. Kloppenborg Verbin, *Excavating Q* (Minneapolis: Fortress Press, 2000).

72. Nickelsburg, *1 Enoch 1,* 59–60.

73. *1 Enoch* 2–5; 100:1—102:3; see ibid., 150–64, 505–10.

74. Nickelsburg, *1 Enoch 1,* 86–78. One must, however, distinguish *1 Enoch* and the Qumran texts on significant issues. For example, *1 Enoch* shows an openness to the Gentiles not found at Qumran (ibid., 52–53); by contrast with Qumran and its Community Rule, we know very little about the community that created and preserved the Enochic traditions (ibid., 64–65). On the possible functions of the Enochic material at Qumran see ibid., 76–78.

75. Collins, "Symbol," 164–70.

76. George W. E. Nickelsburg, "Abraham the Convert: A Jewish Tradition and Its Use by the Apostle Paul," in Michael E. Stone and Theodore A. Bergren, eds., *Biblical Figures outside the Bible* (Harrisburg, Pa.: Trinity Press International, 1998) 151–75.

77. See the commentary and bibliographies in Joseph A. Fitzmyer, *Romans* (AB 33; New York: Doubleday, 1993) 539–636.

78. Nickelsburg, "Incarnation." I take Rom 10:23 to refer to Jews who have not yet accepted Christ, but who may. The "mystery" in 10:25 I understand to refer to God's whole plan—that Israel must first reject Christ, so that the Gentiles may be saved, and Israel's subsequent salvation—rather than to Israel's future salvation through an eschatological act of God.

79. Here I follow Wolfgang Trilling, *Das Wahre Israel: Studien zur Theologie des Matthäus-Evangelium* (3d ed.; SANT 10; Munich: Kösel, 1964). A strong case for an alternative view is made by Anthony J. Saldarini, *Matthew's Christian-Jewish Community* (Chicago: Univ. of Chicago Press, 1994). Many of his points are well taken, and they deserve a more detailed discussion than is possible here. He is correct in asserting that Matthew sees his group as true Jews rather than as Christians-rather-than-Jews. He also correctly notes Matthew's emphasis on the observance of the Torah. However, while he may be correct that "the people" in 27:25 refers to those in Pilate's presence (pp. 32–34), the shift from "crowd" to "people," a word with technical meanings, needs to be explained. Furthermore, while the phrase "all the nations" can (and probably did) include Jews, I see no assertion by Matthew that he is optimistic about a substantial number of Jews accepting Jesus as the Messiah. To the contrary, the plot and the wording of 28:19 ("all the nations") point away from an emphasis on the Jews as the object of mission activity and as a substantial component in the "nation that will bear fruit" (21:43). In short, I think that second-century interpreters of Matthew intuit Matthew's attitude about the Jews more correctly than Saldarini allows (p. 11).

80. Jacob Jervell, *Luke and the People of God: A New Look at Luke-Acts* (Minneapolis: Augsburg, 1972) 41–69, 153–83; Robert Maddox, *The Purpose of Luke-Acts* (Edinburgh: T. & T. Clark, 1982) 31–65, 183–85.

81. Norman R. Petersen, *The Gospel of John and the Sociology of Light: Language and Characterization in the Fourth Gospel* (Valley Forge, Pa.: Trinity Press International, 1993).

82. Exactly when the majority in the church shifted from Jews to Gentiles is difficult to determine. Commonly accepted wisdom places the split between the church and the synagogue in the decades after 70 C.E. Saldarini (*Community*) disputes this and sees Matthew as evidence of a group within Judaism, though deviant from the mainstream. He allows, however, that the balance is shifting by the end of the first century. On the basis of sociological theory, Rodney Stark (*The Rise of Christianity: A Sociologist Reconsiders History* [Princeton, N.J.: Princeton Univ. Press, 1996] 49–71) has argued that the mission to the Jews in the second century "probably worked" far better than has usually been assumed, and he points to some textual and material evidence to support his case. His arguments need to be evaluated carefully to see to what extent this evidence proves his case.

### 4. Agents of God's Activity

1. For a summary discussion of NT christology see John Reumann, "Jesus and Christology," in Eldon Jay Epp and George W. MacRae, eds., *The New Testament and Its Modern Interpreters* (Philadelphia: Fortress Press; Atlanta: Scholars Press, 1989) 508–14. For a major "constructive" article see James D. G. Dunn, "Christology (NT)," *ABD* 1:979–91. It sum-

marizes his book *Christology in the Making* (Philadelphia: Westminster, 1980). Three works on christology based on titles are Vincent Taylor, *The Names of Jesus* (New York: St. Martin's, 1953); Oscar Cullmann, *The Christology of the New Testament* (2d rev. ed.; Philadelphia: Westminster, 1963); and a more historically oriented work, Ferdinand Hahn, *The Titles of Jesus in Christology: Their History in Early Christianity* (New York: World, 1969). Norman R. Petersen suggests in his comments on this manuscript that the first scholar to deal with christological models rather than titles may have been Eduard Schweizer, *Lordship and Discipleship* (SBT 1/28; Naperville, Ill.: Allenson, 1960).

2. Robert C. Tannehill, "The Gospel of Mark as Narrative Christology," *Semeia* 16 (1980) 57–95; Elizabeth Struthers Malbon, "The Christology of Mark's Gospel: Narrative Christology and the Markan Jesus," in Mark-Allan Powell and David R. Bower, eds., *Who Do You Say That I Am?* (Louisville: Westminster John Knox, 1999) 33–48.

3. For many of these texts in translation see George W. E. Nickelsburg and Michael E. Stone, *Faith and Piety in Early Judaism* (Philadelphia: Fortress Press, 1983) 161–201.

4. On the king and justice see Keith W. Whitelam, "King and Kingship," *ABD* 4:44–46.

5. For a Hasmonean reference see George W. E. Nickelsburg, *Jewish Literature between the Bible and the Mishnah* (Philadelphia: Fortress Press, 1981) 203–4, 207. For a reference to Herod the Great see Kenneth Atkinson, "On the Herodian Origin of Militant Davidic Messianism at Qumran: New Light from *Psalm of Solomon* 17," *JBL* 118 (1999) 435–99.

6. On the relationship between the king and the temple cult in ancient Israel, as attested especially in the canonical psalms, see Aubrey R. Johnson, *Sacral Kingship in Ancient Israel* (2d ed.; Cardiff: Univ. of Wales Press, 1967); John H. Eaton, *Kingship and the Psalms* (2d ed.; Sheffield: JSOT Press, 1986).

7. For the fragmentary Qumran texts that refer to a future Davidic king, see John J. Collins, *The Scepter and the Star: The Messiahs of the Dead Sea Scrolls and Other Ancient Literature* (New York: Doubleday, 1995) 56–68. The best known of these texts (4Q285) has been interpreted to refer to a dying messiah, but most likely describes the king as killing his enemy (ibid., 58–60).

8. See *4 Ezra* 11–13; *2 Baruch* 29–30, 72.

9. On "the redeemer figure" in *4 Ezra* see Michael E. Stone, *4 Ezra: A Commentary on the Book of Fourth Ezra* (Hermeneia; Minneapolis: Fortress Press, 1990) 207–13, as well as his commentary on chaps. 11–13 in ibid. On the relationship of the "Anointed One" in *4 Ezra* and *2 Baruch* to the Son of Man, see George W. E. Nickelsburg, "Son of Man," *ABD* 6:140–41.

10. On the pronouncement of the priestly benediction see Sir 50:20; *m. Tamid* 7:2.

11. On a brief discussion of the Qumran Aramaic Levi document, the Geniza MS, and the *Testament of Levi,* as well as bibliography on the details, see Michael E. Stone, "Levi, Aramaic," in Lawrence H. Schiffman and James C. VanderKam, eds., *Encyclopedia of the Dead Sea Scrolls* (2 vols.; Oxford: Oxford Univ. Press, 2000) 1:486–88. For the texts of the Qumran fragments see DJD 22:1–72.

12. Jonas C. Greenfield and Michael E. Stone, "Remarks on the Aramaic Testament of Levi from the Genizah," *RB* 85 (1979) 226–27.

13. George W. E. Nickelsburg, "1 and 2 Maccabees—Same Story, Different Meaning," *CTM* 42 (1971) 518–21. Reprinted in Jacob Neusner and Alan J. Avery-Peck, eds., *George W. E. Nickelsburg in Perspective: An Ongoing Dialogue of Learning* (JSJSup 80:2; Leiden: Brill, 2003) 659–74; see esp. pp. 663–67.

14. For the texts and a translation see Florentino García Martínez and Eibert J. C. Tigchelaar, eds., *The Dead Sea Scrolls Study Edition* (2 vols.; Leiden: Brill; Grand Rapids: Eerdmans, 1997) 2:1082–95. See also Florentino García Martínez, ed., *The Dead Sea Scrolls Translated: The Qumran Texts in English,* trans. Wilfred G. E. Watson (2nd ed.; Leiden: Brill; Grand Rapids: Eerdmans, 1996) 271–75; Geza Vermes, *The Complete Dead Sea Scrolls in English* (New York: Allen Lane/Penguin, 1997) 532–36.

15. See 1QS 5:21; 9:7; 1QSa 1:16, 23; 2:13; 1QM 7:10. "Aaron" also appears as a reference for the priests; see George W. E. Nickelsburg, "Aaron," *RAC* Sup 1:4.

16. See Martha Himmelfarb, "The Wisdom of the Scribe, the Wisdom of the Priest, and the Wisdom of the King according to Ben Sira," in Randal A. Argall, Beverly A. Bow, and Rodney A. Werline, eds., *For a Later Generation: The Transformation of Tradition in Israel, Early Judaism, and Early Christianity* (Harrisburg: Trinity Press International, 2000) 98; she reads Sir 47:22 as "apparently" a reference to the fulfillment of the promise in the past. The double occurrence of "never" suggests to me, however, that the promise has implications for the future of Israel.

17. Collins, *Scepter,* 74–101.

18. For two talmudic passages on which this viewpoint was based, see *b. Sanh.* 11a; *b. Soṭ.* 48.

19. On this text see Rebecca Gray, *Prophetic Figures in Late Second Temple Jewish Palestine: The Evidence from Josephus* (New York: Oxford Univ. Press, 1993) 7–34.

20. Richard A. Horsley and John S. Hanson, *Bandits, Prophets, and Messiahs: Popular Movements in the Time of Jesus* (Minneapolis: Winston, 1985) 135–89; Gray, *Prophetic Figures,* 112–63.

21. George W. E. Nickelsburg, *1 Enoch 1: A Commentary on the Book of 1 Enoch Chapters 1–36; 81–108* (Hermeneia; Minneapolis: Fortress Press, 2001) 30–32, 59–60.

22. Idem, *Jewish Literature,* 176–79; and, in more detail, idem, *Resurrection, Immortality, and Eternal Life in Intertestamental Judaism* (HTS 26; Cambridge: Harvard Univ. Press, 1972) 58–65.

23. Otto Betz, *Offenbarung und Schriftforschung in der Qumransekte* (Tübingen: Mohr/Siebeck, 1960). See also George W. E. Nickelsburg, "The Nature and Function of Revelation in 1 Enoch, Jubilees, and Some Qumranic Documents," in Esther G. Chazon and Michael E. Stone, eds., *Pseudepigraphical Perspectives: The Apocrypha and Pseudepigrapha in Light of the Dead Sea Scrolls, Proceedings of the International Symposium of the Orion Center for the Study of the Dead Sea Scrolls and Associated Literature, 12–14 January, 1997* (STDJ 31; Leiden: Brill, 1999) 107–14.

24. See Gray, *Prophetic Figures.*

25. On the *mal'ak yahweh* see Gerhard Kittel, *"angelos," TDNT* 1 (1964) 77–78.

26. Nickelsburg, *1 Enoch 1,* 140–41.

27. Ibid., 207.

28. Ibid., 208–10.

29. Nickelsburg, *Resurrection,* 11–15.

30. Ibid.

31. Nickelsburg, *1 Enoch 1*, 145.

32. Idem, *Resurrection*, 13–14, 29. See also idem, *1 Enoch 1*, 227–28.

33. On this text see Annette Steudel, "Melchizedek," in Schiffman and VanderKam, eds., *Encyclopedia*, 2:536; Collins, *Scepter*, 161–63.

34. On the interpreting angel in apocalyptic literature see Nickelsburg, *1 Enoch 1*, 294–95.

35. On the complex variations of this tradition see ibid., 191–93.

36. On the two ways and the two spirits in 1QS 3–4 and related texts, such as *Shepherd of Hermas, Epistle of Barnabas, Testaments of XII Patriarchs,* and *Testament of Abraham,* see idem, *Resurrection,* 157–62; idem, "Eschatology in the Testament of Abraham: A Study of the Judgment Scenes in the Two Recensions," in idem, ed., *Studies on the Testament of Abraham* (SBLSCS 6; Missoula, Mont.: Scholars Press, 1976) 27–29.

37. John J. Collins, *Daniel: A Commentary on the Book of Daniel* (Hermeneia; Minneapolis: Fortress Press, 1993) 294–324.

38. For a discussion of the options for the mythic background of this text see ibid., 280–94.

39. Nickelsburg, "Son of Man," 138–40.

40. For aspects of the Servant that parallel those of the Israelite king, see ibid., 138.

41. Nickelsburg, *Resurrection,* 58–65.

42. On the Servant see p. 206, nn. 43–48.

43. On the use of Second and Third Isaiah in a variety of texts that do not posit the presence of a Davidic Messiah, see Daniel 11–12 (Nickelsburg, *Resurrection,* 19–26); *1 Enoch* 1–36 (idem, *1 Enoch 1,* 161–62, 227–28, 315, 318–19); *Jubilees* 23 (idem, *Resurrection,* 31–33); *1 Enoch* 37–71 (idem, "Son of Man," 138–40); Tobit 13 and Baruch (idem, *Jewish Literature,* 33, 112–13), Wisdom of Solomon (idem, *Resurrection,* 63–66); *Psalms of Solomon* 11 (idem, *Jewish Literature,* 206).

44. Matt 9:27; 12:23; 15:22; 20:30-31||Mark 10:47-48; Luke 18:38-39; Matt 21:9, 15||Mark 11:10; Matt 22:42-45|| Mark 12:35-37; Luke 20:42-44; Acts 2:25-35; 13:33-37; 15:16; Rom 1:3; 2 Tim 2:8; Rev 3:7; 5:5; 22:16.

45. Tertullian, *On Baptism* 7:1; Cyril of Jerusalem, *Catech. Lectures* 10:1; 21:5-6; *De uno domine* 11; *De sacro chrism.* 5–6; Pseudo-Clement, *Rec.* 1.44.6—48.6; Armenian *Penitence of Adam* 41–42; *Adam and Eve* 41–42.

46. George W. E. Nickelsburg, "Salvation without and with a Messiah: Developing Beliefs in Writings Ascribed to Enoch," in Jacob Neusner, William S. Green, and Ernest Frerichs, eds., *Judaisms and Their Messiahs* (New York: Cambridge Univ. Press, 1987) 49–68.

47. Idem, "Son of Man," 142–47.

48. Ibid., 147.

49. For Pauline texts in which Jesus is depicted as judge, cf. 1 Cor 4:1-5; 2 Cor 5:10; 1 Thess 2:19-20; 3:13; see ibid., 147–48.

50. See Nickelsburg,, "Resurrection: Early Judaism and Christianity," *ABD* 5:688.

51. See idem, "Son of Man," 144. The motif of persecution and vindication and an occasional use of language from Isaiah 52–53 again point to the kind of interpretation of

Second Isaiah attested in the Wisdom of Solomon. Moreover, the references to the suffering and resurrection of the "Son of Man" are also pertinent, since the scenes in *1 Enoch* that describe the naming of and judgment by the son of man/Chosen One are, in part, expressions of the same traditional interpretation of Second Isaiah (chaps. 48–49, 62–63); see Nickelsburg, "Son of Man," 140. The juxtaposition of the term "the Christ" and the saying about the suffering and resurrection of the "son of man" (Mark 8:29-31; cf. the same juxtaposition in 13:21-27; 14:61-62) parallels the use of both terms in *1 Enoch* to describe the exalted heavenly figure; see Nickelsburg, "Son of Man," 143–44.

52. Idem, "The Genre and Function of the Markan Passion Narrative," *HTR* 73 (1980) 153–84.

53. Idem, "Passion Narratives," *ABD* 5:173, of Mark; John S. Kloppenborg Verbin, *Excavating Q* (Minneapolis: Fortress Press, 2000) 373.

54. Nickelsburg, "Passion Narratives," 174–77.

55. See Bruce Chilton and Craig A. Evans, eds., *Studying the Historical Jesus: Evaluations of the State of Current Research* (NTTS 19; Leiden: Brill, 1994).

56. Joachim Jeremias, *"pais theou,"* *TDNT* 5 (1967) 701–2.

57. See Hans Conzelmann, *The Theology of Saint Luke* (London: Faber & Faber, 1961) 180–83. Note the string of references to the Holy Spirit in 4:1, 14, 18.

58. Kloppenborg Verbin, *Excavating Q,* 369–79.

59. On Colossians see Eduard Lohse, *Colossians and Philemon: A Commentary on the Epistles to the Colossians and to Philemon* (Hermeneia; Philadelphia: Fortress Press, 1971) 41–46. On Hebrews see Harold W. Attridge, *Hebrews: A Commentary on the Epistle to the Hebrews* (Hermeneia; Philadelphia: Fortress Press, 1989) 40–47.

60. See the important and compelling article by Daniel Boyarin, "The Gospel of the *Memra*: Jewish Binitarianism and the Prologue of John," *HTR* 94 (2001) 243–84.

61. For the literature see Jerome Murphy-O'Connor, "Christological Anthropology in Phil., II, 6-11," *RB* 83 (1976) 25, n. 1.

62. The case was first made in detail by Murphy-O'Connor, ibid., 25–50; then by Dunn, *Christology,* 114–21; see also Stanley K. Stowers, *A Rereading of Romans* (New Haven: Yale Univ. Press, 1994) 219–20. Jouette Bassler ("The Faith of Christ, the Obedience of Christ, and the Spirit of Christ: Response to 'The Incarnation: Paul's Solution to the Universal Human Predicament," in Neusner and Avery-Peck, *George W. E. Nickelsburg in Perspective,* 2:600–609) cites this literature in a critique of Nickelsburg, "The Incarnation: Paul's Solution to the Universal Human Predicament," in Birger A. Pearson, ed., *The Future of Early Christianity: Essays in Honor of Helmut Koester* (Minneapolis: Fortress Press, 1991) 348–57.

63. For a discussion of *isa theō* ("equality with God") see Murphy-O'Connor, "Anthropology," 38–39.

64. On the Servant motif here see Jeremias, *TDNT* 5:711–12. The motif, as mediated through the Wisdom of Solomon, is emphasized by Dieter Georgi, "Der vorpaulische Hymnus Phil 2,6-11," in Erich Dinkler, ed., *Zeit und Geschichte: Dankesgabe an Rudolf Bultmann zum 80. Geburtstag* (Tübingen: Mohr/Siebeck, 1964) 269–76. Murphy-O'Connor ("Anthropology," 32–41) also notes the connection with the Servant Song, but employs the the-

ology of the Wisdom of Solomon to explain the hymn's Adam christology. For a contrary opinion see Morna D. Hooker, *Jesus and the Servant: The Influence of the Servant Concept of Deutero-Isaiah in the New Testament* (London: SPCK, 1959) 121.

65. Jeremias, *TDNT* 5:711; Murphy-O'Connor, "Anthropology," 40.

66. On this tradition, see above, pp. 18–19. See also 2 Macc 9:10-11, an expression of this tradition (Nickelsburg, *Resurrection*, 79–80), and the reading *isothea* ("equal to God") in some MSS of v 12.

67. Stowers, *Rereading*, 220. Bassler's response to my article also notes the ambiguity of the evidence, above, p. 222, n. 62. My hesitation about removing any reference to preexistence is related to a mythic text that I have not seen cited in the literature, called to my attention by Norman R. Petersen in comments on this manuscript. In the account of creation in the *Corpus Hermeticum* 1:12-14, one finds the collocation of the terms *autō [theō] ison* ("like him" [God]), the *eikon* and *morphē* ("image, form") of God, and becoming a *doulos* ("slave") as a human being. Could Phil 2:6-11 have reflected an old mythic pattern later attested in the *Hermeticum?*

68. Nickelsburg, "Genre," 173; cf. Heb 5:7.

69. Nickelsburg, "Genre," 174–75. My insights in this respect are based on conversations over the years with Norman R. Petersen, who spells some of them out in "Elijah, the Son of God, and Jesus: Some Issues in the Anthropology of Characterization in Mark," in Argall et al., *Later Generation*, 232–40.

70. Nickelsburg, "Son of Man," 143–44.

71. For a bibliography on the topic see Gerd Theissen, *Miracles Stories of the Early Christian Tradition* (Philadelphia: Fortress Press, 1973) 303–15.

72. The parallel was pointed out to me by Norman R. Petersen. For his exposition of Tobit see idem, "Tobit," in Bernhard W. Anderson, ed., *The Books of the Bible* (2 vols.; New York: Scribner's, 1989) 2:36–42.

73. For this same expression cf. John 16:5, in a text that is very much about the descent and ascent of a heavenly figure, and whose resurrection appearance in 20:19-23 has the characteristics of an angelophany. See below, n. 75.

74. Johannes Munck, *Paul and the Salvation of Mankind* (London: SCM, 1959) 11–35.

75. For the resurrection accounts as commissioning stories see Benjamin J. Hubbard, *The Matthean Redaction of a Primitive Apostolic Commissioning: An Exegesis of Matthew 28:16-20* (SBLDS 19; Missoula, Mont.: Scholars Press, 1974) 69–136. On the account of the Emmaus appearance, as an exception, see Nickelsburg, "Resurrection," *ABD* 5:690. In its similarities to accounts of angelophanies, however, it resembles the other resurrection stories. On the resurrection accounts and traditions about the appearance of angels, see Joseph E. Alsup, *The Post-Resurrection Appearance Stories of the Gospel Tradition: A History of Tradition Analysis with Text-Synopsis* (Calwer Theologische Monographien 5; Stuttgart: Calwer, 1975). See also James M. Robinson, "Jesus from Easter to Valentinus (or to the Apostles' Creed)," *JBL* 101 (1982) 5–37.

76. Though much out of date, the comments of Albert Schweitzer (*The Quest of the Historical Jesus: A Critical Study of Its Progress from Reimarus to Wrede* [New York: Macmillan, 1910]

388–97) are not as improbable as many have thought. It is uncertain to what extent Schweitzer may have drawn his ideas from a text like the *Testament of Moses*, which was published in 1861 and would have been at his disposal.

## 5. Eschatology

1. Johannes Weiss, *Jesus' Proclamation of the Kingdom of God* (Philadelphia: Fortress Press, 1971), translation of 1892 German 1st edition. See also the discussion by Norman Perrin, *The Kingdom of God in the Teaching of Jesus* (NTL; Philadelphia: Westminster, 1963) 13–36.

2. Albert Schweitzer, *Das Messianitäts- und Leidensgeheimnis: Eine Skizze des Lebens Jesu* (Tübingen: Mohr/Siebeck, 1901); idem, *The Quest of the Historical Jesus: A Critical Study of Its Progress from Reimarus to Wrede* (New York: Macmillan, 1956) 238–41, translation of German first published in 1906; idem, *The Mysticism of Paul the Apostle* (New York: Macmillan, 1955) 75–100, translation of German first published in 1930.

3. See the summary discussion by David E. Aune, "Eschatology: Early Christian," *ABD* 2:599–602.

4. Ernst Käsemann, "The Beginnings of Christian Theology" (translation of 1960 article), in *New Testament Questions of Today* (Philadelphia: Fortress Press, 1969) 102.

5. Rudolf Bultmann, *Jesus and the Word* (New York: Scribner's, 1958), reprint of 1934 translation of 1926 German edition; idem, "New Testament and Theology," in Hans Werner Bartsch, ed., *Kerygma and Myth: A Theological Debate* (London: SPCK, 1953) 1–44, translation of 1941 address.

6. C. H. Dodd, *The Parables of the Kingdom* (New York: Scribner's, 1935); idem, *The Interpretation of the Fourth Gospel* (Cambridge: Cambridge Univ. Press, 1960) 7–8, 396–406. For a discussion see Perrin, *Kingdom*, 58–64.

7. George W. E. Nickelsburg, "Eschatology (Early Jewish Literature)," *ABD* 2:592–93.

8. Paul D. Hanson, *The Dawn of Apocalyptic* (Philadelphia: Fortress Press, 1975) 1–31; idem, "Apocalypticism," *IDBSup* 29–34.

9. For a general picture see idem, "Israelite Religion in the Early Postexilic Period," in Patrick D. Miller Jr., Paul D. Hanson, and S. Dean McBride, eds., *Ancient Israelite Religion: Essays in Honor of Frank Moore Cross* (Philadelphia: Fortress Press, 1987) 485–508.

10. Nickelsburg, "Eschatology," *ABD* 2:582–85.

11. On the dating of the early strata of *1 Enoch* see James C. VanderKam, *Enoch and the Growth of an Apocalyptic Tradition* (CBQMS 16; Washington, D.C.: Catholic Biblical Association of America, 1984) 179–88; George W. E. Nickelsburg, *1 Enoch 1: A Commentary on the Book of 1 Enoch Chapters 1–36; 81–108* (Hermeneia; Minneapolis: Fortress Press, 2001) 169–71.

12. Ibid., 57–58.

13. On this form in Third Isaiah see Hanson, *Dawn*, 106–7, 119–20, 143–45, 162–63, 170–71.

14. George W. E. Nickelsburg, *Resurrection, Immortality, and Eternal Life in Intertestamental Judaism* (HTS 26; Cambridge: Harvard Univ. Press, 1972) 20–21, 24–26.

15. On Daniel see ibid., 11–27; on *1 Enoch* see Nickelsburg, *1 Enoch 1*, 48–50.

16. See above, p. 220, n. 16.

17. George W. E. Nickelsburg, *Jewish Literature between the Bible and the Mishnah* (Philadelphia: Fortress Press, 1981) 110–13.

18. Devorah Dimant, "The Library of Qumran: Its Content and Character," in Lawrence H. Schiffman, Emanuel Tov, and James C. VanderKam, eds., *The Dead Sea Scrolls Fifty Years after Their Discovery: 1947–97* (Jerusalem: Israel Exploration Society, 2000) 170–76; Emanuel Tov, "Further Evidence for the Existence of a Qumran Scribal School," in ibid., 199–216.

19. Note the references to seeing what is hidden and to light and glory and to what is engraved in God's presence. All references to the Qumran *hodayot* give the column number now regularly in use and in parentheses the column number formerly in use.

20. Frank M. Cross, *The Ancient Library of Qumran* (3d ed.; Minneapolis: Fortress Press, 1995) 89–93.

21. Geza Vermes, *The Dead Sea Scrolls in English* (4th ed.; Sheffield: Sheffield Academic Press, 1995) 343.

22. George W. E. Nickelsburg, "The Books of Enoch at Qumran: What We Know and What We Need to Look For," in Bernd Kollmann, Wolfgang Reinbold, and Annette Steudel, eds., *Antikes Judentum und Frühes Christentum: Festschrift für Hartmut Stegemann zum 65. Geburtstag* (BZNW 97; Berlin: de Gruyter, 1999) 100–101; idem, *1 Enoch 1*, 78.

23. Idem, *1 Enoch 1*, 398–400.

24. Heinz-Wolfgang Kuhn, *Enderwartung und gegenwärtiges Heil: Untersuchungen zu den Gemeindeliedern von Qumran* (SUNT 4; Göttingen: Vandenhoeck & Ruprecht, 1966); Nickelsburg, *Resurrection*, 152–56.

25. On these texts see John J. Collins, *The Scepter and the Star: The Messiahs of the Dead Sea Scrolls and Other Ancient Literature* (New York: Doubleday, 1995) 74–84.

26. On the text see above, p. 205, n. 32. On its eschatology see Nickelsburg, *Jewish Literature*, 260–61; idem, "Stories of Biblical and Early Post-Biblical Times," in Michael E. Stone, ed., *Jewish Writings of the Second Temple Period* (CRINT 2/2; Assen: Van Gorcum; Philadelphia: Fortress Press, 1984) 67–68.

27. On eschatology in the Wisdom of Solomon see Nickelsburg, *Resurrection*, 162–64.

28. Nickelsburg, *Jewish Literature*, 244–48, 269–70, n. 35.

29. See John J. Collins, "The Genre Apocalypse in Hellenistic Judaism," in David Hellholm, ed., *Apocalypticism in the Mediterranean World and the Near East: Proceedings of the International Colloquium on Apocalypticism, Uppsala, August 12–17, 1979* (Tübingen: Mohr/Siebeck, 1983) 531–48.

30. See above, pp. 90–108.

31. Perrin, *Kingdom*, 178–80.

32. Anna Maria Schwemer, "Gott als König und sein Königsherrschaft in den Sabbatliedern aus Qumran," in Martin Hengel and Anna Maria Schwemer, eds., *Königsherrschaft Gottes und himmlischer Kult im Judentum, Urchristentum und in der hellenistischen Welt* (WUNT 55; Tübingen: Mohr/Siebeck, 1991) 45–118.

33. Nickelsburg, *Resurrection,* 177–80.

34. See *1 En.* 38:3-4; 39:4-5; 45:4-5. See the comments by John J. Collins and my response to them in Jacob Neusner and Alan J. Avery-Peck, *George W. E. Nickelsburg in Perspective: An Ongoing Dialogue of Learning* (JSJSup 80:2; Leiden: Brill, 2003) 377–78, 411.

35. On the land see Doron Mendels, *The Land of Israel as a Political Concept in Hasmonean Literature: Recourse to History in Second Century B.C. Claims to the Holy Land* (TSAJ 15; Tübingen: Mohr/Siebeck, 1987); Robert W. Wilken, *The Land Called Holy: Palestine in Christian History and Thought* (New Haven: Yale Univ. Press, 1992) 21–45.

36. For two discussions of the history of modern apocalyptic studies, see Heinrich Hoffmann, *Das Gesetz in der frühjüdischen Apokalyptik* (SUNT 23; Göttingen: Vandenhoeck & Ruprecht, 1999) 22–70; and, focusing on the more recent discussion, Andreas Bedenbender, *Der Gott der Welt Tritt auf auf den Sinai: Entstehung, Entwickelung und Funktionweise der frühjüdischen Apokalyptik* (Arbeiten zur neutestamentliche Theologie und Zeitgeschichte 8; Berlin: Institut Kirche und Judentum, 2000) 32–87.

37. Christopher Rowland, *The Open Heaven: A Study of Apocalyptic in Judaism and Early Christianity* (New York: Crossroad, 1982) 23–48; Michael E. Stone, "The Books of Enoch and Judaism in the Third Century B.C.E.," *CBQ* 40 (1978) 479–92.

38. Klaus Koch, *The Rediscovery of Apocalyptic* (SBT 2/22; Naperville, Ill.: Allenson, 1972) 18–35.

39. George W. E. Nickelsburg, "Apocalyptic Writings," in Lawrence H. Schiffman and James C. VanderKam, eds., *Encyclopedia of the Dead Sea Scrolls* (2 vols.; Oxford: Oxford Univ. Press, 2000) 1:33–34.

40. See, e.g., Günther Borkamm, *Jesus of Nazareth* (New York: Harper, 1960) 38–39.

41. George W. E. Nickelsburg, "Tobit and Enoch: Distant Cousins with a Recognizable Resemblance," *SBLSP* 27 (1988) 60–62. One may ask whether the author of Tobit thinks that his hero's testamentary prediction was inspired.

42. Nickelsburg, *1 Enoch 1,* 396–98.

43. Cf. 2 Samuel 3–12; 1 Kings 3–10; Ps 68:19; 110:2-4; Ezek 34:22-27; Mic 4:3; Zech 8:12.

44. On the date of Judith see Nickelsburg, *Jewish Literature,* 108–9.

45. Emil Schürer, *Geschichte des jüdischen Volkes im Zeitalter Jesu Christi* (1907; 3 vols.; reprint Hildesheim: Olms, 1970) 2:579–651 (the work was first published in 1890); Wilhelm Bousset and Hugo Gressmann, *Die Religion des Judentums im späthellenistischen Zeitalter* (HNT 21; Tübingen: Mohr/Siebeck, 1926) 202–301; R. H. Charles, *A Critical History of the Doctrine of a Future Life in Israel, Judaism, and Christianity* (London: Black, 1899); Paul Volz, *Die Eschatologie der jüdischen Gemeinde im neutestamentlichen Zeitalter* (Tübingen: Mohr/Siebeck, 1934).

46. On the teaching of John see Joan E. Taylor, *The Immerser: John the Baptist within Second Temple Judaism* (Grand Rapids: Eerdmans, 1997) 101–54.

47. Ibid., 281–88.

48. Cf. Mark 6:14-29 and 1 Kings 18–21. As Jezebel prodded Ahab to destroy Elijah, so Herodias prompts Antipas to take John's life. A similar triangulating element occurs in the Markan passion narrative, where the Jewish leaders use Pilate (a ruler) as their agent

to rid themselves of Jesus. Thus, beginning with the Elijah model for John's martyrdom, the evangelist creates a model for the events leading up to Jesus' death, which story is also heavily influenced by another Jewish model (see above, p. 111).

49. For an extensive discussion see Taylor, *Immerser,* 15–48.

50. For a summary discussion of NT eschatology in its Jewish and Greco-Roman contexts see Aune, "Eschatology," 594–609. For present and future eschatology in the teaching of Jesus see Werner Georg Kümmel, *Promise and Fulfillment* (SBT 1/23; London: SCM, 1961); Kuhn, *Enderwartung,* 188–204.

51. See Perrin, *Kingdom.*

52. Philipp Vielhauer, "Gottesreich und Menschensohn in der Verkündigung Jesu," in idem, *Aufsätze zum Neuen Testament* (Theologische Bücherei 31; Munich: Kaiser, 1965) 55–91.

53. Matt 10:32-34||Luke 12:8-9||Mark 8:38; see George W. E. Nickelsburg, "Son of Man," *ABD* 6:142–43.

54. See *2 Bar.* 21:8 for the same expression that occurs in the Syriac translation of Gal 4:4.

55. On resurrection as an accomplished fact, see Col 2:9-15; Eph 1:15-23; for the associated ethical exhortations, see Colossians 3; Ephesians 4.

56. Nickelsburg, "Son of Man," 145, on 18:1-8. See idem, "Riches, the Rich, and God's Judgment in 1 Enoch 92–105 and the Gospel according to Luke," *NTS* 25 (1979) 338–39.

57. Raymond E. Brown, *The Birth of the Messiah* (Garden City, N.Y.: Doubleday, 1977) 235–469.

58. See Nickelsburg, "Riches," 338–40. For a similar cosmology see *1 Enoch* 22. On the comparison see idem, *1 Enoch 1,* 307.

59. On the *Shepherd of Hermas* see Nickelsburg, *Resurrection,* 160; cf. also 4 Macc 7:19; 16:25, on which text see Nickelsburg, *Resurrection,* 110.

60. See Dodd, *Fourth Gospel,* 364–65. See also Wis 3:2: the righteous only seem to have died.

61. On 5:28–29 I find convincing the explanation of Rudolf Bultmann, *The Gospel of John* (Philadelphia: Westminster, 1971) 261.

62. On John and Qumran in general see the collection edited by James H. Charlesworth, *John and the Dead Sea Scrolls* (New York: Crossroad, 1990).

63. Nickelsburg, *Resurrection,* 88–90.

64. See, e.g., Rom 4:24; 8:11; and cf. Heb 13:20 with Isa 63:11. On the parallel formulation see Otto Michel, *Der Brief an die Römer* (Göttingen: Vandenhoeck & Ruprecht, 1963) 127, n. 3.

65. On passages that contain this motif see George W. E. Nickelsburg, "Resurrection: Early Judaism and Christianity," *ABD* 5:688, 690.

66. John E. Alsup, *The Post-Resurrection Appearance Stories of the Gospel Tradition* (Calwer Theologische Monographien 5; Stuttgart: Calwer, 1975) 246–65, esp. 263–65.

67. James M. Robinson, "Jesus from Easter to Valentinus (or to the Apostles' Creed)," *JBL* 101 (1982) 5–37.

68. On Tobit see Norman R. Petersen, "Tobit," in Bernhard W. Anderson, ed., *The Books of the Bible* (2 vols.; New York: Scribner's, 1989) 2:36–41; and, on the specific characteristics

in chaps. 5 and 12 that are shared with biblical and postbiblical accounts of angelophanies, see Alsup, *Appearance Stories,* 260–61. Note in John 16:5 the same formula that occurs in Tob 12:20.

69. Ernst Käsemann, *The Testament of Jesus: A Study of the Gospel of John in the Light of Chapter 17* (Philadelphia: Fortress Press, 1968) 9.

70. Harold W. Attridge, *The Epistle to the Hebrews: A Commentary on the Epistle to the Hebrews* (Hermeneia; Philadelphia: Fortress Press, 1989) 46. The relevant passages are 1:3; 8:1; 10:12; 12:2.

## 6. Contexts and Settings

1. However, for an example of how an archaeologist can integrate material evidence with literary sources, to the clarification of both, see Jodi Magness, *The Archaeology of Qumran and the Dead Sea Scrolls* (Grand Rapids: Eerdmans, 2002).

2. Erich Gruen reminded me of this complicating factor (personal correspondence, July 1, 2002).

3. See, e.g., *1 En.* 103:5-6, and, by contrast, vv 9-16. On the Deuteronomic language in the latter passage, see George W. E. Nickelsburg, *1 Enoch 1: A Commentary on the Book of 1 Enoch Chapters 1–36; 81–108* (Hermeneia; Minneapolis: Fortress Press, 2001) 526–27.

4. On Judaism in the Diaspora see Erich S. Gruen, *Diaspora: Jews amidst Greeks and Romans* (Cambridge: Harvard Univ. Press, 2002).

5. See Nickelsburg, "Excursus: Sacred Geography in 1 Enoch 6–16," in *1 Enoch 1,* 238–47.

6. For some examples in a popular treatment see Brian Leigh Molyneaux, *The Sacred Earth* (Boston: Little, Brown, 1995).

7. See 1QS 8:12-16 and its interpretation of Isa 40:3. On the tradition that associates John the Baptist with the same passage, see Joan E. Taylor, *The Immerser: John the Baptist within Second Temple Judaism* (Grand Rapids: Eerdmans, 1997) 25–28.

8. George W. E. Nickelsburg, "Enoch, Levi, and Peter: Recipients of Revelation in Upper Galilee," *JBL* 100 (1981) 575–600. Reprinted with a response by Hanan and Esther Eshel in Jacob Neusner and Alan Avery-Peck, eds., *George W. E. Nickelsburg in Perspective: An Ongoing Dialogue of Learning* (JSJSup 80:2; Leiden: Brill, 2003) 427–57.

9. On these issues see Douglas E. Oakman, *Jesus and the Economic Questions of His Time* (Studies in the Bible and Early Christianity 8; Lewiston, N.Y.: Mellen, 1986) 17–35. A sensitivity to these issues can also be found in Joachim Jeremias, *The Parables of Jesus* (rev. ed.; New York: Scribner's, 1963).

10. For the identification of Hellenistic Judaism with the Diaspora and in contrast to Palestinian Judaism, see Paul Volz, *Die Eschatologie der jüdischen Gemeinde im neutestamentlichen Zeitalter* (1934; reprint Hildesheim: Olms, 1966) 53–54. For a sharp contrast between Palestinian and Diaspora Judaism, see Wilhelm Bousset and Hugo Gressmann, *Die Religion des Judentums im späthellenistischen Zeitalter* (HNT 21; Tübingen: Mohr/Siebeck, 1926) 432–37. For some qualification, however, see ibid., 484. See also Claude J. G. Montefiore, *Judaism and St. Paul* (New York: Dutton, 1915) 92–93, who contrasts Hellenistic and Rab-

binic Judaism; and see the critique by W. D. Davies, *Paul and Rabbinic Judaism* (London: SPCK, 1958) 1–16.

11. See Morton Smith, *Palestinian Parties and Politics That Shaped the Old Testament* (New York: Columbia Univ. Press, 1971) 56–81; the monumental work by Martin Hengel, *Hellenism and Judaism* (2 vols.; Philadelphia: Fortress Press, 1974); Saul Liebermann, *Hellenism in Jewish Palestine: Studies in the Literary Transmission, Beliefs, and Manners of Palestine in the I Century B.C.E.–IV Century C.E.* (New York: Jewish Theological Seminary of America, 1950); John J. Collins and Gregory R. Sterling, eds., *Hellenism in the Land of Israel* (Christianity and Judaism in Antiquity 13; Notre Dame, Ind.: Univ. of Notre Dame Press, 2001). For a critique of Hengel see Lester L. Grabbe, *Judaism from Cyrus to Hadrian* (2 vols.; Philadelphia: Fortress Press, 1992) 1:150–53.

12. On the Wisdom of Solomon see C. Larcher, *Études sur le Livre de la Sagesse* (EBib; Paris: Gabalda, 1969) 178–236; David Winston, *Wisdom of Solomon* (AB 43; Garden City, N.Y.: Doubleday, 1979) 25–58; on 4 Maccabees see David A. de Silva, *4 Maccabees* (Sheffield: Sheffield Academic Press, 1998) 51–75.

13. George W. E. Nickelsburg, *Jewish Literature between the Bible and the Mishnah* (Philadelphia: Fortress Press, 1981) 165–69.

14. See above, p. 228, n. 10.

15. See Hengel, *Judaism and Hellenism*, 2:147–49.

16. See Nickelsburg, *1 Enoch 1*, 170; for other Hellenistic aspects see ibid., 62.

17. George W. E. Nickelsburg, *Resurrection, Immortality, and Eternal Life in Intertestamental Judaism* (HTS 26; Cambridge: Harvard Univ. Press, 1972) passim.

18. On lists of vices and virtues in Greco-Roman texts see Abraham J. Malherbe, *Moral Exhortation: A Greco-Roman Sourcebook* (LEC 4; Philadelphia: Westminster, 1986) 73, 130, 138–39; but on an "anti-hellenizing attitude" among the Qumranites see Magness, *Archaeology*, 199–203.

19. On these texts see Nickelsburg, *Jewish Literature*, 73–90, 114–21.

20. Cf., e.g., *1 En.* 99:7; *Jub.* 20:7-9; 22:16-18.

21. For a summary of some findings and the ambiguity of the issue, see George W. E. Nickelsburg, ed., *Studies on the Testament of Joseph* (SBLSCS 5; Missoula, Mont.: Scholars Press, 1975) 11.

22. Jonathan A. Goldstein, *1 Maccabees* (AB 41; Garden City, N.Y.: Doubleday, 1976) 34, and the references listed in n. 70. See also Gruen, *Diaspora*, 174–81.

23. See the collection of papers in Mark W. Chavalas and K. Lawson Younger Jr., eds., *Mesopotamia and the Bible: Comparative Explorations* (JSOTSup 341; Sheffield: Sheffield Academic Press, 2002).

24. Rudolf Bultmann, *Theology of the New Testament* (2 vols.; New York: Scribner's, 1951–55) 1:63; Hans Conzelmann, *An Outline of the Theology of the New Testament* (NTL; New York: Harper & Row, 1969) 9–25.

25. Conzelmann, *Outline*, 29–93.

26. Oscar Cullmann, "Immortality of the Soul or Resurrection of the Body," in Krister Stendahl, ed., *Immortality and Resurrection* (New York: Macmillan, 1965) 9–53.

27. Adolf von Harnack, *The Mission and Expansion of Christianity in the First Three Centuries* (New York: Harper, 1961) 60–64.

28. See Frederick J. Murphy, *The Religious World of Jesus: An Introduction to Second Temple Palestinian Judaism* (Nashville: Abingdon, 1991) 71–91.

29. On Third Isaiah see, e.g., Paul D. Hanson, *The Dawn of Apocalyptic* (Philadelphia: Fortress Press, 1975) 177–79, 245–46; see also Smith, *Palestinian Parties,* 126–92.

30. *2 Bar.* 10:18; *Apoc. Abr.* 25–27, on which see Nickelsburg, *Jewish Literature,* 296–98.

31. The old standard works were J. Simon, *Jerusalem in the Old Testament: Researches and Theories* (Leiden: Brill, 1952); L.-Hughes Vincent and M.-A. Steve, *Jérusalem de l'Ancien Testament: Recherches d'Archéologie et d'Histoire* (3 parts; Paris: Gabalda, 1954–56). On more recent excavations see Nahman Avigad, *Discovering Jerusalem* (New York: Nelson, 1980); Eilat Mazar and Benjamin Mazar, *Excavations in the South of the Temple Mount: The Ophel of Jerusalem* (*Qedem* 29; Jerusalem: Hebrew Univ. Press, 1989); Hillel Geva and Nahman Avigad, "Jerusalem: The Second Temple Period," in Ephraim Stern, ed., *The New Encyclopedia of Archaeological Excavations in the Holy Land* (4 vols.; New York: Simon and Schuster, 1993) 2:717–57. For collections of articles see Yigael Yadin, ed., *Jerusalem Revealed: Archaeology in the Holy City 1968–74* (Jerusalem: Israel Exploration Society, 1975); Leen and Kathleen Ritmeyer, *Secrets of Jerusalem's Temple Mount* (Washington, D.C.: Biblical Archaeology Society, 1998).

32. For the archaeological problems relating to the temple on Mount Gerizim, see the literature cited by Robert T. Anderson, "Samaritans," *ABD* 5:942.

33. The monumental building at Iraq el-Emir in Transjordan has been considered to be a temple; see Paul W. Lapp and Nancy L. Lapp, "Iraq el-Emir," in Stern, ed., *Encyclopedia* 2:648–49. However, see Ehud Netzer, "Floating in the Desert: A Pleasure Palace in Jordan," *Archaeology Odyssey* 2 (1999) 46–55.

34. On *1 Enoch* 90 see Nickelsburg, *1 Enoch 1,* 404–5. The New Jerusalem text has been preserved in six texts (1Q32, 2Q24, 4Q232, 4Q554–555, 5Q15, 11Q18).

35. See, e.g., Alfred Edersheim, *The Life and Times of Jesus the Messiah* (1886; 3d ed.; 2 vols.; reprint: Grand Rapids: Eerdmans, 1950) 1:430–50; Emil Schürer, *Geschichte des jüdischen Volkes im Zeitalter Jesu Christi* (1907; 3 vols.; reprint Hildesheim: Olms, 1970) 491–544; Bousset and Gressmann, *Religion,* 171–78.

36. Eric Meyers, "Synagogue," *ABD* 6:259.

37. For two major recent treatments see Donald D. Binder, *Into the Temple Courts: The Place of the Synagogues in the Second Temple Period* (SBLDS 169; Atlanta: Society of Biblical Literature, 1999); and the magisterial work by Lee I. Levine, *The Ancient Synagogue: The First Thousand Years* (New Haven: Yale Univ. Press, 2000). For a summary discussion see Gruen, *Diaspora,* 105–23. On the term *synagōgē,* as well as a discussion of the institution, see Wolfgang Schrage, "*synagōgē,*" *TDNT* 7 (1971) 798–841.

38. For a summary of the three options see Levine, *Synagogue,* 22–23. On the problem of putting the question of "origins," see Gruen, *Diaspora,* 119–23.

39. On the Hebrew terms and their Septuagintal translations see Schrage, *TDNT* 7:800–805. On *kenishta* see Isaiah Sonne, "Synagogue," *IDB* 4:477.

40. Schrage, *TDNT* 7:802–5.

41. See Levine, *Synagogue,* 75–76. For a critical edition of these inscriptions, see William Horbury and David Noy, *Jewish Inscriptions of Graeco-Roman Egypt* (Cambridge: Cambridge Univ. Press, 1992) 35–37, 201–3.

42. For discussions of these texts see Levine, *Synagogue,* 75–82; Binder, *Temple Courts,* 233–54.

43. Binder, *Temple Courts,* 249–52; Levine, *Synagogue,* 82–84.

44. Levine, *Synagogue,* 89–96; Binder, *Temple Courts,* 257–63.

45. Philo and Josephus mention Roman synagogues; a synagogue has been excavated at Ostia, with its earliest stratum most likely dating to the first century; Binder, *Temple Courts,* 317–36; Levine, *Synagogue,* 97–99.

46. On the problem see Levine, *Synagogue,* 100–105; Binder, *Temple Courts,* 297–317.

47. Levine, *Synagogue,* 111–12; Binder, *Temple Courts,* 286–88.

48. Binder, *Temple Courts,* 274–76; Levine, *Synagogue,* 113–15.

49. Binder, *Temple Courts,* 285–86.

50. See the discussion in Levine, *Synagogue,* 116–18; Binder, *Temple Courts,* 264–68.

51. For an earlier occurrence of the term cf. Ps 149:1.

52. See Binder, *Temple Courts,* 162–72; Levine, *Synagogue,* 51–52.

53. See Binder, *Temple Courts,* 172–85; Levine, *Synagogue,* 58–60.

54. For inclusion of Qumran in this group and for other references to such structures in the Qumran literature, see Levine, *Synagogue,* 60–63; and Binder, *Temple Courts,* 453–68. On the archaeology of Qumran see Magness, *Archaeology.*

55. Binder (*Temple Courts,* 186–93) agrees with the excavators that the lowest stratum beneath the fourth-century synagogue reveals a first-century synagogue on the location. Levine (*Synagogue,* 66–67) is less certain.

56. On the inscription see Levine, *Synagogue,* 54–56. On the likelihood of a plurality of synagogues in Jerusalem see ibid., 56–58.

57. On Dor and Caesarea see ibid., 63–64; and on Tiberias, ibid., 49–51.

58. For details see ibid., 65–69.

59. See, e.g., Edersheim, *Life and Times,* 1:430–50, who also refers occasionally to Philo and Josephus; George Foot Moore, *Judaism in the First Centuries of the Christian Era, the Age of the Tannaim* (3 vols.; Cambridge: Harvard Univ. Press, 1927) 1:281–307, who cites, in addition, a few passages from the Apocrypha and Pseudepigrapha; and Ismar Ellbogen, *Der jüdische Gottesdienst in seiner geschichtlichen Entwicklung* (3d ed.; Hildesheim: Olms, 1931), who relies mainly on talmudic sources, but cites a good deal of secondary literature.

60. Binder, *Temple Courts,* 391–99; Levine, *Synagogue,* 70, 97, 100, 106–7.

61. Levine, *Synagogue,* 135–47; Binder, *Temple Courts,* 399–404; see also Hippolytus *Haer.* 9.17 on the Law and the Prophets among Essenes.

62. On the Aramaic Targumim see Levine, *Synagogue,* 147–51. It is uncertain whether in the Diaspora the Scriptures were read in Greek or in Hebrew, followed by a Greek translation (ibid., 148).

63. See the discussions by Levine, *Synagogue,* 151–58; and Binder, *Temple Courts,* 404–15. See also Esther Glickler Chazon, "Prayers from Qumran and Their Historical Implications,"

*DSD* 1 (1994) 280–81; idem, "Psalms, Hymns, and Prayers," in Lawrence H. Schiffman and James C. VanderKam, eds., *Encyclopedia of the Dead Sea Scrolls* (2 vols.; Oxford: Oxford Univ. Press, 2000) 2:714; idem, "Hymns and Prayers in the Dead Sea Scrolls," in Peter W. Flint and James C. Vanderkam, eds., *The Dead Sea Scrolls after Fifty Years: A Comprehensive Assessment* (2 vols.; Leiden: Brill, 1998) 2:257–58.

64. See especially E. Fleischer, "On the Beginnings of Obligatory Jewish Prayer," *Tarbiz* 59 (1991) 397–441; and with regard to the Sabbath, Heather A. McKay, *Sabbath and Synagogue: The Question of Sabbath Worship in Ancient Judaism* (Religions in the Greco-Roman World 122; Leiden: Brill, 1994). For critiques of Fleischer see Levine, *Synagogue,* 153–54; and the literature cited by Chazon, "Prayers," 280, n. 60. For a critique of McKay see Binder, *Temple Courts,* 404, 409–11.

65. Levine, *Synagogue,* 153–55.

66. Ibid., 155–58.

67. Chazon, "Prayers."

68. Ibid., 279–84.

69. On penitential prayers in the Second Temple period see Rodney A. Werline, *Penitential Prayer in Second Temple Judaism: The Development of a Religious Institution* (SBLEJL 13; Atlanta: Scholars Press, 1998).

70. Levine, *Synagogue,* 144–46; McKay, *Sabbath and Synagogue.*

71. Binder, *Temple Courts,* 415–26; Levine, *Synagogue,* 129–30.

72. This point is emphasized by Levine, *Synagogue,* 128–34.

73. Binder, *Temple Courts,* 426–35.

74. Ibid., 436–49; Levine, *Synagogue,* 131–32.

75. We learn this from the Theodotus inscription; see Levine, *Synagogue,* 54–55.

76. All these points are documented in great detail by Binder, *Temple Courts,* and summarized on pp. 479–93.

77. This is the thesis of Binder, ibid., 493, who cites pagan models, 478–79.

78. See the extensive discussion by Levine, *Synagogue,* 160–606; and two excellent collections of essays: Steven Fine, ed., *Sacred Realm: The Emergence of the Synagogue in the Ancient World* (New York: Oxford Univ. Press and Yeshiva Univ. Museum, 1996); Alan J. Avery-Peck and Jacob Neusner, eds., *Judaism in Late Antiquity,* part 3: *Where We Stand: Issues and Debates in Ancient Judaism,* vol. 4: *The Special Problem of the Synagogue* (HO 1/55; Brill: Leiden, 2001).

79. For Jesus' presence in the synagogue on the Sabbath, see, e.g, Mark 1:21; 3:1-2; Luke 4:16; 13:10. On Paul and the synagogue see Acts 13:14, 27, 42-44; 15:21; 17:2; 18:4.

80. See Luke 4:16-27, where Jesus' expounds a prophetic text. For the reading of the Torah and the Prophets on the Sabbath, see Acts 13:15, 27; cf. 15:21. For preaching on the Sabbath see all of the above texts.

81. Acts 16:13.

82. For *ekklēsia* as an alternative Septuagintal translation of *qahal* and `*ēdah,* see Schrage, *TDNT* 7:802–3. For the Christian use of *ekklēsia,* in relation to both the Septuagint and parallels in Greco-Roman culture, see Wayne A. Meeks, *The First Urban Christians: The Social World of the Apostle Paul* (New Haven: Yale Univ. Press, 1983) 79, 108. See also the extensive

article by Karl Ludwig Schmidt, "*ekklēsia*," *TDNT* 3 (1965) 501–36. The NT propensity for *ekklēsia* (and not *synagōgē*) for the Christian community as the people of God is noteworthy. Cf. the repeated use of *ekklēsia* in Revelation 2–3 and the reference to *synagōgē* of Satan in 2:9 and 3:9.

83. See Hans Conzelmann, *1 Corinthians: A Commentary on the First Epistle to the Corinthians* (Hermeneia; Philadelphia: Fortress Press, 1975) 296, n. 20.

84. A connection between Jewish and Christian practice is assumed by Levine, *Synagogue*, 130. In the NT see Acts 2:42, 46-47; 6:1-2; 1 Cor 11:22-34. This last passage indicates that "the Lord's Supper" was celebrated in the context of a larger meal where people could overeat and overdrink. On the nature of the meals in the Acts passages see Joseph A. Fitzmyer, *The Acts of the Apostles* (AB 18C; New York: Doubleday, 1998) 270–71. On the Qumran meals see Dennis E. Smith, "Meals," in Schiffman and VanderKam, eds., *Encyclopedia*, 1:530–32. For problems on the possible relationship between the Qumran meals and early Christian meals, see Dennis Smith, "The Messianic Banquet," in Birger Pearson, ed., in collaboration with A. Thomas Kraabel, George W. E. Nickelsburg, and Norman R. Petersen, *The Future of Early Christianity: Essays in Honor of Helmut Koester* (Minneapolis: Fortress Press, 1991) 64–73. The literature on this topic, which is surprisingly sparse, is cited in the two articles by Smith. On the so-called agape meal of early Christianity, see Massey H. Shepherd, "Agape," *IDB* 1:53–54.

85. According to Justin (*1 Apol.* 67), "the memoirs of the apostles or the writings of the prophets are read, as time permits," after which the president exhorts and encourages the group to imitate these things.

86. On the Pharisees, Sadducees, and Essenes, see *J.W.* 2.119-66; *Ant.* 13.171-73; 18.11-22. On the Fourth Philosophy see *Ant.* 18.23-25. On the Zealots in Josephus see David Rhoads, "Zealots," *ABD* 6:1043–54. On the Sicarii see *J.W.* 2.254-57; 7.254-58; and for a brief discussion see ibid., 1048. See also Morton Smith, "Zealots and Sicarii," *HTR* 64 (1971) 1–19.

87. On the Essenes see *Prob.* 75–91; *Hypoth.* 11.1-11. On the Theraputae see *De Vita Contemplativa.*

88. For the Sadducees see Mark 12:18 | | Matt 22:23-24 and Luke 20:27; Acts 4:1; 5:17. Most often they are paired with the Pharisees, especially in Matthew, who has a particular dislike for the latter: 3:7; 16:1, 6, 11, 12; see also Acts 23:6-8. On the Herodians see Matt 22:16; Mark 3:6; 12:13. References to the Pharisees are too frequent to cite.

89. Hippolytus *Haer.* 9.18-29. On the relationship of this description to that of Josephus, see Morton Smith, "The Description of the Essenes in Josephus and the Philosophoumena," *HUCA* 29 (1958) 273–93.

90. See J. Thomas, *Le Mouvement Baptiste en Palestine et Syrie (150 av. J.C.–300 ap. J.C.)* (Gembloux: J. Duculot, 1935); and for a summary see Charles H. H. Scobie, *John the Baptist: A New Quest for the Historical John* (London: SCM, 1964) 35–37.

91. See Anthony J. Saldarini, *Pharisees, Scribes, and Sadducees in Palestinian Society* (Wilmington, Del.: Glazier, 1988) 199–237.

92. See, e.g., R. H. Charles on the *Assumption of Moses*, in *APOT* 2:411; G. Buchanan Gray on the *Psalms of Solomon*, ibid., 630.

93. See, e.g., Orville S. Wintermute, "Jubilees," *OTP* 2:45; John Priest, "Testament of Moses," *OTP* 1:921–22; Patrick A. Tiller, *A Commentary on the Animal Apocalypse of 1 Enoch* (SBLEJL 4; Atlanta: Scholars Press, 1993) 101–16.

94. For a lucid exposition of the situation, as it applies to scholarship on the Pharisees, see Anthony J. Saldarini, "Pharisees," *ABD* 5:289–303.

95. For an example of the method see R. H. Charles, *The Apocalypse of Baruch* (London: Black, 1896) lviii–lxiv.

96. For two examples of the holistic study of Josephus that take literary issues into account, see Harold W. Attridge, *The Interpretation of Biblical History in the Antiquitates Judaicae of Flavius Josephus* (HDR 7; Missoula, Mont.: Scholars Press, 1976), esp. pp. 29–70; Steve Mason, *Flavius Josephus on the Pharisees: A Composition-Critical Study* (SPB 39; Leiden: Brill, 1991).

97. Here credit is due especially to the pioneering work of Jacob Neusner, notably *The Rabbinic Traditions about the Pharisees before 70* (3 vols.; Leiden: Brill, 1971). For an appraisal see Anthony J. Saldarini, "Reconstructions of Rabbinic Judaism," in Robert A. Kraft and George W. E. Nickelsburg, eds., *Early Judaism and Its Modern Interpreters* (Philadelphia: Fortress Press; Atlanta: Scholars Press, 1986) 459.

98. See Jacob Neusner, *From Politics to Piety: The Emergence of Pharisaic Judaism* (Englewood Cliffs, N.J.: Prentice-Hall, 1973) 4–7; Charlotte Klein, *Anti-Judaism in Christian Theology* (Philadelphia: Fortress Press, 1978); Saldarini, "Pharisees," 289–91.

99. For an excellent introduction with full bibliography see John H. Elliott, *What Is Social-Scientific Criticism?* (Guides to Biblical Scholarship; Minneapolis: Fortress Press, 1993).

100. For early sensitivity to these issues see Anthony J. Saldarini, *Pharisees*. See esp. his methodologically self-conscious introduction, 3–34.

101. On conflict theory and its limitations see Richard A. Horsley, *Sociology and the Jesus Movement* (New York: Crossroad, 1989) 156–65.

102. See Bryan Wilson, *Religious Sects: A Sociological Study* (London: Weidenfeld and Nicolson, 1970) 21–47; and see the discussion below, pp. 181–82.

103. For an example see the discussion of *1 Enoch* by Tiller, *Commentary*, 123–26; and Nickelsburg, *1 Enoch 1*, 64–65.

104. We are best in a position to do this with the Essenes, thanks to the accounts of Philo, Josephus, and Hippolytus and the discovery of the Qumran Community Rule. See below, pp. 167–75. In other instances we have very little information.

105. See Saldarini's comments on the scholarship on the Pharisees, "Pharisees," 289.

106. On this notion of tradition, see, e.g., the concurrence of Mark 7:3-8 and Josephus, *Ant.* 13.297.

107. See the extensive discussion by Neusner, *Politics to Piety*, 67–80, 88–90, 97–122. So also Saldarini, "Pharisees," 300.

108. Saldarini, *Pharisees*, 220–25.

109. Neusner, *Politics to Piety*, 90.

110. For these accounts as they relate to the Pharisees see Josephus, *J. W.* 2.162-63; *Ant.* 18.12-15. For discussions of these texts and other references to the Pharisees in Josephus,

see Neusner, *Politics to Piety*, 45–66; Saldarini, *Pharisees*, 107–33; and in great detail, Mason, *Flavius Josephus*, 82–324.

111. Cf. Acts 23:6-8; and see Mason, *Flavius Josephus*, 156–70.

112. For an unargued assertion about Pharisaic eschatology and apocalypticism see Saldarini, *Pharisees*, 289–90. See also W. D. Davies, "Apocalyptic and Pharisaism," *ExpTim* 59 (1948) 233–37, republished in idem, *Christian Origins and Judaism* (Philadelphia: Westminster, 1962) 19–30. Davies's evidence is drawn from Pseudepigrapha that are not verifiably Pharisaic or that are late, and from the rabbinic corpus. For a nonapocalyptic Jewish text that posits resurrection, see the discussion of the *Psalms of Solomon* in Nickelsburg, *Resurrection*, 131–34.

113. See Saldarini, *Pharisees*, 280–87.

114. For details on this historical material see Neusner, *Politics to Piety*, 57–64; and Saldarini, *Pharisees*, 81–95. I take the story of John Hyrcanus and the Pharisees (*Ant.* 13.288-98) to reflect some basic historical reality, but whether the Pharisees would have attended such a banquet depends on whether close table fellowship was as central to their self-understanding and practice at that time as it was later.

115. Saldarini, *Pharisees*, 95–101.

116. For a discussion of the Pharisees in the post-70 period, see Jacob Neusner, *Eliezer ben Hyrcanus: The Tradition and the Man* (2 vols.; SJLA 3-4; Leiden: Brill, 1973); idem, *Politics to Piety*, 81–141, and the summary on pp. 143–54; idem, "The Formation of Rabbinic Judaism: Yavneh (Jamnia) from A.D. 70–100," *ANRW* 2/19.2:3–42. According to Saldarini (*Pharisees*, 131–32), the Pharisees rose to religious power and gained recognition by Rome over the course of a number of decades.

117. In this respect it is useful to compare what we know of the Pharisees with the information we can glean about the Essenes, both from Josephus and Philo and from the Qumran Scrolls. For some suggestions about the Pharisees see Saldarini, *Pharisees*, 282–89.

118. Note the unusual expression, "scribes of the Pharisees," in Mark 2:16. That the Pharisees as a group did not constitute "a lay scribal movement," see Saldarini, *Pharisees*, 228–31, 284, who critiques the contrary opinion of Ellis Rivkin, *A Hidden Revolution: The Pharisees' Search for the Kingdom Within* (Nashville: Abingdon, 1978) 125–79; idem, "Defining the Pharisees: The Tannaitic Sources," *HUCA* 40–41 (1969–70) 205–49. For Rivkin's most recent discussion see "Who Were the Pharisees?" in Alan J. Avery-Peck and Jacob Neusner, eds., *Judaism in Late Antiquity*, part 3: *Where We Stand: Issues and Debates in Ancient Judaism*, vol. 3 (HO 1/53; Leiden: Brill, 2000) 1–33, which, however, makes no reference to Saldarini's 1988 critique in *Pharisees*.

119. See Saldarini, *Pharisees*, 43–44, 284; but cf. pp. 139–41, where he sees the apostle Paul as an exception to the rule.

120. Ibid., 39–45, 87–88, and 284, where he identifies such retainers as "subordinate officials, bureaucrats, judges, and educators."

121. In his *Politics to Piety*, Neusner emphasizes this difference in the sources and expounds as his thesis the transition expressed in the book's title. In this he is followed by

Saldarini; Mason *(Flavius Josephus)* emphasizes their influence and political role, but in this he is opposed by Lester Grabbe, "The Pharisees: A Response to Steve Mason," in Avery-Peck and Neusner, eds., *Judaism in Late Antiquity,* 3/3:35–47. See also idem, "Sadducees and Pharisees," in Jacob Neusner and Alan J. Avery-Peck, eds., *Judaism in Late Antiquity,* part 3: *Where We Stand: Issues and Debates in Ancient Judaism,* vol. 1 (HO 1:40; Leiden: Brill, 1999) 35–62.

122. Saldarini, *Pharisees,* 147–48, 197–98, 291–97. On the Pharisees in Galilee see Richard A. Horsley, "The Pharisees and Jesus in Galilee and Q," in Alan J. Avery-Peck, Daniel Harrington, and Jacob Neusner, eds., *When Judaism and Christianity Began: Essays in Memory of Anthony J. Saldarini* (Leiden: Brill, forthcoming).

123. Charles E. Carlston, "The Things That Defile (Mark VI.14) and the Law in Matthew and Mark," *NTS* 15 (1968–69) 75–96.

124. See, e.g., Matt 3:7; 6:5; 23:1-36; Luke 15:2; 16:14-25.

125. For an example of a Jewish polemic against hypocrisy, see *Psalms of Solomon* 4. Ironically, Marie-Joseph LaGrange (*Le Judaïsme avant Jésus-Christ* [Paris: Gabalda, 1931] 160) uses this text to paint a vilifying portrait of the Pharisees. His conclusions are problematic not only because of his exaggerations, but also because the Pharisaic provenance of this text cannot be proven; see below, pp. 177–78.

126. On this text see especially Gerhard Maier, *Der Mensch und freie Wille* (WUNT 12; Tübingen: Mohr/Siebeck, 1971) 282–83, 293–301, 325–42. Horsley ("Pharisees") suggests that with a predominantly oral society, it is no accident that we possess no literature written by Pharisees.

127. See the brief comment by John Strugnell, *JBL* 89 (1970) 485. On *4 Ezra* see the comment by Michael E. Stone, *Fourth Ezra: A Commentary on the Book of Fourth Ezra* (Hermeneia; Minneapolis: Fortress Press, 1990) 38. For a discussion of the importance of Torah as a solution to the disaster of 70 c.e., see Gwendolyn B. Sayler, *Have the Promises Failed? A Literary Analysis of 2 Baruch* (SBLDS 72; Chico, Calif.: Scholars Press, 1984).

128. See George W. E. Nickelsburg, "Jews and Christians in the First Century: The Struggle over Identity," *Neot* 27 (1993) 365–90.

129. Bruce Chilton ("James and the [Christian] Pharisees," in Avery-Peck, Harrington, and Neusner, eds., *Judaism and Christianity*) suggests that the tension between Jesus and the Pharisees depicted in the Gospels may reflect the dispute between Paul and James, on the one hand, and the Christian Pharisees, on the other hand, over the issue of circumcision (Acts 15). However one evaluates that explanation, it rightly brings into the equation the first-century Christians of Pharisaic persuasion. On the portrayal of the Pharisees in Q, see Horsley, "Pharisees."

130. See the discussions by Gary G. Porton, "Diversity in Post-Biblical Judaism," in Kraft and Nickelsburg, eds., *Early Judaism,* 66–68; idem, "Sadducees," *ADB* 5:892–94; and Saldarini, *Pharisees,* 298–308, and the literature cited by them.

131. Saldarini, *Pharisees,* 121, 298–300; Porton, "Sadducees," 894.

132. Albert C. Sundberg, ("Sadducees," *IDB* 4:160) and Porton ("Sadducees," 892) agree on this derivation, but draw, respectively, maximal and minimal conclusions from it.

133. For a discussion of the passages see Saldarini, *Pharisees,* 231–35; Porton, "Sadducees," 892–93.

134. Saldarini, *Pharisees,* 231–35; Porton, "Sadducees," 892–93.

135. Saldarini, *Pharisees,* 303–4; Porton, "Sadducees," 893.

136. Sundberg, "Sadducees," 162; Saldarini, *Pharisees,* 302–3; Porton, "Sadducees," 894.

137. Saldarini, *Pharisees,* 304.

138. See the comment of Porton ("Diversity," 68), who calls for a careful reappraisal of all the sources.

139. See Sundberg ("Sadducees," 160–62), whose section on "History" treats mainly aspects of the history of the priesthood, punctuated with the use of adverbs like "probably" and "possibly."

140. For the archaeological evidence that ties the Scrolls to the community see Magness, *Archaeology,* 43–44, 78–88.

141. The bibliography on Scrolls research is voluminous. For a bibliography of bibliographies on the Scrolls see Joseph A. Fitzmyer, *The Dead Sea Scrolls: Major Publications and Tools for Study* (rev. ed.; Atlanta: Scholars Press, 1990) 97–98. Fitzmyer's volume is itself a valuable bibliographic tool. For a series of detailed bibliographies see William Sanford LaSor, *Bibliography of the Dead Sea Scrolls: 1948–1957* = *Fuller Library Bulletin* 31 (1958) (Pasadena: The Library, Fuller Theological Seminary, 1958); B. Jongeling, *A Classified Bibliography of the Finds in the Desert of Judah: 1958–69* (STDJ 7; Leiden: Brill, 1971); and Florentinio García Martinez and Donald W. Parry, eds., *A Bibliography of the Finds in the Desert of Judah 1970–95* (STDJ 19; Leiden: Brill, 1996). For a major survey of Qumran scholarship see Jerome Murphy-O'Connor, "The Judean Desert," in Kraft and Nickelsburg, eds., *Early Judaism,* 119–56. For a recent and perceptive summary see Eileen Schuller, "Going on Fifty: Reflections on the Study of the Dead Sea Scrolls," *The Canadian Society of Biblical Studies Bulletin & Abstracts 1995/96* 55 (1996) 20–45. For some trends in Qumran research see George W. E. Nickelsburg, "Currents in Qumran Scholarship: The Interplay of Data, Agendas, and Methodology," in Robert A. Kugler and Eileen M. Schuller, eds., *The Dead Sea Scrolls at Fifty* (SBLEJL 15; Atlanta: Scholars Press, 1999) 79–99. For some recent survey volumes see Devorah Dimant and Uriel Rappaport, eds., *The Dead Sea Scrolls: Forty Years of Research* (STDJ 10; Leiden: Brill; Jerusalem: Magnes, 1992); Hershel Shanks, ed., *Understanding the Dead Sea Scrolls* (New York: Random House, 1992); Eugene Ulrich and James VanderKam, eds., *The Community of the Renewed Covenant: The Notre Dame Symposium of the Dead Sea Scrolls* (Christianity and Judaism in Antiquity Series 4; Notre Dame, Ind.; Univ. of Notre Dame Press, 1993); Kugler and Schuller, eds., *Dead Sea Scrolls at Fifty*; Peter W. Flint and James C. VanderKam, eds., *The Dead Sea Scrolls after Fifty Years: A Comprehensive Assessment* (2 vols.; Leiden: Brill, 1998–99). For three recent introductions to the Scrolls see James C. VanderKam, *The Dead Sea Scrolls Today* (Grand Rapids: Eerdmans, 1994); Lawrence H. Schiffman, *Reclaiming the Dead Sea Scrolls* (New York: Doubleday, 1994); and Hartmut Stegemann, *The Library of Qumran* (Grand Rapids: Eerdmans, 1998). For an English translation of the Scrolls and major Scroll fragments, see Geza Vermes, *The Complete Dead Sea Scrolls in English* (Allen Lane: Penguin, 1997). For a more selective collection see idem, *The Dead Sea Scrolls in English* (4th ed.; London: Penguin, 1995).

142. Josephus, *J. W.* 2.119-62; *Ant.* 18.18-22; Philo, *Prob.* 75–91; *Hypoth.* 11.1-11; Hippolytus, *Haer.* 9.18-29. For a detailed comparison of Josephus's account with the Scrolls see Todd S. Beall, *Josephus' Description of the Essenes Illustrated by the Dead Sea Scrolls* (SNTSMS 58; Cambridge: Cambridge Univ. Press, 1988); and, more briefly, VanderKam, *Dead Sea Scrolls Today,* 71–98. On the common source of Josephus and Hippolytus, see Morton Smith, "Description."

143. Pliny, *Nat.* 5.15.73. On this text see Magness, *Archaeology,* 40–41, 45. For a cautious discussion see Robert A. Kraft, "Pliny on Essenes, Pliny on Jews," *DSD* 8 (2001) = *Qumran Studies Presented to Emanuel Tov on His Sixtieth Birthday,* 255–61.

144. For early proponents of the Essene hypothesis see Nickelsburg, "Currents," 91–92.

145. See Lawrence H. Schiffmann, "The Sadducean Origins of the Dead Sea Sect," in Shanks, ed., *Understanding,* 35–49; and idem, *Reclaiming,* 83–112, 154–57.

146. See, in response to Schiffmann's article, James C. VanderKam, "The People of the Dead Sea Scrolls: Essenes or Sadducees," in Shanks, ed., *Understanding,* 50–52. See also the detailed discussion of the halakah in 4QMMT by Ya'akov Sussmann in DJD 10:179–200, and its carefully phrased conclusion on p. 200. On references to the Sadducees in the Mishnah see Joseph A. Fitzmyer, "The Qumran Community: Essene or Sadducean," *HeyJ* 35 (1995) 467–76, who sees these as references to Zadokite, i.e., Qumranic, halakah.

147. On determinism see VanderKam, "People," 54–55. On the afterlife, angels, and spirits see Fitzmyer, "Qumran Community," 473. See also Nickelsburg, *Resurrection,* 152–59, 166–69.

148. Schiffman, *Reclaiming,* 97–104. Admittedly, the points of discrepancy are relatively few; see Beall, *Description,* 129.

149. See especially Albert I. Baumgarten, "The Rule of the Martian as Applied to Qumran," *Israel Oriental Studies* 14 (1994) 121–42; and much greater detail, idem, *The Flourishing of Jewish Sects in the Maccabean Era: An Interpretation* (JSJSup 55; Leiden: Brill, 1997).

150. On the Teacher see VanderKam, *Dead Sea Scrolls Today,* 100–104. For a reference to another leader or leaders see CD 6:2-11.

151. Cf. CD 1:8—2:1; 1QS 2:4-18. For other polarities see George W. E. Nickelsburg, "Religious Exclusivism: A Worldview Governing Some Texts Found at Qumran," in Michael Becker and Wolfgang Fenske, eds., *Das Ende der Tage und die Gegenwart des Heils: Begegnungen mit dem Neuen Testament und seiner Umwelt: Festschrift für Heinz-Wolfgang Kuhn zum 65. Geburtstag* (Leiden: Brill, 1999) 46–59.

152. Cf. also CD 6:2-11. For a parallel cf. *Jub.* 23:26.

153. On the calendrical material at Qumran see Shemaryahu Talmon, "Calendars and Mishmarot," in Schiffman and VanderKam, eds., *Encyclopedia,* 1:117–20; James C. VanderKam, *Calendars in the Dead Sea Scrolls: Measuring Time* (London: Routledge, 1998).

154. See, e.g., Sussmann, DJD 10: 196–200; Schiffman, *Reclaiming,* 249–52; Joseph M. Baumgarten, DJD 18:18–22; Lawrence H. Schiffman, "The Pharisees and Their Legal Traditions according to the Dead Sea Scrolls," *DSD* 8 (2001) 262–77.

155. For a discussion of the Essene ablutions and the *mikvaot* and Qumran, see Magness, *Archaeology,* 132–58.

156. See esp. 1QS 6:2—7:25. For a discussion of some of the details see Aharon Shemesh, "Expulsion and Exclusion in the Community Rule and the Damascus Document," *DSD* 9 (2002) 44–74. Cf. the many parallels that are the substance of the accounts in Philo, Josephus, and Hippolytus.

157. See Gary A. Anderson, "Aaron," in Schiffman and VanderKam, eds., *Encyclopedia,* 1:1–2; Philip R. Davies, "Zadok, Sons of," in ibid., 2:1005–7.

158. John J. Collins, *The Scepter and the Star: The Messiahs of the Dead Sea Scrolls and Other Ancient Literature* (New York: Doubleday, 1995) 74–89.

159. See Hannah K. Harrington, "Purity," in Schiffman and VanderKam, eds., *Encyclopedia,* 2:724–28.

160. On Qumran attitudes about the temple, see, e.g., Joseph M. Baumgarten, "The Essenes and the Temple," in idem, *Studies in Qumran Law* (SJLA 24; Leiden: Brill, 1977) 57–74; Francis Schmidt, *La pensée du Temple de Jérusalem à Qoumrân* (Paris: Seuil, 1994).

161. See also the very fragmentary introduction to the Damascus Document (4Q266:1-8), which appears to allude to a two-ways document.

162. See Frank M. Cross, *The Ancient Library of Qumran* (3d ed.; Minneapolis: Fortress Press, 1995) 89–93.

163. See Heinz-Wolfgang Kuhn, *Enderwartung und gegenwärtiges Heil: Untersuchungen zu den Gemeindeliedern von Qumran* (SUNT 4; Göttingen: Vandenhoeck & Ruprecht, 1966); Nickelsburg, *Resurrection,* 152–56.

164. Fragments of seven copies of the War Scroll and related texts were found in Qumran caves 1, 4, and 11. For a list see DJD 39:132. While this indicates the popularity of the work, we cannot be certain how large a role it played in Qumran thought and practice, and when.

165. On notions of revelation at Qumran, see George W. E. Nickelsburg, "The Nature and Function of Revelation in 1 Enoch, Jubilees, and Some Qumranic Documents," in Esther G. Chazon and Michael E. Stone, eds., *Pseudepigraphical Perspectives: The Apocrypha and Pseudepigrapha in Light of the Dead Sea Scrolls; Proceedings of the International Symposium of the Orion Center for the Study of the Dead Sea Scrolls and Associated Literature, 12–14 January, 1997* (STDJ 31; Leiden: Brill, 1999) 107–17; John J. Collins, "Apocalypticism and Literary Genre in the Dead Sea Scrolls," in Flint and VanderKam, eds., *Dead Sea Scrolls after Fifty,* 403–30.

166. On the MSS of parts of *1 Enoch* see J. T. Milik, *The Books of Enoch: Aramaic Fragments of Qumran Cave 4* (Oxford: Clarendon, 1976). For the fragments of Aramaic Levi see Jonas C. Greenfield and Michael E. Stone, DJD 22:2–72. On the Visions of Amram see idem, "Amram," in Schiffman and VanderKam, eds., *Encyclopedia,* 1:23–24; and on the Testament of Qahat see Michael E. Stone, "Qahat," in ibid., 2:731–32. On Moses see John Strugnell, "Moses the Pseudepigrapher at Qumran," DJD 19:131–36.

167. Collins, *Scepter,* 102–23.

168. On the discrepancy between Josephus, who ascribes a belief in immortality to the Essenes, and Hippolytus, who mentions resurrection, see Nickelsburg, *Resurrection,* 167–69.

169. Beall, *Description.*

170. A belief in immortality and an interest and an adeptness in prophecy (cf. Josephus, *J. W.* 2.154-59) hardly add up to the Scrolls' eschatological worldview.

171. See, however, Magness (*Archaeology,* 190–99), who argues that the Essenes' white linen garments mentioned by Josephus may have denoted priestly status.

172. See Murphy-O'Connor, "Judean Desert," 125.

173. Note also how his Hellenistic description of the activity of John the Baptist (*Ant.* 18.116-19) differs from the Gospels' apocalyptic portrayals.

174. See Martin Goodman, "A Note on the Qumran Sectarians, the Essenes and Josephus," *JJS* 46 (1995) 161–66; Baumgarten, *Sects,* 1, n. 1.

175. See the bibliographies cited above on p. 237, n. 141.

176. For details see George W. E. Nickelsburg, "Currents in Qumran Research," and the responses to it in Kugler and Schuller, eds., *Dead Sea Scrolls at Fifty,* 79–146. The topic is worthy of a whole monograph, written by a social historian.

177. *Discoveries in the Judaean Desert* (Oxford: Clarendon, 1955–). For the overview of the series by Emanuel Tov, see DJD 39:1–25.

178. See the 1991 statement by the Society of Biblical Literature presented by James C. VanderKam, "Ethics of Publication of the Dead Sea Scrolls: Panel Discussion," in Michael O. Wise, Norman Golb, John J. Collins, and Dennis G. Pardee, eds., *Methods of Investigation of the Dead Sea Scrolls and the Khirbet Qumran Site: Present Realities and Future Prospects* (Annals of the New York Academy of Sciences 722; New York: New York Academy of Sciences, 1994) 462–63.

179. On the technologies see, e.g., Scott R. Woodward, Gila Kahila, Patricia Smith, Charles Greenblatt, Joe Zias, and Magen Broshi, "Analysis of Parchment Fragments from the Judean Desert Using DNA Techniques," in Donald W. Parry and Stephen D. Ricks, eds., *Current Research and Technological Developments on the Dead Sea Scrolls: Conference on the Texts from the Judean Desert, Jerusalem, 30 April 1995* (STDJ 20; Leiden: Brill, 1995) 215–38; Bruce Zuckerman and Kenneth Zuckerman, "Photography and Computer Imaging," in Schiffman and VanderKam, eds., *Encyclopedia,* 2:669–75; Gregory L. Doudna, "Dating the Scrolls on the Basis of Radiocarbon Analysis," in Flint and VanderKam, eds., *Dead Sea Scrolls after Fifty,* 1:430–71; Gregory Bearman, Stephen J. Pfann, and Sheila I. Spiro, "Imaging the Scrolls: Photographic and Direct Digital Acquisition," in ibid., 1:472–95; Donald W. Parry, David V. Arnold, David G. Long, and Scott R. Woodward, "New Technological Advances: DNA, Databases, Imaging Radar," in ibid., 1:496–515; Annette Steudel, "Assembling and Reconstructing Manuscripts," in ibid., 1:516–534; Esther Boyd-Alkalay and Elena Libman, "Preserving the Dead Sea Scrolls and Qumran Artifacts," in ibid., 1:535–44; see further the articles in Donald W. Parry, ed., *The Provo International Conference on the Dead Sea Scrolls: Technological Innovations, New Texts, and Reformulated Issues* (STDJ 30; Leiden: Brill, 1999) 5–43.

180. On the history of the problem see John Kampen, *The Hasideans and the Origin of Pharisaism: A Study in 1 and 2 Maccabees* (SBLSCS 24; Atlanta: Scholars Press, 1988) 1–43; Philip R. Davies, "Hasidim in the Maccabean Period," *JJS* 28 (1977) 127–40; Nickelsburg, "Social Aspects," 647–48.

181. For recent discussions and hypotheses on Qumran origins see F. García Martínez and Julio C. Trebolle Barrera, *The People of the Dead Sea Scrolls* (Leiden: Brill, 1995); Philip R. Davies, *Sects and Scrolls: Essays on Qumran and Related Topics* (South Florida Studies in the History of Judaism 134; Atlanta: Scholars Press, 1996); and Gabriele Boccaccini, *Beyond the Essene Hypothesis: The Parting of the Ways between Qumran and Enochic Judaism* (Grand Rapids: Eerdmans, 1998). For a discussion of Boccaccini see Wido van Peursen, "Qumran Origins: Some Remarks on the Enochic/Essene Hypothesis," *RevQ* 20 (2001) 243–53.

182. For a discussion of the issue see Nickelsburg, *1 Enoch 1,* 67, 238–47, 271, 394–95, 447.

183. On the *dorshê hahalaqot* and the Pharisees see Schiffman, "Pharisees," 269.

184. For some forays into these issues see Carol A. Newsom, "The Case of the Blinking I: Discourse of the Self at Qumran," *Semeia* 57 (1992) 13–23; idem, "Knowing as Doing: The Social Symbolics of Knowledge at Qumran," *Semeia* 59 (1992) 139–53; idem, "Disciplinary Power in the Serek ha-Yahad: Rewards and Punishments from a Foucauldian Perspective," unpublished paper given at the 1997 Annual Meeting of the Society of Biblical Literature; idem, "Apocalyptic Subjects: Social Construction of the Self in the Qumran Hodayot," *JSP* 12 (2001) 3–35; Jean Duhaime, "Relative Deprivation in New Religious Movements and the Qumran Community," *RevQ* 16 (1993–94) 265–76; Baumgarten, "Rule of the Martian"; idem, *Sects.*

185. On the texts, especially, see Eileen Schuller, "Women in the Dead Sea Scrolls," in Flint and VanderKam, eds., *Dead Sea Scrolls after Fifty,* 117–44. On the archaeology see Magness, *Archaeology,* 160–84.

186. On these meanings see Cross, *Library,* 54, n. 1, 183.

187. See VanderKam, *Dead Sea Scrolls Today,* 92.

188. Kampen, *Hasideans,* 161–71; idem, "The Cult of Artemis and the Essenes in Syro-Palestine," *DSD* 10 (forthcoming 2003).

189. For early literature on the Scrolls and the NT see Lasor, *Bibliography,* 84–89; Jongeling, *Classified Bibliography,* 111–29. See also the discussion by A. Dupont-Sommer, *The Essene Writings from Qumran* (Cleveland and New York: Word, 1967) 369–78; Cross, *Library,* 143–70.

190. Books devoted to the topic include: F. F. Bruce, *Second Thoughts on the Dead Sea Scrolls* (Grand Rapids: Eerdmans, 1956); William Sanford LaSor, *The Amazing Dead Sea Scrolls and the Christian Faith* (Chicago: Moody, 1957); Krister Stendahl, ed., *The Scrolls and the New Testament* (New York: Harper & Brothers, 1957); Matthew Black, *The Scrolls and Christian Origins: Studies in the Jewish Background of the New Testament* (New York: Nelson, 1961); and James H. Charlesworth, ed., *John and the Dead Sea Scrolls* (New York: Crossroad, 1991). For a summary of the discussion see Murphy-O'Connor, "Qumran and the New Testament."

191. For a summary see Cross, *Library,* 143–70; VanderKam, *Dead Sea Scrolls Today,* 159–85.

192. That the Enochic corpus was the product of a group, see Tiller, *Commentary,* 101–26; Nickelsburg, *1 Enoch 1,* 64.

193. Stating the issue in a slightly different way, Krister Stendahl (*Scrolls and the New Testament,* 10–17) made this point early on in the discussion, comparing Qumran and early Christian eschatology.

194. On the general lack of Jewish interest in mission among the Gentiles see Martin Goodman, *Mission and Conversion* (Oxford: Clarendon, 1994) 38–90. On *1 Enoch* and the Gentiles see Nickelsburg, *1 Enoch 1,* 52–53.

195. See the patristic citations in A. F. J. Klijn and G. J. Reinink, *Patristic Evidence for Jewish-Christian Sects* (NovTSup 36; Leiden: Brill, 1973) 307–8. On Matthew and the Torah see Anthony J. Saldarini, *Matthew's Christian-Jewish Community* (Chicago: Univ. of Chicago Press, 1994) 124–64.

196. For a summary of scholarship on the Hasidim see Kampen, *Hasideans,* 1–43. For an earlier critique of oversimplifying claims about the Hasidim see Davies, *Hasidim.* Totally different is the approach of Baumgarten (*Sects,* 26, n. 79), who, writing in 1996, refers to "the ill-defined group of Hasidim," citing Davies's 1977 article but not Kampen's 1988 book.

197. See, e.g., Victor Tcherikover, *Hellenistic Civilization and the Jews* (Philadelphia: Jewish Publication Society of America, 1961) 125–26, 196–230; Otto Plöger, *Theocracy and Eschatology* (Richmond: John Knox, 1968) 7–9, 17, 23–24; Hengel, *Judaism and Hellenism,* 1:174–247, 250–54. I also worked with the scheme; see Nickelsburg, *Resurrection,* 16–23.

198. Although Kampen prefers the translation "leading citizens," he acknowledges the military connotations of the term (*Hasideans,* 107, 114). See also Daniel R. Schwartz ("Hasidim in 1 Maccabees 2:42?" *SCI* 13 [1994] 7), who knows Kampen's book, but assumes the translation "mighty warriors."

199. Kampen, *Hasideans,* 144.

200. For this Schwartz ("Hasidim") make a compelling text-critical argument, which was called to my attention by Erich Gruen (personal correspondence, July 1, 2002). My only hesitation is that Schwartz ("Hasidim," 7) fails to mention the references from 11QPs[a] and the *Psalms of Solomon,* cited below, which suggest that "assembly of the pious" was a cliché.

201. Kampen, *Hasideans,* 52–53.

202. Ibid., 135–48.

203. Throughout his book Kampen (ibid.) makes a cumulative argument for the Hasidim as the parent group of the Pharisees, but concludes without any certainty ("It may well be . . . ," p. 222). His discussion of the Essenes and the Hasidim is primarily a critique of one of the standard etymologies of "Essene," 150–85. However that may be, one must be cautious of assuming a simple social map of second-century Jewish religious groups.

204. For the text see the edition of James A. Sanders, DJD 4.

205. See Peter W. Flint, *The Dead Sea Psalms Scrolls and the Book of Psalms* (STDJ 17; Leiden: Brill, 1997) 198–200, who cites (p. 176, n. 25) Dieter Lührmann, "Ein Weisheitspsalm aus Qumran (11QPs[a] XVIII)," *ZAW* 80 (1968) 87–98; and Robert Polzin, "Notes on the Dating of the Non-Massoretic Psalms of 11QPs[a]," *HTR* 60 (1967) 468–76.

206. On the original language of the *Psalms of Solomon* see Herbert E. Ryle and Montague Rhodes James, *Psalmoi Solomōntos: Psalms of the Pharisees Commonly Called The Psalms of Solomon* (Cambridge: Cambridge Univ. Press, 1891) lxxvii–lxxxvii.

207. 2:36(40); 3:8(10); 4:6(7), 8(9); 8:23(28), 34(40); 9:3(6); 12:4(5), 6(7); 13:10(9), 12(11); 14:3(2), 10(7); 15:3(5), 7(9).

208. On these groups see above, p. 333, n. 86.

209. For the evidence of a community behind the Enochic writings see Nickelsburg, *1 Enoch 1*, 64.

210. On the relationship of the Enoch community or communities to known groups, see ibid., 64–65. For one approach see Boccaccini, *Essene Hypothesis*.

211. On *Jubilees'* use of the Enochic traditions see Nickelsburg, *1 Enoch 1*, 71–76.

212. On *1 Enoch* and the Mosaic tradition see ibid., 60–61.

213. For the MSS of *Jubilees* at Qumran and some related texts see VanderKam, DJD 13:1–185.

214. See Michael E. Stone, "Levi, Aramaic Levi," in Schiffman and VanderKam, eds., *Encyclopedia*, 1:486–88.

215. On the authorship see Collins, *Daniel*, 66–69. For a list of the Qumran texts and the locus of their publication see DJD 39:47–48. On Daniel and the Enochic tradition see, e.g., Nickelsburg, *1 Enoch 1*, 254, n. 5; idem, "Son of Man," 138–39.

216. Nickelsburg, "Son of Man," 142–49.

217. See idem, *Jewish Literature*, 80–83.

218. Ibid., 142–45.

219. On John the Baptist see Scobie, *Baptist*; and most recently the thorough treatment by Taylor, *Immerser*.

220. See the extensive discussion by Taylor, *Immerser*, 15–48. Hermann Lichtenberger ("The Dead Sea Scrolls and John the Baptist: Reflections on Josephus' Account of John the Baptist," in Dimant and Rappaport, eds., *Dead Sea Scrolls*, 340–46) finds that Josephus describes John as an Essene, but is not certain that he actually was. See also Scobie, *John the Baptist*, 32–48; and Robert L. Webb, "John the Baptist," in Schiffman and VanderKam, eds., *Encyclopedia*, 1:418–21.

221. On John's disciples see Scobie, *John the Baptist*, 131–41; Taylor, *Immerser*, 105–6, 109–11.

222. See Kampen, *Hasideans*, 67–71.

223. For parallels cf. *T. Moses* 9 and the case of Taxo and his son (see Nickelsburg, *Resurrection*, 97–102); and the *Martyrdom of Isaiah* (Nickelsburg, *Jewish Literature*, 142–45). Whether the verb "seek" here connotes a process of exegeting the Scriptures is uncertain; for that usage see Werline, *Penitential Prayer*, 111–14.

224. Wilson, *Religious Sects*, 23–47.

225. Baumgarten, *Sects*, 13.

226. Nickelsburg, "Religious Exclusivism," 46. In a response to a reprinted form of my article, Carol Newsom suggests that my narrow definition of "sect" may obscure how such groups fit in the broader continuum of religious groups. For the article, her response, and my response to her, see Neusner and Avery-Peck, eds., *Perspective*, 2:139–75. By citing Wilson but maintaining my definition here, I attempt to indicate both continuity and uniqueness. For definitions of "sect" similar to mine, which combine sociological

and theological elements, see Shaye J. D. Cohen, *From Maccabees to Mishnah* (LEC 7; Philadelphia: Westminster, 1987) 125, "A sect is a small organized group that separates itself from a large religious body and asserts that it alone embodies the ideals of the larger group because it alone understands God's will"; and Jutta M. Jokiranta, "'Sectarianism' of the Qumran 'Sect': Sociological Notes," *RevQ* 20/78 (2001) 223–39, who emphasizes "the tendency to view oneself as *uniquely legitimate,* or the tendency to set up *boundaries* against others."

227. See the detailed discussion of Baumgarten, *Sects,* passim.

228. On the possible liturgical use of the Enochic Woes see Nickelsburg, *1 Enoch 1,* 429.

229. See Nickelsburg, "Son of Man," 142–49.

230. See idem, *1 Enoch 1,* 103–4.

231. Ibid., 87–108.

232. A discussion of the social settings of Second Temple Judaism should include the topics of kinship, marriage, home, and gender. New literary and epigraphic sources and archaeological evidence, as well as social scientific methods and feminist concerns, have shed considerable light on these matters. I have not treated them here because, as I noted above (pp. 7–8), I have limited myself to issues in Judaism that also enlighten our understanding of early Christianity and its relationship to Judaism. In these particular instances I have not found the discussions that make such a comparison possible. (See also the caution of Ross S. Kraemer, "Jewish Women and Christian Origins: Some Caveats," in Ross Shepard Kraemer and Mary Rose D'Angelo, eds., *Women and Christian Origins* [New York: Oxford Univ. Press, 1999] 46.) For some introduction to these issues see K. C. Hanson and Douglas E. Oakman, *Palestine in the Time of Jesus: Social Structures and Social Conflicts* (Minneapolis: Fortress Press, 1998) 19–61; Amy Jill Levine, ed., *"Women Like These": New Perspectives on Jewish Women in the Greco-Roman World* (SBLEJL 1; Atlanta: Scholars Press, 1991); Kraemer and D'Angelo, eds., *Women and Christian Origins.*

## 7. Conclusions and Implications

1. See above, p. 201, n. 3.

2. See Rodney A. Werline, "The Transformation of Pauline Arguments in Justin Martyr's Dialogue with Trypho," *HTR* 92 (1999) 79–93.

# Index of Passages Cited

## Hebrew Bible

### Genesis

| | |
|---|---|
| 1:1-5 | 113 |
| 1:2 | 63 |
| 1:27 | 56 |
| 2:6 | 104 |
| 3:5 | 113 |
| 4:10 | 99 |
| 6:1-4 | 12, 63, 102 |
| 6:5 | 99, 102 |
| 6:13 | 102 |
| 12:1-3 | 210 |
| 12:3 | 75 |
| 14 | 101 |
| 15:6 | 39, 52 |
| 17:4 | 75 |
| 22 | 39, 52 |
| 30:14-24 | 14 |
| 33 | 15 |
| 34 | 93 |
| 37–45 | 19, 106, 111 |
| 38 | 14 |
| 49 | 14 |

### Exodus

| | |
|---|---|
| 14:13 | 212 |
| 15:2 | 212 |
| 20:2-17 | 209 |
| 21–23 | 211 |
| 32:25-29 | 93 |

### Leviticus

| | |
|---|---|
| 8:1-13 | 93 |

### Numbers

| | |
|---|---|
| 21:18 | 47 |
| 25 | 71, 93 |
| 25:6-8 | 94 |

### Deuteronomy

| | |
|---|---|
| 6:2 | 211 |
| 6:5 | 211 |
| 10:20 | 211 |
| 11:1 | 211 |
| 13:3-4 | 211 |
| 24:1-4 | 56 |
| 28–32 | 16, 45, 66 |
| 28:1-14 | 32 |
| 28:15-29 | 32 |
| 28:59-60 | 214 |
| 29:22-28 | 214 |
| 30:1-10 | 32, 47, 68 |
| 30:6 | 211 |
| 32:1-43 | 69 |
| 32:8 | 98 |
| 32:19-21 | 62 |
| 32:36 | 19 |
| 33 | 14, 91 |
| 33:2 | 91, 98 |

### Joshua

| | |
|---|---|
| 24:2-3 | 13 |

### Judges

| | |
|---|---|
| 5:20 | 98 |
| 15:18 | 212 |

### Ruth | 75

### 1 Samuel

| | |
|---|---|
| 14:45 | 212 |
| 15:22-23 | 213 |

### 2 Samuel

| | |
|---|---|
| 3–12 | 226 |
| 7:4-17 | 91 |
| 15:10 | 212 |

### 1 Kings

| | |
|---|---|
| 3–10 | 226 |
| 17 | 214 |
| 18–21 | 226 |
| 18 | 93 |
| 22:1-40 | 97 |
| 22:19-23 | 63, 98 |

### 2 Kings

| | |
|---|---|
| 4 | 214 |
| 5 | 214 |

**1 Chronicles**

| | |
|---|---|
| 21:1 | 63 |

**Ezra** 34, 122

| | |
|---|---|
| 9–10 | 76 |
| 9 | 17, 66, 68 |

**Nehemiah** 34, 122

| | |
|---|---|
| 1 | 17, 68 |
| 9 | 66, 68 |

**Esther** 106, 111

**Job** 35

| | |
|---|---|
| 1–2 | 13, 63, 64 |
| 16:19 | 99 |
| 19:25 | 99 |

**Psalms**

| | |
|---|---|
| 2 | 24, 91, 105 |
| 2:2 | 20 |
| 2:4 | 107 |
| 2:7 | 107 |
| 2:9 | 92 |
| 2:10 | 107 |
| 3:8 | 212 |
| 22 | 69, 210 |
| 27 | 69 |
| 38 | 214 |
| 40:6 | 23 |
| 45 | 91 |
| 45:4 | 91 |
| 45:7 | 91 |
| 51:3 | 213 |
| 51:9 | 213 |
| 51:10-11 | 68 |
| 51:12 | 213 |
| 68:19 | 226 |
| 69 | 69, 210 |
| 69:1 | 212 |

| | |
|---|---|
| 72 | 91 |
| 72:3-4 | 91 |
| 72:12-14 | 91 |
| 74:12-14 | 63 |
| 74:12 | 212 |
| 82 | 63, 98 |
| 89 | 92 |
| 110:1 | 109 |
| 110:2-4 | 226 |
| 110:4 | 109 |
| 149:1 | 231 |

**Proverbs**

| | |
|---|---|
| 8 | 103–4 |

**Ecclesiastes** 35

**Isaiah**

| | |
|---|---|
| 1:11-14 | 213 |
| 7:14 | 23 |
| 7:20 | 62 |
| 9:1-7 | 91 |
| 11 | 24, 105 |
| 11:1-9 | 91 |
| 11:2-4 | 18, 20 |
| 11:2 | 92 |
| 11:3 | 92 |
| 11:4 | 92 |
| 14 | 19, 63, 64 |
| 14:13-14 | 100, 114 |
| 30:10 | 212 |
| 38:20 | 213, 214 |
| 38:21 | 214 |
| 40–66 | 130, 132 |
| 40:2 | 65 |
| 40:3-5 | 121 |
| 40:3 | 228 |
| 40:4 | 121 |
| 40:9-11 | 121 |
| 42:1-4 | 18, 75 |
| 42:1-2 | 112 |

| | |
|---|---|
| 42:1 | 20, 105 |
| 43:25 | 213 |
| 44:22 | 209, 213 |
| 45 | 92, 121, 133 |
| 45:2 | 121 |
| 48:8, 10 | 20 |
| 49 | 105 |
| 49:1-6 | 20 |
| 49:2 | 18 |
| 49:3-7 | 121 |
| 49:6 | 75, 106 |
| 50:4-9 | 18, 106 |
| 50:4 | 18, 19, 24 |
| 51:3 | 121 |
| 51:9-11 | 121 |
| 51:9 | 63 |
| 52:11-12 | 121 |
| 52:13—53:12 | 17–20, 67, 79, 97, 105–7, 121, 129, 206, 216, 221 |
| 52:13-15 | 18 |
| 52:13 | 18 |
| 52:14 | 19 |
| 53:10-11 | 65 |
| 53:10 | 18, 20 |
| 53:11 | 18, 105 |
| 53:12 | 114 |
| 55:3-4 | 92 |
| 56–66 | 121, 123, 153 |
| 60 | 75 |
| 61:1 | 112 |
| 61:13 | 92 |
| 63–66 | 121 |
| 63:11 | 227 |
| 65–66 | 122, 124, 131 |

| | | | | | |
|---|---|---|---|---|---|
| 65:17-25 | 124, 144 | 3:17-18 | 38 | **Jonah** | 75 |
| 66:15-16 | 121 | 3:28-30 | 77 | | |
| 66:24 | 124 | 4:37 | 77 | **Micah** | |
| | | 6 | 19, 24, | 1 | 91 |
| **Jeremiah** | | | 37, 38, | 4:3 | 226 |
| 3 | 209 | | 106, 111 | 6:6-9 | 213 |
| 3:1 | 209 | 6:26-28 | 77 | | |
| 3:12 | 209 | 7–12 | 77, 126, | **Habakkuk** | |
| 3:22 | 209 | | 133 | 2:1-2 | 16 |
| 4:1 | 209 | 7 | 103–7 | | |
| 7:21-23 | 213 | 7:10 | 98 | **Haggai** | 122 |
| 23:1-8 | 91 | 7:13-14 | 20, 110 | | |
| 23:5-6 | 91 | 7:14 | 130 | **Zechariah** | 122, 153 |
| 23:7-8 | 121 | 8:11 | 100 | 4:14 | 94 |
| 31:31-34 | 121 | 8:16 | 102 | 8:12 | 226 |
| 46–51 | 76 | 9 | 68, 75, | 14:9-21 | 75 |
| | | | 125 | | |
| **Ezekiel** | | 9:2 | 126 | **Malachi** | 122, 153 |
| 1:5-14 | 99 | 9:21-27 | 102, 126 | 3:7 | 209 |
| 16 | 209 | 10–12 | 70, 71 | 4:1 | 135 |
| 24–33 | 76 | 10 | 103 | | |
| 34–37 | 121 | 10:13 | 100 | | |
| 34 | 191, 121 | 10:21 | 100 | | |
| 34:22-27 | 226 | 11–12 | 221 | | |
| 34:40 | 92 | 11:33-35 | 37 | | |
| 36:22-36 | 121 | 11:34 | 71 | | |
| 36:22-32 | 65 | 12:1 | 99, 100, | | |
| 36:26-27 | 68 | | 103 | | |
| 37 | 65, 121 | 12:2-3 | 123 | | |
| 38–39 | 76 | 12:3 | 18, 124, | | |
| 47:22-23 | 76 | | 143 | | |
| | | 12:12 | 133 | | |
| **Daniel** | 15, 36, | | | | |
| | 180 | **Hosea** | | | |
| 1–6 | 40, 77 | 2 | 209 | | |
| 1 | 37 | 11:1 | 209 | | |
| 2 | 133 | 14:1 | 209 | | |
| 2:47 | 77 | | | | |
| 3 | 19, 24, | **Amos** | | | |
| | 37, 38, | 5:21-23 | 213 | | |
| | 106, 111 | 9:11 | 47 | | |

## Apocrypha and Pseudepigrapha

| | |
|---|---|
| *Adam, Penitence of* | |
| 41–42 | 221 |
| | |
| *Adam and Eve* | 14 |
| 12–17 | 64 |
| 41–42 | 221 |
| | |
| *Apocalypse* | 78, 85, |
| *of Abraham* | 153, 215 |
| 1–9 | 210 |
| 1–8 | 203 |
| 25–27 | 230 |
| | |
| *Aristeas, Letter of* | 77, 85, |
| | 151 |

**Baruch**

| | |
|---|---|
| 1:1—3:8 | 68, 125 |
| 1:15—2:5 | 158 |
| 3:9—4:4 | 104, 125, 209 |
| 4:5—5:9 | 39, 125 |

| | |
|---|---|
| *2 Baruch* | 133, 165, 210 |
| 10:18 | 230 |
| 13:4-11 | 66 |
| 21:8 | 227 |
| 29—30 | 219 |
| 49—51 | 143 |
| 72 | 219 |

| | |
|---|---|
| *3 Baruch* | 210 |

**Bel and the Dragon** — 78, 215

| | |
|---|---|
| 28 | 77 |
| 41 | 77 |

| | |
|---|---|
| *1 Enoch* | 41–42, 46–47, 73–74, 126, 151, 175, 182, 210, 221 |
| 1—5 | 123 |
| 1 | 46, 96 |
| 1:1-8 | 91 |
| 1:4 | 100 |
| 1:9 | 100 |
| 2—5 | 217 |
| 5 | 123 |
| 6—11 | 12, 63, 64, 131, 151, 203 |
| 8 | 14, 64 |
| 8:1 | 72 |
| 9—10 | 99, 102 |

| | |
|---|---|
| 9 | 100, 109 |
| 9:1 | 99, 102 |
| 10 | 199, 100 |
| 10:1-3 | 101, 102 |
| 10:4-5 | 101 |
| 10:7 | 72 |
| 10:8 | 100 |
| 10:20-22 | 101 |
| 10:20 | 69 |
| 10:21 | 76 |
| 12—16 | 48, 50, 64, 96, 98 |
| 14:22 | 98 |
| 14:23 | 98 |
| 20—36 | 99, 102 |
| 21—32 | 102 |
| 21 | 102 |
| 22 | 227, 301 |
| 24—27 | 123, 131 |
| 24:2—25:7 | 103, 131 |
| 26—27 | 131 |
| 37—71 | 20, 23, 104, 107, 112, 131–32, 180, 221 |
| 37:1 | 74 |
| 38:1 | 156 |
| 38:3-4 | 226 |
| 39:3 | 83 |
| 39:4-5 | 226 |
| 39:6—40:10 | 217 |
| 39:12 | 98 |
| 40:9 | 72, 101 |
| 42 | 104 |
| 45:4-5 | 226 |
| 46:1—49:4 | 217 |
| 46:1-3 | 104 |
| 46:1 | 20 |
| 46:8 | 156 |
| 47 | 104 |
| 48 | 105 |

| | |
|---|---|
| 48:1-6 | 20 |
| 48:3 | 105 |
| 48:8-10 | 105 |
| 49:3-4 | 105 |
| 49:3 | 20 |
| 49:4 | 20 |
| 50:1-3 | 77 |
| 51 | 144 |
| 53:6 | 156 |
| 61—63 | 217 |
| 62—63 | 20, 52, 105, 107 |
| 62:2-3 | 105 |
| 62:2 | 20 |
| 62:8 | 156 |
| 62:13-16 | 105 |
| 69:26-29 | 217 |
| 71:8 | 98 |
| 72—82 | 102, 103 |
| 81—82 | 211 |
| 81:5—82:3 | 41, 46, 74 |
| 82:2-3 | 74 |
| 85—90 | 14, 71, 76, 131, 133, 179 |
| 89—90 | 99 |
| 89:29-35 | 46 |
| 89:61-64 | 99 |
| 89:76-77 | 99 |
| 90:28-30 | 216 |
| 90:37-38 | 76 |
| 91 | 211 |
| 91:11-17 | 76, 131, 133, 179 |
| 91:14 | 76 |
| 92—105 | 41, 42, 46, 55, 76, 179, 182, 212 |
| 93:1-10 | 76, 131, 133, 179 |
| 93:10 | 74 |

| | |
|---|---|
| 94–103 | 96 |
| 94:1-2 | 211 |
| 94:3-4 | 40 |
| 94:5 | 104 |
| 95:3 | 71 |
| 97–104 | 99, 109 |
| 98:9—99:10 | 96, 211 |
| 98:9 | 47 |
| 98:12 | 71 |
| 99:2 | 46 |
| 99:6-9 | 78, 215 |
| 99:7 | 229 |
| 99:10 | 47 |
| 100:1—102:3 | 217 |
| 100:4 | 100 |
| 100:6 | 77 |
| 102–104 | 131 |
| 103:5-6 | 228 |
| 103:9-16 | 228 |
| 104:2-4 | 143 |
| 104:12—105:1 | 46, 74, 77 |

*4 Ezra* / 133, 165, 210
3:20-22 / 216

*Isaiah, Martyrdom/ Ascension of* / 24, 180, 210, 243
5:1 / 207

**Jeremiah, Letter of** / 78, 215

*Joseph and Aseneth* / 215
12 / 210
12:9-10 / 215
15:5 / 128
18:9 / 128

*Jubilees* / 15, 27, 45–46, 48, 49, 78, 151, 179–80
1 / 131
4:15-26 / 13
4:25 / 102
5:1-12 / 13
7:20-39 / 13
8:1-4 / 13
10 / 64
10:1-17 / 13
10:7-11 / 78
10:10-13 / 72
11–12 / 210
11:3—12:21 / 13
11:4 / 78
12:1-13 / 13
12:1-5 / 78
17:8 / 52
17:15—19:8 / 217
17:15—18:19 / 13, 39
17:17-18 / 210
19:7 / 13
20:7-9 / 78, 229
22:16-18 / 229
22:18 / 78
23 / 16, 45, 47, 221
23:11-15 / 45
23:16-29 / 179
23:26 / 45, 48, 179, 238
23:31 / 131
30:17-19 / 95
32 / 95

**Judith** / 38
16:17 / 134

**1 Maccabees** / 36, 70, 71
1:50-64 / 37
1:62-63 / 37
2:10-26 / 71
2:19-22 / 37
2:23-26 / 93, 94, 95
2:29-41 / 71
2:29-38 / 37, 181
2:29 / 57, 212
2:42-43 / 71
2:42 / 176, 178
2:45-48 / 55
2:50-61 / 52
2:50 / 37
2:52 / 39, 52
3:1 / 94
4:46 / 76
5:61-62 / 94
7:12-18 / 177
9:23-31 / 94
13:8-9 / 94
14:41 / 96
14:4-15 / 95, 133

**2 Maccabees** / 16, 36, 66, 70, 71, 151–52
6–7 / 37, 71, 79
6:12-17 / 66
6:27-28 / 37
7 / 16, 19, 24, 27, 38, 106, 111, 116, 131, 206, 210
7:2 / 37
7:6 / 16, 19
7:9 / 37, 38
7:10 / 19
7:11 / 37, 38
7:12 / 19
7:23 / 37, 38
7:29 / 38
7:36 / 38

| | | | | | |
|---|---|---|---|---|---|
| 7:37-38 | 20 | 4:21 | 211 | 17:22 | 68 |
| 7:37 | 37 | 4:23 | 211 | 17:30 | 93 |
| 7:38 | 67 | 4:25 | 211 | 17:32 | 93 |
| 8:5 | 20, 67 | 5 | 134 | 17:36 | 93 |
| 9 | 19 | 5:18 | 211 | 17:37 | 92 |
| 9:10-11 | 223 | 6:5 | 211 | 17:40 | 92, 93 |
| 14:6 | 176 | 7:8-10 | 66 | 17:43 | 93 |
| | | 8 | 50, 134 | 17:46 | 130 |
| *4 Maccabees* | 27, 66, | 8:11-12 | 93, 95, | | |
| | 79, 131, | | 212 | *Pseudo-Philo (Book* | 14 |
| | 151, 206, | 8:12 | 68 | *of Biblical Antiquities)* | |
| | 210, 217 | 8:23 | 211 | 4:16—7:5 | 203 |
| 7:19 | 227 | 8:34 | 211 | 6 | 210 |
| 16:25 | 227 | 9 | 134 | | |
| 17:20-22 | 67 | 9:3 | 211 | *Sibylline Oracles* | |
| 17:22 | 20 | 10:1-4 | 66 | 3 | 77, 85 |
| | | 10:3 | 211 | | |
| *Paraleipomena* | 14, 25 | 10:6 | 177 | **Sirach** | 39, 40, |
| *of Jeremiah* | | 11 | 90, 125, | | 41, |
| 9:22 | 207 | | 132, 211 | | 151–52 |
| | | 12:4 | 211 | Prol. 8–10 | 10 |
| **Prayer** | 68 | 12:6 | 211 | Prol. 24–25 | 10 |
| **of Azariah** | | 13 | 134 | 3:1-16 | 40 |
| | | 13:9-10 | 66 | 3:3 | 40, 213 |
| **Prayer** | 68, 210 | 13:10 | 60, 211 | 3:30 | 213 |
| **of Manasseh** | | 13:12 | 211 | 7:29-31 | 213 |
| | | 14 | 134 | 11:18-20 | 212 |
| *Psalms of Solomon* | 68, 134, | 14:1 | 211 | 13:24—14:10 | 212 |
| | 165, 221 | 14:3 | 211 | 15:17 | 50 |
| 2 | 50, 134 | 14:10 | 211 | 24 | 41–42, |
| 2:3 | 68, 93, 95, | 15 | 134 | | 50, 54, |
| | 211, 212 | 15:3 | 211 | | 210 |
| 2:33 | 211 | 15:7 | 211 | 24:3 | 104 |
| 2:36 | 211 | 15:13 | 211 | 24:23-34 | 39, 74 |
| 3 | 43, 134 | 16 | 134 | 24:32-34 | 96 |
| 3:8 | 68, 211 | 17 | 92, 115, | 24:32-33 | 11 |
| 3:12 | 211 | | 125 | 24:32 | 18 |
| 4 | 43 | 17:1-3 | 130 | 34:18—35:3 | 213 |
| 4:1 | 177 | 17:5-12 | 92 | 35:1-2 | 67 |
| 4:6 | 211 | 17:16 | 177 | 35:4-11 | 213 |
| 4:8 | 211 | 17:22-24 | 92 | 36:1-17 | 90, 158 |

| | | | | | |
|---|---|---|---|---|---|
| 36:1-7 | 125 | 1–4 | 78 | 2:1-8 | 67 |
| 36:15-16 | 125 | 2–3 | 1 | 3:2-5 | 43 |
| 38:1-8 | 72 | | | 3:7-8 | 72 |
| 39:1-11 | 96 | *Testament of Joseph* 217 | | 4:7-11 | 212 |
| 40:12 | 10, 213 | | | 4:7 | 40 |
| 44–49 | 10 | *Testament of Judah* | | 5 | 228 |
| 44:16-26 | 10 | 10–13 | 14 | 6:1-5 | 73 |
| 44:16-17 | 10 | 24 | 94 | 8:1-3 | 73 |
| 44:20-21 | 39 | | | 11:7-12 | 73 |
| 45:1—49:7 | 10 | *Testament of Levi* | 94 | 11:15 | 66 |
| 45:16 | 213 | 12 | 94 | 12 | 228 |
| 45:20 | 52 | 14–18 | 94 | 12:8-10 | 212 |
| 45:23-26 | 95 | 18 | 94 | 12:8 | 56 |
| 46:15 | 124 | 18:2 | 94 | 12:9-10 | 67 |
| 46:20 | 213 | 18:5 | 94 | 12:15 | 99 |
| 47:1-11 | 95 | 18:6-7 | 110 | 12:20 | 113, 115, |
| 47:11 | 125 | 18:7 | 94 | | 228 |
| 47:22 | 125, 220 | | | 13 | 90, 124 |
| 48:10 | 125, 135 | *Testament* | 14, 16, 38, | 13-14 | 132 |
| 48:22-25 | 10 | *of Moses* | 70–71, | 13:2 | 66 |
| 48:24-25 | 124 | | 75, 77, | 13:5 | 66 |
| 49:6-7 | 10 | | 116, 125, | 13:9 | 66 |
| 49:6 | 124 | | 131, 180, | 14:4-5 | 124 |
| 49:8-9 | 10 | | 224 | 14:4-7 | 124, 133 |
| 49:10 | 10 | 6 | 133 | | |
| 49:11-13 | 10 | 9 | 37, 70 | **Wisdom** | 58, 128, |
| 49:14 | 10 | 9:6 | 37 | **of Solomon** | 131, 151, |
| 50 | 94 | 10 | 38, 70 | | 221–22 |
| 50:20 | 219 | 10:1-10 | 91, | 1:1—6:11 | 107 |
| | | | 130–31 | 1:1-8 | 104 |
| *Testament of Abraham* | | 10:2 | 91, 101 | 1:4-5 | 114 |
| 10–11B | 100 | 10:3 | 69 | 2–5 | 19, 22, 97, |
| 11–12A | 100 | | | | 104, 106, |
| | | *Testament* | 40–41, 95 | | 111, 129, |
| *Testament* | 14 | *of the XII Patriarchs* | | | 131, 141 |
| *of Issachar* | | | | 2:12-15 | 106 |
| | | **Tobit** | 39–41, | 2:17-20 | 106 |
| *Testament of Job* | 14, 24, | | 77, 101 | 3:2 | 227 |
| | 40, 129, | 1:1-8 | 43 | 3:6 | 20 |
| | 131, 212, | 1:3-9 | 66 | 3:8 | 107 |
| | 215, 217 | 1:16-18 | 67 | 4:18 | 107 |

| | | | | | |
|---|---|---|---|---|---|
| 5:2 | 19 | 3:13—4:26 | 41, 51, 54, 81, 102, 128, 151, 169 | 4Q247 | 202 |
| 5:3-5 | 107 | | | 4Q266:1-8 | 239 |
| 5:4-5 | 216 | | | | |
| 5:22-23 | 57 | | | 4Q285 | 219 |
| 14–15 | 22 | 4:9-11 | 55 | | |
| | | 4:20-22 | 69, 136 | 4Q398 (MMT) | |
| **Dead Sea Scrolls** | | 5:7-9 | 47, 127, 169 | 7 10 | 202 |
| | | | | 14-17 2:4-8 | 48 |
| 1QApGen | 14, 203 | 5:9 | 47, 97, 169 | | |
| (Genesis | | | | 4QAmram | 95 |
| Apocryphon) | | 5:10-20 | 169 | | |
| 20 | 73, 83 | 5:14-20 | 170 | 4QInstruction | 41 |
| | | 5:21 | 169, 220 | (Musar le Mevin) | |
| **1QH** | | 5:22 | 47 | | |
| 9(1):24 | 126 | 6:2—7:25 | 239 | 4QLevi | 180 |
| 11(3):19-23 | 128, 141, 170 | 6:6-8 | 47, 179 | | |
| | | 6:14-15 | 47 | 4QpIsa<sup>c</sup> | 212 |
| 12(4):22 | 97 | 8–9 | 127 | 2:10-11 | 267 |
| 14(6):22-29 | 169 | 8 | 47 | | |
| 15(7):10 | 19 | 8:1-10 | 68 | 4QpNahum | |
| 16(8):36 | 19 | 8:4-10 | 47, 80 | 2:2 | 212 |
| 19(11):3-14 | 128, 141, 170 | 8:12-16 | 169, 228 | 2:4-5 | 212 |
| | | 8:12 | 47 | 3:6-7 | 212 |
| | | 8:15 | 47 | | |
| **1QpHab** | 78 | 8:24 | 47 | 4QPrayer | 73 |
| (Habakkuk | | 9:3-7 | 169 | of Nabonidus | |
| Commentary) | | 9:7 | 220 | | |
| 7:1-5 | 16, 127 | 9:11 | 95, 97, 169 | 4QQahat | 95 |
| 7:4-5 | 97 | | | | |
| 7:7-13 | 133 | 10:24-25 | 170 | 4QSongs | 131 |
| 7:16—8:3 | 210 | 11:3-9 | 126 | of the Sabbath | |
| 8:3—10:12 | 95 | 11:9-15 | 51 | Sacrifice | |
| | | | | | |
| **1QM (War Scroll)** | | **1QSa** | | 4QTestimonia | 97 |
| 7:10 | 220 | 1:16 | 220 | | |
| 9:15-16 | 99, 100 | 1:23 | 220 | 11QMelchi- | 69, 101 |
| 17:6-8 | 100 | 2:11-22 | 95, 169 | zedek | |
| | | 2:13 | 220 | | |
| **1QS** | 60 | | | 11QPs<sup>a</sup> | 179 |
| (Community Rule) | | **4Q180–181** | 202 | 18:10-12 | 177 |
| 2:4-18 | 238 | | | | |

| | | | | | | |
|---|---|---|---|---|---|
| 18:10 | 177 | 13:171-73 | 170, 233 | A.5 | 166 |
| 19:8 | 177 | 13:288-98 | 167, 235 | | |
| 22:3 | 177 | 13:293 | 166 | **Babylonian Talmud** | |
| | | 13:297 | 166, 167, | *Sanhedrin* | |
| **11Q Temple** | 27, 48 | | 234 | 11a | 220 |
| **Scroll** | | 18:11-22 | 233 | 90b | 166 |
| | | 18:12-15 | 234 | *Sotah* | |
| **CD** | 48–50 | 18:14-16 | 166 | 48 | 220 |
| (**Damascus** | | 18:18-22 | 238 | | |
| **Document**) | | 18:23-25 | 233 | **Mishnah** | |
| 1:8—2:1 | 238 | 18:116-19 | 181, 240 | *Tamid* | |
| 1:13—2:1 | 170 | 20:17 | 166 | 7:2 | 219 |
| 1:18 | 212 | 20:197-203 | 166 | | |
| 3 | 48 | *Jewish War* | | New Testament | |
| 4:15—5:15 | 47, 48 | 2:119-66 | 233, 238 | | |
| 4:17-18 | 95 | 2:120-21 | 174 | **Matthew** | 15 |
| 4:21 | 56 | 2:131 | 171 | 1—2 | 109 |
| 5 | 47 | 2:154-59 | 240 | 3:2-12 | 81 |
| 5:6-7 | 95 | 2:154-58 | 171 | 3:6 | 81 |
| 6:2-11 | 127, 238 | 2:160-61 | 172, 174 | 3:7 | 233, 236 |
| 6:2-4 | 47 | 2:162-66 | 166, 167 | 5 | 57 |
| 6:4-5 | 47 | 2:162-63 | 234 | 5:5 | 144 |
| 9—14 | 47 | 2:254-57 | 233 | 5:18-21 | 56 |
| 15—16 | 47 | 7:254-58 | 233 | 6:5 | 236 |
| 16:2-4 | 202 | *Life* | | 6:16-18 | 56 |
| 20:1 | 95 | 11 | 181 | 6:19-21 | 57 |
| | | | | 6:33 | 57 |
| **New Jerusalem** 230 | | **Philo of Alexandria** | | 7:24-27 | 57 |
| (1Q32, 2Q24, 4Q232, | | *De Abrahamo* | | 9:27 | 221 |
| 554–555, 5Q15, 11Q18) | | 66-68 | 203 | 10:6 | 86 |
| | | *Hypothetica* | | 10:32-33 | 112, 227 |
| Other Jewish | | 11:1-11 | 233, 238 | 11:7-15 | 135 |
| Texts | | 11:14-17 | 174 | 12:23 | 221 |
| | | *De migratione Abrahami* | | 15:20 | 56 |
| | | 1:176-86 | 203 | 15:22 | 221 |
| **Flavius Josephus** | | *Quod omnis probus liber sit* | | 16:1 | 233 |
| *Against Apion* | | 75-91 | 233, 238 | 16:6 | 233 |
| 1:40 | 96 | | | 16:11 | 233 |
| *Antiquities* | 14 | **Rabbinical texts** | | 16:12 | 233 |
| *of the Jews* | | *Abot Rabbi Nathan* | | 16:13-19 | 80 |
| 1:154-57 | 203 | 4 5:2 | 213 | 18:12-14 | 81, 137 |
| 10:288-98 | 166 | | | | |

| | | | | | |
|---|---|---|---|---|---|
| 19:9 | 57 | 5:1-13 | 83 | 14—15 | 22 |
| 19:28-30 | 109 | 5:7 | 114 | 14:22-24 | 79 |
| 20:1-6 | 81 | 6:7-13 | 83 | 14:60-64 | 110 |
| 20:28 | 80 | 6:14-29 | 226 | 14:61-62 | 110, 114, |
| 20:30 | 221 | 7:1-13 | 55-56 | | 222 |
| 21:9 | 221 | 7:3-8 | 234 | 14:62 | 110 |
| 21:28-32 | 81 | 7:14-23 | 55 | 15:39 | 114 |
| 21:43 | 218 | 7:19 | 56 | | |
| 22:16 | 233 | 7:21 | 55 | **Luke** | 23, 42 |
| 22:23-24 | 233 | 8:29-31 | 222 | 1—2 | 109, 207 |
| 22:42-45 | 221 | 8:31-34 | 216 | 1:1 | 140 |
| 23:1-36 | 236 | 8:31 | 111, 216 | 3:2-18 | 81 |
| 24:42-44 | 111 | 8:34-36 | 82 | 3:11-13 | 81 |
| 25:31-46 | 52, 110 | 8:36 | 57 | 4:1 | 222 |
| 26:27-28 | 79 | 8:38 | 227 | 4:14 | 222 |
| 27:25 | 208, 218 | 9:7 | 114 | 4:16-27 | 232 |
| 28:16-20 | 86, 142 | 9:31 | 111, 216 | 4:16 | 332 |
| 28:18-20 | 115 | 10:2-12 | 56 | 4:18 | 222 |
| 28:19 | 85, 218 | 10:11-12 | 57 | 4:21 | 140 |
| | | 10:17-31 | 137 | 5:29-32 | 211 |
| **Mark** | | 10:17-25 | 57 | 6 | 57 |
| 1:5 | 81 | 10:32-34 | 111 | 6:47-49 | 57 |
| 1:10 | 83 | 10:45 | 80, 111, | 7:24-28 | 135 |
| 1:11 | 114 | | 216 | 7:34-50 | 211 |
| 1:12-13 | 83 | 10:47-48 | 221 | 7:50 | 216 |
| 1:21 | 232 | 11:10 | 221 | 8:12 | 216 |
| 1:23-26 | 83 | 12:13 | 233 | 8:36 | 216 |
| 1:24 | 114 | 12:18-27 | 143, 166 | 8:50 | 216 |
| 1:34 | 83, 114 | 12:18 | 233 | 12:8-9 | 112. 227 |
| 1:48 | 81 | 12:25-27 | 144 | 12:13-34 | 57 |
| 2:7 | 114 | 12:25 | 167 | 12:16-21 | 81 |
| 2:13-17 | 81 | 12:35-37 | 109, 221 | 12:35-40 | 212 |
| 2:15-17 | 56 | 13 | 15 | 12:37-40 | 111 |
| 2:16 | 235 | 13:4-37 | 139 | 13:10 | 232 |
| 2:18-23 | 55, 56 | 13:9-10 | 82 | 13:23 | 216 |
| 2:23—3:6 | 56 | 13:10 | 85 | 14:15-24 | 211 |
| 2:28 | 114 | 13:17 | 212 | 15:1-32 | 211 |
| 3:1-2 | 232 | 13:21-27 | 222 | 15:1-7 | 81, 137 |
| 3:6 | 233 | 13:21-22 | 110 | 15:2 | 236 |
| 3:11-12 | 83, 114 | 13:26-27 | 110 | 15:6 | 216 |
| 3:22-26 | 83 | 13:26 | 110 | 15:8 | 216 |
| 4:41 | 114 | 13:32-37 | 212 | 15:9 | 216 |

| | | | | | |
|---|---|---|---|---|---|
| 15:11-31 | 81 | 3:18 | 141 | 6:8—9:21 | 82 |
| 15:21 | 81 | 3:36 | 141 | 6:8-11 | 216 |
| 15:24 | 216 | 5:24-25 | 141 | 6:12—7:53 | 216 |
| 15:32 | 216 | 5:24 | 141 | 6:15 | 216 |
| 16:1-13 | 57 | 5:28-29 | 141, 227 | 7:53 | 24 |
| 16:1-9 | 81, 137 | 6:44 | 141 | 7:54 | 216 |
| 16:14-25 | 236 | 6:54 | 141 | 7:55-56 | 216 |
| 16:22-31 | 140 | 10:11 | 80 | 7:56 | 140 |
| 17:19 | 216 | 10:15 | 80 | 9:1-9 | 142 |
| 18:1-8 | 227 | 10:17-18 | 80 | 9:20-21 | 216 |
| 18:9-14 | 211 | 11:23-27 | 141 | 11:14 | 216 |
| 18:31-33 | 81 | 11:51 | 80 | 13:14 | 232 |
| 18:38-39 | 221 | 13:31 | 141 | 13:15 | 232 |
| 19:1-10 | 81, 137, | 14:1-3 | 144 | 13:27 | 332 |
| | 211 | 15:13 | 80 | 13:33-37 | 221 |
| 19:10 | 81, 216 | 16:5 | 113, 223, | 13:42-44 | 232 |
| 20:27 | 233 | | 228 | 15 | 236 |
| 20:38 | 140 | 18-19 | 208 | 15:1 | 216 |
| 20:42-44 | 221 | 19:34 | 143 | 15:11 | 216 |
| 21:7-36 | 139 | 20:11-18 | 142 | 15:16 | 221 |
| 21:8-9 | 139 | 20:19-29 | 142, 223 | 15:21 | 232 |
| 21:10-11 | 139 | 21 | 143 | 16:13 | 232 |
| 21:12 | 139 | | | 16:20 | 216 |
| 21:20-24 | 139 | | | 16:31 | 216 |
| 21:25-28 | 139 | **Acts** | | 17:2 | 232 |
| 21:34-36 | 111, 212 | 1:6-8 | 140 | 17:31 | 140 |
| 21:36 | 140 | 1:6 | 109 | 18:4 | 232 |
| 22:19-20 | 81 | 2 | 25 | 19:9 | 216 |
| 22:30 | 109 | 2:21 | 216 | 21:26 | 80 |
| 23:39-43 | 140 | 2:25-35 | 221 | 22:3-11 | 142 |
| 24:13-32 | 142 | 2:40 | 216 | 23:1-10 | 166 |
| 24:36-49 | 142 | 2:42 | 233 | 23:6-8 | 233 |
| 24:37 | 142 | 2:46-47 | 233 | 23:8 | 167 |
| 24:44 | 202 | 2:46 | 80 | 24:12 | 157 |
| 24:47 | 85 | 2:47 | 216 | 26:10-19 | 142 |
| | | 3—4 | 80 | 27:20 | 216 |
| | | 4:1 | 166, 233 | 27:31 | 216 |
| **John** | 84, 86, | 4:9 | 216 | | |
| | 113, 114 | 4:12 | 216 | **Romans** | |
| 1:1-18 | 113 | 5:17 | 166, 233 | 1—5 | 53 |
| 1:14 | 143 | 6—8 | 55 | 1—2 | 54 |
| 3:14 | 141 | 6:1-9 | 157 | 1 | 22 |
| 3:16 | 141 | 6:1-2 | 233 | | |

| | | | | | |
|---|---|---|---|---|---|
| 1:3 | 109, 221 | 7:10-11 | 58 | 1:15-23 | 227 |
| 1:18 | 82 | 8:4 | 215 | 2:6 | 139 |
| 2:1-16 | 52–53 | 9:1 | 143 | 2:19-22 | 80 |
| 2:1-11 | 138 | 10 | 85 | 4 | 227 |
| 2:1-2 | 82 | 10:11-13 | 138 | | |
| 2:9-10 | 53 | 10:20-22 | 215 | **Philippians** | |
| 2:17-28 | 135 | 11:22-34 | 233 | 1:21-24 | 143 |
| 3–5 | 54 | 11:23-25 | 79 | 2:5 | 216 |
| 3:9 | 81 | 15 | 138, 142 | 2:6-11 | 58, 113, |
| 3:19-20 | 82 | 15:3 | 79 | | 216, 223 |
| 3:25 | 79 | 15:8 | 143 | 2:7 | 216 |
| 4 | 58 | 15:24-28 | 142 | 2:10 | 142 |
| 4:24-25 | 79, 216 | 15:48-50 | 143 | 3 | 53 |
| 4:24 | 111, 227 | 15:49-54 | 144 | 3:5-6 | 54 |
| 6–8 | 53, 54 | 15:49 | 143 | 3:20-21 | 143 |
| 6:11 | 138 | 15:51 | 138 | 3:20 | 144 |
| 6:16-19 | 58, 81 | | | 3:21 | 143, 144 |
| 7–8 | 58, 81 | **2 Corinthians** | | | |
| 7:9-12 | 81 | 4:6 | 143 | **Colossians** | |
| 7:14-25 | 51 | 4:16—5:10 | 138 | 1:3—3:4 | 13 |
| 7:17-20 | 81, 82 | 5:10 | 221 | 1:15-20 | 113 |
| 8 | 54, 58, | 5:16-21 | 138 | 1:24 | 216 |
| | 82, 138 | 12:7 | 83 | 2:9-15 | 227 |
| 8:3 | 82 | | | 3 | 227 |
| 8:11 | 142, 227 | **Galatians** | | | |
| 8:18-25 | 144 | 1:12-16 | 115 | **1 Thessalonians** | |
| 8:34 | 109 | 1:13-14 | 54 | 1:9-10 | 81, 215 |
| 9–11 | 53, 86 | 1:16 | 85 | 1:9 | 85 |
| 10:9 | 142 | 2–3 | 53 | 1:10 | 53 |
| 10:23 | 218 | 3–4 | 85 | 2:19-20 | 221 |
| 10:25 | 218 | 3:6—4:7 | 138 | 3:12-13 | 53 |
| 11:23 | 86 | 3:19 | 24 | 3:13 | 221 |
| 11:26 | 86 | 4:4-5 | 216 | 4–5 | 119 |
| 11:33-36 | 86 | 4:4 | 138, 227 | 4:3-7 | 185 |
| 12–14 | 53, 54 | 5 | 58 | 4:3-6 | 53 |
| | | 5:18-21 | 55 | 4:13-17 | 143 |
| **1 Corinthians** | 53 | 5:16—6:10 | 53, 54 | 4:15-17 | 110, 138 |
| 1:7 | 138 | | | 4:15 | 58 |
| 4:1-5 | 221 | **Ephesians** | | 4:17 | 144 |
| 6:9-20 | 85 | 1–2 | 139 | 5:1-11 | 58, 212 |

| | |
|---|---|
| 5:2 | 111 |
| 5:3-17 | 111 |

**2 Thessalonians**
| | |
|---|---|
| 2 | 119 |

**2 Timothy**
| | |
|---|---|
| 2:8 | 221 |

**Hebrews** 15, 113
| | |
|---|---|
| 1:1-4 | 113 |
| 1:3 | 109, 143, 228 |
| 2:9 | 143 |
| 2:14-17 | 109 |
| 2:17 | 109 |
| 4:14-16 | 109, 143 |
| 4:16 | 109 |
| 5 | 80 |
| 5:7-10 | 143 |
| 5:7 | 223 |
| 5:10 | 109 |
| 7–9 | 80 |
| 7:25 | 109 |
| 7:26 | 109 |
| 8:1 | 109, 228 |
| 9:11-14 | 109 |
| 9:24 | 109 |
| 10:5-12 | 109 |
| 10:5-10 | 23 |
| 10:12 | 228 |
| 10:32-39 | 82 |
| 10:35-39 | 52 |
| 11:1—12:2 | 52, 217 |
| 11:35-38 | 24 |
| 12:1-5 | 216 |
| 12:1-4 | 82 |
| 12:2 | 143, 228 |
| 12:3-13 | 52 |
| 13:20 | 227 |

**James**
| | |
|---|---|
| 2:14-26 | 52 |
| 2:21-25 | 52 |
| 2:21-23 | 52 |
| 5:11 | 24 |

**1 Peter**
| | |
|---|---|
| 2:4-10 | 80 |
| 2:18-25 | 82 |
| 2:21-25 | 111, 216 |
| 2:21 | 216 |

**Jude**
| | |
|---|---|
| 14—15 | 23 |

**Revelation** 15, 83, 84
| | |
|---|---|
| 1–2 | 143 |
| 1:7 | 110 |
| 1:9 | 217 |
| 1:16 | 24 |
| 2:2-3 | 217 |
| 2:9 | 233 |
| 2:19 | 217 |
| 2:27 | 24 |
| 3:7 | 221 |
| 3:9 | 233 |
| 3:10 | 217 |
| 4:1 | 83 |
| 5:5 | 221 |
| 5:6 | 24 |
| 5:12 | 24 |
| 6:9-11 | 143 |
| 10:15 | 24 |
| 10:18 | 24 |
| 11:5 | 24 |
| 12 | 64, 108 |
| 13:10 | 217 |
| 14:12 | 217 |
| 21:1—22:5 | 80, 144 |
| 22:16 | 221 |

# Early Christian Literature

*Apocryphon of John* 210

**Cyril of Jerusalem**
*Catechetical Lectures*
| | |
|---|---|
| 10:1 | 221 |
| 21:5-6 | 221 |

*De sacro chrismate*
| | |
|---|---|
| 5-6 | 221 |

*De uno domine*
| | |
|---|---|
| 11 | 221 |

*Didache*
| | |
|---|---|
| 9 | 84 |

**Hippolytus**
*Heresies*
| | |
|---|---|
| 9:13 | 174 |
| 9:18-29 | 233, 238 |
| 9:23 | 72, 174 |

**Justin**
*1 Apology*
| | |
|---|---|
| 67 | 233 |

*Pseudo-Clementine Recognitions*
| | |
|---|---|
| 1.44.6—48.6 | 221 |

**Tertullian**
*On Baptism*
| | |
|---|---|
| 7:1 | 221 |

# Other Texts

*Corpus Hermeticum*
| | |
|---|---|
| 1:12-14 | 223 |

**Pliny**

*Natural History*

5.15.73            238

# Index of Authors

Alsup, Joseph E., 223, 227, 228
Anderson, Bernhard W., 202, 209, 223, 227
Anderson, Gary A., 204, 213, 239
Anderson, Robert T., 230
Argall, Randal A., 202, 214, 220, 223
Arnold, David V., 240
Atkinson, Kenneth, 219
Attridge, Harold W., 204, 222, 228, 234
Aune, David E., 224, 227
Auwers, J.-M., 202
Avery-Peck, Alan, 208, 212, 220, 222, 226, 228, 232, 235, 236, 243
Avigad, Nahman, 230

Bachmann, Theodore, 212
Baltzer, Klaus, 206, 209
Barrett, C. K., 207
Barth, Gerhard, 217
Barton, John M., 205, 210, 213
Bartsch, Hans Werner, 224
Bassler, Jouette, 222
Bauer, Walter, 201
Baumgarten, Albert I., 238, 240, 241, 242, 244
Baumgarten, Joseph M., 211, 238, 239
Baumgartner, Walter, 209
Beall, Todd S., 238, 239
Bearman, Gregory, 240
Becker, Michael, 201, 214, 238
Bedenbender, Andreas, 226

Bergren, Theodore A., 203, 217
Betz, Otto, 220
Billerbeck, Paul, 207
Binder, Donald D., 230, 231, 232
Black, Matthew, 241
Bloch, Renée, 203, 205
Boccaccini, Gabriele, 241, 243
Bogaert, Pierre-Maurice, 204
Bornkamm, Günther, 217, 226
Bousset, Wilhelm, 215, 226, 228, 230
Bow, Beverly A., 208, 220
Bower, David R., 219
Boyarin, Daniel, 222
Boyd-Alkalay, Esther, 240
Brock, Sebastian P., 204
Broshi, Magen, 240
Brown, Raymond E., 208, 217, 227
Brownlee, William, 203
Bruce, F. F., 241
Budick, Sanford, 205
Bultmann, Rudolf, 224, 227, 229
Burchard, Christoph, 205

Carlston, Charles E., 212, 236
Catchpole, David R., 212
Cazeaux, Jacques, 204
Charles, R. H., 204, 205, 226, 233, 234
Charlesworth, James H., 217, 227, 241
Chavalas, Mark W., 229
Chazon, Esther G., 204, 205, 214, 220, 231, 232, 239

Chilton, Bruce, 222, 236
Cohen, Naomi G., 204
Cohen, Shaye J. D., 204, 244
Collins, John J., 203, 204, 207, 210, 212, 214, 215, 217, 219, 220, 221, 225, 226, 229, 239, 240, 243
Conzelmann, Hans, 222, 229, 233
Cook, D., 205
Crawford, Sidnie White, 202
Crenshaw, James L., 209
Cross, Frank M., 203, 225, 239, 241
Cullmann, Oscar, 219, 229

D'Angelo, Mary Rose, 244
Davies, Philip R., 214, 239, 240, 241, 242
Davies, W. D., 215, 229, 235
De Silva, David A., 229
Delling, Gerhard, 205
Di Lella, Alexander A., 202
Di Tomasso, Lorenzo, 201
Didier, M., 205
Dimant, Devorah, 225, 237, 243
Dinkler, Erich, 222
Dodd, C. H., 209, 224, 227
Doudna, Gregory L., 240
Duhaime, Jean, 241
Dungan, David L., 212
Dunn, James D. G., 218, 222
Dupont-Sommer, A., 241

Eaton, John H., 219
Edersheim, Alfred, 230, 231
Ellbogen, Ismar, 231
Elliott, John H., 234
Epp, Eldon J., 218
Eppel, Robert, 210
Eshel, Esther, 228
Eshel, Hanan, 228
Evans, Craig A., 222

Feldman, Louis H., 204
Fenske, Wolfgang, 201, 215, 238

Fine, Steven, 232
Fishbane, Michael, 205
Fitzmyer, Joseph A., 202, 203, 217, 233, 237, 238
Fleischer, E., 232
Flint, Peter W., 202, 211, 232, 237, 239, 240, 241, 242
Foakes Jackson, F. J., 207
Fohrer, Georg, 213
Fox, Michael V., 210
Frerichs, Ernest D., 215, 221
Fritsch, Charles T., 202

García Martínez, Florentino, 208, 212, 220, 237, 241
Georgi, Dieter, 222
Geva, Hillel, 230
Golb, Norman, 240
Goldstein, Jonathan A., 229
Goodman, Martin, 240, 242
Gottwald, Norman, 210
Grabbe, Lester, 214, 229, 236
Gray, G. Buchanan, 233
Gray, Rebecca, 220
Green, William Scott, 221
Greenblatt, Charles, 240
Greenfield, Jonas C., 202, 205, 219, 239
Greenspoon, Leonard J., 202
Gressmann, Hugo, 215, 226, 228, 230
Gruen, Erich, 228, 229, 230, 242

Hadas, Moses, 208
Haenchen, Ernst, 207
Hahn, Ferdinand, 219
Halpern-Amaru, Betsy, 204
Hanson, John S., 220
Hanson, K. C., 244
Hanson, Paul D., 224, 230
Harnack, Adolf von, 208, 230
Harrelson, Walter, 209
Harrington, Daniel J., 203, 204, 211, 236
Harrington, Hannah K., 211, 239

Hartman, Geoffrey H., 205
Hauck. Friedrich, 213
Held, Heinz Joachim, 217
Hellholm, David, 225
Hengel, Martin, 210, 225, 229, 242
Herzer, Jens, 205
Himmelfarb, Martha, 220
Hoffmann, Heinrich, 226
Holladay, William, 209
Hollander, Harm W., 204, 210, 212
Hooker, Morna D., 206, 223
Horbury, William, 231
Horgan, Maurya P., 203, 205
Horsley, Richard A., 220, 234, 236
Hubbard, Benjamin J., 223
Hübner, Hans, 207

James, Montague Rhodes, 242
Jeremias, Joachim, 206, 211, 222, 223, 228
Jervell, Jacob, 218
Jobes, Karen, 207
Johnson, Aubrey R., 219
Johnson, Luke T., 207
Jokiranta, Jutta M., 244
Jonge, H. J. de, 202
Jonge, M. de, 204, 210, 212
Jongeling, B., 237, 241

Kahila, Gila, 240
Kampen, John, 214, 240, 241, 242, 243
Käsemann, Ernst, 224, 228
Kittel, Gerhard, 220
Klein, Charlotte, 208, 211, 234
Klein, Ralph W., 209
Klijn, A. F. J., 242
Kloppenborg, John S., 212, 217, 222
Knibb, Michael E., 205
Koch, Klaus, 226
Koehler, Ludwig, 209
Koester, Helmut, 201, 217
Kollmann, Bernd, 225
Kraabel, A. Thomas, 233

Kraemer, Ross, 205, 215, 244
Kraft, Robert A., 201, 204, 205, 207, 211, 234, 236, 237, 238
Krodel, Gerhard, 201
Kselman, John S., 210
Kugel, James, 205
Kugler, Robert, 204, 214, 237, 240
Kuhn, Heinz-Wolfgang, 201, 225, 227, 239
Kuhn, Thomas S., 201
Kümmel, Werner G., 227

LaGrange, Marie-Joseph, 236
Lake, Kirsopp, 207
Lapp, Nancy L., 230
Lapp, Paul W., 230
Larcher, M., 207, 212, 229
LaSor William Sanford, 237, 241
Leenhardt, Andreas, 201
Lehmann, Helmut T., 212
Levine, Amy-Jill, 204, 244
Levine, Lee, 230, 231, 232, 233
Libman, Elena, 240
Licht, Jacob, 215
Lichtenberrger, Hermann, 243
Lieberman, Saul, 229
Lim, Timothy H., 205
Lohse, Eduard, 222
Long, David G., 240
Lührmann, Dieter, 242

MacRae, George W., 218
Maddox, Robert, 218
Magness, Jodi, 228, 229, 231, 237, 238, 240, 241
Maier, Gerhard, 236
Malherbe, Abraham J., 229
Mason, Steve, 234, 235, 236
Mays, James L., 214
Mazar, Benjamin, 230
Mazar, Eilat, 230
McBride, S. Dean, 224

McDonald, Lee, 202
McKay, Heather A., 232
McKenzie, Steven J., 209
Meeks, Wayne A., 232
Mendels, Doron, 226
Mendenhall, George, 209
Metso, Sarianna, 211
Metzger, Bruce M., 207
Meyer, Rudolf, 213
Meyers, Eric, 230
Michel, Otto, 227
Milik, J. T., 239
Miller, Patrick D., 224
Molyneaux, Brian, 228
Montefiore, Claude J. G., 228
Moore, George Foot, 208, 231
Morgenstern, Matthew, 203
Muddiman, John, 210, 213
Munck, Johannes, 223
Murphy, Richard J., 204, 230
Murphy, Roland P., 209
Murphy-O'Connor, Jerome, 222, 223, 237, 240, 241

Netzer, Ehud, 230
Neusner, Jacob, 207, 208, 212, 215, 220, 221, 222, 226, 228, 232, 234, 235, 243
Newsom, Carol A., 241, 243
Nickelsburg, George W. E., passim
North, Christopher R., 206
Noy, David, 231

Oakman, Douglas E., 228, 244
Olyan, Saul, 213

Pardee, Dennis G., 240
Parry, Donald, 203, 237, 240
Pearson, Birger A., 212, 216, 222, 233
Pelikan, Jaroslav, 208
Perrin, Norman, 224, 225, 227
Perrot, Charles, 204

Petersen, Norman R., 214, 216, 217, 218, 219, 223, 227
Peursen, Wido van, 241
Pfann, Stephen J., 240
Plöger, Otto, 242
Polzin, Robert, 242
Pope, Marvin, 210
Porton, Gary G., 236, 237
Powell, Mark Allan, 219
Priest, John, 204, 234
Purintun, Ann-Elisabeth, 205

Qimron, Elisha, 203

Rad, Gerhard von, 213
Rappaport, Uriel, 237, 243
Reinbold, Wolfgang, 225
Reinink, G. J., 242
Reumann, John, 218
Rhoads, David, 233
Richardson, M. E. J., 209
Ricks, Stephen D., 240,
Ritmeyer, Kathleen, 230
Ritmeyer, Leen, 230
Rivkin, Ellis, 235
Robinson, James M., 201, 217, 223, 227
Robinson, S. E., 205
Rowland, Christopher, 226
Ryle, Herbert E., 242

Saldarini, Anthony J., 207, 211, 212, 218, 233, 234, 235, 236, 237, 242
Sanders, E. P., 209
Sanders, James A., 202, 242
Sandmel, Samuel, 207
Sarna, Nahum, 209
Sayler, Gwendolyn B., 236
Schiffmann, Lawrence H., 202, 208, 214, 219, 221, 225, 226, 232, 233, 237, 238, 239, 240, 241, 243
Schmidt, Francis, 239

Schmidt, Karl Ludwig, 233

Schrage, Wolfgang, 230, 232

Schuller, Eileen, 214, 237, 240, 241

Schürer, Ernst, 226, 230

Schwartz, Daniel R., 242

Schweitzer, Albert, 208, 223, 224

Schweizer, Eduard, 219

Schwemer, Anna Maria, 225

Scobie, Charles H. H., 233, 243

Seeley, David. R., 206

Segbroeck, F. van, 205

Shanks, Hershel, 237, 238

Shemesh, Aharon, 239

Shepherd, Massey H., 233

Silva, Moses, 207

Simon, J., 230

Sivan, Daniel, 203

Skehan, Patrick W., 202

Smith, Dennis, 233

Smith, Morton, 229, 230, 233, 238

Smith, Patricia, 240

Soares Prabhu, George M., 208

Sonne, Isaiah, 230

Spiro, Sheila I., 240

Spittler, Russell P., 204

Stadelmann, H., 213

Stamm, Johann Jacob, 209

Stark, Rodney, 218

Stegemann, Hartmut, 237

Stendahl, Krister, 208, 212, 229, 241

Sterling, Gregory R., 229

Stern, Ephraim, 230

Steudel, Annette, 221, 225, 240

Steve, M.-A., 230

Stone, Michael E., 202, 203, 204, 205, 210,
    211, 214, 215, 216, 217, 219, 220, 225,
    226, 236, 239, 243

Stowers, Stanley K., 222, 223

Strack, Hermann L., 207

Strecker, Georg, 201

Strugnell, John, 211, 214, 236, 239

Struthers-Malbon, Elisabeth, 219

Sundberg, Albert C., 236, 237

Sussmann, Ya'akov, 238

Svartik, Jesper, 212

Swanson, Dwight W., 201

Sweet, J. P. M., 204

Synge, F. C., 205

Talmon, Shemaryahu, 238

Tannehill, Robert, 219

Taylor, Joan E., 226, 227, 228, 243

Taylor, Michael J., 217

Taylor, Vincent, 219

Tcherikover, Victor, 210, 242

Theisohn, Johannes, 207

Theissen, Gerd, 223

Thomas, J., 233

Thornhill, R., 204

Tigchelaar, Eibert J. C., 212, 220

Tiller, Patrick A., 234, 241

Tomson, Peter J., 212

Tov, Emanuel, 202, 203, 225, 240

Trebolle Barrera, Julio C., 241

Trilling, Wolfgang, 218

Ulrich, Eugene C., 202, 203, 237

VanderKam, James C., 202, 203, 204, 208,
    211, 214, 219, 221, 224, 225, 226, 232,
    233, 237, 238, 239, 240, 241, 243

Vermes, Geza, 203, 205, 220, 225, 237

Vielhauer, Philipp, 227

Vincent, L.-Hughes, 230

Volz, Paul, 226, 228

Webb, Robert L., 243

Weiss, Johannes, 224

Werline, Rodney, A., 206, 209, 211, 212,
    213, 220, 232, 244

Whitelam, Keith W., 219

Wilken, Robert L., 226

Williams, Sam K., 206, 216
Wilson, Bryan, 234, 243
Winston, David, 229
Wintermute, Orville S., 203, 234
Wise, Michael O., 240
Woodward, Scott R., 240
Wright, Benjamin G., 213
Wright, G. Ernest, 209

Würthwein, E., 213

Yadin, Yigael, 230
Younger, K. Lawson, 229

Zias, Joseph, 240
Zuckerman, Bruce, 240
Zuckerman, Kenneth, 240